DATE			

© THE BAKER & TAYLOR CO.

THE MANY-FACETED
JACKSONIAN ERA

Recent Titles in
Contributions in American History
SERIES EDITOR: Jon L. Wakelyn

A New Birth of Freedom: The Republican Party and Freedmen's Rights,
1861 to 1866
Herman Belz

When Farmers Voted Red: The Gospel of Socialism in the Oklahoma
Countryside, 1910-1924
Garin Burbank

Henry Highland Garnet: A Voice of Black Radicalism in the Nineteenth
Century
Joel Schor

Blacks in the American Revolution
Philip S. Foner

The Prophet's Army: Trotskyists in America, 1928-1941
Constance Ashton Myers

American Revolutionary: A Biography of General Alexander McDougall
William L. MacDougall

Working Dress in Colonial and Revolutionary America
Peter F. Copeland

In the Almost Promised Land: American Jews and Blacks, 1915-1935
Hasia R. Diner

Essays in Nineteenth-Century American Legal History
Wythe Holt, editor

A Right to the Land: Essays on the Freedmen's Community
Edward Magdol

Essays on American Music
Garry E. Clarke

Culture and Diplomacy: The American Experience
Morrell Heald and Lawrence S. Kaplan

Voting in Provincial America: A Study of Elections in the Thirteen Colonies,
1689-1776
Robert J. Dinkin

The French Forces in America, 1780-1783
Lee Kennett

Cold War Political Justice: The Smith Act, the Communist Party, and
American Civil Liberties
Michal R. Belknap

The many-faceted Jacksonian era

NEW INTERPRETATIONS

edited by Edward Pessen

Contributions in American History, Number 67

 Greenwood Press
WESTPORT, CONNECTICUT • LONDON, ENGLAND

Library of Congress Cataloging in Publication Data

Main entry under title:

The Many-faceted Jacksonian era.

(Contributions in American history ; no. 67 ISSN 0084-9219)
Bibliography: p.
Includes index.
CONTENTS: Society: Pessen, E. The egalitarian myth and the
American social reality. Welter, B. The cult of true womanhood,
1820-1860. Knights, P. R. Out-migration from Boston, 1830-1860.
Curry, L. P. Urbanization and urbanism in the Old South.—The
economy: Temin, P. The Jacksonian economy: Montgomery, D. The
shuttle and the cross, weavers and artisans in the Kensington riots of
1844. Gutman, H.G. The occupational structure and the alleged social
mobility of slaves. Fogel, R.W. How important were railroads to the
antebellum economy?—Politics: Brown, R.H. The Missouri crisis,
slavery, and the politics of Jacksonianism. Wilson, M.L. What Whigs
and Jacksonian Democrats meant by freedom. Ershkowitz, H. and
Shade, W.G. Consensus or conflict? Political behavior in the state legislatures during the Jacksonian Era. [etc.]
    1. United States—Economic conditions—To 1865—Addresses,
essays, lectures. 2. United States—Social conditions—To 1865—
Addresses, essays, lectures. 3. United States—Politics and government—1815-1861—Addresses, essays, lectures. I. Pessen, Edward,
1920-
HC105.M34   309.1'73'056   77-24621
ISBN 0-8371-9720-1

Library of Congress Catalog Card Number: 77-24621
ISBN: 0-8371-9720-1
ISSN: 0084-9219

First published in 1977

Greenwood Press, Inc.
51 Riverside Avenue, Westport, Connecticut 06880

Printed in the United States of America

To Adam

CONTENTS

THE MANY-FACETED
JACKSONIAN ERA

INTRODUCTION

Until recently many scholars treated history as though its chief, if not its only, theme was past politics. In dealing with the second quarter of the nineteenth century they focused above all on the administrations of Andrew Jackson and on the dramatic warfare waged by Jacksonian Democracy against its great political rivals, the National Republicans and the Whigs. That historians called the period the "Jacksonian Era" only reflected their preoccupation with its political issues and their conviction that the seventh president was the dominant figure of his time.

Another popular rubric for the period, "the Era of the Common Man," is yet another sign of historians' fixation on its political themes. The common man supposedly came into his own during the era, first by winning the right to vote, then by taking over the process of nominating candidates for office, and finally by rewarding at the polls the parties and candidates that ostensibly best represented his interests. Both labels, the Jacksonian Era and the Era of the Common Man, attest to the scholarly belief in the centrality of politics.

Who can deny the importance of politics, particularly the dramatic politics of the age of Jackson? The point of this book is not that Jacksonian politics were insignificant but rather that they shared center stage with other themes. To understand Jacksonian America it is necessary to be familiar with its social and economic as well as its political developments. For that matter the recent unearthing of great quantities of new social and economic evidence has thrown important new light on the politics of the period. Political issues do not after all develop in a social vacuum. It matters a great deal, for example, whether a procedural reform that democratizes politics occurs against a backdrop of social inequality and rigid class barriers or in a happier social setting. What would be dismissed as a superficial improvement in the one context might be applauded as a meaningful change in the other. The recent research on social reform and economic and social developments not only highlights previously neglected aspects of the Jacksonian era but it also enriches our understanding of the politics of the period.

Modern historians have not only been investigating new topics but they have been investigating them in new ways, employing innovative methodologies and approaches. This collection contains a cross section of the "new histories" that have enlivened this generation's discussion of the American past. While its editor makes no claim to comprehensiveness, he has no doubt that the selections that follow better reflect the complex reality of the antebellum United States than do books that are confined to the politics of the era.

The interpretations offered here are of course not the only interpretations possible. As a matter of fact I disagree strongly with a number of them. The principle of selection followed for this book is concerned more with the level of interest and the intellectual provocativeness of an essay than with its particular viewpoint. While I am in the habit of regarding my own judgments and interpretations as the right ones, I believe I have sufficient wit to have discovered not only that historians disagree with me as well as with one another, but that with the passage of time I often come to disagree at least in part with my own earlier views. The purpose of this book therefore is to present not a coherent interpretation, the separate chapters of which are logically consistent, but rather a series of stimulating interpretations that challenge scholars and students alike to rethink some of their pet ideas about the Era of the Common Man.

Part One: SOCIETY

EDWARD PESSEN

THE EGALITARIAN MYTH AND THE AMERICAN SOCIAL REALITY: WEALTH, MOBILITY, AND EQUALITY IN THE "ERA OF THE COMMON MAN"

Alexis de Tocqueville's version of an antebellum society characterized by the relative absence both of great fortunes and poverty, a rough equality of condition, and incessant movement up and down the social ladder, was for a long time accepted as an accurate perception. Actually, Tocqueville's social portrait was based on very slight documentation, a product above all of the brilliant Frenchman's deductive flair and his lively sociological imagination. As his most ardent admirers conceded, Tocqueville had little interest in "mere facts." The essay that follows put Tocqueville's influential generalizations to the empirical test—at least for the great cities of the Northeast during the second quarter of the nineteenth century. Drawing its evidence from assessors' notebooks, wills, genealogies, private correspondence, diaries, and journals, among other sources, it discloses a society markedly unlike the egalitarian one depicted by Tocqueville. Adding force to its conclusions are the numerous recent studies indicating that the extremes of wealth and poverty, the worsening maldistribution of wealth, and the slight vertical mobility prevalent in the older cities along the Atlantic seaboard also prevailed in the newer and smaller communities of the West and South.

Alexis de Tocqueville's *Democracy in America,* a work whose insights into the American mind and soul have proven to be almost frighteningly prescient, has been justly acclaimed as the most penetrating single book yet writ-

Originally published in the *American Historical Review,* 76 (October 1971), 989-1034. Copyright © 1971 by Edward Pessen.

ten on American civilization. The book also contains the most influential as well as the most durable interpretation of Jacksonian America yet offered. For while older sectional and class analyses of the great political issues have been largely forsaken by scholars in our own time. Tocqueville's egalitarian version of Jacksonian society continues to command their wide support. The polemic and controversy that have marked the discussion of party battles in the age of Clay and Calhoun have been strangely missing from the consideration of the era's social developments. Jacksonians and anti-Jacksonians, now as earlier, subscribe to the Tocquevillean interpretation of antebellum American society.[1]

Tocqueville was not alone in depicting the American society of the second quarter of the nineteenth century in egalitarian terms. Many contemporaries, native Americans and European visitors alike, observed—or thought they observed—the same fluid social scene discerned by the brilliant young aristocrat.[2] Their joint perception of American society is Tocquevillean not in the sense that its central propositions were original with Tocqueville but rather because no one else formulated the egalitarian thesis so comprehensively, so lucidly, so logically as he. Tocqueville's social portrait is a model of internal consistency.

According to the egalitarian thesis the United States was a society dominated by the great mass of the people, who composed the middling orders. Unfortunate minorities aside, few men here were either very poor or very rich. For that matter the rich here were rich only by American standards, their wealth not comparing in magnitude to the great fortunes accumulated by wealthy European families. What rich men there were in America were typically self-made, born to poor or humble families. Nor did they long hold on to their wealth. Flux ruled this dynamic society; riches and poverty were ephemeral states in this kaleidoscopic milieu. The limited extent and the precariousness of wealth helped explain the dwindling influence of its possessors. At a time when the most liberal of European states was grudgingly permitting some wealthy bourgeois to share the suffrage with great landholders, America was brushing aside all important restrictions on voting. Deference gave way to the strident rule of the masses, as the beleaguered rich turned their backs on a politics permeated by vulgarity, opportunism, and other loveless expressions of popular power. Social and economic democracy followed on the heels of, as they were in part caused by, political democracy. In a society that exalted work over status, class barriers loosened and diminished in significance. And a near if not a perfect equality of condition resulted from the unparalleled equality of opportunity that in Tocqueville's time complemented the abundant natural resources, the technological advances, and the human energy that had been present in America since its settlement.[3]

Tocqueville's comprehensive evaluation of American civilization, stressing as it did the ambivalent values and beliefs of the people, was of course more complex than the preceding passage suggests. The purpose of this essay, however, is not to assess the subtle social philosophy of Alexis de Tocqueville but rather to consider those elements in his appraisal of America that have been widely subscribed to and that form what I call the egalitarian thesis.

The egalitarian thesis has not gone unchallenged. A few contemporary men of affairs joined spiritual and secular perfectionists and labor radicals in dissenting from the consensus as a whole or from particular parts of it. A number of recent publications have also questioned one or another aspect of the traditional interpretation.[4] It is no disparagement to note that the modern criticisms have for the most part focused on other themes; they have either touched on only one facet of the egalitarian thesis or examined only one community; and they have been impressionistic in their methodology.[5] That is, their data are random and inconclusive.

I have gathered much evidence—or what nowadays is called "quantitative data"—from major cities of the Northeast in order to subject the thesis of antebellum egalitarianism to the kind of detailed check it has hitherto been largely spared. What follows is a report on how well several fundamental axioms of the egalitarian theory stand up to the test of empirical verification. Since it is better to be intelligible than modish, clear prose and simple mathematical terms have been used wherever possible in preference to esoteric charts or terminology.[6] Serious historians, even those ancients who had the quaint notion that their purpose was to tell an interesting story well, did much research in the evidence after all. It would be dismaying to think that the amassing of data obliges the scholar to foresake plain English for a mode of communication more characteristic of the computer that may have abetted his research than of the historian who must communicate his findings and his audience who must read them.

"In a democratic society like that of the United States," wrote Tocqueville, "fortunes are scanty," since "the equality of conditions [that] gives some resources to all the members of the community . . . also prevent any of them from having resources of great extent."[7] Tocqueville's reasoning was flawless. As always the great question is whether his logic is borne out by the facts.

It is of course impossible to define objectively "resources of great extent" or riches. The terms may be said to contain both a relative and an absolute component. Riches or great wealth will be owned by relatively few, giving each of their possessors a portion of the community's goods that equals or surpasses in value the total wealth owned by hundreds or even thousands of poorer men. And riches make possible lives marked by material comfort, costly even sumptuous possessions, servants or retainers to perform menial tasks, much leisure time and attractive and expensive means of spending or using it. Since a number of contemporary sources indicated the quantity of wealth required to live the life of the rich, the question to be answered concerns the numbers who attained such wealth.

Digging out evidence of this sort is, however, much harder than devising plans to do so. That few scholarly tasks are more difficult than determining the precise wealth owned by individuals at a given point in their lifetimes prior to death is made abundantly clear by the admitted inexactness of the estimates of wealth made by the few outstanding economic historicans who have tried to deal with the problem. Authorities in this esoteric field offer not precise attributions of wealth but informed estimates.[8]

Nor have many attempts been made by scholars to date to fix the wealth of the great accumulators.[9] In effect the supply of authoritative information is slim, while what is authoritive is unavoidably inexact. If precise scholarly appraisals are lacking, there exists interesting contemporary published evidence that in effect takes up the question: were there very few or no Americans who had substantial fortunes during the era?

Not accoridng to the estimates made by Moses Yale Beach, erstwhile publisher of the New York *Sun* and of lists of New York City's wealthiest one thousand during the 1840s and 1850s.[10] In an 1845 edition of his list John Jacob Astor's wealth was placed at $25,000,000 while twenty other eminent men were adjudged millionaires. Another one thousand New Yorkers were estimated to be worth varying sums ranging from $100,000 to $800,000 for each. The problem with Beach's rating, however, is that in addition to its careless errors and the mystery of its sources—faults noted but accepted by the many scholars who used it because they believed they had no alternative—it was riddled with inconsistencies, was put together shoddily if not irresponsibly, relied on much guesswork, evidently had little or no standing with informed contemporaries, and omitted hundreds of persons who were worth at least the minimum sum required by Beach for inclusion in his pamphlet.[11] Lists similar to Beach's, published for Philadelphia, Brooklyn, Boston, and a number of New England towns, also claimed large fortunes for various luminaries, but the cryptic treatment of the sources of these estimates does not inspire confidence in their accuracy.[12] Probate inventories, while invaluable for particular individuals and general trends, were certain to be incomplete as a clue to the wealth owned by a large group of persons. In the absence of other reliable data the manuscript tax assessment records of the nation's wealthiest cities were consulted, therefore, in order to determine who were the rich and how great were their fortunes.

Urban residents were taxed not on incomes but on the total wealth, real and personal, they owned within the city. During the era Boston printed annual records of all persons who paid taxes on twenty-five dollars or more. New York City, unfortunately, did not. Lists of New York City's taxpayers for 1828 and 1845 were thus created out of the unindexed assessment data: over 100,000 separate items, which in their raw form simply listed, street by street, location by location, the assessed value of each property or estate owned in the city, and alongside it the name of its owner, agent, trustee, administrator, or executor. A John Jacob Astor, who owned hundreds of separate properties, appeared hundreds of times in the original records. Similar lists were drawn up for the then separate—and wealthy—city of Brooklyn.[13] (Philadelphia's tax records did not permit such treatment, since assessors there did not distinguish between owners and users of real property.)

Such lists, if not requiring "a lifetime of research," were indeed time consuming to prepare. Their redeeming value is that they make possible not only the creation of reliable lists of comparative wealth,[14] but answers to a number of important questions raised by the egalitarian thesis.

The assessments have a number of weaknesses, the chief one being their undervaluation of the estates, particularly the personal estates of wealthy men.[15] Tax officials bemoaned the practice of great merchants, men known to be owners of vast real-estate holdings and substantial shareholders in banks and insurance companies, coolly to swear that they possessed no personal wealth whatever. Who could say them nay in view of the incorporeality and the impossibility of tracking down this form of wealth? Boston's property owners may have been unusual in disclosing to assessors much personal wealth, yet officials even in that highly moral city were rightly convinced that property there was assessed substantially below its market value.[16] The consoling feature of the sums disclosed by the tax records is that they are solid bedrock. Charles Hoyt in 1841 was worth at least the $242.226 Brooklyn's assessors of his real property said he was; Hezekiah B. Pierrepont was worth at least the $629,000 that his many lots were assessed for—although if the poor chap could be believed he had not a penny in liquid assets.

Even when the assessed valuations are taken at face value, New York City at the time of Tocqueville's visit had about one hundred persons worth $100,000 or more, while Boston had seventy-five worth at least that sum. A decade later, shortly after the second volume of *Democracy in America* appeared, New York's tax data disclosed that John Jacob Astor and Peter G. Stuyvesant were millionaires, while three hundred other persons were worth $100,000 or more. Boston by then had 150 individuals worth the latter sum, in addition to Peter Chardon Brooks, the millionaire.[17] Brooklyn, by 1841 the nation's seventh city, had twenty-six individuals assessed for $100,000 or more, if none at one million. While Philadelphia's assessments, in not distinguishing between owners and users of real property, do not indicate the total assessed wealth owned by citizens within the city, there is evidence that the Wealthy Citizens listing for that city, like the similar lists for Boston and Brooklyn, was reliable in important respects.[18] Its publisher claimed that Philadelphia had eleven millionaires and another 350 persons each worth $100,000 or more. In any case, the death in 1831 of Stephen Girard, that city's great banker, revealed that he was worth more than $6,000,000, or almost precisely what he was listed for.[19]

The $100,000 figure that many hundreds of Northeasterners were assessed at may not appear to be an impressive sum. Yet even if one makes the most unrealistic assumption that the assessment figures accurately recorded the extent of an individual's wealth, the sums in question were hardly paltry. According to John Jacob Astor's grandson—and he was in a good position to know—a member of the "exclusives" could in 1850 have devoted himself entirely to the good life, including leisurely travel in Europe, on ten thousand a year, in "dollars not pounds," as he hastened to add.[20]

The dollar of the 1830s was capable of wondrous things. William E. Dodge was able to rent a two-story house on Bleecker Street in New York City for an annual rental of $300, while one or two hundred dollars more could pay for an elegant place on "aristocratic Park Place among the Motts, Hones, Costers, Haggertys, Austins, Beekmans, and Hosacks," the *creme de la creme* of New York City society.[21] Room and board at the new Astor House cost $1.50 in 1836, that sum paying for four meals consisting of "all the delicacies of the season . . . served in a most ample manner." Philip Hone, who was sufficiently demanding a gourmet to have found the famed Delmonico's Restaurant wanting, thought the fare at the Astor House capital; he had never seen "a table better set out, better provided, or a dinner better cooked." A wealthy Philadelphian of mid-century held that fifty dollars "constituted the millionairism of money aristocracy of those days," since this sum enabled a man to keep a carriage. According to Sidney George Fisher of Philadelphia, his annual income of less than $3,000 gave him "a comfortable house—servants, a good table—wine—a horse—books—'country quarters,'—a plentiful wardrobe—the ability to exercise hospitality," while an additional one thousand would have enabled him to live like a truly rich man. In view of the prices of other representative goods and services, one understands better why as late as 1852 an informant could advise Carl Schurz that in New York City $150,000 was considered a fortune.[22] There is good reason to believe that men assessed at $100,000 were typically worth many times that sum.

In the absence of income taxes, as well as the presence of a local tax that characteristically took less than one per cent of what a man claimed to be worth, assessed wealth of $100,000 made him a functional millionarie several times over, in terms of modern costs and prices. His real estate was undervalued conservatively by half. Personal estate, regarded by tax authorities and insiders as typically equal in value to real, was almost totally masked. Possessions and investments outside the city were treated by assessors as non-existent. Not one penny was yielded up to a federal tax bureau that in our own era appropriates a substantial portion of a rich man's wealth. In view of the fact, finally, that the dollar of 1840 appeared to be worth roughly between five and six and one-half dollars of 1970, wealth that 130 years ago was assessed at $100,000 is the equivalent of about forty times that gross amount in our own day.[23]

In 1845, when John Jacob Astor's assessed wealth came to $3,074,705, there is good reason to think that he was worth at least five times that sum.[24]

From a Philip Hone notation that "Mr. Astor once remarked that riches did not bring happiness, a man may be as happy with half a million as if he was rich,"[25] one can decide for himself how many times "half a million" the author of that statement was worth. The great merchant banking house of Brown Brothers, led by Alexander Brown of Baltimore and his sons, one of whom, James, was resident in New York City, and another, John A., in Philadelphia, was regarded as one of the greatest international banks; by the mid-1830s its various branches were worth at least $6,000,000.[26] Nor can there be any question that such families as the Stuyvesants, Lorillards, Whitneys, Rhinelanders, Kings, Brookses, Appletons, Greenes, Lawrences, Pierreponts, and Ridgways were then each worth $1,000,000 or more.

Even before the end of the eighteenth century Thomas Willing, the Philadelphia financier, and William Bingham had each accumulated millions.[27] By the 1830s hundreds of families in the nation's northeastern cities had amassed great fortunes based on commerce, insurance, finance, shipbuilding, manufactures, landholding, real-estate speculation, and the professions. The resources and the style of living enjoyed by the Eckfords, Masons, Hendrickses, Beekmans, Lenoxes, Joneses, Costers, and Gouverneurs in New York City, the Bownes, Bergens, Howlands, Leffertses, Cortelyous, Trotters, and Hickses in Brooklyn, the Brimmers, Codmans, Cushings, Parkmans, Phillipses, Quincys, Greenes, Derbys, Otises, Searses, Shaws, Welleses, and Williamses in Boston, and the Becks, Copes, Cadwaladers, McKeans, Walns, Shippens, Biddles, Whartons, Wetherills, and Willings in Philadelphia, not to mention the great families of the antebellum South, were very far from scanty and would have been regarded as substantial wealth anywhere in the world.

The wealth of the American rich, unlike that of the contemporary English aristocracy, derived largely from commerce and when from land, often took the form of real properties recently accumulated in speculations rather than estates held in the family for centuries as was the case with the Bedfords, Northumberlands, or Devonshires overseas.[28] The American rich were a working class, however, only in a technical rather than an actual sense. The preference shown by many of them for attending to business rather than to pleasurable uses of leisure was a matter of taste rather than necessity and can be compared to the preoccupation shown by some peers with the details of managing their estates. By almost any criterion opulent Americans lived lives comparable to those enjoyed by their English and Continental counterparts and were evidently able to do so with significantly smaller expenditures of money. (The ten thousand dollars per annum said by William B. Astor's nephew to be required for lavish living was evidently from one-third to one-quarter the amount needed to achieve a similar standard abroad.)

The town houses of David Sears, Nathaniel Prime, William B. Astor,

William Bedlow Crosby, Peter Schermerhorn, Samuel Ward, Harrison Gray Otis, or Henry Brevoort would have been adjudged magnificent anywhere. If the lavish country residences of David Hosack, John C. Stevens, or James Gore King did not match the awesome size and cost of the duke of Northumberland's Alnwick Castle, neither did the mansions and estates of Northumberland's fellow aristocrats in England. Corps of servants, impressive libraries, elaborate furniture (often manufactured by Duncan Phyfe), sumptuous furnishings, stores of the finest wines, and expensive artworks filled the interiors of the homes of the American economic elite. In the warm weather months the rich retreated to the delights of the Rockaways and other ocean resorts or to the waters of Saratoga and regularly traveled to Havre in ships filled with their own kind, blessed with lavish accommodations, and in Hone's words, with "every day as good a table as the most fastidious gastronome could desire." Their lives at home during the workaday year were enlivened by a constant round of expensive parties, dazzling balls, extravagant fetes and excursions, binding more closely together the leading families both within and between the great cities. The birthday of the beautiful Elizabeth Willing in 1835 was celebrated on Long Island with a trotting match, won by Robert Goelet, a "splendid ball," and a cotillion. On a sparkling fall day later that year "in the beautiful Bay of Boston," aboard a pleasure schooner once owned by David Hosack and Robert Hone, among others, a fishing party of New York City's swells joined with the Brookses, Forbeses, Sturgises, and Bryants in sampling chowder and enjoying great quantities of champagne and fine madeira, to compensate for the mere handful of cod and haddock they had caught.

A fashionable marriage, such as the one uniting Charles A. Heckscher and the daughter of John G. Coster in late 1834, triggered off a round of balls and parties that left even inveterate pleasure seekers somewhat exhausted and a trifle dismayed at their extravagance. The great ball given by Henry Brevoort on February 28, 1840, excited widespread attention for its opulence, but much space in Hone's more than ten thousand pages is given over to description of many dozens of smaller scale but equally exclusive and splendid affairs. A *fête champêtre* of unusual elegance, such as that held at Thomas W. Ludlow's villa on the Hudson, in Phillipsburgh, near Yonkers, on June 26, 1845, could attract several hundred of the leading "judges, lawyers, merchants, men of leisure and millionaires" of New York City to a "picnic" adorned with "every delicacy," fine band music for outdoors, waltzes, polkas, and cotillions within the house, the entire scene enlivened by the presence of several private yachts that circled the private steamer hired for the occasion by Ludlow to carry his guests to and from the festivities. Theater, Italian opera, soirees, and musical evenings also occupied the elite. Fastidious foreign visitors mocked the pretentiousness of the American urban elite's high life, but there could be no denying its expensiveness.

Those who referred to the paltriness of American fortunes doubtless had European wealth in mind. Unfortunately the wealth of the great European accumulators has not been and probably cannot be fixed with precision. For Old World riches as for New, informed estimates rather than precise sums have been offered by scholars. The estate of Nathan Mayer Rothschild, regarded as the wealthiest member of the great family and the richest man in Europe, "was generally assumed to be between £5,000,000 and £6,000,000," or roughly between $21,100,000 and $25,700,000, at the time of his death in 1836. The greatest figure in French finance in the early nineteenth century, Gabriel Julien Ouvrard, who alone in that nation dared think of rivaling the Rothschilds as international financier, could in 1820 "offer a prospective son-in-law a dowry of a million francs." At a high point in Ouvrard's career his worth has been estimated at slightly more than $5,000,000[29]. The duke of Bedford's great estates in 1839 were worth about $10,000,000, to judge from his indebtedness of £551,940, an annual net remittance for the preceding seven years of slightly over £100,000, and the small rate of profit typically earned on his landed property during the period. Only a handful of the three hundred or so families constituting England's landed aristocracy could approximate such wealth, with others such as the earl of Clarendon worth closer to $375,000. Sir Francis Baring, whose fortune may have been matched or exceeded in England in the entire nineteenth century by Queen Victoria, Sir Robert Peel, the dukes of Bedford, Northumberland, Bridgewater, and Devonshire, and hardly any others, has been judged to have been worth slightly less than $5,000,000 during the period, while his son Alexander had real-estate investments worth close to that sum. Lord Overstone, described by a modern authority as the chief figure of Britain's "new commercial aristocracy," had a fortune that at its height, decades after Tocqueville's visit here, has been estimated to have been about $17,000,000.[30]

While these were vast fortunes indeed, they appear to have been approximated by those of the wealthiest Americans. John Jacob Astor's wealth was close to Rothschild's. Dozens of American families commanded riches similar to what has been attributed to Ouvrard and the Barings. For that matter, Alexander Baring's fortune had been substantially abetted both by his marriage to William Bingham's eldest daughter and by his purchase of Bingham's vast Maine properties. European landed wealth of course was much older than American, a fact that possibly led contemporaries to question the extent as well as the vulgarity of the Yankee nouveaux riches. Herman Thorn, a fashionable New Yorker who, in marrying the niece of William Jauncey had also come into much of the latter's fortune, stayed in Paris during the 1830s. Thorn was said to have "lived in a style of princely splendor that eclipsed all rivalry, to the great astonishment of the French, who failed to comprehend where in America he had acquired such funds." In 1836 he was reported "to have spent $8,000 on a single fancy dress ball in his Paris home [actually, a splendid palace]." According to Philip Hone his friend Thorn talked "about hundreds of thousands with the air of a man who has been born and brought up in the midst of gold, silver and precious stones."[31] Yet although Thorn was a rich man, there were close to one hundred families in New York City alone whose wealth surpassed his. The notion that antebellum America lacked substantial fortunes is not borne out by the evidence, primarily, as will be noted, because of its faulty assumption concerning the alleged distribution of "resources to all the members of the community."

"In America," wrote Tocqueville, "most of the rich men were formerly poor."[32] The idea that, in the words of Henry Clay, the wealthy and successful were "self-made men," came close to being an article of faith, so widely was it subscribed to by Americans during the era. The common man was constantly reminded that "the most exalted positions" or great wealth were accessible to men of humble origin, since in this country "merit and industry" rather than "exclusive privileges of birth" determined the course of one's career. The merchant prince, William E. Dodge, offered the estimate that seventy-five per cent of the era's wealthy men "had risen from comparatively small beginnings to their present position."[33] If few modern historians would commit themselves to a precise ratio, many have nevertheless agreed that a remarkable movement up the social and economic ladder characterized the second quarter of the nineteenth century.[34] We have evidently convinced our colleagues in sociology, including some of the leading students of social mobility and stratification, that for the Jacksonian period the facts are in: intergenerational economic and occupational mobility were the rule. Actually it is not the facts that are in but rather a continuing series of firmly stated generalizations that essentially do nothing more than assume that the facts would bear them out.[35]

That Tocqueville in some instances was ready to spin his marvelous social theorems by reference more to logic than to pedestrian data is well known.[36] What is fascinating is the extent to which scholars, ordinarily skeptical of unverified observation, have relied on it in discussing the origins of the rich in the "age of the common man."

The social origins and parental status of wealthy citizens of Boston, Philadelphia, New York City, and Brooklyn have been investigated in order to test the belief that typically they were born poor. Information has been gathered on the several hundred wealthiest citizens in each of these great cities.[37] The evidence indicates that some of the best known among the wealthy citizens did in fact have the kind of background ascribed to them by the egalitarian thesis.

John Jacob Astor's story is perhaps improperly described as a rise from rags to riches. There is some question as to the precise wealth or status of his father. Whether the latter was a "very worthy" minor officeholder, as some described him, or a poor man devoted more to tippling than to industry, as he was depicted by others—for the moment I am prepared to regard the two judgments as contradictory—it seems fairly certain that the great merchant was indeed a self-made man of humble origin. The same can be said, with even more certainty, of his sometime partner, Cornelius Heeney, who migrated from Ireland apparently with less than a dollar in his pockets, to become one of the wealthiest residents in Brooklyn.[38] Lewis A. Godey, publisher of the popular *Ladies' Book,* John Grigg, and Joseph Sill were wealthy Philadelphians of humble beginnings, while Daniel P. Parker, Ebenezer Chadwick, John R. Adan, and the three Henshaw brothers in Boston also appear to have been of poor or humble birth, as were such New York eminences as Anson G. Phelps, Marshall O. Roberts, Gideon Lee, Saul Alley, and possibly the Lorillard brothers. Stephen Girard's claim that he, too, had been a destitute youth was evidently accepted by most contemporaries, although there is some doubt as to whether it was well founded.[39] Evidence is thus not lacking that some rich men had in fact been born poor. The most interesting feature of such evidence, however, is its uncommonness.

During the age of alleged social fluidity, the overwhelming majority of wealthy persons appears to have been descended of parents and families who combined affluence with high social status. The small number of these families that had been less than rich had typically been well to do.[40] Only about two per cent of the Jacksonian era's urban economic elite appear to have actually been born poor, with no more than about six per cent of middling social and economic status. Included in the middle are the families of Peter Cooper, William E. Dodge, Gerard Hallock, Joseph Sampson, Cornelius Vanderbilt, Moses Yale Beach, Peter Chardon Brooks, Amos and Abbot Lawrence, Thomas H. Perkins, George C. Shattuck, George Hall, Thomas Everitt, Jr., Samuel R. Johnson, Cyrus P. Smith and Samuel Smith, all of whom appeared to have been both better off and of higher status occupations than the mechanics, cartmen, milkmen, and laborers who predominated in the cities. The middle category was composed of ministers, petty officials, professionals other than successful lawyers and doctors, shopkeepers, skilled artisans who doubled as small tradesmen, and independent or moderately prosperous farmers. The evidence for these generalizations, inevitably imperfect, requires explanation.

It was of course impossible to obtain reliable information on the family status of all persons, but fortunately abundant evidence exists on the backgrounds of most of the wealthiest persons in the great cities. Data were secured on ninety per cent of the more than one hundred New Yorkers who in 1828 were assessed for $100,000 and upward, and in 1845 at $250,000 or more; on eighty-five per cent of the more than one hundred Bostonians worth $100,000 or better in 1833, and $200,000 or more in 1848; and on about ninety per cent of the seventy-five Brooklynites who in 1841 were evaluated at $60,000 or more. For Philadelphia, as was indicated earlier, the nature of the tax records does not permit them to be used to disclose the assessed total wealth of individuals. One can differentiate the "super rich" of that city from other rich or well-to-do persons only by accepting at face value the sums attributed in the anonymous *Memoirs and Auto-Biography of Some of the Wealthy Citizens of Philadlephia.* (Information was obtained on seventy per cent of the 365 persons each claimed by the *Memoirs* to be worth $100,000 or more.) The pattern of the social backgrounds of the urban rich was strikingly similar for all the Northeastern cities. About ninety-five per cent of New York City's one hundred wealthiest persons were born into families of wealth or high status and occupation; three per cent came of "middling" background; only two per cent were born poor. As small a portion of Boston's one hundred wealthiest citizens started humble, with perhaps six per cent originating from middling families. Phladelphia's statistics differ from Boston's only in that four per cent of the former city's 365 richest citizens were born into families of middling status; two per cent of her wealthiest citizens started poor. Cornelius Heeney and John Dikeman were the only wealthy Brooklynites of truly humble origins, with sixteen per cent born into middling status, and the remaining eighty-one per cent of wealthy or high-status families.

Evidence was not as freely available for the "lesser rich" of the great cities. Data were obtained on about seventy per cent of the more than 450 New Yorkers assessed at between $25,000 and $100,000 in 1828, and for sixty-three per cent of the 950 New Yorkers who in 1845 were worth between $45,000 and $250,000; on close to sixty-five per cent of the 260 Bostonians evaluated at between $50,000 and $200,000, in 1833, and on the same percentage of the four hundred Bostonians similarly assessed in 1848; and sixty-three per cent of the one hundred Brooklynites assessed in 1841 at $30,000 to $60,000. It is of course possible that the backgrounds of the "missing persons" were unlike those of the much larger number of persons for whom information was obtained. It could be argued that the omissions concern less eminent persons, whose families probably were not as wealthy or of as high status as the families whose careers and records are better publicized.[41] Yet a significant feature of the evidence is its disclosure that there appeared to be no difference in the patterns of social origin among the "lesser wealthy" as against the "super rich"; or in the patterns of family background of the relatively little known or unknown rich for whom information was obtained as against the eminent rich.

Many of the eras richest men, while born into relative affluence, managed to carve out fortunes that far surpassed their original inheritances. Such prsons were self-made only in a special sense, their careers hardly illustrating what publicists of the era meant by that term. That the children of high-status parents, living in an age of dynamic growth, convert their original advantages into fortunes of unprecedented scope is—as Jackson Turner Main has noted in another context—hardly a sign of social mobility. A family whose adult heads for four or five generations were among the economic elite of their city or community cannot be said to have experienced upward social movement because their always inordinate wealth kept increasing.

The rags-to-riches ideology had so penetrated American thought during the era that publishers whose own compilations contradicted the thesis could manage to convince themselves that it was nevertheless true. Freeman Hunt, devoted and enthusiastic admirer of America's merchants, whom he extolled in his charming *Merchants' Magazine,* could somehow describe Walter Restored Jones of the old, eminent, and wealthy family of Cold Spring, Long Island, truly one of fortune's favorites, as a "self-taught and self-made man."[42] Popular ideology notwithstanding, the era of the common man was remarkable above all for how few rich men were in fact descended of common folk.

When it is compared with earlier periods in American history, the age of egalitarianism appears to have been an age of increasing social rigidity. According to a recent study of seventeenth-century Salem, while "some members of the rapidly emerging elite began their careers propertyless and benefited from the opportunities for investment . . . more often they emigrated with considerable wealth which was further augmented by fortuitous investment."[43] Jackson Main has concluded that there was "remarkable opportunity for the man of modest property to become rich" in the late eighteenth century. Main's admittedly imperfect and partial data on the three greatest cities of the Northeast are of special interest. He finds that about one-third of the sixty wealthiest Bostonians of 1771 had started with little or nothing; in 1789 only one-half of a small number of the city's wealthiest merchants had been born into "wealthy or well-to-do families," with the rest scattered among middling or lower status occupations. Of a group of one hundred wealthy Philadelphians, about "one third had made their own fortunes." He found that "between one third and two fifths of the merchants in pre-Revolutionary New York City [actually, members of the Chamber of Commerce] were self-made men," while in the years immediately after the Revolution the high "mobility rate" actually went up: "probably sixty per cent at the least [of a number of merchants in 1786] were self-made men," and in 1791 fifty per cent of the wealthiest citizens of the east ward had risen from humble origins.[44]

A recent study of post-Revolutionary New York City concludes that for the period ending in 1815 "the evidence of upward social mobility is marked. Almost two thirds of the attorneys and merchants in public office had risen above the occupational level of their fathers who were mechanics or farmers."[45] The evidence on the earlier period, scattered and partial though it may be, suggests that a substantial upward economic mobility that had characterized Northeastern urban life came to a halt during the so-called age of the common man. The self-made man, recently shown by William Miller and his students to have been more fantasy than fact in the post-Civil War decades,[46] was evidently a creature of the imagination a generation earlier, at the very time that the great Henry Clay was asserting the phantom's corporeality and ubiquitousness.

A related belief holds that the second quarter of the nineteenth century was "a highly speculative age in which fortunes were made and lost overnight, in which men rose and fell . . . with dexterous agility."[47] Tocqueville believed that fortunes here were both scanty and "insecure," wealth ostensibly circulating with "inconceivable rapidity." Contemporary American merchants insisted that theirs was the most precarious of callings, incapable of attaining the "security which accompanied the more pedestrian occupations."[48] True, the eminent Philip Hone had noted the resiliency of businessmen: "Throw down our merchants ever so flat [and] they roll over once and spring to their feet again"; but this optimistic judgment was confided to his private diary.[49] The prevailing view was that the pre-industrial decades were characterized by great intragenerational economic mobility.[50] It has recently been shown, however, that antebellum Philadelphia witnessed slight movement up and down the occupational ladder or to and from residential districts of clearly differentiated wealth and status.[51] Another recent study examines the changing economic circumstances of thousands of Bostonians and New York City residents of different wealth levels over the course of a generation.[52] Some generalizations, drawn from its detailed findings, follow.

The richest Bostonians of the early Jacksonian era were invariably among the very richest Bostonians late in the period. Very few persons of the upper-middle wealth level—only seven per cent of that group—moved upward into the wealthy category whose members were each assessed for $50,000 or more. The extent of an individual's early wealth was the major factor determining whether he would be among the rich later. Absolute increases in wealth of any sort followed the rule: the greater an individual's initial wealth, the greater the amount by which it was augmented. A companion rule was that the greater one's original riches, the more likely was he to enjoy an increase. Since the population by mid-century had increased substantially in two decades the ranks of the later rich necessarily had to be filled by many persons who earlier were not among the wealthy. More often than not these newly rich taxpayers were younger members of old families, since fewer than ten per cent of the later group of Boston's rich were new men. Not one member of the $100,000 group of mid-century who had paid taxes earlier had paid them on less than the $20,000 owned by the wealthiest two per cent of the Boston population. Since many contemporaries claimed that the careers of successful merchants followed an erratic course in this kaleido-scopic economy, changes over short-run periods were also investigated to determine whether persons who started and ended the race strong may have lagged in between. They did not. In Boston "few new great families sprang up while fewer still fell away" during the era.

New York City's statistics for the period were not an exact replica of the Boston evidence. Since New York was richer all categories of wealth from the upper middle on up experienced greater gains in absolute wealth than did their counterparts in Boston. For the rest the general pattern was re-markably similar for the two great cities. Between the period of Andrew Jackson's first election to the presidency and his death not quite two decades later only one of New York City's fifty richest persons fell from the class of the rich, and even he barely failed to qualify. As in Boston the few New Yorkers who rose from the upper-middle wealth level to the rich during the course of the era "were more often than not from families of great wealth." The "newcomers" were younger members of the great Hendricks, Jones, Lenox, Lorillard, Barclay, Cruger, Grinnell, Bronson, Grosvenor, Hone, Lawrence, Post, Murray, Storm, Ward, Remsen, Schieffelin, and Van Rensselaer families or of "others of like distinction." About seventy-five per cent of the New York City families constituting the plutocracy of the so-called industrial era of the mid-1850s were families that comprised the elite of the merchant-capitalist era of a generation earlier.[53]

Brooklyn assessment data exist for 1810 and 1841. If the earlier date falls before what even the most flexible classifications would consider the "Jack-sonian era," that fact hardly detracts from its value. If anything the earlier starting point permits those so inclined to draw conclusions about economic fluidity between the "Jeffersonian" and "Jacksonian" periods. Brooklyn's wealthiest families of the early nineteenth century remained among the wealthiest families of the 1840s. Only one of the truly rich of 1810 fell by the wayside and not because of poverty but because of death. In Brooklyn, as in its mighty neighbor, riches achieved by early in the nineteenth century appeared to be the surest guarantee to the possession of wealth a generation later. The many wealthy persons of 1841 who were relative newcomers to the city had achieved their success almost without exception "as a result of a great boost given them at birth by wealthy or comfortably situated parents or relatives."

The pursuit of wealth in Jacksonian America was marked not by fluidity but by stability if not rigidity. Great fortunes earlier accumulated held their own through all manner of vicissitudes.[55] The tax records indicate that the panic of 1837 appeared to have no effect on the minuscule rate by which the mighty fell or the puny rose during the years surrounding that economic convulsion. The Boston tax records disclose that of the owners of the modest property evaluated at between $5,000 and $7,000 prior to the panic of 1837, less than one per cent became significantly wealthier in its wake, while slightly more than one-third were badly hurt by the cataclysm or compelled to leave the city. In contrast, only two of the nearly one hundred Bostonians worth $100,000 or more each suffered substantial losses, while about twenty-three per cent of them enjoyed gains of $20,000 or better in the immediate aftermath of the financial crisis.

That the rich typically were well born and held on to or increased their wealth does not prove that there was no social mobility during the era. The vast and swelling sociological literature on the related topics of "vertical mobility" and social stratification makes clear that the concept of social mobility is a most complex one, not least because it involves the intangible of status. As has recently been pointed out, "there are a host of different ways of measuring mobility. And mobility has many varied contours."[56] No last word can ever be said concerning a subject so elusive and for which the data are so often imperfect.[57]

If, as Ralf Dahrendorf has written, "the concept of social mobility is too general to be useful," there is much to be said for dealing with specific aspects of it rather than with the concept as a whole. All of which is to say that if no data can measure the immeasurable—social mobility in general—the evidence pointing to the upper-class backgrounds of the Jacksonian era's elite and the tenacity with which they held on to their wealth undermines two of the main supports of the long-popular belief in antebellum mobility.

The final question to be considered in this discussion concerns the distribution of wealth in the age of equality. Did the rich command an inordinate share and did it increase or dwindle during the period?

A keystone of the egalitarian intellectual structure is the belief that, in Tocqueville's words, a "general equality of condition" prevailed here. A perfect equality was of course out of the quesiton. Pariah ethnic groups and hordes of unwashed new immigrants obviously were not in on the feast. But that the cornucopia was almost equally available to most others, like other elements in the egalitarian canon, remains a living belief.[58] Even a modern scholar who dissents from the consensus, finding that in New York State "heavy immigration and industrialization" after 1830 widened the gulf between the classes, concedes that earlier "there did not appear to be any contradiction between the notion of equality of opportunity and a general equality of condition."[59] By this version, the prefactory age, or what economic historians have called the age of merchant capitalism, was indeed an age of equality. The comprehensive evidence I have gathered on what almost every urbanite was worth early and late in the era makes possible an empirical test of this thesis. The fact that other scholars have performed similar quantitative studies of the distribution of wealth for earlier periods and that useful evidence exists for the Civil War years and later permits us to compare the degree of equality in the "age of egalitarianism" with that of other periods in American history.

During the colonial era wealth had become more unequally distributed with the passing years. This at least is the burden of the modern studies of scattered towns and villages. In Chester County, Pennsylvania, the richest ten per cent of the population owned slightly less than one-quarter of the wealth in 1693. Over the course of the next century their share increased to slightly under two-fifths, from 23.8 per cent to 38.3 per cent of the total, at the same time as the proportion owned by the poorest three-fifths of the population declined from 38.5 per cent to 17.6 per cent. Wealth was distributed less equally in commercial or seaport towns, and the tempo of increasing maldistribution was swifter in such communities. Where the wealthiest five per cent of property owners in Salem owned about one-fifth of its wealth during the quarter century before 1660, by 1681 their portion had risen to about one-half of the prospering Massachusetts town's total. In colonial Boston the wealthiest one per cent of the population owned about one-tenth, the richest five per cent about one-quarter, and the upper fifteen per cent about one-half of the city's real and personal estate in 1687. By 1771 the wealthiest three per cent of Boston's population held slightly over one-third of the city's wealth, while the upper ten per cent owned about fifty-five per cent of the property of a Boston community that had become "more stratified and unequal." Precisely the same share was owned by Philadelphia's upper tenth of "potential wealthholders" in 1774. On the eve of the Revolution, the richest ten per cent of Northerners owned about forty-five per cent of the wealth, a figure slightly greater than the amount of net worth controlled by the richest tenth of the middle colonies for 1774.[60] A less detailed comparison of New York City between 1789 and 1815 notes that the wealthiest thirty per cent of the city's fourth ward increased slightly their share, from seventy-one to seventy-six per cent of the community's wealth during that quarter of a century.[61]

Was the inegalitarian trend reversed in the nineteenth century? During the "age of equality" wealth in Boston became more unequally distributed than ever before.[62] On the eve of the Revolution Boston's richest tenth had held slightly more than one-half of the city's wealth. Very little change evidently occurred over the course of the next half century, according to a local census report, whose table of Boston's tax payments for 1820 indicated that the upper one per cent controlled about one-sixth of the city's wealth, while the richest tenth continued to own the slightly more than one-half they had held in 1771.[63] Significant changes occurred over the following decade, since by 1833 the pattern of distribution had been sharply altered. The inegalitarian trend accelerated during the next fifteen years. (See tables 1 and 2.)

Actually the richest Bostonians owned a larger share of their city's wealth than tables 1 and 2 indicate. In Boston as elsewhere a small number of rich men appeared to own most of the capital of their city's great financial institutions. A careful check reveals that Boston's wealthiest merchants and businessmen were the officers and directors, and therefore the major shareholders, of the city's fifty largest banks and insurance companies. The disparity between the actual proportion of Boston's entire wealth owned by the elite and the share indicated in the tables 1 and 2 (based on the assessments) is not as great, it will be shown, as were the disparities for New York City and Brookyn. Boston banks and insurance companies were assessed only on their real estate, a relatively small component of the city's wealth. Private individuals who owned corporate wealth were evidently assessed for their holdings; in sharp contrast to New York City and Brooklyn, therefore, taxpayers in Boston were assessed for personal property almost equal in value to their real estate. The fact, however, that in Boston as elsewhere the undervaluation of all property favored the rich above all, since they had the most to hide, is the chief assurance that actual wealth was more unequally distributed than was assessed wealth.

A contemporary yeasayer wrote that in Jacksonian New York City, "wealth [was] universally diffused."[64] Even the normally optimistic Philip Hone disagreed, noting disconsolately that his beloved New York City late in the

Table 1. Distribution Wealth in Boston in 1833

Level of Wealth	Percentage of Population	Approximate Total Wealth Owned[a]	Percentage Non-corporate Wealth
$75,000 or more	1%	$19,439,000	33%
$30,000 to $75,000	3%	$15,000,000	26%
$ 5,000 to $30,000	10%	$16,047,400	27%
Under $5,000	86%	$ 8,331,000	14%

[a]*In 1833 Boston wealth was listed at one-half its assessed value. In this table, therefore, the sums are doubled.*

Table 2. Distribution of Wealth in Boston in 1848

Level of Wealth	Percentage of Population	Approximate Total Wealth Owned	Percentage Non-corporate Wealth
$90,000 or more	1%	$47,778,500	37%
$35,000 to $90,000	3%	$34,781,800	27%
$ 4,000 to $35,000	15%	$40,636,400	32%
Under $4,000	81%	$ 6,000,000	4%

era had "arrived at the [unhappy] state of society to be found in the large cities of Europe," in which "the two extremes of costly luxury in living, expensive establishments and improvident waste are presented in daily and hourly contrast with squalid misery and hopeless destitution." The evidence bears out Hone's gloomy assessment.

In the year of Andrew Jackson's election to the presidency the wealthiest four per cent of the population of New York City, in owning almost half the wealth, controlled a larger proportion of the city's wealth than the richest ten per cent had evidently owned in the urban Northeast as a whole a half century earlier. By 1845 the disparities had sharply increased.

To judge from the New York City evidence, the rate by which the rich got proportionately richer became much more rapid during the nineteenth century than it had been during the seventeenth or eighteenth. As for the city's inequality in 1828 and 1845, its full extent is not disclosed in the assessment figures for these years.

A committee of the Common Council had reported that it was persons of "very extensive capital" who paid taxes on personal property "far less in proportion than those in moderate and low circumstances." In view of the way in which the underassessments of all wealth masked the true wealth of the rich above all, it is clear that the proportion of the city's wealth owned by a small upper crust was greater than the figures indicate. If, as contemporary municipal officials believed, the richest of the rich owned most of the hidden personal wealth, the proportion of the city's total wealth they controlled goes up by a figure dependent on the percentage of the undisclosed wealth that is attributed to them. On the basis that the personal property of the rich equaled the worth of their real estate, and that the wealthiest four per cent owned about nine-tenths of New York City's unassessed personal property, the upper one per cent would have owned about thirty-five per cent and the next wealthiest three per cent about twenty-two per cent of all noncorporate wealth in 1828. In 1845, by this reckoning, the richest one per cent would have owned about forty-seven per cent, while the next wealthiest three per cent would have held an additional thirty-two per cent of the

Table 3. Distribution of Wealth in New York City in 1828

Level of Wealth	Percentage of Population	Approximate Non-corporate Wealth Owned[a]	Percentage Non-corporate Wealth
$35,000 or more	1%	$25,517,000	29%
$ 7,500 to $35,000	3%	$17,520,000	20%

[a]The figures used here for the city's total wealth are slightly less than the figures given in Thomas F. Gordon's *Gazeteer of the State of New York* (New York, 1836), because I have excluded the assessments on partnerships.

city's noncorporate wealth. Nor do these estimates take into account the likelihood that the actual worth of the real property owned by the largest wealth holders was also undervalued. Perhaps the latter distortion can be compensated for or canceled out by an adjustment that attempts to take into account the ownership of corporate wealth.

In 1828 corporations, mainly banks and insurance companies, were assessed for $23,984,660 or twenty-one per cent of the city's total estate of $112,019,533 (exclusive of partnerships). It is probably impossible to track down the owners of all corporate wealth; records, inadequate to begin with, have been lost. Yet for all the imprecision attending the attribution of corporate capital, certain conclusions can be drawn that affect significantly the distribution of wealth.

Poor men and for that matter the great bulk of the city's population owned either nothing or merely minuscule portions of such capital. The minimum cost of a share, typically fifty dollars to one hundred dollars, priced out such people. As Cadwallader C. Colden and Peter A. Jay pointed out in behalf of the Bank for Savings in 1823, "a depositor is not a stockholder."[66] The directors of the corporations regularly listed in the annual New York City directories were overwhelmingly the merchant elite, many of the same individuals forming a kind of interlocking directorate over the great city's banks and insurance companies.[67] These directors were required to own stock in their corporations. According to an insider, himself an officer in several New York City banks during the era, directors usually "own[ed] in the aggregate a considerable portion of the stock" in their companies. They had been chosen in the first place "for their wealth, commercial experience, and influence in attracting to the institution a good class of dealers."[69] Precise information available for a number of contemporary banks and insurance companies discloses that a small number of directors owned almost all the capital in their corporations.[70] When allowance is made for the inordinate share of corporate wealth owned by the elite it is likely that in New York City the richest one per cent actually owned as much as forty-one per cent and the next wealthiest three per cent owned twenty-two per cent of all wealth in 1828. By 1845 the wealthiest one per cent would have owned one-half of all wealth, while the upper four per cent owned eighty-one per cent of the city's total wealth.[71]

Table 4. Distribution of Wealth in New York City in 1845

Level of Wealth	Percentage of Population	Approximate Noncorporate Wealth Owned	Percentage Noncorporate Wealth
$55,000 or more	1%	$85,804,000	40%
$20,000 to $55,000	3%	$55,000,000	26%

The evidence for Brooklyn is unusually interesting because it permits a comparison of the degree of equality that obtained in the village of 1810, populated by fewer than 5,000 persons, with the bustling city of 1841, whose population of about 41,000 placed Brooklyn seventh among the nation's cities. The richest wealth holders of the early nineteenth-century village held a slightly larger portion of Brooklyn's wealth than had typically been controlled by the upper tenth in the urban Northeast late in the "Revolutionary era."

Although the poorer half of the population owned only a tiny fraction of Brooklyn's wealth in 1810, the fact that seven out of eight families paid taxes on some property, even if slight, suggests that few residents of the community could be classified as propertyless proletarians. By 1841 important changes had occurred.

The distribution of wealth in the commercial Brooklyn of 1841 was strikingly similar to the division that obtained in its great neighbor across the East River. By 1841 the poorest two-thirds of Brooklyn's population owned

Table 5. Distribution of Wealth in Brooklyn in 1810

Level of Wealth	Percentage of Population	Approximate Non-corporate Wealth Owned	Percentage Non-corporate Wealth
$15,000 or more	1%	$262,400	22%
$ 4,000 to $15,000	7%	$383,122	33%
$ 2,500 to $ 4,000	6%	$137,944	11%
$ 1,000 to $ 2,500	20%	$290,000	25%
$ 500 to $ 1,000	12%	$ 67,500	6%
Under $500	54%	$ 30,000	3%

Table 6. Distribution of Wealth in Brooklyn in 1841

Level of Wealth	Percentage of Population	Approximate Non-corporate Wealth Owned	Percentage Non-corporate Wealth
$50,000 or more	1%	$10,087,000	42%
$15,000 to $50,000	2%	$ 4,000,000	17%
$ 4,500 to $15,000	9%	$ 5,730,000	24%
$ 1,000 to $ 4,500	15%	$ 2,804,000	12%
$ 100 to $ 1,000	7%	$ 1,000,000	4%
Under $100	66%	—	—

less than one per cent of its wealth, with only about one out of five families (exclusive of nonresident taxpayers) taxed on any property at all. Corporate wealth had come to be a factor of some significance, accounting for seven per cent of the total. As in New York City, this type of wealth was evidently monopolized by the elite. Data on the holdings and ownership of the Fulton Ferry, the Brooklyn White Lead Company, the Long Island Bank, and the Brooklyn Fire Insurance Company—firms assessed for about seventy-five per cent of the city's corporate wealth—indicate that the percentage of assessed wealth owned by the richest one per cent was closer to forty-five than forty-two per cent.[72] In addition, Brooklyn's wealthiest taxpayers for the most part admitted to no personal wealth whatever. If the personal wealth of the richest one per cent is treated as though it equaled in value their real property, and when the underassessement of the latter form of property is accounted for by working into our estimate an adjustment that presumes ownership of three-quarters of corporate capital by Brooklyn's elite (outsiders owned close to one-quarter), Brooklyn's richest one per cent emerge with one-half of their city's wealth.

The trend toward increasingly unequal distribution of wealth in the antebellum era was not confined to the great cities of the Northeast. While the pattern of distribution in rural communities and small towns was not as skewed as it was in large urban centers, inequality in the former milieus was dramatic and worsening. In Hamilton, Ontario, "a small commercial lakeport almost entirely lacking in factory industry, with a population just over 14,000" shortly after mid-century, the poorest four-fifths of the population owned less than four per cent of the town's property, in contrast to the richest tenth, who owned almost ninety per cent.[73] As small Massachusetts communities, such as Worcester, became increasingly urbanized, the rich became relatively richer, the numbers of propertyless citizens increased drastically, and "patterns of ownership" became "sharply skewed."[74]

Recent research indicates that on the eve of the Civil War the pattern of maldistribution in Philadelphia and in a number of Southern and Western cities was quite similar to the inequality that prevailed in New York City, Brookyn, and Boston in the 1840s. By 1860 the wealthiest one per cent of Philadelphia's population evidently owned one-half, while the lower eighty per cent held only three per cent of the city's wealth. In Baltimore, New Orleans, and St. Louis the richest one per cent of the population owned about two-fifths, the richest five per cent better than two-thirds, and the upper ten per cent more than four-fifths of the wealth. An impressionistic recent account of Galveston at mid-century finds that the affluent social and economic elite were one hundred times wealthier than their fellow citizens, the wealth of the former group contrasting "strikingly with that of their nearest neighbors." The division of property was not as unequal in rural counties, Southern or Western, although even in such areas the distribution has been found to have been skewed to a surprising extent. In cotton counties the wealthiest five per cent of landholders held more than two-fifths of the wealth, while the upper ten per cent owned almost three-fifths. (According to Gavin Wright, a close student of rural wealth distribution, the actual degree of inequality was greater than the census data indicate.) While wealth was more equally distributed on the northeastern frontier, even there the upper tenth by 1860 held close to two-fifths of taxable wealth. In the words of two modern students, property holding on the Michigan frontier became "more concentrated" with the passage of time, while the distribution of wealth "scarcely supports the typical American image of the frontier as the land of promise for the poor, ambitious young man."[75]

During the age of egalitarianism wealth became more unequally distributed with each passing season. Shared less equally, even at the era's beginnings, than it had been a generation or two earlier, in the aftermath of the Revolution, wealth became concentrated in the hands of an ever smaller percentage of the population. The trend persisted through the 1850s, resulting in wider disparities than ever by the time of the Civil War.[76] Far from being an age of equality, the antebellum decades were featured by an inequality that surpasses anything experienced by the United States in the twentieth century.[77]

According to Gerhard Lenski, the central question in studying social stratification is: "Who gets what and why?"[78] For the era of Tocqueville the answer to the first part of this question is clear enough. The few at the top got a share of society's material things that was disproportionate at the start and became more so at the era's end. Why they did is of course more difficult to explain.

It may be, as Lenski has argued, that in a free market system "small inequalities tend to generate greater inequalities and great inequalities still greater ones."[79] Even if Lenski's comment is true, it is more descriptive than analytical, while leaving unanswered the question: Why? The explanation, popular since Karl Marx's time, that it was industrialization that pauperized the masses, in the process transforming a relatively egalitarian social order, appears wanting. Vast disparities between urban rich and poor antedated industrialism. Commercial wealth, as surely as industrial, enabled its fortunate inheritors to command a disproportionate share of society's good things and the children of the fortunate to hold a still greater share. A massive internal migration, above all of younger, marginal persons of little standing, into and out of the nation's cities increased both the power and the share of wealth commanded by more substantial and therefore more stable elements.[80] It is hard to disagree with Robert Gallman's generalization that "there were forces at work in the American economy during the nineteenth century that tended to produce greater inequality in the distribution of wealth over time."[81] A not insignificant task of future scholarship will be to ascertain as precisely as possible the nature of these "forces." I would venture the judgment that the transportation revolution and the *de facto* single national market it helped create made possible and indeed decisively fostered great increases in profit-making opportunities even before the victory of industrialism, while the system of inheritance and the minimal influence of the non-propertyowning classes enabled private accumulators to command a larger share of society's product than they would be able to in a later era of vastly greater absolute productivity and profits. Amid all the hulabaloo about the "common man" during the era, he in fact got what was left over.

It has long been argued that equality of opportunity if not of condition prevailed in antebellum America, the era's numerous success stories testifying to the rule of the former principle. In David Potter's language, in America equality did not mean the possession of uniform wealth so much as "parity in competition."[82] The evidence, however, indicates that if dramatic upward climbs were more fanciful than real in Jacksonian America, competition was also marked by anything but parity. The absence of legal disabilities did not mean that poor men started the race for success on equal terms with their more favored contemporaries.

According to Charles Astor Bristed, the young man who hoped to gain entry into New York's upper one thousand was one who, possessed of "fair natural abilities, adds to these the advantages of inherited wealth, a liberal education and foreign travel."[83] It need hardly be pointed out that the travel and liberal education mentioned by Bristed were not available to most Americans.[84] Rather, they were accessible to men such as Abram C. Dayton, son of "an opulent merchant" of New York City, who had "all the accomplishments that education, travel and wealth could give." They were available to Andrew Gordon Hamersley, who inherited from his father a fortune, which, by "judicious management," he succeeded in substantially enlarging. Like other of his golden contemporaries he never went into business, owing his success rather to his name, his original possessions, and his "entertaining conversation and courtly manner." They were available to John Collins Warren, Valentine Mott, David Hosack, and Philip Syng Physick, brilliant physicians all, who from childhood had moved in the most rarified circles, attending the greatest universities and studying with the most learned masters at home and abroad, accumulating much wealth largely because they had much to begin with. Means rather than need gave one access to the services of these eminences.[85]

It is of course possible that innate ability or a fortunate genetic inheritance accounted for the success achieved by most of the era's socioeconomic elite, Such traits no doubt played a significant part in some cases. The biographical data indicate, however, that a material inheritance was the great initial advantage that enabled most of those fortunate enough to have it to become worldly successes. Robert A. Dahl has contended that the era was marked by a "cumulative inequality: when one individual was much better off than another in one resource, such as wealth, he was usually better off in almost every other resource," including political influence.[86] It is clear that almost all of the eras successful and wealthy urbanites had initially been much better off than their fellows in possessing the "resource" of wealth.

The race was indeed to the swift, but unfortunately the requisite swiftness was beyond the power of ordinary men to attain. For this swiftness was of a special sort. Unlike the speed of thoroughbred horses, which is a rare but a natural if inbred gift, the ability to cover great ground in the race for human material success appeared to depend less on the possession of innate abilities than on the inheritance of the artificial gifts of wealth and standing. During the "age of the common man" opportunity was hardly more equal than was material condition.

The evidence presented here has been drawn primarily from four large Northeastern cities, communities that were hardly typical of the nation as a whole. Yet, as has been indicated, earlier detailed if not quantitative studies of antebellum Natchez, Detroit, Cincinnati, and other Southern and Western cities revealed patterns of increasing inequality and social rigidity along the "urban frontier."[87] Recent quantitative studies have disclosed that wealth was distributed most unequally in agricultural areas, in small towns, and in Baltimore, New Orleans, and St. Louis, even if the precise patterns of maldistribution were not quite as skewed as for the great cities of the Northeast. The data on the origins, the immensity, the durability, and the distribution of wealth in the United States during the second quarter of the nineteenth century therefore suggest that egalitarianism, in accord with Webster's definition of a myth, may have existed more in the imagination of men than in the lives they led.

The limitation of such evidence lies precisely in its inability to penetrate the imagination or the thinking and feeling of men, in Freudian terms, their conscious and unconscious. A significant component of what I have called the "egalitarian myth," in being immaterial or metaphysical, is resistant to the quantitative method. There appear to be important questions that quantitative studies have not answered and may be unable to answer.[88] Who would aspire to a comprehensive grasp of the "age of egalitarianism" must consider such questions. What has been attempted in this article has been the measurement of the measurable—or, to be more precise, the measurement of some of the measurable. The behavior and influence of the rich, phenomena that are measurable if difficult to gauge, remain to be evaluated.[89] It may be, as one scholar has recently written, that the latter kind of information is "more crucial for history than the social origins" of the elite.[90] The purpose of this investigation has not been the grandiose one of answering the most crucial questions—whatever they may be—about Jacksonian society. I have chosen, rather, to discuss important questions, the answers to which may be crucial to an understanding of that society. The evidence on the backgrounds and the wealth of the rich indicates that the second quarter of the nineteenth century was something other than an age of egalitarianism.

Since ancient historical rubrics confirmed by long usage are powerfully resistant to scholarly attempts to discard them, historians might spend their time more fruitfully by rethinking their estimates of the period in the light of the new evidence than by trying to replace old labels with new. Truer captions will follow on the heels of truer explanations of the nature of the era.

APPENDIX:
A Note on Sources of Information on the
Families of the Rich

Since several sources were consulted for each of two thousand individuals, and valuable material, though sometimes in snippets, was obtained from many of the nongenealogical writings, any attempt even to list all of these sources would run into dozens of pages. I sought clues in many hundreds of manuscript and printed sources for each of the cities studied and was assisted by cooperative librarians who simply turned me loose in their stacks, enabling me to examine every published item on the period.

Unless their data were confirmed by reliable contemporaries, little stock was placed on the evidence of the famous biographical encyclopedias, primarily for its thinness but also for its unreliability. See Allan Nevins, *The Gateway to History* (Boston, 1938) (especially p. 202 of the reprint of a portion of Nevins' essay, in Robin W. Winks, ed., *The Historian as Detective: Essays in Evidence* [New York, 1969]), for a discussion of the actual invention of material in Appleton's *Cyclopaedia of American Biography;* and Nicholas B. Wainwright, ed., *A Philadelphia Perspective: The Diary of Sidney George Fisher Covering the Years 1834-1871* (Philadelphia, 1967), iii, on an inaccuracy in the *Dictionary of American Biography.* The problem with the latter estimable source for our purposes is that so many of its contributors had little interest in the parental status of their subjects. See Daniel Scott Smith, "Cyclical, Secular, and Structural Change in American Elite Composition," *Perspectives in American History,* 4 (1970): 370, for a brief discussion of some of the inadequacies of the *DAB* material. I have discounted entirely Moses Beach's Wealthy Citizens pamphlets, since Beach's cavalier methods in publishing these listings disqualify them as reliable sources. I also agree with the editor of the authoritative *New York Genealogical and Biographical Record,* who said of Joseph Scoville's *Old Merchants of New York* that "the character of this entertaining, gossipy work is not such as to entitle it to any weight," for all its author's ability and experience. *NYGBR,* 3 (1872): 180. Specific Scoville errors are also pointed out in *ibid.,* 61 (1930): 342-43. Genealogical data are hardly foolproof, even when drawn from such reliable sources as the *NYGBR,* the *New England Historical and Genealogical Register* (hereafter *NEHGR*), the *Publications of the Genealogical Society of Pennsylvania,* and the *Pennsylvania Magazine of History and Biography* (the journal of the Historical Society of Pennsylvania) and even when every item in every issue of these sources, commencing with the first issue of the *NEHGR* in January 1847, was scrutinized for useful leads. Family genealogies were also examined. If, after consulting an early volume of the former sources, the researcher is confident that he has secured accurate data, he would be disappointed to discover that subsequent volumes sometimes modify drastically previous biographical statements. As for the latter sources, the tendency of some genealogists to attribute a too exalted status to families of their subjects is counterbalanced somewhat by the disposition to attribute humble origins to substantial men. For comment on the latter tendency, see Benjamin D. Silliman, "Personal Reminiscences of Sixty Years at the New York Bar," 1: 226-43; and John F. Watson, *Annals of Philadelphia in the Olden Time* (Philadelphia, 1842), 1: 530. For a pointed criticism of the tendency of too many geneaologists to prefer biographical to social data, see Edward P. Cheyney, "Thomas Cheyney, A Chester County Squire: His Lesson for Genealogists," *Pennsylvania Magazine of History and Biography,* 60 (1936): 209, 221-22. Other informative criticisms are Roy F. Nichols, "The Genealogist and the Historian," *Publications of the Genealogical Society of Pennsylvania,* 14 (1942): 1-2; and Z. S. Fink, "Some Genealogical Absurdities," *NYGBR,* 52 (1921): 295-96. A useful essay, written from a different point of view, is John F. Lewis, "Some Genealogical Obstacles Considered," *Publications of the Genealogical Society of Pennsylvania,* 3 (1906): 81-104. Among the sources consulted at the historical societies and in other libraries were the private papers of such families as the Stuyvesants, Hendrickses, Fishes, Hones, Grosvenors, Beekmans, Lorillards, Suydams, Schermerhorns, Tillotsons, Strongs, Van Rensselaers, Brinckerhoffs, Astors, Hallocks, Noahs, Kings, Bennetts, Livingstons, Griswolds, Brevoorts, Dodges, Allens, Phelpses, Enos, Whitneys, Aspinwalls, Emmets, Bories, Fishers, Careys, Brimmers, Appletons, Searses, Lawrences, Brookses, Everetts, and Furmans. While such sources are invaluable for many purpsoes, they yield less fruitful data on the status of families, in some cases, than do some of the excellent local histories written in the nineteenth century by contemporary historians and genealpgists, see the correspondence between Latting Latting, early editor of the *NYGBR,* had studied law under Francis B. Cutting and worked with Caleb S. Woodhull. Latting's perfectionism in authenticating the most minute items, as he rummaged through probate records, published and unpublished documents, or sought out survivors, is assurance of his reliability. For examples of the comforting finickiness of this man, who was widely respected and sought after by contemproary historians and genealogists, see the correspondence between Latting and the historian of Long Island, Henry Onderdonk, Jr., in the Onderdonk Papers at the Long Island Historical Society. That Henry Simpson, mid-nineteenth-century biographer of Philadelphia's elite, was aided in his research by such eminences as Horace Binney, Samuel Breck, Henry W. Gilpin, Charles J. Biddle, and Thomas Balch, adds to the credibility of his *Lives.* John F. Watson's personal encounters with some of the elite whose family histories he sketched in 1842 similarly induce respect for his portrayals; see J. Thomas Scharf and Thompson Westcott, *History of Philadelphia, 1609-1884* (Philadelphia, 1884), 2: 1169. Certainly the value of Abraham Ritter's charming and anecdotal account of *Philadelphia and Her Merchants* (Philadelphia, 1860) is enhanced by the evidence that dozens of the early nineteenth-century merchants he discusses respected his judgments. Of course the character of a genealogist is a surer clue to his reliability than the fact that he was contemporary with his subject. And even sensible biographers had foibles. Thompson Westcott was an indefatigable researcher and invaluable source for all things Philadelphian in the mid-nineteenth century. Yet I have discovered that some of his biographical vignettes either ignored or omitted pertinent data and in a few cases simply repeated unverified versions written by predecessors. See Westcott, comp., *Biographies of Philadelphians* (Philadelphia, 1861), and Westcott's four-volume "Historical Scrap

Book concerning the City of Philadelphia," collected 1848-52, which is at the Historical Society of Pennsylvania. Unusually helpful were Horace Lyman Weeks, *Prominent Families of New York* (New York, 1897); Stephen Winslow, *Biographies of Successful Philadelphia Merchants;* Mary Louise Booth, *History of the City of New York* (New York, 1859); Charles Andrew Ditmas, *Historic Homesteads of Kings County* (New York, 1909); Freeman Hunt, *Lives of American Merchants* (New York, 1857), and Hunt's *Merchants' Magazine;* Martha Lamb and Mrs. Burton Harrison, *History of the City of New York* (New York, 1877-96); Frank Willing Leach, *Old Philadelphia Families* (Philadelphia, 1907-13); Charles Morris, *Makers of Philadelphia* (Philadelphia, 1894); John William Leonard, *History of the City of New York 1609-1909* (New York, 1910); James J. Levick, *The Early Physicians of Philadelphia* (Philadelphia, 1886); Benson J. Lossing, *History of New York City* (New York, 1884); Ellis Paxon Oberholtzer, *Philadelphia, A History* (Philadelphia, n.d.); Oberholtzer, *Literary History of Philadelphia* (Philadelphia, 1906); I.N. Phelps Stokes, *Iconography of Manhattan Island* (New York, 1916-28); Josiah Quincy, *Figures of the Past* (Boston, 1883); Edwin A. Stone, *A Century of Boston Banking* (Boston, 1894); John F. Trow, ed., *Boston Past and Present* (Boston, n.d.); George H. Blelock, *Boston Past and Present* (Boston, 1874); John Langdon Sibley, *Biographical Sketches of Graduates of Harvard University* (Cambridge, Mass., 1881); Clifford K. Shipton, *Biographical Sketches of Those Who Attended Harvard College in the Classes 1690-1700* (Cambridge, Mass., 1933); William R. Cutter, *Genealogical and Personal Memoirs Relating to Families of Boston and Eastern Massachusetts* (New York, 1908); and Mary Caroline Crawford, *Famous Families of Massachusetts* (Boston, 1930). For testimony on the reliability of Crawford, Lamb, and Weeks, see the *New York Genealogical and Biographical Record,* 61 (1930): 219; 24 (1893): 92; 29 (1898): 182. Modern scholarly biographies such as Philip L. White's *The Beekmans of New York in Politics and Commerce;* James A. Rawley, *Edwin D. Morgan, 1811-1883, Merchant in Politics* (New York, 1955); D. G. Brinton Thompson, *Ruggles of New York: A Life of Samuel B. Ruggles* (New York, 1946); Richard Lowitt, *A Merchant Prince of the Nineteenth Century: William E. Dodge* (New York, 1954); Bertram Wyatt-Brown, *Lewis Tappan and the Evangelical War Against Slavery* (Cleveland, 1969); and Elva Tooker, *Nathan Trotter, Philadelphia Merchant, 1787-1853* (Cambridge, 1955)—to name only a few—are first rate on particular families. The twenty-eight folio volumes containing Philip Hone's diary, like the manuscript diaries of George Templeton Strong (for the brave soul who can manage Strong's handwriting) and Edward Neufville Tailer, all at the New-York Historical Society, the diary of Sidney George Fisher at the Historical Society of Pennsylvania, or the journals of Gabriel Furman and John Baxter in the Long Island Historical Society are filled with intimate glimpses into the backgrounds of the urban elite by men who knew them because they were of them. James G. Wilson's *Memorial History of the City of New York* including an "anonymously" edited fifth biographical volume; Justin Winsor's *Memorial History of Boston* (Boston, 1884); and John Russell Young's *Memorial History of the City of Philadelphia* (New York, 1895), are examples of the "memorial histories," histories of bench and bar, the medical, religious, and business histories, and many dozens of local accounts that offer invaluable data on the elite of the great cities. For Brooklyn nothing compares in value with Henry R. Stiles monumental *Civil, Political, Professional and Ecclesiastical History and Commercial and Industrial Record of the County of Kings and the City of Brooklyn New York from 1683 to 1884.* (New York, 1884), a sprawling, detailed account filled with family vignettes written by an insider who was an indefatigable genealogist. Stiles was a founder and the first librarian of the Long Island Historical Society as well as the first president of the New York Genealogical and Biographical Society. Indispensable for Brooklyn, too, are the 160 scrapbooks at the Long Island Historical Society, a treasurehouse filled with much trivia side by side with invaluable manuscript and other data on the Cortelyou, Hoyt, Gerritson, Couwenhoven, Martense, Rapelye, Schermerhorn, Remsen, Hicks, Willoughby and other elite families.

Notes

1. Alexis de Tocqueville, *Democracy in America* (Paris, 1835, 1840). References in this article are to an edition edited by Phillips Bradley (New York, 1954). For useful recent discussions of the political historiogrpahy, see Alfred A. Cave, *Jacksonian Democracy and the Historians* (Gainesville, 1964); Charles G. Sellers, Jr., "Andrew Jackson versus the Historians," *Mississippi Valley Historical Review,* 44 (1958): 615-34; and, Edward Pessen, *Jacksonian America; Society, Personality, and Politics* (Homewood, 1969), 352-93. Among the modern works that subscribe to one or more of the central tenets of the egalitarian theory are David M. Potter, *People of Plenty* (Chicago, 1958); Carl N. Degler, *Out of Our Past* (rev. ed.; New York, 1970), 144-45; Marvin Meyers, *The Jacksonian Persuasion* (Stanford, 1957); Lee Benson, *The Concept of Jacksonian Democracy: New York As a Test Case* (Princeton, 1961); Marcus Cunliffe, *The Nation Takes Shape, 1789-1837* (Chicago, 1965); John William Ward, "The Age of the Common Man," in John Higham, ed., *Reconstruction in American History* (New York, 1962), 82-97; David Riesman, Nathan Glazer, and Reuel Denney, *The Lonely Crowd* (New York, 1953); Rowland Berthoff, "The American Social Order: A Conservative Hypothesis," *AHR,* 65 (1959-60); 499; and Stuart Bruchey, *The Roots of American Economic Growth, 1607-1861* (New York, 1968).

2. For a discussion of the individuals who helped shape the egalitarian viewpoint, see Pessen, *Jacksonian America,* 39-46.

3. Tocqueville, *Democracy in America,* 1: 53-54; 2: 105, 138, 164, 199, 234, 237, 239, 250, 251, 258, 263, *passim.*

4. For a discussion of some of the era's dissenters, see Arthur E. Bestor, Jr., *Backwoods Utopias* (Philadelphia, 1950), and Edward Pessen, *Most Uncommon Jacksonians* (Albany, 1967). For recent publications, see Richard C. Wade, *The Urban Frontier: The Rise of Western Cities, 1790-1830* (Cambridge, 1959), 203-30; D. Clayton James, *Antebellum Natchez* (Baton Rouge, 1968); Kenneth W. Wheeler, *To Wear a City's Crown: The Beginnings of Urban Growth in Texas, 1836-1865* (Cambridge, Mass., 1968); Robert A. Dahl, *Who Governs? Democracy and Power in an American City* (New Haven, 1961); Douglas T. Miller, *Jacksonian Aristocracy: Class and Democracy in New York, 1830-1860* (New York, 1967); Miller, "Immigration and Social Stratification in Pre-Civil War New York," *New York History,* 49 (1968): 157-68; Pessen, *Jacksonian America;* Sidney H. Aronson, *Status and Kinship in the Higher Civil Service* (Cambridge, Mass., 1964); and Gary B. Nash, "The Philadelphia Bench and Bar, 1800-1861," *Comparative Studies in Society and History,* 7 (1965): 203-20.

5. Exceptions to the impressionistic approach are a number of recent quantitative studies of particular communities, some of them yet unpublished. Particularly valuable are Stuart Mack Blumin, "Mobility in a Nineteenth-Century American City: Philadelphia, 1820-1860" (Ph.D. dissertation, University of Pennsylvania, 1968), a condensed summary of which appears under the title "Mobility and Change in Ante-Bellum Philadelphia," in Stephan Thernstrom and Richard Sennett, eds., *Nineteenth-Century Cities: Essays in the New Urban History* (New Haven, 1969), 165-208; Alexandra McCoy, "The Political Affiliations of American Elites: Wayne County, Michigan, 1844-1860, as a Test Case" (Ph.D. dissertation, Wayne State University, 1965); and two papers read at the annual meeting of the Organization of American

Historians, April 19, 1971, in New Orleans: Robert Doherty, "Property Distribution in Jacksonian America," on New England; and Michael B. Katz, "Patterns of Inequality, Wealth and Power in a Nineteenth-Century City," on Hamilton, Ontario.

6. In dealing with the distribution of wealth, for example, it has appeared to me as sensible and more economical to make simple statements of the proportions of wealth owned by different levels of wealth holders than to use the Lorenz curve as the means of indicating graphically the difference between a perfect equality of distribution and the actual inequality that inevitably obtains. It is perhaps more revealing to say that the poorest ninety per cent of Philadelphians owned only ten per cent of the wealth in 1860 than to note that the Schutz coefficient of inequality for the same data is .79 (with 0 representing perfect equality and .999 the greatest possible degree of inequality). Similarly, I fail to see the need to refer to the Gini coefficient of concentration, which would be zero on the case of perfect equality of distribution and approaches closer to 1.0 as the area between the diagonal line, representing perfect equality of distribution (in a graph in which the vertical pole measures wealth and the horizontal, population) and the Lorenz curve (connecting the points that indicate the proportions of wealth owned by varying percentages of the population—"deciles," where the latter are divided into tenths) enlarges, in an instance in which the richest tenth owning better than forty per cent of the wealth and the poorest half less than fifteen per cent, produces a Gini coefficient of .54.

7. *Democracy in America*, 2:250,258. Writing more recently, Marcus Cunliffe advises that in America "sizable fortunes were made, but not astronomical fortunes and not static fortunes." *The Nation Takes Shape*, 169.

8. See Ralph Hidy, *The House of Baring in American Trade and Finance: English Merchant Bankers at Work, 1763-1861* (Cambridge, 1949), 40, 46; Kenneth W. Porter, *John Jacob Astor, Business Man* (New York, 1966), 2: 939n.; and Philip L. White, *The Beekmans of New York in Politics and Commerce, 1647-1877* (New York, 1956), 214. Wills, while useful, disclose only what a man was worth at his death—if they do that. In many cases wills affixed no monetary value to the items they listed, See, for example, Leo Hershkowitz, comp., *Wills of Early New York Jews, 1704-1799* (New York, 1967), or the will of William Hamersley, in Lawrence Roth, ed., *Colonial Families of America* (New York, 1946), 25: 16. While probate inventories are invaluable, they, too, are imperfect, typically omitting real property as well as transfers of property before death, depending on the ability of particular valuers, and not existing in sufficient numbers to permit a comprehensive comparison of the relative wealth owned by diverse individuals and wealth-holding groups in a given community. See, for example, "Inventory of the Personal Estate of Peter G. Stuyvesant, December 30, 1847," Stuyvesant Papers, New-York Historical Society. For critiques of the weaknesses of the inventories by scholars who have made effective use of the inventories' strengths, see Jackson Turner Main, *The Social Structure of Revolutionary America* (Princeton, 1965), 288-91; Richard Grassby, "The Personal Wealth of the Business Community in Seventeenth-Century England," *Economic History Review*, 2d ser., 23 (1970): 220; and Alice Hanson Jones, "Wealth Estimates for the American Middle Colonies, 1774," *Economic Development and Cultural Change*, 18 (1970): x, 1-172. Mrs. Jones makes brilliant use of slightly more than two hundred inventories in effect to infer the proportions of wealth held by all levels of wealth holders, a process that of course could not be used to determine the wealth held by particular living individuals.

9. Peter N. Stearns advises me that the extant European literature is sparse. The contemporary *Zeitgeist* may be a contributing factor, since for England, he has written me, "for the most part social historians have stressed the poor rather than the rich in their studies." Whatever the reasons, the relevant bibliography is a small one. The situation evidently has not changed very much from what it was almost a half century ago, when Sorokin wrote that "wealthy men as a specific social group have been studied very little up to this time." Pitirim A. Sorokin, "American Millionaires and Multimillionaires: A Comparative Statistical Study," *Journal of Social Forces*, 3 (1925): 627. Sorokin's method for determining "millionaires," particularly for the nineteenth century, relied heavily on surmise. Robert E. Gallman has recently estimated that there were sixty "millionaire families in the United States in 1840," but

unfortunately his estimate is based on undocumented contemporary listings of "wealthy citizens." Gallman, "Trends in the Nineteenth Century: Some Speculations," in Leo Soltow, ed., *Six Papers on the Size Distribution of Wealth and Income* (New York, 1969), 15. See below for a discussion of the various Wealthy Citizens listings.

10. In New York, beginning in 1842, Beach and his son published thirteen editions of a pamphlet that typically contained the names, the estimated wealth, and biographical vignettes of the purportedly one thousand wealthiest citizens of New York City. The title most often used for these listings was *Wealth and Biography of the Wealthy Citizens of New York City.*

11. See Edward Pessen, "Moses Beach Revisited: A Critical Examination of His Wealthy Citizens Pamphlets," *Journal of American History,* 58 (1971): 415-26.

12. Among the listings were "A Member of the Philadelphia Bar," *Wealth and Biography of the Wealthy Citizens of Philadelphia* (Philadelphia, 1845); "A Merchant of Philadelphia," *Memoirs and Auto-Biography of Some of the Wealthy Citizens of Philadelphia* (Philadelphia, 1846); John Lomas and Alfred S. Peace, *The Wealthy Men and Women of Brooklyn and Williamsburgh* (Brooklyn, 1847); William Armstrong, *The Aristocracy of New York: Who They Are and What They Were* (New York, 1848); Thomas L. Wilson, *Aristocracy of Boston* (Boston, 1848), a unique listing in that it offered no estimates of wealth; A Forbes and J. W. Green, *The Rich Men of Massachusetts* (Boston, 1852); and *"Our First Men": A Calendar of Wealth, Fashion and Gentility* (Boston, 1846). The authorship of the latter pamphlet has been attributed to the historian Richard Hildreth. See Donald E. Emerson, *Richard Hildreth* (Baltimore, 1946), 126, 169. "Our First Men" was published by the printers David H. Ela and Abner Forbes. Ela was a lawyer who had served in the Treasury Department and written on financial subjects; see the *New England Historical and Genealogical Register*, 79 (1926); 89-90. In a letter written December 6, 1892, Frank H. Forbes, son of Abner Forbes, claimed that he and his father had written the pamphlet (which he does not name by title); the letter is located in the Department of Rare Books and Manuscripts of the Boston Public Library.

13. The New York City assessment records for the period are located in the New York City Municipal Archives and Records Center. The Brooklyn assessments for 1810 and 1841 are at the Long Island Historical Society.

14. See Edward Pessen, "The Wealthiest New Yorkers of the Jacksonian Era: A New List," *New-York Historical Society Quarterly,* 54 (1970): 145-72.

15. For a discussion of the strengths and weaknesses of tax data as a clue to the wealth of individuals, see Pessen, "The Wealthiest New Yorkers of the Jacksonian Era," 148-52, and note 23 below.

16. Before 1842 assessments were openly made at one-half the estimated value of property. See Lemuel Shattuck, *Report to the Committee of the City Council Appointed to Obtain the Census of Boston for the year 1845* (Boston, 1846), app., 59; William Minot, Jr., *Taxation in Massachusetts* (Boston, 1877), 7; and *Report of the Committee to Consider . . . Measures . . . that will improve the method of assessing, abating and collecting the Taxes of the City,* City Doc. No. 9 (Boston, 1848).

17. See *List of Persons, Copartnerships, and Corporations, Taxed in the City of Boston for the Year[s] 1833 [and 1843]* (Boston, 1834, 1844).

18. A detailed examination of Lomas and Peace's Brooklyn list shows that most of its estimates were close to the assessed valuations of wealth. As for Boston's *Calendar of Wealth, Fashion and Gentility,* approximately 85 per cent of the close to 400 individuals it listed among the city's 420 most heavily assessed persons. (By way of contrast, fewer than 50 per cent of Moses Beach's "top 1,000" were among the 1,000 New Yorkers assessed for the most wealth.) Guided by the ingenious methodology of Blumin's "Social Mobility in a Nineteenth-Century American City," which identified a small number of occupations and residential districts with great wealth, I have checked the occupations and residences of the 1,128 individuals listed in the *Memoirs and Auto-Biography of . . . the Wealthy Citizens of Philadelphia,* for occupation and residence. Not only was the pamphlet accurate in recording occupations—that is, it was borne out by directories and other evidence—the occupations were over-

whelmingly the high status occupations associated with great wealth. Seventy-seven per cent were classified as merchants; 11 per cent as lawyers and doctors; 6 per cent as manufacturers; and only one per cent as "mechanics"—some of the latter of whom might well have been entrepreneurs. Compare Jackson Turner Main's finding that of Philadelphia's richest 100 in 1765, "more than half . . . were merchants. Nearly one out of five were professional men, mostly lawyers and doctors. . . . Less than one-tenth were artisans or manufacturers." *The Social Structure of Revolutionary America,* 192. Of the 800 wealthy Philadelphians whose residences were located, a majority lived in the wealthy eastern wards whose per capita assessed wealth was more than three times as great as the wealth of most of the other wards in the city. That a house was not located between the Delaware and Seventh Street, running east to west, or between Mulberry and Walnut Streets, north to south, was hardly a sign of the poverty of its owner, however. By the 1840s many of Philadelphia's wealthiest and most notable persons lived in "Girard Row," the row of houses on the north side of Chestnut Street, between Eleventh and Twelfth Streets. According to Willis P. Hazard, who published a revised edition of John F. Watson's *Annals of Philadelphia in the Olden Time* (Philadelphia, 1927), 3: 247, although the eastern wards were still substantially wealthier than the western in 1835, a sharp narrowing of the gap between them had begun by 1829 and continued thereafter. Many a "mansion" stood in the "poorer" wards of Philadelphia, the wealth of the mansion's occupant not sufficient to change significantly the average wealth of all of the district's inhabitants. (This pattern existed in Brooklyn as well. Although Brooklyn Heights was clearly the center of fashion and wealth, many wealthy persons continued to inhabit homes put up by their families generations earlier, in what had now become poorer neighborhoods. See Edward Pessen, "A Social and Economic Portrait of Jacksonian Brooklyn," scheduled for publication in the October 1971 issue of the *New-York Historical Society Quarterly.*) Another indirect sign of the Philadelphia list's worth is the fact that it contained about 85 per cent of the persons who belonged to the exclusive Philadelphia Club in the mid-1840s.

19. Stephen Simpson, *Biography of Stephen Girard* (Philadelphia, 1832), 213; Harry Emerson Wildes, *Lonely Midas: The Story of Stephen Girard* (New York, 1943), 247.

20. Charles Astor Bristed, *The Upper Ten Thousand: Sketches of American Society* (New York, 1852), 18. According to Bristed, an upper 10,000 was a great exaggeration, "for the people so designated are hardly as many hundreds" (p. 271).

21. Abram C. Dayton, *Last Days of Knickerbocker Life in New York* (New York, 1871), 97; William E. Dodge, *Old New York: A Lecture* (New York, 1880), 17. To compare the cost of living for a Western merchant, see Daniel Aaron, "Cincinnati, 1818-1838: A Study of Attitudes in the Urban West" (Ph.D. dissertation, Harvard University, 1942), 67.

22. The latter quotation is from Robert G. Albion, *The Rise of New York Port, 1815-1850* (New York, 1939), 258. The "Philadelphian" is cited in Elizabeth M. Geffen, "Joseph Sill and His Diary," *Pennsylvania Magazine of History and Biography,* 94 (1970): 303. Fisher's comment is from the diary of Sidney George Fisher, Jan. 17, 1842. Historical Society of Pennsylvania. Other sources are Benjamin Silliman, "Personal Reminiscences of 60 Years at the New York Bar," in David McAdam *et al.,* eds., *History of the Bench and Bar of New York* (New York, 1897), 1: 232; *History of the Chemical Bank, 1823-1913* (New York, 1913), 118-19; Freeman Hunt, *Lives of Eminent Merchants* (New York, 1857), 1: 475-76; Asa Greene, *A Glance at New York* (New York, 1837), 18; I. N. Phelps-Stokes, *The Iconography of Manhattan Island* (New York, 1916, 1918, 1922, 1926, 1928), 3: 528; and the MS diary of Philip Hone, 13: 249. The twenty-eight folio volumes are at the New-York Historical Society. The massive unpublished segments in particular, which constitute about ninety per cent of Hone's account, are a treasure trove on life among New York City's social and economic elite.

23. It is impossible to make an exact comparison of the value of the dollar in 1840 and 1970. It was possible, however, to work out a rough comparison by using reliable, mainly federal data on changing wholesale and consumer price indexes that trace the changing value of the dollar. My estimate that the 1840 dollar was worth about $6.50 in 1970 is based on Arthur Harrison Cole, *Wholesale Commodity Prices in the United States, 1700-1861* (Cambridge, Mass.,

1938); Horace G. Wadlin, Chief of U.S. Bureau of Statistics, *Comparative Wages and Prices, 1860-1897* (Boston, 1898); U.S. Department of Labor, Bureau of Labor Statistics, Index Numbers of Wholesale Prices on Pre-War Base, 1890 to 1927 (Washington, 1928); Robert A. Sayre, National Industrial Conference Board, *Consumers' Prices 1914-1948* (New York, 1948); U.S. Senate, Joint Economic Committee Report, with U.S. Department of Labor, Bureau of Labor Statistics, *Frequency of Changes in Wholesale Prices: A Study of Price Flexibility* (Washington, 1959); and information on 1956-70 furnished me by the U.S. Department of Labor, Bureau of Labor Statistics, Regional Office 11, for New York, New Jersey, Puerto Rico, and the Virgin Islands, Using different data, Alice Hanson Jones has worked out a devaluation from 1774 to 1967, in which a later dollar is worth one-sixth the earlier, "Wealth Estimates for the American Middle Colonies," 127-29. She advises me, I am glad to say, that in the judgment of the authoritative Jack E. Triplett, neither estimate is right or wrong; different data yield different conclusions; perfection is out of the question in price estimates. See Jack E. Triplett, "Quality Bias in Price Indexes and New Methods of Quality Measurement," in Zvi Griliches, ed., *Price Indexes and Quality Changes,* scheduled for publication in 1971. It is also consoling that in Mrs. Jones' judgment the difference between her skilled estimate and my rough effort is not significant. The changing price index undoubtedly underestimates the devaluation that has occurred in the "rich man's dollar." Mrs. Jones, who was formerly with the Department of Labor, informs me that the CPI "is the price of a 'market basket' of goods and services commonly purchased by *wage earners and clerical workers.*" (My italics.) My formula for estimating the contemporary gross-dollar value of the rich man's assessed wealth of 130 years ago treats personal estate as equal in value to real, and out-of-city real holdings as worth one-half of city properties. See John C. Schwab, *History of the New York Property Tax: An Introduction to the History of State and Local Finances in New York* (Baltimore, 1890), 87; *Report of the Special Committee of the Common Council of the City of Brooklyn, on Finances, Indebtedness, etc. of the City* (Brooklyn, 1838). In Hone's notes the prices realized by a number of wealthy New Yorkers on the sale only of portions of their city properties were more than twice the amount of their total wealth as reported by assessors. The charge that assessments measured only a small fraction of the wealth of the rich appears in *Minutes of the Common Council of the City of New York, 1784-1831* (New York, 1917), 8: 437; New York State, *Report of the Tax Commissioners of New York* (New York, 1871), 30; "Report of the Special Committee of the Board of Supervisors Appointed to examine the Assessment Rolls, and ascertain whether valuations in each Ward bear a just relation to the aggregate valuations in all the Wards," New York City, Sept. 4, 1829, in City Clerk Filed Papers, Location 3012, New York City Municipal Archives and Records Center; G. N. Bleecker, Comptroller, "Communication from the Comptroller on Subject of the Defective Manner of Assessing Personal Property in This City," New York, Jan. 24, 1820, City Clerk Filed Papers, Location 3216; and in other sources discussed in Pessen, "The Wealthiest New Yorkers of the Jacksonian Era," 151 n.9.

24. The leading student of Astor's finances, Kenneth W. Porter, is skeptical of Astor's claim that his real estate in 1846 was worth only $5,184,340. Porter notes that seven years earlier the great merchant conceded that his real property was worth $5,445,525; subsequently he amassed more property, while the value of his older properties had appreciated. *John Jacob Astor,* 2: 939, 951-52.

25. MS diary of Philip Hone, 22: 356.

26. The Philadelphia Wealthy Citizens list modestly estimated Brown's wealth at $500,000. See the letter of an officer of the firm to the governor of the Bank of England, cited in John Crosby Brown, *A Hundred Years of Merchant Banking: A History of Brown Brothers and Company* (New York, 1909), 83; see also David S. Landes, *Bankers and Pashas: International Finance and Economic Imperialism in Egypt* (London, 1958), ch. 1, and Benson J. Lossing, *History of New York City* (New York, 1884), 2: 583.

27. Burton Alva Konkle, *Thomas Willing and the First American Financial System* (New York, 1937), 120-21; Robert C. Alberts, *The Golden Voyage: The life and Times of William Bingham, 1752-1804* (Boston, 1969), ix, 429; Henry Simpson, *The Lives of Eminent Phila-*

delphians (Philadelphia, 1859), 87; Margaret L. Brown, "Mr. and Mrs. William Bingham of Philadelphia," *Pennsylvania Magazine of History and Biography,* 61 (1937): 286-324; Brown, "William Bingham, Eighteenth Century Magnate," *Ibid., 387-434;* William Otis Sawtelle, "William Bingham of Philadelphia and His Maine Lands," *Publications of the Genealogical Society of Pennsylvania,* 9 (1926): 207-26.

28. My view of English landed wealth is derived mainly from F. M. L. Thompson, *English Landed Society in the Nineteenth Century* (London, 1963); David Spring, *The English Landed Estate in the Nineteenth Century: Its Administration* (Baltimore, 1963); and from conversations in which Mr. Spring was kind enough to give me the benefit of his unsurpassed knowledge of the Bedford and the other English landed families.

29. David Landes has advised me that it is impossible to determine precisely what Nathan Rothschild was worth, in view of the tangled nature of the great family's finances and the difficulties posed by Rothschild's will. Bertrand Gille's authoritative *Histoire de la Maison Rothschild, Des Origines à 1848* (Geneva, 1965) and *Histoire de la Maison Rothschild, 1848-1870* (Geneva, 1967) focus on the family's corporate assets rather than the personal wealth of its members. For an informed estimate, see Cecil Roth, *The Magnificent Rothschilds* (London, 1939), 25-26. In arriving at the dollar value of the pound for the period I have followed Ralph Hidy's estimate, "calculating the dollar at 4 shillings and 8 pence," in "The House of Baring and the Second Bank of the United States, 1826-1836," *Pennsylvania Magazine of History and Biography,* 68 (1944): 270. Arthur-Lévy, *Un Grand Profiteur de Guerre: Gabriel Julien Ouvrard, 1770-1846* (Paris, 1929), 1; Otto Wolff, *Ouvrard, Speculator of Genius, 1770-1846* (London, 1962), xiv, 148, 187. The estimate of Ouvrard's wealth in dollars is drawn from Arthur-Lévy's work and from Wolff's judgment that "during most of Ouvrard's lifetime the rate of exchange was twenty-five francs to the pound." *Ouvrard,* xiv.

30. Spring, *English Landed Estate,* 35, 41; Thompson, *English Landed Society,* 25. Mr. Spring has suggested to me that multiplying the landed income of the great aristocrats by thirty and then subtracting their indebtedness yields a useful if rough approximation of their worth. Hidy, *House of Baring,* 40, 46; Thompson, *English Landed Society,* 39. Overstone had spent £1,670,000 in the purchase of estates, and by his death in 1883 he left £2,118,804 in stocks, shares, and other forms of personal property.

31. MS diary of Philip Hone, 10: 76; *New York Genealogical and Biographical Record* (hereafter NYGBR), 91 (1960): 91.

32. *Democracy in America,* 1: 54; see also 2: 138.

33. See Dodge, *Old New York,* 38-40; Joseph Scoville, *The Old Merchants of New York* (New York, 1862-63), *passim;* Hunt, *Lives of Eminent Merchants, passim;* John W. Francis, *Old New York* (New York, 1866), ix; Calvin Colton, *Junius Tracts* (New York, 1844), 7: 15; Paul Goodman, "Ethics and Enterprise: The Values of a Boston Elite, 1800-1860," *American Quarterly,* 18 (1966): 440, 447; Moses Yale Beach, editorials in the New York *Sun,* Jan. 8, 11, 13, 18, 1845, and preface to *Wealth and Pedigree of the Wealthy Citizens of New York* (New York, 1842); *Memoirs of the Wealthy Citizens of Philadelphia,* the preface of which reported that "our wealthy citizens . . . pride themselves for having made their own money"; *Charles Humphreys, Philadelphia Merchant* (Philadelphia, n.d.); and Stephen N. Winslow, *Biographies of Successful Philadelphia Merchants* (Philadelphia, 1864), viii, 111, 137. The popularity of the belief during the antebellum period is discussed in John G. Cawalti, *Apostles of the Self-Made Man* (Chicago, 1965), and Irvin G. Wyllie, *The Self-Made Man in America: The Myth of Rags to Riches* (New York, 1966), 14-20.

34. One well-known textbook states that "of the successful businessmen of the period before the Civil War, almost fifty per cent came from the lower social and economic strata of society." Dexter Perkins and Glyndon G. Van Deusen, *The United States of America: A History* (New York, 1968), 1: 446. For variations on the theme of the self-made Jacksonian rich, see Carl R. Fish, *The Rise of the Common Man: 1830 to 1850* (New York, 1927), 9; Berthoff, "American Social Structure," 499-500; Benson, *Concept of Jacksonian Democracy,* 165; Cunliffe, *The Nation Takes Shape,* 164; Morton Borden, *The American Profile* (Lexington, 1970), 114;

Samuel Eliot Morison, *Oxford History of the American People* (New York, 1965), 475; Stuart Bruchey, *Roots of American Economic Growth,* 201, 207; and P. M. G. Harris, "The Social Origins of American Leaders: The Demographic Foundations," *Perspectives in American History,* 3 (1969): 218. According to Douglas Miller social lines hardened in New York after 1830, but earlier, "poor-boy-made-good examples abounded" in this socially mobile society. *Jacksonian Aristocracy,* 23, 59, 60, 181.

35. See Seymour M. Lipset and Hans L. Zetterberg, "A Theory of Social Mobility," in Reinhard Bendix and Seymour Martin Lipset, eds., *Class, Status, and Power: Social Stratification in Comparative Perspective* (2d ed.; New York, 1966), 561. In arguing for a shift from descriptive to interpretive research that places greater stress on causes and consequences, the authors state that there is by now "enough descriptive material" on the "background of members of elite groups." See also Harold M. Hodges, *Social Stratification: Class in America* (Cambridge, 1964), 1; Leonard Reissman, *Class in American Society* (New York, 1959), 11, 243; and Sorokin, "American Millionaires and Multimillionaires," 635-36. Stephan Thernstrom's recent observation that "systematic studies of social mobility in nineteenth-century America are still woefully absent" is very much to the point. See Thernstrom, "Notes on the Historical Study of Social Mobility," in Don Karl Rowney and James Q. Graham, Jr., eds., *Quantitative History* (Homewood, 1969), 100. See also Stuart Blumin, "The Historical Study of Vertical Mobility," *Historical Methods Newsletter,* 1 (Sept. 1968): 1.

36. For discussions of Tocqueville's predilection for the deductive method, see Lynn L. Marshall and Seymour Drescher, "American Historians and Tocqueville's Democracy," *Journal of American History,* 55 (1968): 517; Seymour Drescher, "Tocqueville's Two *Démocraties,*" *Journal of the History of Ideas,* 25 (1964): 211-16; Edward T. Gargan, "Some Problems in Tocqueville Scholarship," *Mid-America,* 41 (1959): 3-26; Gargan, "Tocqueville and the Problem of Historical Prognosis," *AHR,* 68 (1962-63): 332-45; Jack Lively, *The Social and Political Thought of Alexis de Tocqueville* (Oxford, 1962); Marvin Zetterbaum, *Tocqueville and the Problem of Democracy* (Stanford, 1966); and George W. Pierson, *Tocqueville and Beaumont in America* (New York, 1938), 759-60.

37. See the appendix, above, for a discussion of the sources of family data.

38. Porter, *John Jacob Astor,* 1: 4-5; John William Leonard, *History of the City of New York, 1609-1909* (New York, 1910), 2: 500; Thomas F. Meehan, "A Self-Effaced Philanthropist: Cornelius Heeney, 1754-1848," *Catholic Historical Review,* 4 (1918): 4.

39. According to his most recent biographer, who had access to papers not available to earlier commentators, "the facts do not support the myth," propagated above all by Girard himself, as to his boyhood poverty. Wildes, *Lonely Midas,* 4, 5, 10-11, 319. Girard had received a substantial sum from his merchant father before emigrating to America as a junior officer, not a cabin boy. See *Memoirs and Auto-Biography of . . . the Wealthy Citizens of Philadelphia,* app., and Simpson, *Biography of Stephen Girard,* a book that, while it may err on Girard's earlier status, is a fascinating psychological study by a man who knew Girard at firsthand. More prosaic is John B. McMaster, *The Life and Times of Stephen Girard, Mariner and Merchant* (Philadelphia, 1918).

40. Compare Jackson Main's treatment of this issue in *Social Structure of Revolutionary America,* 184. Main concludes that the dozen or so wealthiest Virginians of 1787 whose families were "well-to-do though not wealthy," were not self-made and that those who "inherited *part* of their wealth cannot really be considered mobile." (Italics mine.)

41. For the argument made in a different context, that persons for whom family data are lacking were not necessarily of lower status than those for whom the data exist, see Seymour Martin Lipset and Reinhard Bendix, *Social Mobility in Industrial Society* (Berkeley, 1963), 125-26.

42. Hunt, *Lives of Eminent Merchants,* 1: 428. Jones was an innovative figure in the history of antebellum commercial and marine insurance, yet he owed his start not to any sudden blooming of youthful commercial genius on his part but to his name, his status, and his own family's involvement in the insurance business. As for the self-delusion of the publishers of

the Wealthy Citizens ratings, even when their unsubstantiated biographical sketches are taken at face value, men born rich far outnumbered men born poor. Most of these booklets offered slim biographical material of any sort.

43. Donald Warner Koch, "Income Distribution and Political Structure in Seventeenth-Century Salem, Massachusetts," *Essex Institute Historical Collections,* 105 (1969): 51.

44. Main, *Social Structure of Revolutionary America,* 163, 189-93.

45. Edmund Willis, "Social Origins of Political Leadership in New York City from the Revolution to 1815" (Ph.D. dissertation, University of California, Berkeley, 1967), 171. For a contrasting viewpoint concerning mobility in the Revolutionary era, see Robert A. East, *Business Enterprise in the American Revolutionary Era* (New York, 1938), 213, and Kenneth W. Porter, ed., *The Jacksons and the Lees: Two Generations of Massachusetts Merchants, 1765-1844* (Cambridge, Mass., 1937), 3-150, which stresses the "strong tendency" for businessmen to beget businessmen. Also useful are Nash, "The Philadelphia Bench and Bar," 217-19; McCoy, "Political Affiliations of American Economic Elites," which shows that almost all of Wayne County's successful businessmen were well to do earlier; and for the post-Civil War decades, Clyde Griffin, "Making It in America: Social Mobility in Mid-Nineteenth Century Poughkeepsie," *New York History,* 51 (1970): 479-500.

46. William Miller, "American Historians and the Business Elite," in William Miller, ed., *Men in Business: Essays on the Historical Role of the Entrepreneur* (New York, 1962), 311-28, examines the family status and backgrounds of 200 business leaders of the late nineteenth and early twentieth centuries; Frances W. Gregory and Irene D. Neu, "The American Industrial Elite in the 1870's: Their Social Origins," *ibid.,* 193-211, studies the backgrounds of 300 leaders from textiles, steel, and railroads. Discovering that "poor immigrant boys and poor farm boys actually made up no more than three per cent of the business leaders" he studied, Miller concludes his essay with the statement that poor boys "who become business leaders have always been more conspicuous in American history books than in American history." Herbert G. Gutman, on the other hand, has recently shown that "the most successful Paterson iron, locomotive, and machinery manufacturers" of the late nineteenth century were with few exceptions self-made men who had come to the small New Jersey city as ironworkers or craftsmen who "opened small shops or factories of their own," after completing their apprenticeships. Gutman, "The Reality of the Rags-to-Riches 'Myth': The Case of the Paterson, New Jersey, Locomotive, Iron, and Machinery Manufacturers, 1830-1880," in Thernstrom and Sennett, *Nineteenth-Century Cities,* 98-124. Gutman notes that the biographical material he has drawn from several directories and books refers "*not* [to] a sample" but to an entire group. The group, however, includes only about thirty men, and it is not clear how rich they were. But his study suggests the value in further examinations of the backgrounds of small businessmen and skilled artisans in other communities. It may be that in the early phases of certain manufacturing industries success required a know-how that came only with working in the craft.

47. Bruchey, *Roots of American Economic Growth,* 206.

48. Robert G. Albion, "Commercial Fortunes in New York: A Study in the History of the Port of New York About 1850," *New York History,* 16 (1935): 167-68; Tocqueville, *Democracy in America,* 1: 53, 2: 105, 234, 250-51.

49. MS diary of Philip Hone, 23: 165.

50. For modern variations on this view, see Marcus Cunliffe, *The Nation Takes Shape,* 169; Berthoff, "The American Social Order," 499-500; Ward, "The Age of the Common Man," 86; Potter, *People of Plenty,* 95; Meyers, *The Jacksonian Persuasion,* 46; Degler, *Out of Our Past,* 144.

51. Blumin, "Mobility in a Nineteenth-Century American City," 90, 109, 134-52. Winslow long ago wrote that financial crises "touched Philadelphia with gentle wings." In Philadelphia there was "more real, solid, enduring wealth than in any [other] city in the Union"; *Biographies of Successful Philadelphia Merchants,* vii. For valuable discussions of the relationship between occupational change and social mobility, see Ely Chinoy, "Social Mobility Trends in the United States," *American Sociological Review,* 20 (1955): 180-86; Paul K. Hatt, "Occupation and Social Stratification," *American Journal of Sociology,* 55 (1950): 534; Gerhard E. Lenski,

"Trends in Inter-Generational Occupational Mobility in the United States," *American Sociological Review*, 23 (1958): 514-23; Elton F. Jackson and Harry J. Crockett, Jr., "Occupational Mobility in the United States: A Point Estimate and Trend Comparison," *ibid.*, 29 (1964): 5-15; and Otis Dudley Duncan, "The Trend of Occupational Mobility in the United States," *ibid.*, 30 (1965): 491-98.

52. Edward Pessen, "Did Fortunes Rise and Fall Mercurially in Antebellum America? The Tale of Two Cities: Boston and New York," *Journal of Social History*, 4 (1971): 339-59.

53. Close to fifty of the sixty merchants who contributed $100 each to equip the Seventh Regiment of New York City in 1861 were of the prominent families of an earlier generation. Among the donors were members of the Grinnell, DeForest, Emmet, Wetmore, Blatchford, Minturn, Haggerty, Griswold, Fish, Manice, Blunt, Titus, Knapp, Stout, Stewart, Brown, Alsop, Aspinwall, Chauncey, Bronson, Prime, Coster, Aymar, Oothout, Ward, and Swan families. Martha Lamb and Mrs. Burton Harrison, *History of the City of New York* (New York, 1877, 1880, 1896), 3: 773. For evidence that the New York City upper crust of the late nineteenth and early twentieth centuries continued to consist primarily of descendants of the elite of the Tocqueville era, see the listings of the modern groups in Nathaniel Burt, *First Families: The Making of an American Aristocracy* (Boston, 1970), 285, and Cleveland Amory, *Who Killed Society?* (New York, 1960), 119-20, 132-33.

54. This and the other conclusions about fluidity in nineteenth-century Brooklyn are developed statistically in Pessen, "A Social and Economic Portrait of Jacksonian Brooklyn."

55. The generalization may also apply to the eighteenth century. Seventy-five per cent of the two dozen families assessed for the greatest wealth in New York City in 1674 were still among the city's wealthiest families in 1828. About ninety per cent of New York City's "Successful Business Men" of 1786 as well as the elite personages who appeared on Mrs. John Jay's exclusive "Dinner and Supper List for 1787 and '8," were still among the elite of wealth two generations later. See *Valentine's Manuals* (New York, 1841-42) and James Grant Wilson, *Memorial History of the City of New York* (New York, 1892-93), 1: 362; 3: 87-101.

56. Thomas Fox and S. M. Miller, "Occupational Stratification and Mobility," in Bendix and Lipset, *Class, Status, and Power*, 581. Almost fifteen years ago Bernard Barber noted the vastness of the relevant literature in his *Social Stratification* (New York, 1957), as did Raymond W. Mack, Linton Freeman, and Seymour Yellin, in *Social Mobility: Thirty Years of Research and Theory* (Syracuse, 1957). As even a hasty glance at the articles in the *American Sociological Review* of the past decade would indicate, the pace of publication on the topic has quickened. Allusions to the complexity and variety of definitions of social mobility, as well as to the many ingredients subsumed under the topic, can be found in Sorokin, *Social Mobility* (New York, 1927), 13; Bendix and Lipset, *Class, Status, and Power*, 1, 6, 112; D. V. Glass, ed., *Social Mobility in Britain* (London, 1967), introduction, 5; Ralf Dahrendorf, *Class and Class Conflict in Industrial Society* (Stanford, 1959), 220; R. Mukherjie and J. R. Hall, "A Note on the Analysis of Social Data," in Glass, *Social Mobility in Britain*, 218; Thernstrom, "Notes on the Historical Study of Social Mobility," 107; and Charles F. Westoff, Marvin Bressler, and Philip C. Sagi, "The Concept of Social Mobility: An Empirical Inquiry," *American Sociological Review*, 25 (1960): 375-85, whose list of twenty-two ingredients of mobility is admittedly not comprehensive.

57. The kind of evidence that enabled Stephan Thernstrom to study the occupational movement of working-class children in Newburyport, 1850-80, is not always available. See Thernstrom, *Poverty and Progress* (Cambridge, Mass., 1964); see also Harris, "Social Origins of American Leaders," 161. Valuable criticisms of the methodology employed in earlier mobility studies are offered in Natalie Rogoff, *Recent Trends in Occupational Mobility* (Glencoe, 1953), 13; Otis Dudley Duncan, "Methodological Issues in the Analysis of Social Mobility," in Neil J. Smelser and S. M. Lipset, eds., *Social Structure and Mobility in Economic Development* (Chicago, 1966), 51-97, particularly p. 52; Saburo Yosuda, "A Methodological Inquiry into Social Mobility," *American Sociological Review*, 29 (1964): 16-23; and Gosta Carlsson, *Social Mobility and Class Structure* (Lund, 1958), chs. 5, 6.

58. Marvin Meyers sees a "narrowed spread of property differences, with a heavy concen-

tration in the middle range," *Jacksonian Persuasion,* 47; David M. Potter, an abundance that more than any other factor shaped American ways and values, *People of Plenty, passim;* and Carl R. Fish believed that "there was so close an approximation to economic equality to match the political that effort and ability could raise anyone to the top," *Rise of the Common Man,* 9.

59. Miller, *Jacksonian Aristocracy,* x.

60. The figures for Philadelphia are taken from Alice Hanson Jones, "Wealth Distribution in the American Middle Colonies in the Third Quarter of the Eighteenth Century," paper read at the annual meeting of the Organization of American Historians, Apr. 17, 1971, in New Orleans, as are the figures for the middle colonies in 1774. The figures for the North on the eve of the Revolution are from Main, *Social Structure of Revolutionary America,* 42. The other figures are from Donald Warner Koch, "Income Distribution and Political Structure in Seventeenth-Century Salem," 54, 58, 59, 63; James T. Lemon and Gary B. Nash, "The Distribution of Wealth in Eighteenth Century America: A Century of Changes in Chester County, Pennsylvania, 1693-1802," *Journal of Social History,* 2 (1968): 13; and James Henretta, "Economic Development and Social Structure in Colonial Boston," *William and Mary Quarterly,* 22 (1965): 79, 80, 82, 87, 89, 92.

61. Willis, "Social Origins of Political Leadership in New York City," 110. For the distribution of wealth in a small Connecticut town, see Charles S. Grant, *Democracy in the Connecticut Frontier Town of Kent* (New York, 1961), 34, 96-97.

62. For Boston, New York City, and Brooklyn the distribution of wealth was arrived at by the following process: the total assessed wealth of the city, corporate and noncorporate, was determined for a given year. Taxpayers were grouped according to the level or category of their wealth. The assessed wealth of all members of each category was then added up in order to determine the percentage of the city's total (noncorporate) wealth they owned. In determining the percentage of the city's population represented by the persons in a given wealth category, the denominator used was the number of families in the city rather than the total population. Not to have done so would have suggested a far more drastic inequality than was actually the case, since it would have converted rich men's wives, children, and other dependents into so many "propertyless" individuals.

63. My generalizationa are based on computations performed on the table in Shattuck, *Census of Boston for the Year 1845,* 95.

64. Stephen Girard, *The Merchants' Sketch Book and Guide to New York City* (New York, 1844), 6. Whoever this author may have been, he was not the great Philadelphia merchant, who was dead thirteen years by the date of publication of this pamphlet.

65. MS diary of Philip Hone, 24: 408.

66. Quoted in Charles E. Knowles, *History of the Bank for Savings in the City of New York, 1819-1929* (New York, 1929), 70-71.

67. Appearing over and over again as directors were the names of New York City's mighty; William Bayard; Henry Rutgers; Archibald Gracie; Richard Varick; Duncan P. Campbell; Gilbert and William H. Aspinwall; Peter A. Jay; George Arcularius; Henry Eckford; Philip Hone; Jeremiah Thompson; Henry Remsen; Chancellor James Kent; William Few; I. P. Phoenix; S. B. Ruggles; James and Robert Lenox; Daniel Embury; James De Peyster; John Jacob and William B. Astor; James H. Suydam; J. W. Hamersley; Preserved Fish; Gerard, Henry, and John C. Beekman; Thomas Addis Emmet; Leonard Bleecker; David Hosack; Isaac Kip; John Mason; Peter Schermerhorn; Peter W. Livingston; Nathaniel Prime; Ogden Hoffman; Edward R. and John Q. Jones; Peter Goelet; David S. Kennedy; Aquila G. Stout; Isaac and John Heyer; Arthur Tappan; Mathew Clarkson; Frederick Schuchardt; C. V. S. Roosevelt; John D. Wolfe; A. T. Stewart; Jacob and George Lorillard; Peter Lorillard, Jr.; Al[l]ison Post; John Rankin; Daniel Lord; Jacob LeRoy; Nicholas Dean; John Sampson; Thomas T. Woodruff; Myndert Van Schaick; Ambrose C. Kingsland; David H. Haight; Alonzo A. Alvord; Stephen A. Halsey; William B. Crosby; Caleb O. Halsted; James Brown; Henry Brevoort; Robert C. Cornell; Rufus L. Lord; George Bruce; Gideon Tucker; John T. Irving; and other members of the great city's elite of wealth.

68. When Preserved Fish testified in the case of *City Fire Insurance Company v. Elisha Bloomer* in 1834, in response to the question as to when he resigned as director, Fish answered: "I resigned six months ago. The fact is, rather, that I sold out my stock, which precluded my being a Director after that time." New York City Court for the Correction of Errors, *The City Fire Insurance Company of the City of New-York, Respondents, Elisha Bloomer, Impleader with others [including Richard K. Haight and David H. Haight]* (New York, 1841), 19-20.

69. James Sloane Gibbons, *The Banks of New York* (New York, 1858), 21. See also Winslow, *Biographies of Successful Philadelphia Merchants,* 197, for reference to the large quantity of bank and insurance stock owned by wealthy individuals.

70. The fifteen wealthiest subscribers, all of them in the city's mercantile upper crust, owned more than half the shares of the rechartered Chemical Bank in 1844. *History of the Chemical Bank* (New York, 1913), 34. According to Samuel B. Ruggles' biographer, the $10,000 worth of shares in the Bank of Commerce owned by Ruggles in 1840 was the minimum that a director could own; each of the bank's seventeen directors usually owned more than that amount. D. G. Brinton Thompson, *Ruggles of New York: A Life of Samuel B. Ruggles* (New York, 1946), 39-40. See also *Records of Guaranty Trust Company of New York* (New York, n.d.); Philip G. Hudnut, *The Merchants' National Bank of the City of New York* (New York, 1903), 4; Henry W. Domett, *A History of the Bank of New York 1784-1884* (New York, 1884), much fuller and more valuable than Allan Nevins, *History of the Bank of New York and Trust Company 1784 to 1934* (New York, 1934) Wilson, *Memorial History of the City of New York, Biographical Volume,* 176-77; MS diary of Philip Hone, 19; 83; *Charter of the Seventh Ward Fire Insurance Company of New-York* (New York, 1839); Lossing, *History of New York City,* 2: 487.

71. These figures are based on a formula that attributes half of corporate capital to outsiders (which is probably overgenerous) and the rest to elite taxpayers. The worthwhileness of this rough rule was confirmed by an authority on both statistics and finance. Samuel Richmond, author of *Statistical Analysis* (New York, 1968).

72. The Brooklyn directories for the period list valuable data on boards of directors. See also Henry R. Stiles, *The Civil, Political, Professional and Ecclesiastical History and Commercial and Industrial Record of the County of Kings and the City of Brooklyn New York from 1683 to 1884* (New York, 1884), 1: 143, 154, 2: 213, 436, 620-23; Stiles, *A History of the City of Brooklyn* (Brooklyn, 1867-70), 3; 543; "A Director," *A Historical Sketch of the Fulton Ferry* (Brooklyn, 1839), app., 8-11; *History and Commerce of Brooklyn* (New York, 1893); and *Charter and By-Laws and Regulations of the Brooklyn Savings' Bank* (Brooklyn, 1836).

73. Katz, "Patterns of Inequality."

74. Doherty, "Property Distribution in Jacksonian America," introduction, 2, 4. Doherty found that only towns that languished or stagnated resisted the trend toward greater inequality.

75. George Blackburn and Sherman L. Richards, Jr., "A Demographic History of the West: Manistee County, MIchigan, 1860," *Journal of American History,* 57 (1970): 618, 613; Gavin Wright, "'Economic Democracy' and the Concentration of Agricultural Wealth in the Cotton South, 1850-1860," *Agricultural History,* 44 (1970): 63-94; Blumin, "Mobility in a Nineteenth-Century American City," 46-48; Gallman, "Trends in the Size Distribuiton of Wealth in the Nineteenth Century," 1-25; and Wheeler, *Beginnings of Urban Growth in Texas, 1836-1865,* 131.

76. In New York City by 1863 roughly sixty-one per cent of all income was made by the 1,600 families that constituted the upper one per cent of income earners: computed from the figures in *The Income Record, A List Giving the Taxable Income for the year 1863, of the Residents of New York [City]* (New York, 1865). It is likely that wealth was more badly distribued, since inheritance accounts for so much of it, in contrast to the democratic rule governing income that in a sense all people start from scratch no matter how disparate their earnings. Rufus S. Tucker long ago noted that the 1863 tax record for New York City showed "less concentration and less inequality than actually existed." See Tucker, "The Distribution of Income Among Income Taxpayers in the United States, 1863-1935," *Quarterly Journal of Economics,* 52 (1938): 561-62.

77. Modern scholars differ in interpreting the data on income distribution. Yet even Michael Harrington and Gabriel Kolko, whose estimates reveal the greatest amount of inequality, attribute percentages of income to the upper brackets that are far smaller than the upper one per cent of New York City controlled in income in 1863 or in wealth in 1845. See Kolko, "Economic Mobility and Social Stratification," *American Journal of Sociology,* 63 (1957): 38; Kolko, *Wealth and Power in America: An Analysis of Social Class and Income Distribution* (New York, 1962); and Michael Harrington, *The Other America: Poverty in the United States* (New York, 1962). See also Tucker, "The Distribution of Income Among Income Taxpayers in the United States," 569, 585; Herman P. Miller, *Income of the American People* (New York, 1955); United States Bureau of the Census, *How Our Income is Divided* (Washington, 1963); Robert J. Lampman, *Changes in the Share of Wealth Held by Top Wealth-Holders, 1922-1953* (New York, 1960); and Lampman, *The Share of Top Wealth-Holders in National Wealth, 1922-1956* (Princeton, 1962). For a comparison with Britain, see Roy Perrot, *The Aristocrats, A Portrait of Britain's Nobility and Their Way of Life Today* (New York, 1968), 76-77.

78. Gerhard Lenski, *Power and Privilege: A Theory of Social Stratification* (New York, 1966), 3.

79. *Ibid.,* 341

80. See Doherty, "Property Distribution in Jacksonian America," 4-5; Stephan Thernstrom and Peter R. Knights, "Men in Motion: Some Data and Speculations about Urban Population Mobility in Nineteenth-Century America," *Journal of Interdisciplinary History,* 1 (1970): 29-30; Michael Katz, "Patterns of Inequality," 5; and Stuart Blumin, "The Restless Citizen: Vertical Mobility, Migration and Social Participation in Mid-Nineteenth Century America," a 1970 unpublished version of a paper (on Kingston, New York) presented at the Conference on Social Science Concepts in American Political History, Oct. 24, 1969, at Brockport, New York.

81. Gallman, "Trends in the Size Distribution of Wealth," 11.

82. Potter, *People of Plenty,* 91-92.

83. Bristed, *The Upper Ten Thousand,* 9.

84. In Boston, where the importance of education was hardly understressed, college attendance during the era was confined to the few. In 1829 one person in 620 attended; in 1833, one in 929; in 1837, one in 748; in 1841, one in 873; and in 1845, one in 1,012. Shattuck, *Census of Boston for the Year 1845,* 74. See also Weeks, *Prominent Families of New York,* 524; and Daniel Scott Smith, "Cyclical, Secular, and Structural Changes in American Elite Composition," *Perspectives in American History,* 4 (1970): 369.

85. When Philip Hone's brother John was seriously ill in 1832 he was attended by Hosack, Mott, and the eminent Dr. Hugh McLean. MS diary of Philip Hone, 4: 121.

86. Dahl, *Who Governs?* 85.

87. Wade, *The Urban Frontier;* James, *Antebellum Natchez;* Wheeler, *Beginnings of Urban Growth in Texas;* McCoy, "Political Affiliations of American Economic Elites"; Aaron, "Cincinnati, 1818-1838."

88. Edward Pessen, "*Should* Labor Have Supported Jackson? or Questions the Quantitative Studies Do Not Answer," paper read at the annual meeting of the Organization of American Historians, Apr. 18, 1969, in Philadelphia; published in revised form as "Jacksonian Quantification: On Asking the Right Questions," in Herbert Bass, ed., *The State of American History* (Chicago, 1970), 362-72.

89. I investigated these matters in *Riches, Class, and Power Before the Civil War* (Lexington, Mass., 1973).

90. Daniel Scott Smith, "Cyclical, Secular, and Structural Changes in American Elite Composition," 372. A similar statement is made by Michael H. Frisch, "The Community Elite and the Emergence of Urban Politics: Springfield, Massachusetts, 1840-1880," in Thernstrom and Sennett, *Nineteenth-Century Cities,* 277.

BARBARA WELTER

THE CULT OF TRUE WOMANHOOD: 1820-1860

*Written with charm and verve, Barbara Welter's essay
on the cult of True Womanhood is as entertaining as it is
instructive. Based on a heroically thorough reading of
women's magazines, gift annuals, and religious literature,
it offers diverse literary examples of what antebellum
America regarded as the ultimate female virtues: piety,
purity, submissiveness, and domesticity. The extent to
which American women of the middle and other classes
actually embraced such values is another matter, beyond
the scope of Professor Welter's research. Her article
focuses on the mythical and the ideal, themselves no
less a part of the American reality, if more difficult to
appraise, than was the measurable tangible situation of
women. The patronizing, sentimental, and arrogant
attitudes harbored by male toward female America
provide a glimpse into the American social mind that is
no less illuminating than is the one afforded by the
era's racial or economic beliefs.*

The nineteenth-century American man was a busy builder of bridges and
railroads, at work long hours in a materialistic society. The religious values
of his forebears were neglected in practice if not in intent, and he occasionally
felt some guilt that he had turned this new land, this temple of the chosen
people, into one vast countinghouse. But he could salve his conscience by
reflecting that he had left behind a hostage, not only to fortune, but to all
the values which he held so dear and treated so lightly. Woman, in the cult
of True Womanhood[1] presented by the women's magazines, gift annuals

Barbara Welter, "The Cult of True Womanhood: 1820-1860," *American Quarterly,* Vol.
XVIII (Summer, 1966), pp. 151-174. Copyright © 1966 Trustees of the University of Pennsylvania.

and religious literature of the nineteenth century, was the hostage in the home.[2] In a society where values changed frequently, where fortunes rose and fell with frightening rapidity, where social and economic mobility provided instability as well as hope, one thing at least remained the same—a true woman was a true woman, wherever she was found. If anyone, male or female, dared to tamper with the complex of virtues which made up True Womanhood, he was damned immediately as an enemy of God, of civilization and of the Republic. It was a fearful obligation, a solemn responsibility, which the nineteenth-century American woman had—to uphold the pillars of the temple with her frail white hand.

The attributes of True Womanhood, by which a woman judged herself and was judged by her husband, her neighbors and society, could be divided into four cardinal virtues—piety, purity, submissiveness and domesticity. Put them all together and they spelled mother, daughter, sister, wife—woman. Without them, no matter whether there was fame, achievement or wealth, all was ashes. With them she was promised happiness and power.

Religion or piety was the core of woman's virtue, the source of her strength. Young men looking for a mate were cautioned to search first for piety, for if that were there, all else would follow.[3] Religion belonged to woman by divine right, a gift of God and nature. This "peculiar susceptibility" to religion was given her for a reason: "the vestal flame of piety, lighted up by Heaven in the breast of woman" would throw its beams into the naughty world of men.[4] So far would its candle power reach that the "Universe might be Enlightened, Improved, and Harmonized by WOMAN!!"[5] She would be another, better Eve, working in cooperation with the Redeemer, bringing the world back "from its revolt and sin."[6] The world would be reclaimed for God through her suffering, for "God increased the cares and sorrows of woman, that she might be sooner constrained to accept the terms of salvation."[7] A popular poem by Mrs. Frances Osgood, "The Triumph of the Spiritual Over the Sensual," expressed just this sentiment, woman's purifying passionless love bringing an erring man back to Christ.[8]

Dr. Charles Meigs, explaining to a graduating class of medical students why women were naturally religious, said that "hers is a pious mind. Her confiding nature leads her more readily than men to accept the proffered grace of the Gospel."[9] Caleb Atwater, Esq., writing in *The Ladies' Repository,* saw the hand of the Lord in female piety: "Religion is exactly what a woman needs for it gives her that dignity that best suits her dependence."[10] And Mrs. John Sandford, who had no very high opinion of her sex, agreed thoroughly: "Religion is just what woman needs. Without it she is ever restless or unhappy."[11] Mrs. Sandford and the others did not speak only of that restlessness of the human heart, which St. Augustine notes, that can only find its peace in God. They spoke rather of religion as a kind of tranquilizer for the many undefined longings which swept even the most pious young girl, and about which it was better to pray than to think.

One reason religion was valued was that it did not take a woman away from her "proper sphere," her home. Unlike participation in other societies or movements, church work would not make her less domestic or submissive, less a True Woman. In religious vineyards, said the *Young Ladies' Literary and Missionary Report,* "you may labor without the apprehension of detracting from the charms of feminine delicacy." Mrs. S.L. Dagg, writing from her chapter of the Society in Tuscaloosa, Alabama, was eqully reassuring: "As no sensible woman will suffer her intellectual pursuits to clash with her domestic duties" she should concentrate on religious work "which promotes these very duties."[12]

The women's seminaries aimed at aiding women to be religious, as well as accomplished. Mt. Holyoke's catalogue promised to make female education "a handmaid to the Gospel and an efficient auxiliary in the great task of renovating the world."[13] The Young Ladies' Seminary at Bordentown, New Jersey, declared its most important function to be "the forming of a sound and virtuous character."[14] In Keene, New Hampshire, the Seminary tried to instill a "consistent and useful character" in its students, to enable them in this life to be "a good friend, wife and mother" but more important to qualify them for "the enjoyment of Celestial Happiness in the life to come."[15] And Joseph M' D. Mathews, Principal of Oakland Female Seminary in Hillsborough, Ohio, believed that "female education should be preeminently religious."[16]

If religion was so vital to a woman, irreligion was almost too awful to contemplate. Women were warned not to let their literary or intellectual pursuits take them away from God. Sarah Josepha Hale spoke darkly of those who, like Margaret Fuller, threw away the "One True Book" for others, open to error. Mrs. Hale used the unfortunate Miss Fuller as fateful proof that "the greater the intellectual force, the greater and more fatal the errors into which women fall who wander from the Rock of Salvation, Christ the Saviour. . . ."[17]

One gentleman, writing on "Female Irreligion," reminded his readers that "Man may make himself a brute, and does so very often, but can woman brutify herself to his level—the lowest level of human nature—without exerting special wonder?" Fanny Wright, because she was godless, "was no woman, mother though she be." A few years ago, he recalls, such women would have been whipped. In any case, "woman never looks lovelier than in her reverence for religion" and, conversely, "female irreligion is the most revolting feature in human character."[18]

Purity was as essential as piety to a young woman, its absence as unnatural and unfeminine. Without it she was, in fact, no woman at all, but a member of some lower order. A "fallen woman" was a "fallen angel," unworthy of the celestial company of her sex. To contemplate the loss of purity brought tears; to be guilty of such a crime, in the women's magazines at least, brought madness or death. Even the language of the flowers had bitter words for it:

a dried white rose symbolized "Death Preferable to Loss of Innocence."[19] The marriage night was the single great event of a woman's life, when she bestowed her greatest treasure upon her husband, and from that time on was completely dependent upon him, an empty vessel,[20] without legal or emotional existence of her own.[21]

Therefore all True Women were urged, in the strongest possible terms, to maintain their virtue, although men, being by nature more sensual than they, would try to assault it. Thomas Branagan admitted in *The Excellency of the Female Character Vindicated* that his sex would sin and sin again, they could not help it, but woman, stronger and purer, must not give in and let man "take liberties incompatible with her delicacy." "If you do," Branagan addressed his gentle reader, "You will be left in silent sadness to bewail your credulity, imbecility, duplicity, and premature prostitution."[22]

Mrs. Eliza Farrar, in *The Young Lady's Friend,* gave practical logistics to avoid trouble: "Sit not with another in a place that is too narrow; read not out of the same book; let not your eagerness to see anything induce you to place your head close to another person's."[23]

If such good advice was ignored the consequences were terrible and inexorable. In *Girlhood and Womanhood: Or Sketches of My Schoolmates,* by Mrs. A. J. Graves (a kind of mid-nineteenth-century *The Group*), the bad ends of a boarding school class of girls are scrupulously recorded. The worst end of all is reserved for "Amelia Dorrington: The Lost One." Amelia died in the almshouse "the wretched victim of depravity and intemperance" and all because her mother had let her be "high-spirited not prudent." These girlish high spirits had been misinterpreted by a young man, with disastrous results. Amelia's "thoughtless levity" was "followed by a total loss of virtuous principle" and Mrs. Graves editorializes that "the coldest reserve is more admirable in a woman a man wishes to make his wife, than the least approach to undue familiarity."[24]

A popular and often-reprinted story by Fanny Forester told the sad tale of "Lucy Dutton." Lucy "with the seal of innocence upon her heart, and a rose-leaf on her cheek" came out of her vine-covered cottage and ran into a city slicker. "And Lucy was beautiful and trusting, and thoughtless: and he was gay, selfish and profligate. Needs the story to be told? . . . Nay, censor, Lucy was a child—consider how young, how very untaught—oh! her innocence was no match for the sophistry of a gay, city youth! Spring came and shame was stamped upon the cottage at the foot of the hill." The baby died; Lucy went mad at the funeral and finally died herself. "Poor, poor Lucy Dutton! The grave is a blessed couch and pillow to the wretched. Rest thee there, poor Lucy!"[25] The frequency with which derangement follows loss of virtue suggests the exquisite sensibility of woman, and the possibility that, in the women's magazines at least, her intellect was geared to her hymen, not her brain.

If, however, a woman managed to withstand man's assaults on her virtue, she demonstrated her superiority and her power over him. Eliza Farnham, trying to prove this female superiority, concluded smugly that "the purity of women is the everlasting barrier against which the tides of man's sensual nature surge."[26]

A story in *The Lady's Amaranth* illustrates this dominance. It is set, improbably, in Sicily, where two lovers, Bianca and Tebaldo, have been separated because her family insisted she marry a rich old man. By some strange circumstance the two are in a shipwreck and cast on a desert island, the only survivors. Even here, however, the rigid standards of True Womanhood prevail. Tebaldo unfortunately forgets himself slightly, so that Bianca must warn him: "We may not indeed gratify our fondness by caresses, but it is still something to bestow our kindest language, and looks and prayers, and all lawful and honest attentions on each other." Something, perhaps, but not enough, and Bianca must further remonstrate: "It is true that another man is my husband, but you are my guardian angel." When even that does not work she says in a voice of sweet reason, passive and proper to the end, that she wishes he wouldn't but "still, if you insist, I will become what you wish; but I beseech you to consider, ere that decision, that debasement which I must suffer in your esteem." This appeal to his own double standards holds the beast in him at bay. They are rescued, discover that the old husband is dead, and after "mourning a decent season" Bianca finally gives in, legally.[27]

Men could be counted on to be grateful when women thus saved them from themselves. William Alcott, guiding young men in their relations with the opposite sex, told them that "Nothing is better calculated to preserve a young man from contamination of low pleasures and pursuits than frequent intercourse with the more refined and virtuous of the other sex." And he added, one assumes in equal innocence, that youths should "observe and learn to admire, that purity and ignorance of evil which is the characteristic of well-educated young ladies, and which, when we are near them, raises us above those sordid and sensual considerations which hold such sway over men in their intercourse with each other."[28]

The Rev. Jonathan F. Stearns was also impressed by female chastity in the face of male passion, and warned woman never to compromise the source of her power: "Let her lay aside delicacy, and her influence over our sex is gone."[29]

Women themselves accepted, with pride but suitable modesty, this priceless virtue. *The Ladies' Wreath,* in "Woman the Creature of God and the Manufacturer of Society" saw purity as her greatest gift and chief means of discharging her duty to save the world: "Purity is the highest beauty—the true pole-star which is to guide humanity aright in its long, varied, and perilous voyage."[30]

Sometimes, however, a woman did not see the dangers to her treasure. In that case, they must be pointed out to her, usually by a male. In the nine-teenth century any form of social change was tantamount to an attack on woman's virtue, if only it was correctly understood. For example, dress reform seemed innocuous enough and the bloomers worn by the lady of that name and her followers were certainly modest attire. Such was the reason-ing only of the ignorant. In another issue of *The Ladies' Wreath* a young lady is represented in dialogue with her "Professor." The girl expresses admiration for the bloomer costume—it gives freedom of motion, is health-ful and attractive. The "Professor" sets her straight. Trousers, he explains, are "only one of the many manifestations of that wild spirit of socialism and agrarian radicalism which is at present so rife in our land." The young lady recants immediately: "If this dress has any connexion with Fourierism or Socialism, or fanaticism in any shape whatever, I have no disposition to wear it at all . . . no true woman would so far compromise her delicacy as to espouse, however unwittingly, such a cause."[31]

America could boast that her daughters were particularly innocent. In a poem on "The American Girl" the author wrote proudly:

> Her eye of light is the diamond bright,
> Her innocence the pearl,
> And these are ever the bridal gems
> That are worn by the American girl.[32]

Lydia Maria Child, giving advice to mothers, aimed at preserving that spirit of innocence. She regretted that "want of confidence between mothers and daughters on delicate subjects" and suggested a woman tell her daughter a few facts when she reached the age of twelve to "set her mind at rest." Then Mrs. Child confidently hoped that a young lady's "instinctive modesty" would "prevent her from dwelling on the informaton until she was called upon to use it."[33] In the same vein, a book of advice to the newly-married was titled *Whisper to a Bride*.[34] As far as intimate information was concerned, there was no need to whisper, since the book contained none at all.

A masculine summary of this virtue was expressed in a poem "Female Charms":

> I would have her as pure as the snow on the mount—
>   As true as the smile that to infamy's given—
> As pure as the wave of the crystalline fount,
>   Yet as warm in the heart as the sunlight of heaven.
> With a mind cultivated, not boastingly wise,
>   I could gaze on such beauty, with exquisite bliss;
> With her heart on her lips and her soul in her eyes—
>   What more could I wish in dear woman than this.[35]

Man might, in fact, ask no more than this in woman, but she was beginning to ask more of herself, and in the asking was threatening the third powerful and necessary virtue, submission. Purity, considered as a moral imperative, set up a dilemma which was hard to resolve. Woman must preserve her virtue until marriage and marriage was necessary for her happiness. Yet marriage was, literally, an end to innocence. She was told not to question this dilemma, but simply to accept it.

Submission was perhaps the most feminine virtue expected of women. Men were supposed to be religious, although they rarely had time for it, and supposed to be pure, although it came awfully hard to them, but men were the movers, the doers, the actors. Women were the passive, submissive responders. The order of dialogue was, of course, fixed in Heaven. Man was "woman's superior by God's appointment, if not in intellectual dowry, at least by official decree." Therefore, as Charles Elliott argued in *The Ladies' Repository,* she should submit to him "for the sake of good order at least."[36] In *The Ladies Companion* a young wife was quoted approvingly as saying that she did not think woman should "feel and act for herself" because "When, next to God, her husband is not the tribunal to which her heart and intellect appeals—the golden bowl of affection is broken."[37] Women were warned that if they tampered with this quality they tampered with the order of the Universe.

The Young Lady's Book summarized the necessity of the passive virtues in its readers' lives: "It is, however, certain, that in whatever situation of life a woman is placed from her cradle to her grave, a spirit of obedience and submission, pliability of temper, and humility of mind, are required from her."[38]

Woman understood her position if she was the right kind of woman, a true woman. "She feels herself weak and timid. She needs a protector," declared George Burnap, in his lectures on *The Sphere and Duties of Woman.* "She is in a measure dependent. She asks for wisdom, constancy, firmness, perseverance, and she is willing to repay it all by the surrender of the full treasure of her affections. Woman despises in man every thing like herself except a tender heart. It is enough that she is effeminate and weak; she does not want another like herself."[39] Or put even more strongly by Mrs. Sandford: "A really sensible woman feels her dependence. She does what she can, but she is conscious of inferiority, and therefore grateful for support."[40]

Mrs. Sigourney, however, assured young ladies that although they were separate, they were equal. This difference of the sexes did not imply inferiority, for it was part of that same order of Nature established by Him "who bids the oak brave the fury of the tempest, and the alpine flower lean its cheek on the bosom of eternal shows."[41] Dr. Meigs had a different analogy to make the same point, contrasting the anatomy of the Apollo of the Belvedere (illustrating the male principle) with the Venus de Medici (illustrating the female principle). "Woman," said the physician, with a kind of clinical gallantry, "has a head almost too small for intellect but just big enough for love."[42]

This love itself was to be passive and responsive. "Love, in the heart of a woman," wrote Mrs. Farrar, "should partake largely of the nature of gratitude. She should love, because she is already loved by one deserving her regard."[43]

Woman was to work in silence, unseen, like Wordsworth's Lucy. Yet, "working like nature, in secret" her love goes forth to the world "to regulate its pulsation, and send forth from its heart, in pure and temperate flow, the life-giving current."[44] She was to work only for pure affection, without thought of money or ambition. A poem, "Woman and Fame," by Felicia Hemans, widely quoted in many of the gift books, concludes with a spirited renunciation of the gift of fame:

> Away! to me, a woman, bring
> Sweet flowers from affection's spring.[45]

"True feminine genius," said Grace Greenwood (Sara Jane Clarke), "is ever timid, doubtful, and clingingly dependent; a perpetual childhood." And she advised literary ladies in an essay on "The Intellectual Woman"— "Don't trample on the flowers while longing for the stars."[46] A wife who submerged her own talents to work for her husband was extolled as an example of a true woman. In *Women of Worth: A Book for Girls,* Mrs. Ann Flaxman, an artist of promise herself, was praised because she "devoted herself to sustain her husband's genius and aid him in his arduous career."[47]

Caroline Gilman's advice to the bride aimed at establishing this proper order from the beginning of a marriage: "Oh, young and lovely bride, watch well the first moments when your will conflicts with his to whom God and society have given the control. Reverence his *wishes* even when you do not his *opinions.*"[48]

Mrs. Gilman's perfect wife in *Recollections of a Southern Matron* realizes that "the three golden threads with which domestic happiness is woven" are "to repress a harsh answer, to confess a fault, and to stop (right or wrong) in the midst of self-defense, in gentle submission." Woman could do this, hard though it was, because in her heart she knew she was right and so could afford to be forgiving, even a trifle condescending. "Men are not unreasonable," averred Mrs. Gilman. "Their difficulties lie in not understanding the moral and physical nature of our sex. They often wound through ignorance, and are surprised at having offended." Wives were advised to do their best to reform men, but if they couldn't, to give up gracefully. "If any habit of his annoyed me, I spoke of it once or twice, calmly, then bore it quietly."[49]

A wife should occupy herself "only with domestic affairs—wait till your husband confides to you those of a high importance—and do not give your advice until he asks for it," advised the *Lady's Token*. At all times she should behave in a manner becoming a woman, who had "no arms other than gentleness." Thus "if he is abusive, never retort."[50] *A Young Lady's Guide to the Harmonious Development of a Christian Character* suggested that females should "become as little children" and "avoid a controversial spirit."[51] *The Mother's Assistant and Young Lady's Friend* listed "Always Conciliate" as its first commandment in "Rules for Conjugal and Domestic Happiness." Small wonder that these same rules ended with the succinct maxim: "Do not expect too much."[52]

As mother, as well as wife, woman was required to submit to fortune. In *Letters to Mothers* Mrs. Sigourney sighed: "To bear the evils and sorrows which may be appointed us, with a patient mind, should be the continual effort of our sex. . . . It seems, indeed, to be expected of us; since the passive and enduring virtues are more immediately within our province." Of these trials "the hardest was to bear the loss of children with submission" but the indomitable Mrs. Sigourney found strength to murmur to the bereaved mother: "The Lord loveth a cheerful giver."[53] *The Ladies' Parlor Companion* agreed thoroughly in "A Submissive Mother," in which a mother who had already buried two children and was nursing a dying baby saw her sole remaining child "probably scalded to death. Handing over the infant to die in the arms of a friend, she bowed in sweet submission to the double stroke." But the child "through the goodness of God survived, and the mother learned to say 'Thy will be done.'"[54]

Woman then, in all her roles, accepted submission as her lot. It was a lot she had not chosen or deserved. As *Godey's* said, "the lesson of submission is forced upon woman." Without comment or criticism the writer affirms that "To suffer and to be silent under suffering seems the great command she has to obey."[55] George Burnap referred to a woman's life as "a series of suppressed emotions."[56] She was, as Emerson said, "more vulnerable, more infirm, more mortal than man."[57] The death of a beautiful woman, cherished in fiction, represented woman as the innocent victim, suffering without sin, too pure and good for this world but too weak and passive to resist its evil forces.[58] The best refuge for such a delicate creature was the warmth and safety of her home.

The true woman's place was unquestionably by her own fireside—as daughter, sister, but most of all as wife and mother. Therefore domesticity was among the virtues most prized by the women's magazines. "As society is constituted," wrote Mrs. S. E. Farley, on the "Domestic and Social Claims on Woman," "the true dignity and beauty of the female character seem to consist in a right understanding and faithful and cheerful performance of social and family duties."[59] Sacred Scripture re-enforced social pressure: "St. Paul knew what was best for women when he advised them to be domestic," said Mrs. Sandford. "There is composure at home; there is something sedative in the duties which home involves. It affords security not only from the world, but from delusions and errors of every kind."[60]

From her home woman performed her great task of bringing men back to God. *The Young Ladies' Class Book* was sure that "the domestic fireside is the great guardian of society against the excesses of human passions."[61] *The Lady at Home* expressed its convictions in its very title and concluded that "even if we cannot reform the world in a moment, we can begin the work by reforming ourselves and our households—It is woman's mission. Let her not look away from her own little family circle for the means of producing moral and social reforms, but begin at home."[62]

Home was supposed to be a cheerful place, so that brothers, husbands and sons would not go elsewhere in search of a good time. Woman was expected to dispense comfort and cheer. In writing the biography of Margaret Mercer (every inch a true woman) her biographer (male) notes: "She never forgot that it is the peculiar province of woman to minister to the comfort, and promote the happiness, first, of those most nearly allied to her, and then of those, who by the Providence of God are placed in a state of dependence upon her."[63] Many other essays in the women's journals showed woman as comforter: "Woman, Man's Best Friend," "Woman, the Greatest Social Benefit," "Woman, A Being to Come Home To," "The Wife: Source of Comfort and the Spring of Joy."[64]

One of the most important functions of woman as comforter was her role as nurse. Her own health was probably, although regrettably, delicate.[65] Many homes had "little sufferers," those pale children who wasted away to saintly deaths. And there were enough other illnesses of youth and age, major and minor, to give the nineteenth-century American woman nursing experience. The sickroom called for the exercise of her higher qualities of patience, mercy and gentleness as well as for her housewifely arts. She could thus fulfill her dual feminine function—beauty and usefulness.

The cookbooks of the period offer formulas for gout cordials, ointment for sore nipples, hiccough and cough remedies, opening pills and refreshing drinks for fever, along with recipes for pound cake, jumbles, stewed calves head and currant wine.[66] *The Ladies' New Book of Cookery* believed that "food prepared by the kind hand of a wife, mother, sister, friend" tasted better and had a "restorative power which money cannot purchase."[67]

A chapter of *The Young Lady's Friend* was devoted to woman's privilege as "ministering spirit at the couch of the sick." Mrs. Farrar advised a soft voice, gentle and clean hands, and a cheerful smile. She also cautioned against an excess of female delicacy. That was all right for a young lady in the parlor, but not for bedside manners. Leeches, for example, were to be regarded as "a curious piece of mechanism . . . their ornamental stripes should recommend them even to the eye, and their valuable services to our feelings." And she went on calmly to discuss their use. Nor were women to shrink from medical terminology, since "If you cultivate right views of the wonderful structure of the body, you will be as willing to speak to a physician of the bowels as the brains of your patient."[68]

Nursing the sick, particularly sick males, not only made a woman feel useful and accomplished, but increased her influence. In a piece of heavy-handed humor in *Godey's* a man confessed that some women were only happy when their husbands were ailing that they might have the joy of nursing him to recovery, "thus gratifying their medical vanity and their love of power by making him more dependent upon them."[69] In a similar vein a husband sometimes suspected his wife "almost wishes me dead—for the pleasure of being utterly inconsolable."[70]

In the home women were not only the highest adornment of civilization, but they were supposed to keep busy at morally uplifting tasks. Fortunately most of housework, if looked at in true womanly fashion, could be regarded as uplifting. Mrs. Sigourney extolled its virtues: "The science of house-keeping affords exercise for the judgment and energy, ready recollection, and patient self-possession, that are the characteristics of a superior mind."[71] According to Mrs. Farrar, making beds was good exercise, the repetitiveness of routine tasks inculcated patience and perseverance, and proper management of the home was a surprisingly complex art: "There is more to be learned about pouring out tea and coffee, than most young ladies are willing to believe."[72] *Godey's* went so far as to suggest coyly, in "Learning vs. Housewifery," that the two were complementary, not opposed: chemistry could be utilized in cooking, geometry in dividing cloth, and phrenology in discovering talent in children.[73]

Women were to master every variety of needlework, for, as Mrs. Sigourney pointed out, "Needle-work, in all its forms of use, elegance, and ornament, has ever been the appropriate occupation of woman."[74] Embroidery improved taste; knitting promoted serenity and economy.[75] Other forms of artsy-craftsy activity for her leisure moments included painting on glass or velvet, Poonah work, tussy-mussy frames for her own needlepoint or water colors, stands for hyacinths, hair bracelets or baskets of feathers.[76]

She was expected to have a special affinity for flowers. To the editors of *The Lady's Token* "A Woman never appears more truly in her sphere, than when she divides her time between her domestic avocations and the culture of flowers."[77] She could write letters, an activity particularly feminine since it had to do with the outpourings of the heart,[78] or practice her drawingroom skills of singing and playing an instrument. She might even read.

Here she faced a bewildering array of advice. The female was dangerously addicted to novels, according to the literature of the period. She should avoid them, since they interfered with "serious piety." If she simply couldn't help herself and read them anyway, she should choose edifying ones from lists of morally acceptable authors.[79] She should study history since it "showed the depravity of the human heart and the evil nature of sin." On the whole, "religious biography was best."[79]

The women's magazines themselves could be read without any loss of concern for the home. *Godey's* promised the husband that he would find his wife "no less assiduous for his reception, or less sincere in welcoming his return" as a result of reading their magazine.[80] *The Lily of the Valley* won its right to be admitted to the boudoir by confessing that it was "like its namesake humble and unostentatious, but it is yet pure, and, we trust, free from moral imperfections."[81]

No matter what later authorities claimed, the nineteenth century knew that girls *could* be ruined by a book. The seduction stories regard "exciting and dangerous books" as contributory causes of disaster. The man without honorable intentions always provides the innocent maiden with such books as a prelude to his assault on her virtue.[82] Books which attacked or seemed to attack woman's accepted place in society were regarded as equally dangerous. A reviewer of Harriet Martineau's *Society in America* wanted it kept out of the hands of American women. They were so susceptible to persuasion, with their "gentle yielding natures" that they might listen to "the bold ravings of the hard-featured of their own sex." The frightening result: "such reading will unsettle them for their true station and pursuits, and they will throw the world back again into confusion."[83]

The debate over women's education posed the question of whether a "finished" education detracted from the practice of housewifely arts. Again it proved to be a case of semantics, for a true woman's education was never "finished" until she was instructed in the gentle science of homemaking.[84] Helen Irving, writing on "Literary Women," made it very clear that if women invoked the muse, it was as a genie of the household lamp. "If the necessities of her position require these duties at her hands, she will perform them nonetheless cheerfully, that she knows herself capable of higher things." The literary woman must conform to the same standards as any other woman: "That her home shall be made a loving place of rest and joy and comfort for those who are dear to her, will be the first wish of every true woman's heart."[85] Mrs. Ann Stephens told women who wrote to make sure they did not sacrifice one domestic duty. "As for genius, make it a domestic plant. Let its roots strike deep in your house. . . ."[86]

The fear of "blue stockings" (the eighteenth-century male's term of derision for educated or literary women) need not persist for nineteenth-century American men. The magazines presented spurious dialogues in which bachelors were convinced of their fallacy in fearing educated wives. One such dialogue took place between a young man and his female cousin. Ernest deprecates learned ladies ("A *Woman* is far more lovable than a *philosopher*") but Alice refutes him with the beautiful example of their Aunt Barbara who "although she *has* perpetrated the heinous crime of writing some half dozen folios" is still a model of "the spirit of feminine gentleness." His memory prodded, Ernest concedes that, by George, there was a woman: "When I last had a cold she not only made me a bottle of cough syrup, but when I complained of nothing new to read, set to work and wrote some twenty stanzas on consumption."[87]

The magazines were filled with domestic tragedies in which spoiled young girls learned that when there was a hungry man to feed French and china painting were not helpful. According to these stories many a marriage is jeopardized because the wife has not learned to keep house. Harriet Beecher Stowe wrote a sprightly piece of personal experience for *Godey's*, ridiculing her own bad housekeeping as a bride. She used the same theme in a story "The Only Daughter," in which the pampered beauty learns the facts of domestic life from a rather difficult source, her mother-in-law. Mrs. Hamilton tells Caroline in the sweetest way possible to shape up in the kitchen, reserving her rebuke for her son: "You are her husband—her guide—her protector—now see what you can do," she admonished him. "Give her credit for every effort: treat her faults with tenderness; encourage and praise whenever you can, and depend upon it, you will see another woman in her." He is properly masterful, she properly domestic and in a few months Caroline is making lumpless gravy and keeping up with the darning. Domestic tranquillity has been restored and the young wife moralizes: "Bring up a girl to feel that she has a responsible part to bear in promoting the happiness of the family, and you make a reflecting being of her at once, and remove that lightness and frivolity of character which makes her shrink from graver studies."[88] These stories end with the heroine drying her hands on her apron and vowing that *her* daughter will be properly educated, in piecrust as well as Poonah work.

The female seminaries were quick to defend themselves against any suspicion of interfering with the role which nature's God had assigned to women. They hoped to enlarge and deepen that role, but not to change its setting. At the Young Ladies' Seminary and Collegiate Institute in Monroe City, Michigan, the catalogue admitted few of its graduates would be likely "to fill the learned professions." Still, they were called to "other scenes of usefulness and honor." The average woman is to be "the presiding genius of love" in the home, where she is to "give a correct and elevated literary taste to her children, and to assume that influential station that she ought to possess as the companion of an educated man."[89]

At Miss Pierce's famous school in Litchfield, the students were taught that they had "attained the perfection of their characters when they could combine their elegant accomplishments with a turn for solid domestic virtues."[90] Mt. Holyoke paid pious tribute to domestic skills: "Let a young lady despise this branch of the duties of woman, and she despises the appointments of her existence." God, nature and the Bible "enjoin these duties on the sex, and she cannot violate them with impunity." Thus warned, the young lady would have to seek knowledge of these duties elsewhere, since it was not in the curriculum at Mt. Holyoke. "We would not take this privilege from the mother."[91]

One reason for knowing her way around a kitchen was that America was "a land of precarious fortunes," as Lydia Maria Child pointed out in her book *The Frugal Housewife: Dedicated to Those Who Are Not Ashamed of Economy.* Mrs. Child's chapter "How To Endure Poverty" prescribed a combination of piety and knowledge—the kind of knowledge found in a true woman's education, "a thorough religious *useful* education."[92] The woman who had servants today, might tomorrow, because of a depression or panic, be forced to do her own work. If that happened she knew how to act, for she was to be the same cheerful consoler of her husband in their cottage as in their mansion.

An essay by Washington Irving, much quoted in the gift annuals, discussed the value of a wife in case of business reverses: "I have observed that a married man falling into misfortune is more apt to achieve his situation in the world than a single one . . . it is beautifully ordained by Providence that woman, who is the ornament of man in his happier hours, should be his stay and solace when smitten with sudden calamity."[93]

A story titled simply but eloquently "The Wife" dealt with the quiet heroism of Ellen Graham during her husband's plunge from fortune to poverty. Ned Graham said of her: "Words are too poor to tell you what I owe to that noble woman. In our darkest seasons of adversity, she has been an angel of consolation—utterly forgetful of self and anxious only to comfort and sustain me." Of course she had a little help from "faithful Dinah who absolutely refused to leave her beloved mistress," but even so Ellen did no more than would be expected of any true woman.[94]

Most of this advice was directed to woman as wife. Marriage was the proper state for the exercise of the domestic virtues. "True Love and a Happy Home," an essay in *The Young Ladies' Oasis,* might have been carved on every girl's hope chest.[95] But although marriage was best, it was not absolutely necessary. The women's magazines tried to remove the stigma from being an "Old Maid." They advised no marriage at all rather than an unhappy one contracted out of selfish motives.[96] Their stories showed maiden ladies as unselfish ministers to the sick, teachers of the young, or moral preceptors with their pens, beloved of the entire village. Usually the life of single blessedness resulted from the premature death of a fiancé, or chosen through fidelity to some high mission. For example, in "Two Sisters," Mary devotes herself to Ellen and her abandoned children, giving up her own chance for marriage. "Her devotion to her sister's happiness has met its reward in the consciousness of having fulfilled a sacred duty."[97] Very rarely, a "woman of genius" was absolved from the necessity of marriage, being so extraordinary that she did not need the security or status of being a wife.[98] Most often, however, if girls proved "difficult," marriage and a family were regarded as a cure.[99] The "sedative quality" of a home could be counted on to subdue even the most restless spirits.

George Burnap saw marriage as "that sphere for which woman was originally intended, and to which she is so exactly fitted to adorn and bless, as the wife, the mistress of a home, the solace, the aid, and the counsellor of that ONE, for whose sake alone the world is of any consequence to her."[100] Samuel Miller preached a sermon on women: "How interesting and important are the duties devolved on females as WIVES . . . the counsellor and friend of the husband; who makes it her daily study to lighten his cares, to soothe his sorrows, and to augment his joys; who, like a guardian angel, watches over his interests, warns him against dangers, comforts him under trials; and by her pious, assiduous, and attractive deportment, constantly endeavors to render him more virtuous, more useful, more honourable, and more happy."[101] A woman's whole interest should be focused on her husband, paying him "those numberless attentions to which the French give the title of *petits soins* and which the woman who loves knows so well how to pay . . . she should consider nothing as trivial which could win a smile of approbation from him."[102]

Marriage was seen not only in terms of service but as an increase in authority for woman. Burnap concluded that marriage improves the female character "not only because it puts her under the best possible tuition, that of the affections, and affords scope to her active energies, but because it gives her higher aims, and a more dignified position."[103] *The Lady's Amaranth* saw it as a balance of power: "The man bears rule over his wife's person and conduct. She bears rule over his inclinations: he governs by law; she by persuasion. . . . The empire of the woman is an empire of softness . . . her commands are caresses, her menaces are tears."[104]

Woman should marry, but not for money. She should choose only the high road of true love and not truckle to the values of a materialistic society. A story "Marrying for Money" (subtlety was not the strong point of the ladies' magazines) depicts Gertrude, the heroine, rueing the day she made her crass choice: "It is a terrible thing to live without love. . . . A woman who dares marry for aught but the purest affection, calls down the just judgments of heaven upon her head."[105]

The corollary to marriage, with or without true love, was motherhood, which added another dimension to her usefulness and her prestige. It also anchored her even more firmly to the home. "My Friend," wrote Mrs. Sigourney, "If in becoming a mother, you have reached the climax of your happiness, you have also taken a higher place in the scale of being . . . you have gained an increase of power."[106] The Rev. J. N. Danforth pleaded in *The Ladies' Casket,* "Oh, mother, acquit thyself well in thy humble sphere, for thou mayest affect the world."[107] A true woman naturally loved her children; to suggest otherwise was monstrous.[108]

America depended upon her mothers to raise up a whole generation of Christian statesmen who could say, "All that I am I owe to my angel mother."[109] The mothers must do the inculcating of virtue since the fathers, alas, were too busy chasing the dollar. Or as *The Ladies' Companion* put it more effusively, the father "weary with the heat and burden of life's summer day, or trampling with unwilling foot the decaying leaves of life's autumn, has forgotten the sympathies of life's joyous springtime. . . . The acquisition of wealth, the advancement of his children in worldly honor—these are his self-imposed tasks." It was his wife who formed "the infant mind as yet untainted by contact with evil . . . like wax beneath the plastic hand of the mother."[110]

The Ladies' Wreath offered a fifty-dollar prize to the woman who submitted the most convincing essay on "How May An American Woman Best Show Her Patriotism." The winner was Miss Elizabeth Wetherell who provided herself with a husband in her answer. The wife in the essay of course asked her husband's opinion. He tried a few jokes first—"Call her eldest son George Washington," "Don't speak French, speak American"—but then got down to telling her in sober prize-winning truth what women could do for their country. Voting was no asset, since that would result only in "a vast increase of confusion and expense without in the smallest degree affecting the result." Besides, continued this oracle, "looking down at their child," if "we were to go a step further and let the children vote, their first act would be to vote their mothers at home." There is no comment on this devastating male logic and he continues: "Most women would follow the lead of their fathers and husbands," and the few who would "fly off on a tangent from the circle of home influence would cancel each other out."

The wife responds dutifully: "I see all that. I never understood so well before." Encouraged by her quick womanly perception, the master of the house resolves the question—an American woman best shows her patriotism by staying at home, where she brings her influence to bear "upon the right side for the country's weal." That woman will instinctively choose the side of right he has no doubt. Besides her "natural refinement and closeness to God" she has the "blessed advantage of a quiet life" while man is exposed to conflict and evil. She stays home with "her Bible and a well-balanced mind" and raises her sons to be good Americans. The judges rejoiced in this conclusion and paid the prize money cheerfully, remarking "they deemed it cheap at the price."[111]

If any woman asked for greater scope for her gifts the magazines were sharply critical. Such women were tampering with society, undermining civilization. Mary Wollstonecraft, Frances Wright and Harriet Martineau were condemned in the strongest possible language—they were read out of the sex. "They are only semi-women, mental hermaphrodites." The Rev. Harrington knew the women of America could not possibly approve of such perversions and went to some wives and mothers to ask if they did want a "wider sphere of interest" as these nonwomen claimed. The answer was reassuring. " 'NO!' they cried simultaneously, 'Let the men take care of politics, *we will take care of the children*!' " Again female discontent resulted only from a lack of understanding: women were not subservient, they were rather "chosen vessels." Looked at in this light the conclusion was inescapable: "Noble, sublime is the task of the American mother."[112]

"Women's Rights" meant one thing to reformers, but quite another to the True Woman. She knew her rights,

> The right to love whom others scorn,
> The right to comfort and to mourn,
> The right to shed new joy on earth,
> The right to feel the soul's high worth . . .
> Such women's rights, and God will bless
> And crown their champions with success.[113]

The American woman had her choice—she could define her rights in the way of the women's magazines and insure them by the practice of the requisite virtues, or she could go outside the home, seeking other rewards than love. It was a decision on which, she was told, everything in her world depended. "Yours it is to determine," the Rev. Mr. Stearns solemnly warned from the pulpit, "whether the beautiful order of society . . . shall continue as it has been" or whether "society shall break up and become a chaos of disjointed and unsightly elements."[114] If she chose to listen to other voices than those of her proper mentors, sought other rooms than those of her home, she lost both her happiness and her power—"that almost magic power, which, in her proper sphere, she now wields over the destinies of the world."[115]

But even while the women's magazines and related literature encouraged this ideal of the perfect woman, forces were at work in the nineteenth century which impelled woman herself to change, to play a more creative role in society. The movements for social reform, westward migration, missionary activity, utopian communities, industrialism, the Civil War—all called forth responses from woman which differed from those she was trained to believe were hers by nature and divine decree. The very perfection of True Womanhood, moreover, carried within itself the seeds of its own destruction. For if woman was so very little less than the angels, she should surely take a more active part in running the world, especially since men were making such a hash of things.

Real women often felt they did not live up to the ideal of True Womanhood: some of them blamed themselves, some challenged the standard, some tried to keep the virtues and enlarge the scope of womanhood.[116] Somehow through this mixture of challenge and acceptance, of change and continuity, the True Woman evolved into the New Woman—a transformation as startling in its way as the abolition of slavery or the coming of the machine age. And yet the stereotype, the "mystique" if you will, of what woman was and ought to be persisted, bringing guilt and confusion in the midst of opportunity.[117]

The women's magazines and related literature had feared this very dislocation of values and blurring of roles. By careful manipulation and interpretation they sought to convince woman that she had the best of both worlds—power and virtue—and that a stable order of society depended upon her maintaining her traditional place in it. To that end she was identified with everything that was beautiful and holy.

"Who Can Find a Valiant Woman?" was asked frequently from the pulpit and the editorial pages. There was only one place to look for her—at home. Clearly and confidently these authorities proclaimed the True Woman of the nineteenth century to be the Valiant Woman of the Bible, in whom the heart of her husband rejoiced and whose price was above rubies.

Notes

1. Authors who addressed themselves to the subject of women in the mid-nineteenth century used this phrase as frequently as writers on religion mentioned God. Neither group felt it necessary to define their favorite terms; they simply assumed—with some justification—that readers would intuitively understand exactly what they meant. Frequently what people of one era take for granted is most striking and revealing to the student from another. In a sense this analysis of the ideal woman of the mid-nineteenth century is an examination of what writers of that period actually meant when they used so confidently the vague phrase, "True Womanhood."

2. The conclusions reached in this article are based on a survey of almost all of the women's magazines published for more than three years during the period 1820-60 and a sampling of those published for less than three years; all the gift books cited in Ralph Thompson, *American Literary Annuals and Gift Books, 1825-1865* (New York, 1936), deposited in the Library of Congress, the New York Public Library, the New-York Historical Society, Columbia University Special Collections, Library of the City College of the Unviersity of New York, Pennsylvania Historical Society, Massachusetts Historical Society, Boston Public Library, Fruitlands Museum Library, the Smithsonian Institution and the Wisconsin Historical Society; hundreds of religious tracts and sermons in the American Unitarian Society and the Galatea Collection of the Boston Public Library; and the large collection of nineteenth-century cookbooks in the New York Public LIbrary and the Academy of Medicine of New York. Corroborative evidence not cited in this article was found in women's diaries, memoirs, autobiographies and personal papers, as well as in all the novels by women which sold over 75,000 copies during this period, as cited in Frank Luther Mott, *Golden Multitudes: The Story of Best Sellers in the United States* (New York, 1947) and H. R. Brown, *The Sentimental Novel in America, 1789-1860* (Durham, N. C., 1940). This latter information also indicated the effect of the cult of True Womanhood on those most directly concerned.

3. As in "The Bachelor's Dream," in *The Lady's Gift: Souvenir for All Seasons* (Nashua, N. H., 1849), p. 37.

4. *The Young Ladies' Class Book: A Selection of Lessons for Reading in Prose and Verse,* ed. Ebenezer Bailey, Principal of Young Ladies' High School, Boston (Boston, 1831), p. 168.

5. A Lady of Philadelphia, *The World Enlightened, Improved, and Harmonized by WOMAN!!!* A lecture, delivered in the City of New York, before the Young Ladies' Society for Mutual Improvement, on the following question, proposed by the society, with the offer of $100 for the best lecture that should be read before them on the subject proposed;—What is the

power and influence of woman in moulding the manners, morals and habits of civil society? (Philadelphia, 1840), p. 1.

6. *The Young Lady's Book: A Manual of Elegant Recreations, Exercises, and Pursuits* (Boston, 1830), p. 29.

7. *Woman As She Was, Is, and Should Be* (New York, 1849), p. 206.

8. "The Triumph of the Spiritual Over the Sensual: An Allegory," in *Ladies' Companion: A Monthly Magazine Embracing Every Department of Literature, Embellished With Original Engravings and Music,* XVII (New York) (1842), 67.

9. *Lecture on Some of the Distinctive Characteristics of the Female,* delivered before the class of the Jefferson Medical College, Jan. 1847 (Philadelphia, 1847), p. 13.

10. "Female Education," *Ladies' Repository and Gatherings of the West: A Monthly Periodical Devoted to Literature and Religion,* I (Cincinnati), 12.

11. *Woman, in Her Social and Domestic Character* (Boston, 1842), pp. 41-42.

12. *Second Annual Report of the Young Ladies' Literary and Missionary Association of the Philadelphia Collegiate Institution* (Philadelphia, 1840), pp. 20, 26.

13. *Mt. Holyoke Female Seminary: Female Education. Tendencies of the Principles Embraced, and the System Adopted in the Mt. Holyoke Female Seminary* (Boston, 1839), p. 3.

14. *Prospectus of the Young Ladies' Seminary at Bordentown, New Jersey* (Bordentown, 1836), p. 7.

15. *Catalogue of the Young Ladies' Seminary in Keene, New Hampshire* (n.p. 1832), p. 20.

16. "Report to the College of Teachers, Cincinnati, October, 1840" in *Ladies' Repository,* I (1841), 50.

17. *Woman's Record: or Sketches of All Distinguished Women from 'The Beginning' Till A. D. 1850* (New York, 1853), pp. 665, 669.

18. "Female Irreligion," *Ladies' Companion,* XIII (May-Oct. 1840), III.

19. *The Lady's Book of Flowers and Poetry,* ed. Lucy Hooper (New York, 1842), has a "Floral Dictionary" giving the symbolic meaning of floral tributes.

20. See, for example, Nathaniel Hawthorne, *The Blithedale Romance* (Boston, 1852), p. 71, in which Zenobia says: "How can she be happy, after discovering that fate has assigned her but one single event, which she must contrive to make the substance of her whole life? A man has his choice of innumerable events."

21. Mary R. Beard, *Woman As Force in History* (New York, 1946), makes this point at some length. According to common law, a woman had no legal existence once she was married and therefore could not manage property, sue in court, etc. In the 1840s and 1850s laws were passed in several states to remedy this condition.

22. *Excellency of the Female Character Vindicated: Being an Investigation Relative to the Cause and Effects on the Encroachments of Men Upon the Rights of Women, and the Too Frequent Degradation and Consequent Misfortunes of The Fair Sex* (New York, 1807), pp. 277, 278.

23. By a Lady (Eliza Ware Rotch Farrar), *The Young Lady's Friend* (Boston, 1837), p. 293.

24. *Girlhood and Womanhood: or, Sketches of My Schoolmates* (Boston, 1844), p. 140.

25. Emily Chubbuck, *Alderbrook* (Boston, 1847), 2nd ed., II, 121, 127.

26. *Woman and Her Era* (New York, 1864), p. 95.

27. "The Two Lovers of Sicily," *The Lady's Amaranth: A Journal of Tales, Essays, Excerpts—Historical and Biographical Sketches, Poetry and Literature in General* (Philadelphia), II (Jan. 1839), 17.

28. *The Young Man's Guide* (Boston, 1833), pp. 229, 231.

29. *Female Influence: and the True Christian Mode of Its Exercise; a Discourse Delivered in the First Presbyterian Church in Newburyport, July 30, 1837* (Newburyport, 1837), p. 18.

30. W. Tolles, "Woman The Creature of God and the Manufacturer of Society," *Ladies' Wreath* (New York), III (1852), 205.

31. Prof. William M. Heim, "The Bloomer Dress," *Ladies Wreath,* III (1852), 247.

32. *The Young Lady's Offering: or Gems of Prose and Poetry* (Boston, 1853), p. 283. The

American girl, whose innocence was often connected with ignorance, was the spiritual ancestress of the Henry James heroine. Daisy Miller, like Lucy Dutton, saw innocence lead to tragedy.

33. *The Mother's Book* (Boston, 1831), pp. 151, 152.

34. Mrs. L. H. Sigourney, *Whisper to a Bride* (Hartford, 1851), in which Mrs. Sigourney's approach is summed up in this quotation: "Home! Blessed bride, thou art about to enter this sanctuary, and to become a priestess at its altar!" p. 44.

35. S. R. R., "Female Charms," *Godey's Magazine and Lady's Book* (Philadelphia), XXXIII (1846), 52.

36. Charles Elliott, "Arguing With Females," *Ladies' Repository,* I (1841), 25.

37. *Ladies' Companion,* VIII (Jan. 1838), 147.

38. *The Young Lady's Book* (New York, 1830), American edition, p. 28. (This is a different book than the one of the same title and date of publication cited in note 6.)

39. *Sphere and Duties of Woman* (5th ed., Baltimore, 1854), p. 47.

40. *Women,* p. 15.

41. *Letters to Young Ladies* (Hartford, 1835), p. 179.

42. *Lecture,* p. 17.

43. *The Young Lady's Friend,* p. 313.

44. Maria J. McIntosh, *Woman in America: Her Work and Her Reward* (New York, 1850), p. 25.

45. *Poems and a Memoir of the Life of Mrs. Felicia Hemans* (London, 1860), p. 16.

46. Letter "To an Unrecognized Poetess, June, 1846" (Sara Jane Clarke), *Greenwood Leaves* (2nd ed.; Boston, 1850), p. 311.

47. "The Sculptor's Assistant: Ann Flaxman," in *Women of Worth: A Book for Girls* (New York, 1860), p. 263.

48. Mrs. Clarissa Packard (Mrs. Caroline Howard Gilman), *Recollections of a Housekeeper* (New York, 1834), p. 122.

49. *Recollectins of a Southern Matron* (New York, 1838), pp. 256, 257.

50. *The Lady's Token: or Gift of Friendship,* ed. Colesworth Pinckney (Nashua, N. H., 1848), p. 119.

51. Harvey Newcomb, *Young Lady's Guide to the Harmonious Development of Christian Character* (Boston, 1846), p. 10.

52. "Rules for Conjugal and Domestic Happiness," *Mother's Assistant and Young Lady's Friend,* III (Boston), (April 1843), 115.

53. *Letters to Mothers* (Hartford, 1838), p. 199. In the diaries and letters of women who lived during this period the death of a child seemed consistently to be the hardest thing for them to bear and to occasion more anguish and rebellion, as well as eventual submission, than any other event in their lives.

54. "A Submissive Mother," *The Ladies' Parlor Companion: A Collection of Scattered Fragments and Literary Gems* (New York, 1852), p. 358.

55. "Woman," *Godey's Lady's Book,* II (Aug. 1831), 110.

56. *Sphere and Duties of Woman,* p. 172.

57. Ralph Waldo Emerson, "Woman," *Complete Writings of Ralph Waldo Emerson* (New York, 1875), p. 1180.

58. As in Donald Fraser, *The Mental Flower Garden* (New York, 1857). Perhaps the most famous exponent of this theory is Edgar Allan Poe who affirms in "The Philosophy of Composition" that "the death of a beautiful woman is unquestionably the most poetical topic in the world. . . . ."

59. "Domestic and Social Claims on Woman," *Mother's Magazine,* VI (1846), 21.

60. *Woman,* p. 173.

61. *The Young Ladies' Class Book,* p. 166.

62. T. S. Arthur, *The Lady at Home: or, Leaves from the Every-Day Book of an American Woman* (Philadelphia, 1847), pp. 177, 178.

63. Caspar Morris, *Margaret Mercer* (Boston, 1840), quoted in *Woman's Record*, p. 425.

64. These particular titles come from: *The Young Ladies' Oasis: or Gems of Prose and Poetry*, ed. N. L. Ferguson (Lowell, 1851), pp. 14, 16; *The Genteel School Reader* (Philadelphia, 1849), p. 271; and *Magnolia*, I (1842), 4. A popular poem in book form, published in England, expressed very fully this concept of woman as comforter: Coventry Patmore, *The Angel in the Home* (Boston, 1856 and 1857). Patmore expressed his devotion to True Womanhood in such lines as:

> The gentle wife, who decks his board
> And makes his day to have no night,
> Whose wishes wait upon her Lord,
> Who finds her own in his delight. (p. 94)

65. The women's magazines carried on a crusade against tight lacing and regretted, rather than encouraged, the prevalent ill health of the American woman. See, for example, *An American Mother, Hints and Sketches* (New York, 1839), pp. 28 ff., for an essay on the need for a healthy mind in a healthy body in order to better be a good example for children.

66. The best single collection of nineteenth-century cookbooks is in the Academy of Medicine of New York Library, although some of the most interesting cures were in hand-written cookbooks found among the papers of women who lived during the period.

67. Sarah Josepha Hale, *The Ladies' New Book of Cookery: A Practical System for Private Families in Town and Country* (5th ed.; New York, 1852), p. 409. Similar evidence on the importance of nursing skills to every female is found in such books of advice as William A. Alcott, *The Young Housekeeper* (Boston, 1838), in which, along with a plea for apples and cold baths, Alcott says, "Every female should be trained to the angelic art of managing properly the sick," p. 47.

68. *The Young Lady's Friend*, pp. 75-77, 79.

69. "A Tender Wife," *Godey's*, II (July 1831), 28.

70. "MY WIFE! A Whisper," *Godey's*, II (Oct. 1831), 231.

71. *Letters to Young Ladies*, p. 27. The greatest exponent of the mental and moral joys of housekeeping was the *Lady's Annual Register and Housewife's Memorandum Book* (Boston, 1838), which gave practical advice on ironing, hair curling, budgeting and marketing, and turning cuffs—all activities which contributed to the "beauty of usefulness" and "joy of accomplishment" which a woman desired (I, 23).

72. *The Young Lady's Friend*, p. 230.

73. "Learning vs. Housewifery," *Godey's*, X (Aug. 1839), 95.

74. *Letters to Young Ladies*, p. 25. W. Thayer, *Life at the Fireside* (Boston, 1857), has an idyllic picture of the woman of the house mending her children's garments, the grandmother knitting and the little girl taking her first stitches, all in the light of the domestic hearth.

75. "The Mirror's Advice," *Young Maiden's Mirror* (Boston, 1858), p. 263.

76. Mrs. L. Maria Child, *The Girl's Own Book* (New York, 1833).

77. P. 44.

78. T. S. Arthur, *Advice to Young Ladies* (Boston, 1850), p. 45.

79. R. C. Waterston, *Thoughts on Moral and Spiritual Culture* (Boston, 1842), p. 101. Newcomb's *Young Lady's Guide* also advised religious biography as the best reading for women (p. 111).

80. *Godey's*, I (1828), 1. (Repeated often in *Godey's* editorials.)

81. *The Lily of the Valley*, n. v. (1851), p. 2.

82. For example, "The Fatalist," *Godey's*, IV (Jan. 1834), 10, in which Somers Dudley has Catherine reading these dangerous books until life becomes "a bewildered dream. . . . O passion, what a shocking perverter of reason thou art!"

83. Review of *Society in America* (New York, 1837) in *American Quarterly Review* (Philadelphia), XXII (Sept. 1837), 38.

84. "A Finished Education," *Ladies' Museum* (Providence), I (1825), 42.

85. Helen Irving, "Literary Women," *Ladies' Wreath*, III (1850), 93.

86. "Women of Genius," *Ladies' Companion*, XI (1839), 89.

87. "Intellect vs. Affection in Woman," *Godey's*, XVI (1846), 86.

88. "The Only Daughter," *Godey's*, X (Mar. 1839), 122.

89. *The Annual Catalogue of the Officers and Pupils of the Young Ladies' Seminary and Collegiate Institute* (Monroe City, 1855), pp. 18, 19.

90. *Chronicles of a Pioneer School from 1792 to 1833: Being the History of Miss Sarah Pierce and Her Litchfield School,* compiled by Emily Noyes Vanderpoel; ed. Elizabeth C. Barney Buel (Cambridge, 1903), p. 74.

91. *Mt. Holyoke Female Seminary,* p. 13.

92. *The American Frugal Housewife* (New York, 1838), p. 111.

93. "Female Influence," in *The Ladies' Pearl and Literary Gleaner: ' Collection of Tales, Sketches, Essays, Anecdotes, and Historical Incidents* (Lowell), I (1841), 10.

94. Mrs. S. T. Martyn, "The Wife," *Ladies' Wreath,* II (1848-49), 171.

95. *The Young Ladies' Oasis,* p. 26.

96. "On Marriage," *Ladies' Repository,* I (1841), 133; "Old Maids," *Ladies' Literary Cabinet* (Newburyport), II (1822) (Microfilm), 141; "Matrimony," *Godey's,* II (Sept. 1831), 174; and "Married or Single," *Peterson's Magazine* (Philadelphia) IX (1859), 36, all express the belief that while marriage is desirable for a woman it is not essential. This attempt to reclaim the status of the unmarried woman is an example of the kind of mild crusade which the women's magazines sometimes carried on. Other examples were their strictures against an overly-genteel education and against the affectation and aggravation of ill health. In this sense the magazines were truly conservative, for they did not oppose all change but only that which did violence to some cherished tradition. The reforms they advocated would, if put into effect, make woman even more the perfect female, and enhance the ideal of True Womanhood.

97. *Girlhood and Womanhood,* p. 100. Mrs. Graves tells the stories in the book in the person of an "Old Maid" and her conclusions are that "single life has its happiness too," for the single woman "can enjoy all the pleasures of maternity without its pains and trials" (p. 140). In another one of her books, *Woman in America* (New York, 1843), Mrs. Graves speaks out even more strongly in favor of "single blessedness" rather than "a loveless or unhappy marriage" (p. 130).

98. A very unusual story is Lela Linwood, "A Chapter in the History of a Free Heart," *Ladies' Wreath,* III (1853), 349. The heroine, Grace Arland, is "sublime" and dwells in perfect light while we others struggle yet with the shadows." She refuses marriage and her friends regret this but are told her heart "is rejoicing in its *freedom.*" The story ends with the plaintive refrain:

> But is it not a happy thing,
>   All fetterless and free,
> Like any wild bird, on the wing,
>   To carol merrily?

But even in this tale the unusual, almost unearthly rarity of Grace's genius is stressed; she is not offered as an example to more mortal beings.

99. Horace Greeley even went so far as to apply this remedy to the "dissatisfactions" of Margaret Fuller. In his autobiography, *Recollecitons of a Busy Life* (New York, 1868), he says that "noble and great as she was, a good husband and two or three bouncing babies would have emancipated her from a deal of cant and nonsense" (p. 178).

100. *Sphere and Duties of Woman,* p. 64.

101. *A Sermon: Preached March 13, 1808, for the Benefit of the Society Instituted in the City of New-York, For the Relief of Poor Widows with Small Children* (New York, 1808), pp. 13, 14.

102. *Lady's Magazine and Museum: A Family Journal* (London) IV (Jan. 1831), 6. This magazine is included partly because its editorials proclaimed it "of interest to the English speaking lady at home and abroad" and partly because it shows that the preoccupation with True Womanhood was by no means confined to the United States.

103. *Sphere and Duties of Woman,* p. 102.

104. "Matrimony," *Lady's Amaranth,* II (Dec. 1839), 271.

105. Elizabeth Doten, "Marrying for Money," *The Lily of the Valley,* n. v. (1857), p. 112.

106. *Letters to Mothers,* p. 9.

107. "Maternal Relation," *Ladies' Casket* (New York, 1850?), p. 85. The importance of the mother's role was emphasized abroad as well as in America. *Godey's* recommended the book by the French author Aimeé-Martin on the education of mothers to "be read five times," in the original if possible (XIII, Dec. 1842, 201). In this book the highest ideals of True Womanhood are upheld. For example: "Jeunes filles, jeunes épouses, tendres mères, c'est dans votre âme bien plus que dans les lois du législateur que reposent aujourd'hui l'avenir de l'Europe et les destinées du genre humain," L. Aimeé-Martin, *De l'Education des Meres de famille ou De la civilisation du genre humain par les femmes* (Bruxelles, 1857), II, 527.

108. *Maternal Association of the Amity Baptist Church:* Annual Report (New York, 1847), p. 2: "Suffer the little children to come unto me and forbid them not, is and must ever be a sacred commandment to the Christian woman."

109. For example, Daniel Webster, "The Influence of Woman," in *The Young Ladies' Reader* (Philadelphia, 1851), p. 310.

110. Mrs. Emma C. Embury, "Female Education," *Ladies' Companion,* VIII (Jan. 1838), 18. Mrs. Embury stressed the fact that the American woman was not the "mere playthning of passion" but was in strict training to be "the mother of statesmen."

111. "How May An American Woman Best Show Her Patriotism?" *Ladies' Wreath,* III (1851), 313. Elizabeth Wetherell was the pen name of Susan Warner, author of *The Wide Wide World* and *Queechy.*

112. Henry F. Harrington, "Female Education," *Ladies' Companion,* IX (1838), 293, and "Influence of Woman—Past and Present," *Ladies' Companion,* XIII (1840), 245.

113. Mrs. E. Little, "What Are the Rights of Women?" *Ladies Wreath,* II (1848-49), 133.

114. *Female Influence,* p. 18.

115. *Ibid.,* p. 23.

116. Even the women reformers were prone to use domestic images, i.e., "sweep Uncle Sam's kitchen clean," and "tidy up our country's house."

117. The "Animus and Anima" of Jung amounts almost to a catalogue of the nineteenth-century masculine and female traits, and the female hysterics whom Freud saw had much of the same training as the nineteenth-century American woman. Betty Friedan, *The Feminine Mystique* (New York, 1963), challenges the whole concept of True Womanhood as it hampers the "fulfillment" of the twentieth-century woman.

PETER R. KNIGHTS

OUT-MIGRATION FROM BOSTON, 1830-1860

*In 1846 Lemuel Shattuck, the author of a comprehensive
statistical report on the lives of Bostonians, reported
that the "locomotive habits" of the city's population
made record taking much more difficult than it would
have been for "the more stationary population of the
country." A contemporary of Shattuck noted that it
was "characteristic of the poor everywhere, to be continually shifting their places of abode." In the following
essay, extracted from his book-length study, Peter
Knights in effect submits these earlier impressions to
the quantitative methodology that is increasingly relied
on by modern social historians. While he utilizes such
diverse sources as city directories, cemetery records,
vital statistics, manuscript census schedules, genealogies,
and town histories, Knights freely concedes that his
findings concerning out-migrants and their measurable
characteristics are tentative rather than definitive. His
data base was not a large one; some of the sources
yield pitifully slight and incomplete information on the
questions that interest him. Professor Knights' essay
is included here precisely because of the kinds of
questions it asks and the way it goes about answering
them; in both respects it offers a nice example of the
"new social history."*

The old residents, leaving the low and reclaimed land to foreign laborers, plant themselves in the suburbs. There they build tasteful houses, with flower-plots and gardens; availing [themselves] of the frequent omnibuses, or of special trains run almost hourly, . . . they reach their stores and offices in the morning, and at night

From *The Plain People of Boston, 1830-1860: A Study in City Growth* by Peter R. Knights.
Copyright © 1971 by Oxford University Press, Inc. Reprinted by permission. Notes have
been omitted from this excerpt.

sleep with their wives and children in the suburbs. No time is lost, for they read the morning and evening journals as they go and return.

ELIAS H. DERBY

As it is, our mechanics, clerks, and others, are driven to the country to find suitable places at a moderate rent to live in. Deprived of the society of their families, dining at restaurants, and gradually alienated from their domestic hearths, their moral exposure is greater than can be well calculated.

BOSTON SOCIETY FOR THE
PREVENTION OF PAUPERISM

Ante-bellum Boston not only served as an attraction to population, but also as a point of departure. The passage of people through cities seems to be one of the more neglected aspects of the entire urbanization process. If Boston, with its approximately 40 per cent interdecadal persistence during 1830-60, was filtering through itself each decade from two to six times as many households as lived in the city at the start of any decade, what of Philadelphia, with its persistence rates of 30 to 38 per cent? What of Rochester's 20 per cent persistence during the fifties? It would appear generally that the larger the city, the lower the persistence (during the 1850s) and the more rapid the turnover.

Assuming, for the sake of illustration, that during 1830-60 all American cities over 50,000 displayed residential mobility of 30 per cent per year, half of the population of these cities would have been replaced every two years, or the equivalent of two and one-half times the whole population every decade. Considering this flow, which is about equal to the combined "urban" population of the United States (using a cutoff of 2,500) between 1830 and 1860, suggests the possibility that a goodly proportion of America's nineteenth-century "urban" population may have spent some time in a city of over 50,000 (cf. Table 1). In any event, urbanization was not the "one-way street" we are wont to consider it.

Table 1. Comparison of Population in Areas of Over 2500 and of Over 50,000, United States, 1830-1860

Year	Total Population of All Places Over		3. (2) as Per Cent of (1)	4. (3) (Times 2.5 to Estimate Turnover)
	1. 2,500	2. 50,000		
1830	1,127,247	425,063	37.7	94.3
1840	1,845,055	704,264	38.2	95.4
1850	3,543,716	1,459,023	41.2	102.9
1860	6,216,518	3,090,841	49.7	124.3

Source: U.S. Bureau of the Census, *Historical Statistics of the United States [from] Colonial Times to 1957* (Washington: Government Printing Office, 1961), 14.

This chapter essays a description of the fate of Boston's out-migrants, who were, after all, almost as numerous as its immigrants and in-migrants. As nearly as can be determined, no nineteenth-century urban study has dealt with a city's out-migrants. Out-migrants vanish into a historical limbo, gone but not unmourned. One expert declares that "There is . . . no feasible method of tracing individuals once they disappear from the universe of the community under consideration." This attitude has, regrettably, permeated previous urban studies. But there are at least five sources of information on Boston's out-migrants; all have been used in this study.

First, city directories list suburban dwelling places for increasing numbers of Bostonians after about 1850. Second, the records of Boston area cemeteries contain information on the city's residents who wandered away, yet were returned to stay. Third, the Commonwealth of Massachusetts vital statistics records have information, for and after 1841/1842, on births, deaths, and marriages within the state. Any of several events—a person's death, the death of one of his children, his re-marriage, or the marriage of a child—may betray the presence, far from the Hub, of an ex-Bostonian. Fourth, there is the manuscript census itself. For the 1850 and 1860 federal censuses, which alone during the study period permit positive identification of individuals by comparison of given names, one has but to search the lists of residents in areas surrounding the study area. With practice, millions of names may be screened. For instance, in the present study, in addition to Boston the manuscript census lists (on microfilm) of 128 other Massachusetts cities and towns were checked. And last, genealogies and town histories often mentioned out-migrants' destinations.

Of the sample members in 1830, 1840, and 1850, from 15 to 18 per cent died in the subsequent decade. Another 9.1 to 12.7 per cent were positively identified as out-migrants, while from 36 to 45 per cent remained in Boston at the end of each decade. Between 28 and 36 per cent of each sample could not be accounted for at decades end, and was presumed to have left Boston (and probably Massachusetts). If one assumes the death rate among those not accounted for was about the same as that among those who remained (15-18 per cent), the proportion of living unknowns at decade's end would drop to about 30 per cent. Since the state registration was fairly efficient, one may conclude they had left the state. Until the manuscript census returns for the entire United States are data-processed, these persons must be considered lost. Nevertheless, we may still compare the pre-departure records of the "lost" 30 per cent with those of persons who stayed, thus characterizing some of the qualities of "transients" as against those of "continuous residents."

The general characteristics of those who left Boston were not, in most cases, markedly different from those of persons persisting in the city. The relative socioeconomic status group distributions, for example (Table 2), manifested distinct differences only among the Proprietors, Managers, &

Officials and Unskilled & Menial Service categories. Up to 1850, the former was underrepresented among out-migrants, while after 1840 the latter was over-represented.

Dividing the samples into assessment groups produces similar results. As one might expect, non-assessed males showed a marked tendency to leave Boston. But among those who paid only a poll tax, no especially wide gap opened between transients and "persisters" until the 1850's, when a greater proportion of "poll-tax-only" payers remained in Boston, reversing the previous trend (see Table 3). Persons with only a small amount of property ($200-$1000) were about one and one-fifth to two times as likely to remain in Boston as to leave, as Table 4 demonstrates. An anomaly crops up among the "upper middle" group ($1001-$10,000), though. During the 1830's, persons in this group were almost twice as likely to remain as to leave; the margin opened to three to one during the 'forties, only to reverse in the 'fifties to about three-quarters to one, indicating a substantial out-migration among this group. George Adams, who took the 1850 state census of Boston, may have had this "upper middle" group in mind when he wrote that

> many, especially for the last ten years, doing business in Boston, had become residents of the neighboring towns. These removals have not only been numerous, but many who have entered the City for the purpose of engaging in business have retained their country residences. The multiplied conveniences of traveling have in part induced to this. . . .

The Boston Directory contains the names of nearly 4000 persons doing business in Boston, and residing out of town. . . . it has been estimated that the whole number

Table 2. Socioeconomic Status Group Composition of Persisting and Out-Migrating Sample Members, 1830-1860, by Per Cent

Socioeconomic Status Group	Sample and Per Cent								
	1830			*1840*			*1850*		
	Per-sisting	Out-Mi-grating	Total Sample	Per-sisting	Out-Mi-grating	Total Sample	Per-sisting	Out-Mi-grating	Total Sample
Unskilled & Menial Service	10.5	11.2	11.4	11.4	20.5	14.3	20.4	33.3	27.0
Semi-Skilled & Service	8.0	8.6	8.3	5.1	6.4	6.2	7.0	4.8	5.5
Petty Proprietors, Managers, & Officials	17.8	15.2	16.9	14.2	17.9	16.6	13.4	7.4	9.9
Skilled	17.2	21.8	19.7	17.6	18.6	18.2	31.7	23.3	25.4
Clerical & Sales	4.3	0.7	2.3	1.7	1.3	2.1	2.8	3.7	3.9
Semi-Professional	1.3	2.7	1.8	2.3	0.6	1.6	1.4	—	0.8
Proprietors, Managers, & Officials	20.3	13.9	14.5	35.2	10.9	23.1	11.3	12.2	11.4
Professional	4.9	2.7	3.6	3.4	0.6	2.1	4.2	2.6	3.4
Miscellaneous & Unknown	16.0	23.7	21.3	9.1	23.1	15.8	7.7	12.7	12.7
Total in Sample	163	152	385	183	148	385	142	189	385

Because some sample members died, the sum of "persisting" and "out-migrating" sample members does not equal 385.
Source: Sample data.

Table 3. Assessment Group Composition of Persisting and Out-Migrating Sample Members, 1830-1860, by Per Cent

Sample and Characteristic	N	Assessment Group					
		Not Assessed Male	Female	Under $200	$200-$1,000	$1,001-$10,000	Over $10,000
1830							
Persisting	163	9.2	16.6	28.8	19.0	18.4	8.0
Out-Migrating	152	22.4	17.1	32.9	14.5	11.2	2.0
Total Sample	385	15.6	17.2	33.3	16.1	13.0	4.9
1840							
Persisting	176	5.1	8.0	30.7	19.3	27.8	9.1
Out-Migrating	156	23.7	15.4	33.3	17.3	9.0	1.3
Total Sample	385	13.2	11.9	31.2	19.0	19.2	5.5
1850							
Persisting	142	16.2	7.0	45.8	12.0	7.7	11.3
Out-Migrating	189	33.3	12.7	32.8	6.9	10.1	4.2
Total Sample	385	25.2	10.1	37.1	9.4	10.1	8.1

Because some sample members died, the sum of "persisting" and "out-migrating" sample members does not equal 385.

Source: Sample data.

of individuals doing business in Boston, and residing in the country, including their families, would amount to 20,000.

It is unlikely that Adams referred to the very rich (assessed over $10,000), for as Table 4 shows, up to 1850 these persons were two or three times as likely to stay in Boston as to leave it. Together, Tables 2, 3 and 4 indicate that the persons most likely to leave Boston were (after 1840) generally propertyless unskilled individuals. Those most likely to remain were (up till 1850) the major managers, proprietors, and officials worth more than $1000. After 1850, though, there occurred a considerable departure of this class, forming a noticeable fraction of Boston's outward-flowing population.

Before examining the out-migration patterns revealed by the sample groups, it may be that census data can illuminate the situation somewhat. We are of course handicapped in that antebellum censuses taken in Massachusetts never inquired where persons had lived previously. But in 1850 and 1860 the federal census, and in 1855 the state census, contained nativity questions. This permits a gross separation of population into native-born and foreign-born. Irish predominated in the latter (about 75 per cent). [These foreign-born individuals experienced exceptional mobility into, within, and out of Boston.] Because of their visibility in the census returns, and because their residential mobility formed such a large portion of Boston's residential

Table 4. Persistence Rates of Members of Various Assessment Groups, 1830-1860

Sample and Characteristic	N	Assessment Group					
		Male	Not Assessed Female	Under $200	$200-$1,000	$1,001-$10,000	Over $10,000
1830							
Present in 1830	385	60	66	127	62	50	19
Present in 1840	163	15	27	47	31	30	13
Persistence Rate (Per Cent)	42.4	25.0	40.9	37.0	50.0	60.0	68.4
1840							
Present in 1840	385	51	46	120	73	74	21
Present in 1850	176	9	14	54	34	49	16
Persistence Rate (Per Cent)	45.7	17.6	30.4	45.0	46.6	66.2	76.2
1850							
Present in 1850	385	97	39	143	36	39	31
Present in 1860	142	23	10	65	17	11	16
Persistence Rate (Per Cent)	36.9	23.7	25.6	45.5	47.2	28.2	51.6

Sample	Total of All Assessed		
	Present in Sample Year	Present After Ten Years	Persistence Rate (Per Cent)
1830	257	122	47.5
1840	288	163	56.6
1850	249	112	45.0

Source: Sample data.

mobility, their distribution should show some of the major characteristics of the outflowing population of Boston. This presumes that most Irish who lived in Massachusetts had been "processed" through Boston, and that backflow from New York City (the nearest other major port of entry) was negligible. The first seems likely, given Boston's position as a railroad center after 1845. The second assumption would appear reasonable since interstate migration statistics for native-born individuals show little backflow from New York to Massachusetts.

The 1855 state census provides the period's only town-by-town breakdown of nativity figures; its major results appear in Table 5 (in this census, "foreign-born" did not include native-born children of foreign parents). It shows the marked clustering of foreign-born around Boston. In 1855, some 25.7 per cent of the state's native-born residents lived within ten miles of Boston, as against 44.3 per cent of the foreign-born. The foreign-born were progressively less prevalent farther from Boston, with one foreigner out of four in Massachusetts living in Boston itself, one out of eight in the contiguous cities and towns, and one out of sixteen in the rest of the towns to a distance of ten miles from Boston. Perhaps a good place to look for Boston's out-migrants, or at least quite a few of them, would be in the suburban cities and towns to a distance of ten miles.

Of the 1155 sample members of the 1830, 1840, 1850 samples, 37, 48, and 49, respectively, were definitely identified as out-migrants by being located in a census outside Boston after their disappearance from Boston. These 134 persons represent just over 11 per cent of the 1155, and account for only 27 per cent of the 497 out-migrants during 1830-60 (i.e., 134 "known" and 363 "presumed"). Table 6 compares the socioeconomic status group and assessment group characteristics of the 134 known and 363 presumed out-migrants. Generally, the out-migrants who were tracked down in censuses outside Boston tended to belong to the Petty Proprietors, Managers, & Officials, the Skilled, and the Proprietors, Managers, & Officials socioeconomic status groups and (until 1850) to cluster in the Under $200 and $200-$1000 assessment categories. After $1850, there occurred a sharp shift toward the wealthier tax brackets of $1001 and above.

Although the 134 known out-migrants represented a generally better off, more elevated socioeconomic group than did the 363 presumed out-migrants, nonetheless it should be interesting to glance briefly at the smaller group, since it does constitute the only considerable number of urban out-migrants ever located.

Table 5. Distribution of Total and Foreign-Born Population in Boston and Nearby Areas, 1855

Area	1. Total Population in the Area	2. Foreign-Born[a] Population in the Area	3. (2) as Per Cent of (1)	4. (1) as Per Cent of State Population	5. (2) as Per Cent of Total Foreign-Born in State	6. [(1)-(2)] as Per Cent of Native-Born in State
Boston	160,490	62,353	38.9	14.2	25.4	11.1
Contiguous Cities and Towns	97,411	29,532	30.3	8.8	12.0	7.7
All Other Cities and Towns Within Ten Miles of Boston	77,583	16,823	21.7	7.0	6.9	6.9

[a] Foreign-born does not include native-born children of foreign parents.

Source: Massachusetts. Secretary of the Commonwealth, *Abstract of the Census of the Commonwealth of Massachusetts . . . 1855 . . .* (Boston: William White, 1857), 105-7, 115-21, 123, 126, 132.

Geographically, the known out-migrants tended to settle near Boston; more than half of those located had moved less than ten miles from Boston's Merchants' Exchange. Table 7 suggests that, after the 1840's (when census identification became easier), the proportion of known out-migrants who had moved less than ten miles from Boston rose to about three-quarters. It was during the late 'forties that *commutation* became widespread in Boston; as distinct from the former home-to-work journey, commutation required conveyances. Of course, well-to-do individuals had for some time used their carriages to travel from, say, suburban Roxbury or Brighton into the business section of Boston. (As early as 1846, complaints appeared in a Boston

Table 6. Socioeconomic Status Group and Assessment Group of Known and Assumed Out-Migrants, 1830-1860, by Per Cent

Socioeconomic Status Group	Sample and Per Cent					
	1830 Known/Assumed Out-Migrants		1840 Known/Assumed Out-Migrants		1850 Known/Assumed Out-Migrants	
Unskilled & Menial Service	8.1	12.2	8.3	25.9	2.0	44.3
Semi-Skilled & Service	2.7	10.5	2.1	8.3	6.1	4.3
Petty Proprietors, Managers, & Officials	24.4	12.2	27.1	13.9	8.2	7.1
Skilled	21.7	21.8	22.9	16.7	22.4	23.6
Clerical & Sales	—	0.9	2.1	0.9	10.2	1.4
Semi-Professional	2.7	2.6	—	0.9	—	—
Proprietors, Managers, & Officials	32.5	7.9	25.0	4.6	38.8	2.9
Professional	2.7	2.6	—	0.9	6.1	1.4
Miscellaneous & Unknown	5.4	29.6	12.5	27.8	6.1	15.0
Assessment Group						
Not Assessed—Males	5.4	27.9	6.3	31.5	6.1	42.9
Not Assessed—Females	5.4	20.0	8.3	18.5	6.1	15.0
Under $200	29.8	34.0	33.3	33.3	36.7	31.4
$200-$1,000	27.1	10.5	27.1	13.0	8.2	6.4
$1,001-$10,000	21.7	7.9	20.8	3.7	28.6	3.6
Over $10,000	10.9	—	4.2	—	14.3	0.7
Totals (N)	37	115	48	108	49	140

Source: Sample data.

Table 7. Distances from Boston's Merchants' Exchange at Which Known Out-Migrants Settled, 1830-1860

	Sample					
Number of Miles from Exchange at Which Residing	1830 Known Out-Migrants in 1840		1840 Known Out-Migrants in 1850		1850 Known Out-Migrants in 1860	
	Number	Per Cent	Number	Per Cent	Number	Per Cent
1-5	13	35.1	22	45.8	23	46.9
6-10	7	18.9	10	20.8	13	26.5
11-49	7	18.9	10	20.8	11	22.4
50 and over	5	13.5	6	12.5	2	4.1
Unknown[a]	5	13.5	—	—	—	—
Totals	37	99.9	48	99.9	49	99.9

[a]Distance was deemed "unknown" when individual was known, by death record, to have died outside Boston, yet could not be located in the town of demise in a preceding census; because of frequency of "stage" migration, such persons might have moved to another town from Boston, and then to the town of demise.

Source: Sample data.

newspaper about persons who tied down the reins of their carriages but did not hitch the reins to streetside posts; this allowed horse and carriage gradually to wander along a street, blocking traffic.)

The phenomenon of population dispersion to the suburbs did not escape contemporaries. One of the first to comment on the process was Jesse Chickering:

In consequence of traveling facilities by railroads radiating in every direction from Boston, as a common centre; many merchants and others doing business in the City, have of late been induced to remove to the neighboring towns whence they can go to the places of their daily business as quickly and as cheaply as if they had continued in their former residences.

By 1852, the City Council's Committee on Public Lands noted that

A reference to the census will show that while our foreign population is rapidly augmenting, our native population is in a greater ratio diminishing. The great influx of foreigners is changing entirely the character of various portions of the City. . . .

The older parts of the City are crowded, rents are exorbitant, and it is with extreme difficulty that a comfortable tenement can be obtained.

Many citizens of Boston are erecting houses in the neighboring cities and villages, and increasing the taxable property in those places from the profits of business transacted within our limits. . . .

The Committee are of opinion that the true interest of the City requires that every proper inducement should be offered to incline our citizens to remain within our limits.

And that, of course, was the experience of the more prosperous Bostonians, for a student of Boston's ante-bellum commutation system has described a dichotomy operating in the outward spread of the city's population. The cost of commutation was beyond the means of the ordinary laborer. Thus Boston's population divided into at least three groups: persons remaining in the city, persons commuting from the suburbs, and persons who moved to the suburbs but could not afford to commute. In substantiation of these findings, we have noticed that after 1840 propertyless unskilled individuals contributed heavily to the outward movement. After 1850 there was a considerable admixture of the "upper-middle" commuters whose principal real property in Boston had consisted of their homes, with the bulk of their holdings in "personal estate" at their business locations. It was thus easier for them to remove from the city than it was for persons with extensive real estate holdings; these, the "upper class," tended to remain in Boston.

A prominent feature of previous studies on population mobility has been the assumption that persons who left an area were doing so, among other reasons, because they were not as "successful" as their contemporaries. As far as ante-bellum Boston is concerned, this assumption appears plausible, for, generally, prior economic achievement was a good predictor of persistence in Boston. The fact that the 1850 and 1860 federal censuses contained wealth questions means that persons who left Boston may be compared, as to wealth, with those who remained. The results of such comparisons are presented with some diffidence, for though individuals who refused to "render a true account . . . in the various particulars required in and by" the census act of 1850 might be fined $30, about one household head in 14 lied about his real estate holdings, or omitted to mention them, or was victimized by a clerical omission of their amount (see Table 8). This illustrates the dangers of using any wealth figures derived from the manuscript census alone.

Persons who were assessed in Boston in 1850 (as 1850 sample members) and who were again assessed in 1860, together with a few others whose assessment could be deduced although it was not available, numbered 142. . . . Of these, by 1860 about one in five had advanced to a higher assessment group. About two-thirds remained in the same group, and approximately one-ninth had slipped to a lower group. However, of the 31 persons known to have left Boston in the 1850's for whom 1860 census reports were found, more than two-fifths had moved to the equivalent of a higher assessment group. Nearly half were still in the same bracket, and only one-tenth had dropped to a lower category (see Table 9). Since the known out-migrants were better off in 1850 than were the "persisters," the former would be expected to have enjoyed superior opportunities for advancement. Nevertheless, when we compare the performance of the propertyless individuals

Table 8. Real Estate Assessments, 1850, of Persons Listed in the Federal Manuscript Census as Owning No Real Estate

Assessment Category	Number in Category	As Per Cent of Total Sample (385)
Not Assessed—Male	99	25.7
Not Assessed—Female	39	10.1
Poll Tax Only (Under $200 in Property)	140	36.4
Assessed for Some Personal Property but no Real Estate	42	10.9
(Total Not Assessed for Real Estate)	(320)	(83.1)
$301-$500[a]	4	1.0
$501-$1,000	6	1.6
$1,501-$2,500[a]	6	1.6
$2,501-$5,000	4	1.0
$5,001-$10,000	4	1.0
$10,001-$25,000[a]	4	1.0
(Total Assessed for Real Estate But Not Listed in Census as Owning Real Estate)	(28)	(7.3)
(Total Assessed for Real Estate and Listed in Census as Owning Real Estate)	(37)	(9.6)
Totals	385	100.0

[a]The assessment categories $200-$300, $1,001-$1,500, and $25,001 and over were omitted because their entries were zero.

Source: Sample data.

in each group, we note that of the 98 "persisters" only 24 (24.5 per cent) had obtained property as of 1860. But of the 16 propertyless (as of 1850) who became known out-migrants, 7 (43.8 per cent) owned some property by 1860, suggesting that about twice as many of them had become property-owners of some sort.

These fragmentary data should suffice to indicate that the little-known portion of the urbanization process occurring *after* arrival at a population center is the part currently subject to the most facile (and perhaps least accurate) generalizations. These generalizaions, which concern the relationship of "success" and persistence, have yet to be examined rigorously. The requisite examination would seem, unfortunately, to be beyond the resources of individuals using current methods. Yet the data here presented argue that this very area of concern—which might be called the "post-urban" part of the urbanization process—is not only of great intrinsic importance, but has also been allowed to languish untilled, its boundaries and characteristics those of a *terra incognita*.

Table 9. Comparisons of Changes in Assessment Group, 1850-1860 of 142 "Persisters" and 31 Known Out-Migrants

Assessment Group, 1850	"Persisters" Number in Assessment Groups, 1860					Change	Number	Percent
	N	I	II	III	IV			
I. (Under $200)	98	74	10	13	1			
II. ($200-$1,000)	17	8	4	5	—	Upward	32	22.5
						None	94	66.2
III. ($1,001-$10,000)	11	2	1	5	3	Downward	16	11.3
						Totals	142	100.0
IV. (Over $10,000)	16	1	—	4	11			
Totals	142	85	15	27	15			

Assessment Group, 1850	Known Out-Migrants Numbers in Wealth Categories Corresponding to Assessment Groups, as Listed in the 1860 Manuscript Census					Change	Number	Percent
	N	I	II	III	IV			
I. (Under $200)	16	9	2	5	—			
II. ($200-$1,000)	2	—	—	2	—	Upward	13	41.9
						None	15	48.4
III. ($1,001-$10,000)	9	1	—	4	4	Downward	3	9.7
						Totals	31	100.0
IV. (Over $10,000)	4	1	—	1	2			
Totals	31	11	2	12	6			

Source: Sample data.

LEONARD P. CURRY

URBANIZATION AND URBANISM IN THE OLD SOUTH

Urban history, as the readers of the work of Henri Pirenne and Carl Bridenbaugh will know, is hardly a new subject to historians. Yet the new urban history differs markedly from the old, among other ways by substituting analysis for description, by relying on comprehensive evidence drawn from such sources as directories and censuses rather than on random impressions, and in its preoccupation with the common characteristics of a "composite city" rather than with the inevitable uniquenesses of particular cities. Leonard Curry's essay reflects some of the characteristics of the recent work. While its conclusions rest on the solid evidence of censuses, its focus on the relatively larger cities and its avoidance of comparing total urban populations on both sides of the Mason-Dixon line perhaps leave an impression that southern urbanism was more substantial, quantitatively, than it actually was. Curry's informative discussion of the strikingly similar problems faced by antebellum cities north and south, as well as the similarities in their responses to these problems, provides one more illustration that the sections were not as unlike as we used to think they were.

An examination of urban development in the antebellum South might appear to some to be an exercise in the manipulation of minutiae. So thoroughly has the myth of the plantation (or, at least, rural) Old South been embedded in historical consciousness that there is an overwhelming tendency to dismiss such urban considerations as at best peripheral and atypical, if not insignificant.[1]

Leonard P. Curry, "Urbanization and Urbanism in the Old South: A Comparative View," *Journal of Southern History*, XL (February 1974), 43-60. Copyright © 1974 by the Southern Historical Association. Reprinted by permission of the Managing Editor.

In recent years historians have become increasingly (and commendably) aware of the anthropological concept of the utility of myths, and certainly, understanding of social and intellectual history has been measurably enriched as a result of this awareness. Undoubtedly, some interested historian could profitably examine the remarkable consistency with which a mythic view of the Old South was and has been accepted by the region's defenders and its detractors alike. But for those not directly involved in the study of this particular element of intellectual history, the myth presents a hazard, not an opportunity. It clouds eyes, stops ears, and warps mental processes. Even a cursory examination of readily available evidence suggests the existence of a pre-1850 South of considerable commercial enterprise, some interest in manufacturing, remarkable agricultural diversification, and specifically, relatively substantial urbanization.

Before entering more deeply into this discussion, a few words about the boundaries and purposes of this inquiry are in order. This study will deal primarily with the years 1800-1850, which might be called the heart of the Old South period. Not only is the half century a neat and convenient time span, but terminating the inquiry in 1850 avoids the volatile (and, in some respects, atypical) precursory decade to disunion. Moreover, as a Census Bureau writer observed some thirty years ago, "By 1850, settlement was well under way in most of the States which have now [1939] attained a high percentage of urban population; and since that date . . . the trend of the percentage urban in the country as a whole has been less affected . . . by the expansion of the settled area or by the beginning of urbanization."[2] In other words, the year 1850 roughly marks the end of the seedtime of American urban development, and there is, the Census Bureau writer contends, an observable substantive difference between the urban statistics collected before that date and those of later years.

The initial date of 1800 has some peculiar advantages for the study of southern urban development, since it marks with a fair degree of precision the juncture at which the emerging cotton culture presumably breathed new life into an apparently moribund plantation economy. Ten years earlier American cotton production had totaled a paltry 3,000 bales, and in 1795 the figure had not reached 20,000 bales. But in 1800 production first topped 50,000 bales and the following year touched the 100,000-bale level. The impact of this massive economic shift on southern urban development may be argued to have been commercially stimulative or psychologically inhibitive, but it can hardly have been negligible.[3]

The South that is the subject of this study consisted of the fifteen states and the federal district in which slavery was established by law in 1850, and in which, it might be added, there was no visible prospect of its legal demise. For if there was a South, most assuredly it was the South that slavery made.

This paper will be primarily devoted to a quantitive and qualitative comparison of southern and nonsouthern urban development during this era in an attempt to determine to what extent, if at all, the urban experience in the

South differed from that in the rest of the country. To this will be added a few observations intended to suggest some of the differences between southern urban development in this period and in subsequent years.

In assessing the extent of urbanization in the Old South, perhaps it is best to start at the top. In 1850 this region contained two of the nation's five largest cities, three of the ten largest, and six of the fifteen largest.[4] This distribution very closely approximated the division of the nation's population between the sections; the South in 1850 contained slightly more than two-fifths (41.23 percent) of the total population. Moreover, almost one-third (31.78 percent) of the southern population consisted of people—slaves—who (with minute exceptions) could not voluntarily take up residence in the cities. The South, in fact, contained less than one-third (32.63 percent) of the nation's free population.[5]

The objection may be raised that these six cities—Baltimore, New Orleans, St. Louis, Louisville, Charleston, and Washington—are all located on the periphery of the South—on or near the coast and along the great rivers dividing the two sections—and hence are not truly southern. But this observation applies to the large cities of the North with almost equal force. Of the nine major cities located in the North only Albany can even remotely be considered an interior town, though Pittsburgh is also a few miles removed from the sectional boundary. All the others—Philadelphia, New York, Brooklyn, Providence, Boston, Buffalo, and Cincinnati—are clearly peripheral coastal, lake, and river cities. Or it might be argued that the fact that these large southern cities were to be found in only six political jurisdictions (five states and the District of Columbia) shows how lightly urban life touched the South. The nine largest northern cities, however, were concentrated in only five states (indeed, six of them in two states), and furthermore, these states were entirely contiguous. Thus the dispersion of urban centers was obviously more widespread in the South than in the North, although the peripheral locational pattern was common to both sections.

It should be noted that there is considerable merit in speaking of numbers of urban centers rather than the total populations in these cities when dealing only with the largest urban units. For it is doubtful that, beyond a certain indeterminate point, the urban influence of a city is directly proportional to its population. This is particularly true when the population of a single city constitutes an exceptionally large proportion of the total urban population. In 1850, for instance, New York City contained well over a quarter of the total population of the nation's fifteen largest cities, but it may be doubted that its urban influence, though great, was of proportional magnitude.[6]

The South, of course, contained fewer of the cities of the second rank—substantial and thriving urban centers in many instances but not sufficiently populous to be included in the top fifteen. But if the scope of the inquiry is extended to include all cities with populations of 25,000 or more no massive shifts are observable. In 1850 the North, with roughly three-fifths of the nation's total population and more than two-thirds of the free population, contained just over two-thirds of these cities (fifteen of twenty-two).[7]

It may be urged, however, that revealing (and, perhaps to some, surprising) as these observations on the level of urbanization in the South in 1850 may be, they are not in themselves determinative. Such figures might reflect rather too heavily an early start (Charleston), a territorial annexation which added to the South a relatively large and thriving metropolis (New Orleans) without a commensurate urban accretion to the North, or a sudden spurt in the growth of a particular city (St. Louis) immediately before the date chosen for analysis. Since the primary concern is with the relative urban positions of the North and the South, some of these suggestions would seem to have no great merit; for New York, Boston, Providence, and Albany, at least, had the advantage of earlier starts than Charleston, and the growth of Brooklyn in the 1840s was almost as phenomenal as that of St. Louis. But there is some virtue in the thought that the rate of urban growth during the half century from 1800 to 1850 should also be a matter of concern.

The inadequacy of the Census Bureau definition of urban population is so apparent as to require no belaboring. It is, indeed, this circumstance that explains the concentration, thus far, on the larger cities. But the census figures have the great and undeniable merit of availability, and they do encompass a very large range of so-called urban units. Moreover, the figures may be less misleading (if dealt with in relative terms) for the antebellum era than for later periods, because of the earlier disportionate impact on the indices of the major city populations. In 1850 the fifteen largest cities contained well over one-half of the nation's total urban population (as defined by the Census Bureau); by 1900 this figure had declined to slightly over one-third.[8]

It is, in this regard, necessary to do two things: (1) to determine how the pattern of growth of the urban population in the South compared with that in the North (or, more accurately, the Non-South) throughout the half century from 1800 to 1850 and (2) to show simply and accurately the relative rates of growth of the urban populations in the two areas for the period as a whole. The pattern or urban growth throughout the era is most clearly depicted by constructing a line graph on which the percentages of population urban are plotted for the South, the North, and the nation as a whole (Figure 1). The South, of course, entered the nineteenth century with a much smaller urban population than the North, both relatively and absolutely. Throughout the period, therefore, the South line lies below the North line on the graph, with the national line falling between the two. But the significant point is that during most of the half century these lines move essentially in parallel, with a slight convergence of the North and South lines between 1800 and 1820, a slight divergence between 1820 and 1840, and a more significant widening of the gap between 1840 and 1850 (Figure 2).

FIGURE 1
Regional Percentage of Population Urban Point Deviation from National Percentage
1790–1930

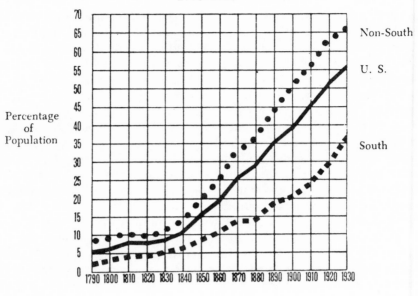

FIGURE 2
Regional and National Percentage of Population Urban
1790–1930

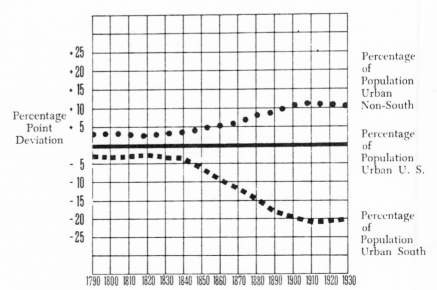

Thus, the course of urban growth in the South can be seen to have conformed closely to the national pattern, except during the final decade of the period under consideration.

To devise a single, simple index (preferably with some intrinsic meaning) to show accurately the comparable rates of urbanization in the two sections is not quite as easy as it appears. There is, of course, no difficulty in computing the percentage of urban population growth for the half century; for the South the figure is 946.52 percent and for the North, 1011.7 percent. It might be noted that even these gross percentages are much closer together than the Old South myth would have suggested. But these figures actually provide little or no necessarily reliable information about the respective rates of urbanization, for they are likely to be strongly affected by the rate of total population growth in the region.

For instance, suppose one assumes the existence of two geographic units, each of which has a population of ten million, 10 percent of which is urban. In a given period of time the population of Unit A increases by two million and that of Unit B by one million. In each unit the percentage of the total population that is urban remains constant. Unit A will thus show a 20 percent increase in its urban population, while Unit B will show a 10 percent increase. Actually, since the percentage of the population that is urban remains unchanged, the comparative urban rate of increase is the same in both units—zero. What is really wanted is the rate at which the population is becoming increasingly (or decreasingly) urbanized. This can, of course, be shown as the percentage increase (*not* the percentage-*point* increase) of the percentage of the population that is urban. This process has the disadvantage, however, of producing a rather abstract index figure, the intrinsic meaning of which may not be immediately apparent.

Another way of comparing the rate of increase in the urban population with the rate of increase in the total population is more likely to be readily comprehended. This is simply to state how much more rapidly the urban population is increasing than the total population is growing. This figure might be denominated the Comparative Urban Rate of Increase (CURI) and is easily computed by dividing the percentage of urban population increase by the percentage of total population increase.[9] The CURI index also has the advantage of almost instant comprehensibility—a CURI factor of 2.0 simply means that the urban population grew twice as fast as the total population in the period under consideration.

Between 1800 and 1850 the urban population of the South increased by 946.52 percent while the total population grew by 268.62 percent; for the North the figures were 1011.7 percent and 403.51 percent, respectively. Thus, the Comparative Rate of Urban Increase for the South was 3.52 and that for the North, 2.50. These figures mean, than, that in the North the urban population was growing two and one half times as rapidly as the total population, while in the South the urban population grew slightly more than three and one-half times as rapidly as the whole population.[10]

Thus, various statistical analyses show urbanization in the Old South to have been a movement of consequence. The section contained roughly its proportional share of the major and secondary cities, these cities were relatively more widely dispersed in the South than in the North, and a peripheral pattern of location was common to both sections. The trend of southern urban growth conformed closely to the national pattern for four-fifths of the period, and the Comparative Urban Rate of Increase was significantly greater in the South than in the rest of the nation.

But it may be argued that despite the statistically demonstrable presence of a respectable and growing urban population, the Old South was, nevertheless, nonurban because these urban centers were in qualitative terms nonsouthern—atypical of the region. In large part, of course, such arguments are mere parrotings of the Old South myth, which would hold urban populations and institutions to be nonsouthern by definition, regardless of their location within the regional boundaries. It would be more logical, obviously, to conclude that because these urban populations and institutions did lie within its regional boundaries, the South cannot be viewed as having been wholly nonurban, the Old South myth to the contrary notwithstanding. While it may be validly urged that New Orleans was not typical of the South, it must also be added that neither was New York typical of the North; and if life in Charleston differed from that in northern Alabama, so did life in Boston differ from that in northern Vermont.

A closely related question does have validity, however, and requires careful consideration. Did southern cities differ qualitatively from northern cities? If southernism did not prevent urbanization, did it so modify the process and the product as to make the southern urban experience distinct from and largely unrelated to the urban experience elsewhere in the country? But the pursuit of the answers to these questions leads to the consideration of that perplexing subject, urbanism—the qualitative nature of the urban experience. Although some urbanologists would deny the existence of urbanism, these questions about the qualitative nature of urban life seem to be worthy of exploration. But masses of evidence dealing with the internal affairs of the major cities suggest that southern cities were more peculiarly urban than peculiarly southern. This is not to say that one city is like every other or to deny that each city has its own peculiarities. Yet cities by their nature share some common problems, opportunities, and purposes, and all constantly draw upon a common pool of urban ideas and experiences.

The patterns of urban government in the South, for instance, were substantially identical with those in northern cities—a legislative body, sometimes of one and sometimes of two houses, elected by wards on the basis of a declining property qualification; a mayor, gradually divesting himself of the remnants of his judicial functions, initially appointive but made elective during this period (1812 in New Orleans, 1820 in Washington, 1833 in Baltimore, and 1838 in Louisville); and a small number of other officers who throughout the period increasingly tended to be elected. Even the unique municipality system in New Orleans was merely an extreme example of the dispersal of municipal function and decision making, which can also be seen at work in the fragmentation of the Brooklyn, Boston, and New York school systems, the ward election of policemen in New York, Washington's use of ward funds as a dominant factor in its fiscal operations, and the almost universal election of such ward officers as assessors, collectors, constables, and overseers of the poor.[11]

Moreover, these southern governments found themselves dealing with the same issues that absorbed the energies of their northern counterparts. Beyond doubt, the development of public education, for instance, in these cities lagged behind the best in the northern area. But rudimentary systems were established in Charleston by 1811, in Washington by 1812, in New Orleans, Baltimore, and Louisville in the 1820s, and in St. Louis before the end of the 1830s. By 1850 New Orleans had a public-school enrollment which, in relative terms, though trailing well behind Boston and Philadelphia, did not compare too unfavorably with New York. The relative position of Baltimore was not quite so good, and those of Louisville and St. Louis were significantly better. Southern as well as northern cities introduced night schools to reach the sizable segment of the cities' youths who were fully employed.[12]

Fire protection followed the national pattern of encouraging the formation of volunteer companies by grants of exemption from jury and militia duty. To this was added municipal financial support in the form of appropriations for equipment and engine houses. In southern as well as northern cities the intense rivalries led to violence.

Southern police protection, too, conformed to practices elsewhere, with forces consisting primarily of night watchmen but with increased introduction of day police as the half century wore on. As in the case of fire protection, the demand for personnel was roughly proportional to population size, though Washington—apparently unusually free from nocturnal crime despite its poor street lighting—was admittedly slow in developing its watch system. New York and New Orleans contended for the distinction of having the most corrupt and criminal police force, and Charlestonians slept peacefully (one presumes) while their streets were patrolled by a force in which major infractions (punishable by fine, imprisonment, suspension, etc.) averaged better than one per year per officer, and the rate of minor infractions (such as absence from duty) ran more than thirty times as high. If northerners complained more loudly, southerners probably suffered no less from the incompetence and corruption of these forces.[13]

In performing the mundane tasks of urban housekeeping, the records of southern city governments like those of their northern counterparts were spotty. Street lighting in Washington, for instance, was almost an impossible task because of the great distances and the sparse population; indeed, for a time the city government abandoned all efforts in this field. Baltimore, on the other hand, in 1818 became the first American city to authorize the lighting of its streets by gas. The last two decades of this period saw the extension of gas lighting to the other major southern cities (including Washington) and in the same era to many of their northern sisters.[14] Street paving also proved difficult for the Washington corporation because of the extreme width of the streets, the small number of property holders to bear the cost, and the reluctance of Congress to assume any financial responsibility for the district. And New Orleans got a late start because it was believed that paving stones would disappear into the swampy earth. By the end of the half century, however, paving was extensive in all the major southern urban centers, and the same methods were being used as in the North, although Washington continued to have special problems, and Charleston relied almost exclusively on gravel, shell, and macadam surfacing.[15]

Filth and garbage in the streets posed the same problems for both southern and northern urbanites; indeed, for climatic reasons, the problems were undoubtedly more acute in the South. Thus, the efforts of southern municipalities were perhaps somewhat more energetic in this field, but the methods employed were the same—and marked by the same lack of complete effectiveness—as those used elsewhere. The same comments may be said to apply to the not unrelated problem of controlling dogs and hogs running at large. In the southern as in the northern cities a debate raged over whether the ever-present swine should be considered health hazards or public benefactors. The issue was stated succinctly by a Baltimorean in 1820. "A hog running at large," he asserted, "is a friend to every one he visits, whilst a hog confined is the most intolerable nuisance."[16] Unable to resolve the controversy, the southern city officials followed the same course as their northern brothers; they passed but did not enforce ordinances prohibiting swine from running at large. Dogs, of course, had none of the theoretical social advantages of swine, but then as now dog owners were a touchy lot. Nominal license fees were imposed (and occasionally collected), and the ordinances providing for the taking up and destruction of unlicensed dogs running at large were spasmodically enforced. Token efforts were also made to curb the growth of the canine population, as when the Washington City Council imposed an annual tax on female dogs roughly equivalent to a week's wages for a skilled laborer, and the St. Louis corporation established a bounty for killing "every slut found running at large . . . during the period of her salacity," but again, evidence of consistent enforcement is nonexistent.[17]

Both health considerations and the need for more nearly adequate fire protection caused cities in both sections to address themselves to the question of water supply. Washington, again because of the vast distances and sparse population, relied on a multiplicity of springs and with minor exceptions piped water only for short distances. The construction of a city-wide system in the nation's capital was thus delayed until the 1850s. The city of Charleston was unsuccessful in its efforts to locate a suitable supply, despite active financial support of artesian-well ventures in the 1840s. Easy access to an unusually abundant supply of largely unpolluted well water postponed Louisville action in this area into the 1850s. The other major cities of the South followed the Philadelphia example of distributing water from a single source through a network of pipes. Baltimore as early as 1807 and New Orleans and St. Louis in the 1820s and 1830s created their waterworks. The southern systems developed somewhat more slowly than some of the northern ones, but by the end of the half century piped water was supplied to roughly one-half of the Baltimore residents, and those of New Orleans were being furnished with about one and one-third million gallons of water daily.[18]

The southern as well as the northern cities bore the responsibility of caring for the poor within their boundaries (an obligation sometimes shared with the counties), and the same practices prevailed in both sections. Almshouses—established before 1800 in Charleston and at relatively early dates elsewhere—cared for increasing numbers and percentages of paupers, while direct donations (whether of money or supplies) to the out-of-doors pensioners tended to decline relatively throughout the period. A growing number of infirmaries and dispensaries provided medical treatment and drugs in all the major southern cities. City orphanages were established in some instances, and in a greater number of cases city funds helped to support private establishments. Almost every city government complained of the disproportionate number of nonresidents who inflated the relief rolls.[19]

Similar practices prevailed in both sections in the field of consumer protection. Market regulations were extensive and detailed; inspectors and measurers abounded; building codes were enacted; ferry rates were established by ordinance, as were rates for hacks, carts, and drays, the operators of which were usually required to be licensed annually. Southern cities seem to have been somewhat more inclined than their northern counterparts to set maximum bread prices (in relation to the cost of flour) than merely to specify the weight and quality of the loaves.[20]

Some of these regulations, of course, were implemented primarily as public-health measures, and this category would also include the many ordinances requiring the draining of cellars and vacant lots. All the major southern cities had boards and officers charged with ensuring the healthfulness of the city, and increasingly these city employees included vaccine physicians, who vaccinated large numbers of the urban population without charge.

It may be suggested that though urban governments perforce deal with essentially the same matters, southern cities differed qualitatively from those of the North in the nature of the non-official institutions that developed. Such a suggestion will not bear close scrutiny.

Southern cities like their northern counterparts (with the exception of Pittsburgh and, to a lesser degree, Cincinnati and Providence) rested on commercial bases and assumed similar roles as regional centers of banking and insurance capital.[21] Southern cities spawned literary societies, professional associations, and debating groups. Their inhabitants were as quick as their northern brothers to fight urban anonymity by joining fraternal and other social organizations; the Masons, Odd Fellows, Redmen, Druids, Sons of Malta, and other orders were established early and developed rapidly. The various ethnic organizations were also present, supported by a large foreign-born population. Although Washington and Charleston seem to have had a lower percentage of foreign-born in their populations in 1850 than the other major cities of the nation, St. Louis and New Orleans appear to have ranked first and third in this category.[22] Public libraries grew, newspapers flourished, theaters appeared early and were well patronized, and some support was accorded to musical groups. First-class hotels were built, sometimes as a matter of civic pride; the St. Charles and St. Louis in New Orleans, the Planters' House in St. Louis, the City in Baltimore, and Louisville's Galt House did not suffer grossly by comparison with Cincinnati's Burnet House, Boston's Tremont House, or the Astor House in New York.[23] The rage for suburban cemeteries so notable in northern cities also touched their southern counterparts, giving rise to Cypress Grove and Greenwood in New Orleans, Cave Hill in Louisville, and Bellefontaine in St. Louis.[24]

Some differences, indeed, there were. Southern urban populations had much larger Negro components than did those north of Mason's and Dixon's line, and blacks obviously had far greater economic opportunities in the southern cities. Lower South cities (but not those of the upper South) appear to have been slightly less subject to rioting—a circumstance that probably resulted form the pervasive fear of the impact of such disorders on the slaves. It is notable that only Charleston and New Orleans had sizable slave populations.

But to an overwhelming degree the pattern that emerges is one of similarities, not differences. Numerous additional examples could doubtless be cited, but surely enough evidence has been presented to establish the fact that quantitatively and qualitatively southern urban development in the first half of the nineteenth century closely approximated national norms.

One final question remains to be considered briefly: How did the pattern of urbanization in the Old South compare with that in the New South? Two preliminary observaitons are in order. First, a qualitative comparison of the urban experience in the antebellum and the postbellum South, however interesting in itself, would contribute little to the understanding of this problem because of intervening technological changes, shifts in economic orientation, a massive modification of the social structure, and the fact that the urban leaders of the New South were building on the foundations laid and advancing from the positions achieved by their predecessors. Second, it is obvious that both the gross size of the southern urban population and the percentage of the southern population classified as urban increased substantially after the middle of the nineteenth century. But these facts standing alone are relatively unimportant. The significant question is what comparison can be drawn between the antebellum and postbellum patterns of urbanization in the South in relation to contemporary national and non-southern norms.

The figures provide an interesting contrast. In 1850 it will be recalled, the South contained about two-fifths of the national population (slightly less than one-third of the nation's free population) and could count within its borders two of the five largest and six of the fifteen largest cities in the United States, together with roughly one-third of all American cities with populations in excess of 25,000. By 1900, however, while the South's share of the national population still stood at a substantial 35.27 percent, the region contained only one of the five largest and four of the fifteen largest cities, and its share of the cities with populations greater than 25,000 had declined to slightly over one-quarter. Of the total population resident in these cities of 25,000 and up, the South in 1850 had, relative to its whole population, 59.71 percent of its proportional share, or 68.67 percent of its proportional share if one considers the free population only; by 1900 this last figure had dropped to 48.14 percent.

The charting of the percentages of the total population classified as urban in the South, the Non-South, and the nation produced for the period 1800-1850 lines that moved essentially in parallel (until 1840); in the post-1850 period, however, these lines diverged acutely and increasingly, at least to 1910 (Figures 1 and 2). In 1850 one-quarter of the southern states (including the District of Columbia) had percentages of their population classified as urban equal to or higher than the figure for the nation as a whole; by 1900 the number had dropped to less than one-fifth and by 1930 to one-eighth.[25] In the Comparative Urban Rate of Increase index—a measurement which probably indicates more accurately the relative rate of urbanization—the New South fares a little better. For the period 1850-1900 the Comparative Urban Rate of Increase was 3.08 for the South as compared to 3.13 for the rest of the country. These figures represent a drop of .44 units for the South and an increase of .63 units for the Non-South over the 1800-1850 figures. For the period 1870-1920 the CURI factor dropped to 2.89 for the South and, more precipitously, to 2.43 for the rest of the country.[26] While the South is thus seen to regain its earlier lead over the Non-South in this index, the advantage is less than one-half of a CURI unit as compared to more than a full unit advantage for the South for the 1800-1850 period. Thus, by almost any statistical measurement the South of about 1900 to 1920 occupied a weaker position in terms of urban development relative to the rest of the country than was true of the Old South.

Clearly then, urban development in the Old South was neither massively different from nor consistently inferior to that in the rest of the United States. And it can validly be argued that similar statements could be made about commercial enterprise and agricultural diversification. Why, then, should these things not be accepted and made the subjects of continuing investigation? Why must such evidence be categorized as atypical and discarded? Probably every discrete historical fact is atypical, however illustrative it may be. It is high time that historians free themselves from the influence of the half-truths, omissions, and the comfortable nostalgia that make up the Old South myth and exorcise this ghost. Then, perhaps, they can, with clearer vision and minds less "cabined, cribbed, [and] confined," seek to rediscover the reality of the Old South.

Notes

1. No space is devoted to urbanization and urbanism in the Old South in such works as Avery O. Craven, *The Growth of Southern Nationalism, 1848-1861* ([Baton Rouge], 1953); Monroe L. Billington, *The American South: A Brief History* (New York, 1971); Ulrich B. Phillips, *The Course of the South to Secession: An Interpretation,* edited by E. Merton Coulter (New York and London, 1939); Frank L. Owsley, *Plain Folk of the Old South* ([Baton Rouge], 1949); and William R. Taylor, *Cavalier and Yankee: The Old South and American National Character* (New York, 1961). Fewer than a half-dozen pages containing substantive information on Old South cities can be found in William B. Hesseltine and David L. Smiley, *The South in American History* (2d ed., Englewood Cliffs, N. J., 1960), and Francis B. Simkins and Charles P. Roland, *A History of the South* (4th ed., New York, 1972); and not more than twice that number in Ulrich B. Phillips, *Life and Labor in the Old South* (Boston, 1929), and Charles S. Sydnor, *The Development of Southern Sectionalism, 1819-1848* ([Baton Rouge], 1948). Some of these writers express their rejection of the conception of southern urbanism in both a positive and a negative fashion, as when Simkins asserts (p. 150), "The genius of the Old South was rural," and when Owsley says of his "plain folk" (p. vii), "Their thoughts, traditions, and legends were rural. . . ." A notable exception to this general pattern among historians of the Old South is Clement Eaton, who evinces some genuine interest in urban life in his excellent *A History of the Old South* (2d ed., New York, 1966), and whose chapter on "Town Life" in his *The Growth of Southern Civilization, 1790-1860* (New York, 1961), 247-70, is, to the best of my knowledge, unique among general histories of the Old South. But even Eaton, of course, is not concerned with the pattern of southern urban growth, nor does he address himself to a comparative analysis of southern and nonsouthern urbanism and urbanization.

2. U. S. Bureau of the Census, *Urban Population in the United States from the First Census (1790) to the Fifteenth Census (1930)* ([Washington, 1939]), 5.

3. U. S. Bureau of the Census, *Historical Statistics of the United States, Colonial Times to 1957* (Washington, 1960), 302.

4. For the purposes of this analysis Philadelphia and its suburbs are treated as a single city, although the actual legal consolidation did not take place until 1854. See J. D. B. De Bow, *Statistical View of the United States . . .* (Washington, 1854), 192; *The Seventh Census of the United States: 1850* (Washington, 1853), *passim.*

5. In this and the next analysis (dealing with cities having populations of 25,000 or more), the populations of California and the territories have been excluded; that of California because of the unreliability and incompleteness of the published figures on urban population and that of the territories because their recent origins and sparse populations rendered the development of urban centers of this size patently impossible. The inclusion of the published figures for these areas would minutely decrease the South's share of the total national population and produce a slightly more significant reduction of the South's proportion of the free population. The result would be to place the South in a slightly stronger urban position than the above analysis indicates. In subsequent analyses (dealing with the Census Bureau definition of urban population) the published figures for these areas are included. The statistics for the quantitative

analyses in this paper are drawn from the sources listed in footnotes 2, 3, and 4, and from the *Twelfth Census of the United States, Taken in the Year 1900:* Vol. I, *Population* (Washington, 1901).

6. The population figures themselves, however, though clearly showing a preponderant share of the major city population to be resident in the North, do not reveal such gross discrepancies as the Old South myth would lead us to anticipate. In 1850 these large cities contained just over a tenth of the northern population—almost precisely twice the southern proportion. But if free population only be considered, then the southern figure rises to almost 7 percent.

7. The cities (in addition to the fifteen previously mentioned) with populations of 25,000 and up were Newark, New Jersey; Rochester, New York; Lowell, Massachusetts; Williamsburg, New York; Chicago, Illinois; Troy, New York; and Richmond, Virginia. The calculation of the proportion of the regional populations resident in this enlarged group of cities leaves the relative position of the sections essentially unchanged from that shown in the analysis of the major city populations only. The figures (together with the increase over similar figures for major cities only) were: North—11.12 percent (up .67 percentage points); South (total population)—5.35 percent (up .29 percentage points); South (free population only)—7.07 percent (up .28 percentage points). The reasons for the insignificance of the change, of course, are the small number of additional cities included and the smallness of their populations, especially in relation to those of the major cities. The cities in question were distributed among seven political jurisdictions in each section.

8. During the same period the percentage of the urban population resident in towns of 10,000 or less population declined only infinitesimally (from 22.93 to 20.23 percent). I am inclined to believe, on the basis of almost cursory spot checks, that the use of Census Bureau urban population figures unduly inflates the North's urban population percentages in the antebellum era.

9. If the percentage of total population growth (%tpg) is greater than the percentage of urban population growth (%upg), then the former must be divided by the latter and the result stated as a negative number. Hence, a CURI factor of −2.0 would indicate that the total population has increased twice as rapidly as the urban population. This index is not designed to deal with absolute decreases. There is, of course, nothing particularly innovative in the use of such a statement as, "The urban population increased X times more rapidly than the population as a whole." I am simply suggesting that this figure be recognized as an index number having very considerable value in comparative studies of urbanization in different locations and at different times.

10. U. S. Bureau of the Census, *Urban Population,* 6-11.

11. A word must be said about documentation practices for the remainder of this paper. Space considerations make it utterly impossible to document this section as fully as I would wish, for a single generalization might require a dozen or more source citations. I have concluded, therefore, to make no effort to include citations documenting generalizations or references to comparable conditions in northern cities. Documentation will be confined to quite specific statements about individual southern cities. In a few instances some illustrative examples will be cited. I regret the necessity of this procedure but perceive no practical alternative. The observations in the text are based on a study of the fifteen major cities previously mentioned. See William W. Howe, *Municipal History of New Orleans* (John Hopkins University, *Studies in Historical and Political Science,* VII, No. 4, Baltimore, 1889), 14; Walter F. Dodd, *The Government of the District of Columbia: A Study in Federal and Municipal Administration* (Washington, 1909), 36-38; Clayton C. Hall, ed., *Baltimore: Its History and Its People* (3 vols., New York and Chicago, 1912), I, 64n; Attia M. Bowmer, "The History of the Government of the City of Louisville, 1780-1870" (unpublished M.A. thesis, University of Louisville, 1948), 35-36.

12. Charleston, *Year Book—1880* (Charleston, 1880), 112-13; Samuel Y. At Lee, *History of*

the Public Schools of Washington City, D. C., from August, 1805, to August, 1875 (Washington, [1876]), 9; Henry Rightor, ed., *Standard History of New Orleans, Louisiana* (Chicago, 1900), 233, 237; Hall, ed., *Baltimore*, I, 559; Gabriel Collins, *The Louisville Directory, for the Year 1836* (Louisville, 1836), 94; J. Thomas Scharf, *History of Saint Louis City and County, from the Earliest Periods to the Present Day* (2 vols., Philadelphia, 1883), I, 836; Baltimore, *The Ordinances of the Mayor and City Council of Baltimore . . . 1851* (Baltimore, 1851), Appendix, Table K, following 232; Helen Borgman, "The History of the Louisville Public Elementary Schools, 1829-1860" (unpublished M.A. thesis, University of Louisville, 1942), 58.

13. Albert A. [E.] Fossier, *New Orleans: The Glamour Period, 1800-1840* (New Orleans, 1957), 164; Charleston City Council, *A Report Containing a Review of the Proceedings of the City Authorities from First September, 1838, to First August, 1839* (Charleston, 1839), 45.

14. Wilhelmus B. Bryan, *A History of the National Capital . . .* (2 vols., New York, 1914-1916), II, 295-98; Baltimore City Council, *Ordinances and Resolutions of the Corporation of the City of Baltimore . . . 1818* (Baltimore, 1877), 25; N. Peabody Poor, comp., *Haldeman's Picture of Louisville, Directory and Business Advertiser, for 1844-1845* (Louisville, 1844), 97; New Orleans City Council, *A Digest of the Ordinances, Resolutions, By-Laws, and Regulations of the Corporation of New Orleans . . .* (New Orleans, 1836), 87; Scharf, *History of Saint Louis,* II, 1438; Charleston City Council, *Ordinances of the City of Charleston, from the 19th of August 1844, to the 14th of September 1854 . . .* (Charleston, 1854), 76.

15. Bryan, *History of the National Capital,* I, 507-509; A. C. Bell, "History and Selection of Street Paving in the City of New Orleans," Association of Engineering Societies, *Journal,* XXII (February 1899), 47-48; Charleston City Council, *Report, 1838-1839,* pp. 30-31; James S. Buckingham, *The Slave States of America* (2 vols., London, [1842]), I, 47.

16. *A Series of Letters and Other Documents Relating to the Late Epidemic or [of] Yellow Fever . . .* (Baltimore, 1820), 66.

17. Washington City Council, *Laws Passed by the Eighth Council of the City of Washington . . . [1810]* (n.p., n.d.), 1; Wilson Primm, ed., *The Revised Ordinances of the City of Saint Louis . . .* (St. Louis, 1836), 94.

18. Bryan, *History of the National Capital,* II, 305-307; Wiliam Elliot, *The Washington Guide* (Washington, 1837), 53, 111-12; Robert Mills, *Water-Works for the Metropolitan City of Washington* (Washington, 1853), 29-31; Charleston, *Year Book—1881* (Charleston, 1881), 264-66; Richard Deering, *Louisville: Her Commercial, Manufacturing and Social Advantages* (Louisville, 1859), 36-37; J. Thomas Scharf, *History of Baltimore City and County, from the Earliest Period to the Present Day* (Philadelphia, 1881), 216; Benjamin H. B. Latrobe, *Impressions Respecting New Orleans: Diary & Sketches, 1818-1820,* edited by Samuel Wilson, Jr. (New York, 1951), xxii-xxiii; Jacob N. Taylor and M. O. Crooks, *Sketch Book of Saint Louis* (St. Louis, 1858), 70-71; James Wynne, "Sanitary Report of Baltimore," American Medical Association, *Transactions,* II (1849), 562; Albert J. Pickett, *Eight Days in New Orleans in February, 1847* ([Montgomery, Ala., 1847]), 26.

19. John Melish, *Travels Through the United States of America, in the Years 1806 & 1807, and 1809, 1810 & 1811* (London, 1818), 199; Robert Mills, *Statistics of South Carolina* (Charleston, 1826), 431; William T. Howard, Jr., *Public Health Administration and the Natural History of Disease in Baltimore, Maryland, 1797-1920* (Washington, 1924), 19; Jacob G. Davies, "Mayor's Communication," Baltimore City Council, *The Ordinances of the Mayor and City Council of Baltimore . . . 1845* (Baltimore, 1845), Appendix, 8; Hall, ed., *Baltimore,* I, 659; *The Louisville Directory for the Year 1832* (Louisville, 1832), 32, 144; Bryan, *History of the National Capital,* I, 541-42; Marie G. Windell, "The Background of Reform on the Missouri Frontier," *Missouri Historical Review,* XXXIX (January 1945), 168.

20. Scharf, *History of Saint Louis,* II, 1235-36; Washington City Council, *Acts of the Corporation of the City of Washington . . . [1815]* (Washington, 1815), 27; Charleston City Council, *A Digest of the Ordinances of the City Council of Charleston, from the Year 1783 to Oct. 1844 . . .* (Charleston, 1844), 28-31.

21. In 1857 New Orleans' banking capital was greater than that of Philadelphia, and Charleston's was only slightly less. See Eugene T. Wells, "St. Louis and Cities West, 1820-1880: A Study in History and Geography" (unpublished Ph.D. dissertation, University of Kansas, 1951), 106.

22. De Bow, *Statistical View of the United States, passim.*

23. Buckingham, *The Slave States,* I, 331-35; Elihu H. Shepard, *The Early History of St. Louis and Missouri, from Its First Exploration by White Men in 1673 to 1843* (St. Louis, 1870), 155; Edward T. Coke, *A Subaltern's Furlough: Descriptive of Scenes in Various Parts of the United States . . . During the Summer and Autumn of 1832* (2 vols., New York, 1833), I, 71; Josiah S. Johnston, ed., *Memorial History of Louisville from Its First Settlement to the Year 1896* (2 vols., Chicago and New York, [1896]), I, 88.

24. Johnston, ed., *Memorial History of Louisville,* I, 92; Logan U. Reavis, *Saint Louis: The Future Great City of the World* (St. Louis, 1875), 56; Thomas O'Connor, ed., *History of the Fire Department of New Orleans, from the Earliest Days to the Present Time* (New Orleans, 1895), 69-70, 75.

25. U. S. Bureau of the Census, *Urban Population,* 6-11. The figures are as follows:

	1850	1900	1930
U.S.	15.3%	39.7%	56.2%
District of Columbia	93.6%	100.0%	100.0%
Maryland	32.6%	49.8%	59.8%
Louisiana	26.0%	—	—
Delaware	15.3%	46.4%	—

26. *Ibid.* It will be recalled that these figures simply mean that during the 1870-1920 period the urban population of the South increased 2.89 times as rapidly as the total population of the region, and in the rest of the country the urban population increased 2.43 times as rapidly as the total population. The figures are as follows:

		South	Other
	1850-1900:		
%upg	%upg	572.93	805.15
	%tpg	185.90	257.54
	CURI	3.08	3.13
	1870-1920		
	%upg	465.26	442.60
	%tpg	160.76	181.81
	CURI	2.89	2.43

Part Two: THE ECONOMY

PETER TEMIN

THE JACKSONIAN ECONOMY

Peter Temin's essay is a provocative but relatively accessible example of what has been called the "new economic history." In contrast to earlier economic histories, which relied largely on random or scattered if sometimes abundant evidence in reaching their conclusions, the new approach emphasizes the necessity of gathering either total or statistically representative *evidence. While the following selection includes the introduction and the conclusion, rather than the heart of Temin's study, it manages to convey some of the main features of his argument. Clearly its author does not suffer from excessive self-doubt about the superiority of his conclusions to those of the scholars whose work he controverts. Arguing that Andrew Jackson's war on the second Bank of the United States has been misinterpreted by almost all previous scholars, Temin also offers a new explanation of the Panics of 1837 1839 and the Depression— or what he calls the deflation— that followed, as well as a challenge to the traditional version of the manifestations or consequences of the Depression. While Temin's arguments are not as convincing, nor his conclusions as definitive, as he seems to think they are, the boldness and the force with which they are presented makes Temin's study an interesting point of departure for all future discussion of the issues it considers.*

The Historiography of the Jacksonian period presents at least one curiosity to the modern observer. The period is noted both for great political changes and dramatic economic fluctuations. Yet while controversy continues to rage about the former, there appears to be an accepted interpretation of the latter that is agreed upon by all major authorities.

According to this interpretation, the economic fluctuations of the 1830's and early 1840's were the direct result of Andrew Jackson's political actions. By vetoing the recharter of the Second Bank of the United States in 1832 and removing the public deposits from the Bank in 1833, Jackson initiated an unsound credit expansion and inflation characterized by unprecedented speculation in public lands. The excesses of this boom would have produced a crisis in any case, but Jackson precipitated the Panic of 1837 by his policies toward the public land sales which had intensified the expansion and produced a surplus in the hands of the Federal Government. Jackson's Specie Circular of 1836 was designed to curb the sales, and the distribution of the surplus in 1837 was an attempt to dispose of the revenue already collected from them. Together they produced the Panic of 1837. After the panic the boom collapsed, and the economy slipped into one of the worst depressions it has known.

This story is clear, logical, and unambiguous. It shows unequivocally how Jackson's political program led the economy step by step to disaster. For those who do not admire Jackson, it has provided ample reason for rejecting his policies. For those who support Jackson, it has represented the dire consequences of good intentions thwarted by the speculative propensities of the American people. In either case, the conviction that Jackson's policies were highly destructive of economic stability is a major starting point for the evaluation of Jacksonian democracy.

Thus Arthur M. Schlesinger, Jr., said, "Above all, the Bank War triumphantly established Jackson in the confidence of the people," but admitted that, "In destroying the Bank, Jackson had removed a valuable brake on credit expansion; and in sponsoring the system of deposit in state banks, he had accelerated the tendencies toward inflation." Richard Hofstadter agreed: "In killing the bank he [Jackson] had strangled a potential threat to democratic government, but at an unnecessarily high cost." Marvin Meyers also concurred: "[T]he bank-boom-bust sequence was the primal experience of Jacksonian life, which fixed the content, tone, and terms of politics for as long as Jacksonianism counted in America." And Bray Hammond asserted, "Although the Bank was by no means the only thing that occupied the Jacksonians, its destruction was apparently esteemed by many of them their finest accomplishment," even though, "over-trading, inflation, and speculation, . . . which Andrew Jackson aimlessly deplored, could not have been more effectively promoted by Jacksonian policies had that been their purpose."[1]

Despite its universal acceptance, this story will not stand close scrutiny; it is negated by the extant data of the 1830's. Jackson's economic policies were not the most enlightened the country has ever seen, but they were by no means disastrous. The inflation and crises of the 1830's had their origin in events largely beyond Jackson's control and probably would have taken place whether or not he had acted as he did. The economy was not the victim of Jacksonian politics; Jackson's policies were the victims of economic fluctuations.

The demonstration of this fact is straightforward. As Albert Gallatin noted at the time: "[T]he charges against the President for having interfered in the currency resolve themselves into the single fact of having prevented the renewal of the charter of the Bank of the United States."[2] As a result, so the story goes, banks expanded their notes and deposits without a corresponding increase in their specie reserves, that is, without just cause. Yet the actual sequence was that bank *reserves* increased rapidly in the 1830's and that banks did not increase the volume of their obligations faster than they received new reserves.[3]

This finding shatters the traditional interpretaton of the 1830's. And as is usual with such findings, it raises more questions than it answers. If Jackson's destruction of the Second Bank did not cause the inflation, what did? And even if Jackson's actions in 1832 and 1833 did not start the boom, did his actions in 1836 stop it? How important was the Bank of the United States, and the political storm it aroused, to the eocnomy? Has Jackson been blamed for economic fluctuations that he did not cause? The following pages will attempt to answer these questions, but a closer look at the traditional story will expose the questions that need answering more precisely.

The Traditional History of the Jacksonian Boom

The traditional story appears in one version or another in almost all the standard secondary works on the Jacksonian period. Some versions are more complete than others, and none is definitive, but they are clearly all variations on a single theme. Before presenting a new version of the Jacksonian boom, it is useful to review the traditional account and the methods by which it was derived.

To show the emotional content of this history and the agreement among the sources, a canonical account has been compiled from the standard secondary sources. Despite occasional differences of emphasis, the concentration of all authors on the role of Jackson and the excessive nature of the banking expansion will be evident. Here, then, is the traditional history of the boom in the words of Hammond, Hofstadter, Meyers, Schlesinger, *et al.*

The story opens with the famous "Bank War" between Andrew Jackson, President of the United States, and Nicholas Biddle, president of the Second Bank of the United States. The most dramatic act of the "war," which ended in the "destruction" of the Second Bank, was Jackson's veto of the bill to recharter the Bank in 1832. "The message accompanying the veto is a famous state paper. It is legalistic, demagogic, and full of sham. Its economic reasoning was said by Professor Catterall, over 50 years ago, to be beneath contempt. Its level is now no higher."[4]

"Pursuing the bank war to its conclusion, Jackson found defeat in victory. Re-elected overwhelmingly on the bank issue in 1832, he soon removed all United States funds from the bank. . . . The federal deposits that Jackson had taken from Biddle were made available to several dozen state banks; these promptly used their new resources to start a credit boom."[5] "The proportion of paper to specie lengthened, gambling in banks, internal improvements and public lands grew more frenzied, and the economic structure became increasingly speculative and unsound."[6]

"[E]verybody who could borrow money bought public land to sell again at the market value, or to hold for a further rise. In this way the deposits were borrowed, paid to the land receiver for land, to be by him deposited in the banks; then the operation was repeated again and again, the growing surplus consisting of bank credits mainly."[7] "Each bank could count the notes of other banks as reserves and expand its notes accordingly; with the general result that the more the banks lent the more they mutually augmented their reserves and the more they were able to lend. No legal requirements governed bank reserves before 1837 . . . and there was now no federal bank maintaining systematic pressure on the banks to redeem their notes."[8]

"It appears inevitable that the gaudy mid-thirties dream of sudden fortune should have collapsed. The credit inflation flowed from a highly vulnerable banking system lacking resources and techniques to sustain its commitments. The land bubble was balanced precariously upon a shaky credit structure, and had to fail as soon as a hard reckoning of values was enforced. The bond issues of the states created large immediate obligations against doubtful, sometimes hopeless, revenue prospects; a process of liquidation could not long be avoided. Briefly, the very excesses of the boom, inherently unstable, defined the necessity for a crisis as soon as faith faltered and bets were called."[9]

"Into this unstable situation, the federal government introduced several measures which aggravated the instability. First, Collectors of the Public Revenue were ordered not to receive small bank notes. Second, it was stipulated that on and after August 15, 1836 [,] public lands must be paid for with gold and silver. . . . This policy had the effect of attracting specie away from banks in the centers of commerce into outlying areas, such as Michigan, where land sales were large. Third, Congress authorized that the surplus in the Treasury above $5,000,000 be distributed to the states in proportion to their population. The distribution was to be made in quarterly installments beginning January 1, 1837."[10]

"Each quarterly installment, in consequence, was to be $9,367,215. Some of this money was in banks situated in the states to which it was to be distributed. Much was not. Some banks had enough cash and collectible loans to enable them to make their payments. Many had not. Over the country as a whole, the banks that had received the surplus were not in general the banks that held the gold and silver in which the surplus was to be distributed, and the funds in the individual states did not match the amounts to be distributed to those states. The requirements of the specie circular [that is, the second measure mentioned in the previous paragraph], aggravated by the distribution, produced absurd disorder."[11]

The federal charter of the Bank of the United States had expired in 1836, but the Bank had not ceased its operations. It had acquired a new charter from the state of Pennsylvania and was active in subsequent events. In fact, it was so active that most accounts of these years are concentrated on the Bank's actions. The Bank suspended specie payments in 1837, resumed them in 1838, suspended them again in 1839, and failed in 1841. Many banks followed suit, and the economy is reported to have had a crisis in 1837, renewed its prosperity in 1838, experienced a new crisis in 1839, and plunged into a severe depression in the early 1840's.[12]

The failure of the Bank of the United States has been analyzed in detail, but the reasons why the economy should have been depressed are less clear. "Many factors contributed to the gravity of the slump. Most important undoubtedly was the violence and speculative nature of the boom that had preceded it. Public land sales had reached in 1836 a level which was never again to be equalled. The renewed suspension of the B. U. S. in 1839, following as it did on the widespread bank failures of 1837, caused a profound public mistrust of banks and bank credit generally. The failure on the part of nine of the states to pay the interest due on their debts destroyed American credit in Europe and made it out of the question for any more loans to be obtained in that way. And the state of the cotton market in Britain after 1840 could scarcely have been less hopeful."[13]

This is the traditional story. It is presented with remarkably little variation in any number of places.[14] The precise cause of the crisis of 1837 is the only subject still in dispute, although the actions of President Jackson figure strongly in most explanations. Historians who say that the boom made a crisis inevitable place the responsibility for the crisis on Jackson's actions initiating the boom. Those who say that the Specie Circular, the distribution of the surplus, or both caused the crisis, also blame Jackson. But a few, who say that the Bank of England produced the crisis, dissent from this view.[15]

A New Approach

This account is in error at three main points. First, the boom did not have its origins in the Bank War. It resulted from a combination of large capital imports from England and a change in the Chinese desire for silver which together produced a rapid increase in the quantity of silver in the United States. Banks did not expand their operations because they were treating the government deposits as reserves, to finance speculation, or because the Bank of the United States was no longer restraining them; they expanded because their true—that is, specie—reserves had risen.[16] Second, the Panic of 1837 was not caused by President Jackson's actions. The "destruction" of the Bank of the United States did not produce the crisis because it did not produce the boom. The Specie Circular and the distribution of the surplus also did not have the effects attributed to them. And third, the depression of the early 1840's was neither as serious as historians assume nor the fault of Nicholas Biddle. It was primarily a deflation, as opposed to a decline in production, and it was produced by events over which Biddle had little control.

These errors have arisen because of the nature of the sources used to compile the traditional account. The most important source, as is usual in historical investigations, has been the opinion of informed contemporaries. There is no doubt that we must rely on the opinions of informed witnesses for an understanding of some aspects of the 1830's, but there is good reason to doubt that we can discover the whole story from their words. Most of these observers were also participants, and their objectivity may be questioned. Nicholas Biddle could not possibly have given a balanced account of Jackson's involvement with the Panic of 1837. Other contemporary observers held ideas about the operation of the economy that we can no longer accept today. Albert Gallatin, for example, former Secretary of the Treasury and dean of the New York banking community, could assert with great finality: "It has always been the opinion of the writer of this essay that a public debt was always an evil to be avoided whenever practicable; hardly ever justifiable except in time of war."[17] And even if the difficulties of personal subjectivity did not exist, the opinions of illustrious contemporaries would still not be a good source. They simply were not sufficiently consistent to provide the raw material for a unified account.

The two opinions most often quoted are those of Nicholas Biddle expressed in an open letter to John Quincy Adams, November 11, 1836, and the 1841 essay of Albert Gallatin from which an opinion was just quoted. Biddle supported one line of argument found in the traditional account by saying: "In my judgment, the main cause of it [the current crisis] is the mismanagement of the revenue—mismanagement in two respects: the mode of executing the distribution law, and the order requiring specie for the public lands." And Gallatin supported a different part of the story by announcing: "Overtrading has been the primary cause of the present crisis in America."[18]

Unfortunately, Biddle did not think much of the opinion expressed by Gallatin, and Gallatin did not agree with Biddle. Biddle noted in his letter that "it is said that the country has overtraded—that the banks have over-issued, and that the purchasers of public lands have been very extravagant. I am not struck by the truth or propriety of these complaints. The phrase of overtrading is very convenient but not very intelligible. If it means anything, it means that our dealings with other countries have brought us in debt to those countries. In that case the exchange turns against our country, and is rectified by an exportation of specie or stocks in the first instance—and then by reducing [the ratio of] the imports to the exports. Now the fact is, that at this moment [November, 1836], the exchanges are all in favor of this country—that is, you can buy a bill of exchange on a foreign country cheaper than you can send specie to that country."[19]

And as we have already noted, Gallatin said, "[T]he charges against the President for having interfered in the currency resolve themselves into the single fact of having prevented the renewal of the charter of the Bank of the United States." He went on to say, "The direct and immediate effects cannot be correctly ascertained; but they have been greatly exaggerated by party spirit. That he found the currency in a sound and left it in a deplorable state is true; but he cannot certainly be made responsible for the aberrations and misdeeds of the bank [of the United States] under either of its charters. The unforeseen, unexampled accumulation of the public revenue was one of the principal proximate causes of the disasters that ensued. It cannot be ascribed either to the President or to any branch of the government, and its effects might have been the same whether the public deposits were in the State banks, or had been left in the national bank, organized and governed as that was."[20]

These divergent views by well-qualified contemporary observers cannot be reconciled by appeals to opinion alone. Reference must be made to the actual events taking place. Such observations comprise the other main source of data for the traditional account, but they have not been used in any systematic fashion. Each author has chosen a few facts about the monetary system or the banking structure to present, but almost no one has tried to put these data into a systematic framework or tried to make explicit the implications of the cited observations.[21] As Brinley Thomas once said in a different context, the empirical data have been used "as a drunk uses lampposts: more for support than for illumination."

This can be seen clearly in the treatment of the core of the traditional story of the boom: the nature of the "credit expansion." It is stated that banks used government deposits and notes of other banks as reserves, and that they expanded their activities without references to their true reserves, that is, specie. As Schlesinger phrased it in the passage just cited: "The proportion of paper [that is, bank obligations] to specie lengthened." Phrased another way, the reserve ratio of banks—the inverse of the ratio of obligations to specie—declined. But not one of the historians repeating this story cites any evidence on the reserve ratio of the banking system. One occasionally sees references to the behavior of individual banks and states, but never is there documentation of how the system as a whole behaved.

This gap in our knowledge of the 1830's has been extremely costly. The behavior of individual banks does not necessarily parallel the behavior of the banking system as a whole, and the experience of any single state is not always a good index of the progress of the Union. The story of the 1830's constructed from accounts of individual banks and states is seriously in error, and it can be corrected only by the use of data about the economy as a whole. Incorporated systematically into a coherent theoretical framework, the aggregate data on the 1830's enable us to discriminate between alternate hypotheses and schemes of causation. As a result, we can say both that the traditional account is invalid and that the alternate account to be presented here is supported at many points by the available data.

* * *

We opened this inquiry with a summary of the traditional story of the Jacksonian boom and its aftermath; we close with a summary of the replacement offered here and some comments about its implications.

To start, the political importance of Jackson's "destruction" of the Second Bank of the United States far outweiɡned the economic. The unsupported bank expansion that the Bank War has been thought to have initiated simply did not take place. Banks did not expand credit without cause, and they do not seem to have regarded government deposits as additions to reserves. They kept more or less constant reserve ratios throughout the boom—excepting 1834, of course—and the supply of money expanded for reasons unconnected with the Bank War.

Unfortunately for Jackson's reputation, the Bank War coincided with two developments, one in England and one in China, that together produced inflation. A series of unusually good harvests in England initiated a boom in that country about 1832, and British eagerness to invest in the United States and to buy American cotton rose and stayed high for several years. For the British to export capital to the United States, the United States had to buy more in Britain than it sold—that is, to run a trade deficit. And in order for the American demand for British goods to rise, prices in the United States had to rise to make imported goods cheaper, and therefore preferable, to domestically produced ones.[22] The British demand for cotton caused prices in America to rise higher than they otherwise would have done; American exports were increasing at the same time as American imports, and a trade deficit was harder to produce.

For prices in America to rise, the supply of money in America had to rise. Since banks were not willing to expand without increased reserves, new reserves—that is, specie—were needed to let the quantity of money rise. This specie could not have come from Britain because the Bank of England was not willing to let its reserves slip across the Atlantic. The Old Lady of Threadneedle Street showed as much by her actions in 1836 and 1837; she would have acted sooner if need had arisen. Consequently, the English boom by itself could not have caused the American inflation.

Coincidentally, however, changes were taking place in the Far East that had important ramifications for this process. The Chinese were buying opium in increasing quantities, and they no longer desired silver to hoard. They wanted silver to exchange for opium, and any silver the United States sent to them would have been sent to England in payment for Indian opium. This transshipment was avoided by substituting American credit for Mexican silver, and the United States retained the silver imports from Mexico that it had sent to the Orient in earlier years. This silver went into bank reserves in America, allowing prices to rise and the demand for imports to increase. It may be said that the Chinese enabled the British to export capital to the United States by releasing silver to be used as a base for American monetary expansion, or that the capital flow from Britain to the United States allowed the Americans to keep their silver instead of sending it to the East.

The high British demand for cotton acted to increase the inflation by reducing the American trade deficit, but it also acted to retard the inflation by setting off a land boom. As the price of cotton soared upward, speculative fever kept pace. Land sales of the Federal Government rose dramatically in 1835 and 1836, and part of the increase in the money supply went into land purchases. The Federal Government accumulated a surplus, and these funds were removed from circulation. It was thought at the time that these funds were used as the basis for further monetary expansion, but we have shown that this did not happen. The government continued to sell land at a constant price, and funds that otherwise would have been used to raise prices rested in the government's surplus. We have no way of knowing whether the net effect of the cotton price's two offsetting influences was positive or negative.

The inflation had to end, and even be replaced by deflation, if the British stopped exporting capital to the United States. The Bank of England thought it was losing specie to the United States in late 1836 and acted to restrain the capital flow. This produced a commercial crisis in the United States, but the breaking point did not come until the price of cotton fell in early 1837. As this important price fell, the credit structure built with cotton as security collapsed. Banks in the United States refused to preserve the convertibility of their notes and deposits into specie and thus into foreign exchange at a fixed rate; the United States effectively devalued for a short time.

Andrew Jackson has been blamed for the Panic of 1837, but it is clear that he was not the villain. The accumulating surplus had created a political problem, and the distribution of the surplus to the states offered a solution. The distribution would have created some hardship for the banking system, but it was not qualitatively different from previous governmental transactions, and it would not have produced a crisis. The Specie Circular, issued to offset the inflationary effects of the distribution, similarly was not a cause of the panic. The boom had been caused by a tenuous balance of independent forces; when this balance was lost, one or the other of the forces was bound to cause trouble. As it turned out, a diminution in the capital flow from England to America was the force that led to the crisis.

The effects of the panic were mild, however, and the economy soon recovered from them. The British continued to lend to the United States once the Bank of England had accumulated a satisfactory volume of reserves, the price of cotton revived in early 1839 due to a short harvest and to the effects of Nicholas Biddle's speculations, and the funds distributed to the states were spent by them on a variety of projects. The first and second of these developments restored the financial system to its pre-panic health and allowed American banks to resume specie payments. The restored financial system cooperated with the demand from the states to produce renewed prosperity in 1839.

This prosperity did not last long. A bad wheat harvest in England in 1838 caused the British to export specie in return for imports of wheat in 1839, and the Bank of England tightened credit once again to replenish its reserves. A bumper crop of cotton in 1839 caused the price of cotton to fall in early 1840, and many banks followed the precedent of 1837 by suspending payments. The panic was not as severe in 1839 as it had been in 1837, but it marked the end of the boom.

States ceased their expenditures and defaulted on their bonds. The British replied by ceasing to export capital to the United States. Simultaneously, banks increased their reserve ratios, and people raised the proportion of their funds they wanted to hold in coin. The cessation of British lending meant the end of the opportunity for the United States to finance a trade deficit. The rise in the two monetary ratios lowered the supply of money, reducing the demand for both American and imported goods. The falling demand for imports ended the trade deficit. The effects of the panic thus produced deflation in two ways: Through its effect on the balance of trade and by its effect on the supply of money. As with the inflation, it is not possible to say that the international capital movements or the change in the quantity of money alone produced the deflation; they acted together, and their results are inseparable.

The deflation was as dramatic as the preceding inflation, and its effect on national income appears to have been as small. Many businesses failed, but the resultant change in ownership did not interrupt production. Agricultural production was unaffected by the deflation, and the growing industrial sector of the economy continued to expand. Only the part of the economy servicing trade and commerce suffered, and the overall effects of the decline in trade were small. There is no evidence of widespread unemployment or of distress not produced by the price fall alone during the early 1840's.

Inflation, crisis, deflation: This was the story of the Jacksonian era. The sequence has been known for a long time, but the roles played by historical personnages have been confused. Contemporary observers blamed Andrew Jackson, and historians have agreed. Yet analysis shows that Jackson was not the prime mover in the inflation, the crises, or the deflation. His policies did not help the economy to adjust to the harsh requirements of external forces, but they were of little importance beside these far stronger influences.

Andrew Jackson, then, did not pay a high cost for his destruction of the Second Bank. He did not initiate a speculative mania, and he did not plunge the economy into crisis and depression. To the extent that these events have been blamed on his actions, he has been victimized by external events. It would not be appropriate here to defend Jackson's policies, but it must be insisted that they were not tested by the events of the 1830's. We cannot say what would have happened had Jackson not entered into his "war" with Biddle, but it is doubtful that the banking system would have reacted any differently to the shocks it received had the Bank of the United States continued as the government's fiscal agent.

The economy was not as unstable as historians have assumed; there do not appear to have been forces within the banking system leading inevitably toward a crisis unless restrained by superior force. The banking system did not have the ability to adapt to external shocks, but it did not produce sharp inflations like the one culminating in 1837 without external help. The antebellum economy was vulnerable to disturbing influences, but it was not a source of them. The distinction is important.

Finally, the economy possessed a structure of some analytic interest. It functioned to a large extent in the fashion described by what we now call classical economic theory. Prices were flexible, they could vary to facilitate capital transfers, and they could change radically without destroying the ability of the economy to operate near capacity. Yet the price-specie-flow mechanism did not operate according to the textbook rules; without a supply of silver from "outside the system," the mechanism would not have worked. And the price level, while variable, was not "neutral." It mattered what the price level was, or at least what the price of cotton was, because a large part of the antebellum financial system used cotton for security. When its price fell, the system broke down, and a decline in prices was considerably more difficult to effect than a rise.

As Gallatin said, Jackson "found the currency of the country in a sound and left it in a deplorable state," but most of the change was not of Jackson's doing. In destroying the Second Bank of the United States, he had closed off an area of possible future experimentation, but he had not precitated a "bank-boom-bust sequence." The economic fluctuations of the Jacksonian era may still be deplored, but they cannot any longer be used as an argument against Jacksonianism.

Notes

1. Arthur M. Schlesinger, Jr., *The Age of Jackson* (Boston: Little, Brown, 1945), pp. 115, 218; Richard Hofstadter, *The American Political Tradition* (New York: Knopf, 1948), p. 63 (page reference from the Vintage edition); Marvin Meyers, *The Jacksonian Persuasion* (Stanford: Stanford University Press, 1960), p. 103; Bray Hammond, *Banks and Politics in America, from the Revolution to the Civil War* (Princeton: Princeton University Press, 1957), pp. 361, 453.

2. Albert Gallatin, *Suggestions on the Banks and Currency of the Several States, in Reference Principally to the Suspension of Specie Payments* (New York, 1841), p. 31.

3. The data are presented in Table 3. Bank notes and deposits were current obligations of banks. In other words, banks promised to pay gold or silver coins on demand for their notes and for checks drawn against their deposits. Gold and silver coins were referred to collectively as "specie," and banks had to keep reserves of specie in order to be able to pay it for their notes or for checks drawn on their deposits.

4. Hammond, p. 405. The reference is to Ralph C. H. Catterall, *The Second Bank of the United States* (Chicago: University of Chicago Press, 1902), p. 239.

5. Hofstadter, p. 63.

6. Schlesinger, p. 217.

7. Edward G. Bourne, *History of the Surplus Revenue of 1837* (New York, 1885), pp. 14-15.

8. Hammond, pp. 452-53.

9. Meyers, p. 114.

10. Walter Buckingham Smith, *Economic Aspects of the Second Bank of the United States* (Cambridge: Harvard University Press, 1953), p. 185.

11. Hammond, p. 456.

12. Smith, Chap. 11; Hammond, pp. 467-90, 502-18; Douglass C. North, in *Growth and Welfare in the American Past* (Englewood Cliffs: Prentice-Hall, 1966), p. 32, said: "Probably the depression of 1839 [to 1843] was the most severe of the century."

13. R. C. O. Matthews, *A Study in Trade-Cycle History: Economic Fluctuations in Great Britain, 1833-1842* (Cambridge, England: Cambridge University Press, 1954), p. 68.

14. This account, or references to it, appears in the following political and biographical studies: Carl Brent Swisher, *Roger B. Taney* (New York: Macmillan, 1935), pp. 331-33; Charles M. Wiltse, *John C. Calhoun, Nullifier, 1829-39* (Indianapolis: Bobbs-Merrill, 1949), pp. 287-88, 345-46; William Nisbet Chambers, *Old Bullion Benton, Senator from the New West* (Boston: Little, Brown, 1956), p. 222; Thomas Payne Govan, *Nicholas Biddle: Nationalist and Public Banker, 1786-1844* (Chicago: University of Chicago Press, 1959), pp. 301-02; Glyndon G. Van Deusen, *The Jacksonian Era: 1828-1848* (New York: Harper & Row, 1959), pp. 105-06; Walter Hugins, *Jacksonian Democracy and the Working Class* (Stanford: Stanford University Press, 1960), pp. 45, 178-79.

It also appears in the following economic studies: William Graham Sumner, *A History of Banking in the United States* (New York, 1896), pp. 230-32; Reginald Charles McGrane, *The Panic of 1837* (Chicago: University of Chicago Press, 1924), pp. 91-94; Oscar and Mary Flug Handlin, *Commonwealth; A Study of the Role of Government in the American Economy: Massachusetts, 1774-1861* (New York: New York University Press, 1947), p. 179; George Rogers Taylor, *The Transportation Revolution* (New York: Holt, Rinehart and Winston, 1951), pp. 340-42.

Additional economic history texts using this story are cited in J. R. T. Hughes and Nathan Rosenberg, "The United States Business Cycle Before 1860: Some Problems of Interpretation," *Economic History Review,* Second Series, XV (1963), 476-93.

It has found its way into standard texts, such as: Samuel Eliot Morison and Henry Steele Commager, *The Growth of the American Republic,* Fifth Edition (New York: Oxford University Press, 1962), I, 484-87; T. H. Williams, R. N. Current, and F. Freidel, *A History of the United States* (New York: Knopf, 1959), I, 385-88; Frank Thistlethwaithe, *The Great Experiment* (Cambridge, England: Cambridge University Press, 1955), p. 143.

Some authors writing about this period, however, do not even mention the boom or the causes of the Panic of 1837. See, for example, Carl Russell Fish, *The Rise of the Common Man, 1830-1850,* Vol. VI of Arthur M. Schlesinger and Dixon Ryan Fix (eds.), *A History of American Life* (New York: Macmillan, 1927); Lee Benson, *The Concept of Jacksonian Democracy* (Princeton: Princeton University Press, 1961); and Richard P. McCormick, *The Second American Party System: Party Formulation in the Jacksonian Era* (Chapel Hill: University of North Carolina Press, 1966).

15. Ralph W. Hidy, *The House of Baring in American Trade and Finance* (Cambridge: Harvard University Press, 1949), p. 207. It is common for historians to note the actions of the Bank of England and even to assert their importance while at the same time continuing to blame Jackson for the crisis. See Hammond, p. 457, for example.

16. Macesich noted that the reserves of the banking system had risen rapidly during the boom. This observation is correct, but Macesich's attempts to formulate a new interpretaton of the boom were not entirely successful and have not been widely accepted. See George Macesich, "Sources of Monetary Disturbances in the U. S., 1834-1845," *Journal of Economic History*, XX (September, 1960), 407-34, and "International Trade and United States Economic Development Revisited," *Journal of Economic History*, XXI (September, 1961), pp. 384-85; Jeffrey G. Williamson, "International Trade and United States Economic Development: 1827-1843," *Journal of Economic History*, XXI (September, 1961), 372-83; Douglass C. North, *The Economic Growth of the United States, 1790-1860* (Englewood Cliffs: Prentice-Hall, 1961), pp. 198-202.

17. Gallatin, pp. 28-29.

18. Nicholas Biddle to J. Q. Adams, Nov. 11, 1836, reprinted in *Niles' Weekly Register*, LI (Baltimore, Dec. 17, 1836), 243-45; Gallatin, p. 26. See also the 1837 comments of Abbot Lawrence, in Hamilton A. Hill, *Memoir of Abbot Lawrence* (Cambridge, 1884), pp. 16-18. Hughes and Rosenberg document the use of the word "overtrading" and the prefix "over-" in the recent literature.

19. *Niles'*, LI, 243-45.

20. Gallatin, pp. 31-32.

21. Exceptions to this rule are provided by Macesich, 1960, and Jeffrey G. Williamson, *American Growth and the Balance of Payments, 1820-1913: A Study of the Long Swing* (Chapel Hill: University of North Carolina Press, 1964).

22. Demand for imports can also rise because national income rises, but the national income in the United States could not rise enough to produce the desired import surplus. There was substantially full employment at the start of the boom, and there were no technological changes that markedly increased the productivity of labor.

DAVID MONTGOMERY

THE SHUTTLE AND THE CROSS: WEAVERS AND ARTISANS IN THE KENSINGTON RIOTS OF 1844

*David Montgomery's essay is a good example of the
new labor history. While it is concerned with the
economic issues and the strikes that were the preoccupation of John R. Commons and the traditional
labor history, it is equally concerned with the religious,
moral, and cultural issues that have commanded the
attention of Edward Thompson in England and
historians like Herbert G. Gutman in this country.
Montgomery demonstrates convincingly that the life
of the working classes in Philadelphia—and probably
elsewhere—cannot be well understood unless ideological
and bread-and-butter themes are woven together into a
single yet complex context. Working men who might
unite on broad economic grounds would split apart on
such issues as religion, nationality, or ethnic background, education, and temperance. Coreligionists in
turn could be divided by skill or along craft lines.
Latent hostilities that remained muted during an inflationary era in which trade union idealism and
economic militance were in the ascendancy, rose to
the surface in the wake of the financial panics of the late
1830s and the bitter depression that ensued. The result
was the meteoric rise of the anti-Irish Catholic (and
anti-weavers) nativist political movement and the
violent rioting of 1844. Adding yet another dimension to
Montgomery's subtle analysis are the roles he assigns to
major party politics and to the urban patriciate during
the period of intense disorder.*

Copyright © 1972, by Peter N. Stearns. Reprinted from the *Journal of Social History*, vol.
V, pp. 411-446, by permission of the editor.

American workers in the nineteenth century engaged in economic conflicts with their employers as fierce as any known to the industrial world, yet in their political behavior they consistently failed to exhibit a class-consciousness. This paradox was evident as early as 1844, when nativist parties triumphed at the polls in Philadelphia, Boston and New York. At the close of a decade and a half of hotly-contested strikes and severe economic hardship, climaxed by the bitter depression of 1837-43, workingmen had divided their votes along ethnic lines. The greater part of them were swept up into an enthusiastic political movement whose negative reference group was not the capitalists, but Roman Catholics. Other workers found their enemy in evangelical Protestantism.

Analysis of the nativist movement and of the bloody riots it spawned in the Philadelphia area suggests that the political behavior of American workingmen in the 1840s was fashioned not so much by the economic impact of industrialization as by the workers' reactions to the political demands made by evangelical Protestantism: the moral content of education, liquor licensing and prohibition, Sabbath closing and the suppression of popular "lewd and tumultous" conduct. Such moral policing as evangelists demanded was in turn urgently needed by the new industrialists, to be sure, for it promised them a disciplined labor force, pacing its toil and its very life cycle to the requirements of the machine and the clock, respectful of property and orderly in its demeanor.[1] Because the responses of various groups of workers to these evangelical issues were determined by their religious outlooks, rather than their economic conditions, however, the working classes were fragmented on election day. Class interests were most clearly evident in trade union activity and in tensions *within* the political parties over questions like the legal ten hour day. Such issues, rising directly from the economic impact of industrialization, set working class against middle class. The pattern of cultural politics generated by the religious impact of industrialization, on the other hand, attached workers to the political leadership of the middle classes of their particular ethnic groups.

The counterpoint of class and ethnic conflict in working-class life was clearly visible in Kensington, a manufacturing suburb of Philadelphia, where crowds of Irishmen and native Americans battled each other for four days in May 1844. While the city proper contained some of the most advanced iron rolling mills, machine shops and locomotive works in the country, only 54 percent of its 16,600 working adults were listed in manufacturing and trades by the census of 1840. Commerce, navigation and the learned professions absorbed the rest. By way of contrast, in Kensington 89 percent of the labor force of slightly under 3,000 people was classified in manufacturing and trades.[2] Few really wealthy men lived there. The richest residents were master weavers, shoemakers, victuallers, gunsmiths and ship builders, whose holdings census takers in 1850 assessed mostly between $2,000 and $10,000. By the Delaware River waterfront one could find the old Pennsylvania

Wainwright family, lumber dealers and co-owners of two large piers. Jonathan Wainwright's real estate holdings valued at $20,000 in 1850 were remarkably large for Kensington, yet his wealth was surpassed by that of the acknowledged leader of the Catholic community, boss weaver Hugh Clark. Michael Keenan, another Catholic master weaver, whose houses were burned by rioters in 1844, estimated his real estate at $18,000 in 1850. Only the most prosperous of the Vandusens, a large clan of lumber merchants, ship builders and ship carpenters who helped lead the Protestant cause, approached this level of wealth.[3]

This was a community of working men and women, and among them that division of labor which Adam Smith termed the mainspring of economic growth was evident in profusion.[4] Interspersed with the larger occupational categories were solitary cloth measurers, artificial limb makers, tooth manufacturers, bird stuffers, lime burners and saw handle makers, not to mention two perfumers, a drum maker and a "comedean." More important, the major occupations encompassed superior craftsmen whose style of work had changed little since the eighteenth century (butchers, cabinet makers, ship carpenters), some factory operatives (in metals and glass works), swarms of outworkers (weaving, tailoring and shoemaking) and the inevitable impoverished laborers, carters, draymen and boatmen.

With the notable exception of the weavers, most of the workmen had been born in the United States. In fact, the manuscript census returns of 1850, the first to record age, occupation and birthplace for each individual, indicate that most were native Pennsylvanians. In contrast to the heavily immigrant weaving areas, concentrated in the second and fifth wards of 1844, the waterfront first, third and fourth wards with their vast tracts of lumberyards, furniture shops, shipbuilding facilities and fishermen's wharves were the special domain of the natives. Alongside only five Englishmen and four Irishmen who worked in shipyard trades could be found 433 Americans. Many of their neighbors on the Delaware's shore worked at one of the two paternalistically managed glass works, where more than 70 percent of the employees were native born.[5] Not only were 92 of the 103 fishermen Pennsylvanian by birth, but they shared among themselves only a handful of family names.

Shoemaking, one of Kensington's largest occupations in 1850, involved 343 natives, 128 Germans, 70 Irishmen, 19 Englishmen, 3 Frenchmen, 2 Scots and a Dutchman. In the newer metal trades of the same area—machinists, boiler makers, molders and rolling mill hands—more than half were Pennsylvanians, and 63 percent were Americans, though numerous Englishmen were to be found in their ranks. Among tailors, on the other hand, German immigrants were preponderant; and in the ranks of cabinet makers Germans almost equalled the natives in number. At the bottom of the occupational ladder, the laborers included 405 Irishmen, 99 Germans and 205 natives.[6]

Among the wage earners were many young recent arrivals in Kensington. The town's population almost doubled between 1840 and 1850, on top of an increase of 88 percent during the twenties and 66 percent in the thirties.[7] Many of the residents lived in boardinghouses, kept mostly by widows or by workingmen's wives. In the home of a New York-born bootmaker dwelt three young families (his own and those of two youthful locally born machinists) and no fewer than four other machinists, one pattern maker, two blacksmiths, two iron molders and a stray cigar maker. All the boarders were Americans in their twenties, except for a molder and a machinist from England.[8] An inn, not far from this menagerie of metallurists, bore a more cosmopolitan aspect. In addition to the owner's family, it housed an Irish hostler and his 18-year-old wife, an English bartender and his blacksmith compatriot, a painter, a ship carpenter, an accountant, a house carpenter and a cordwainer—all from Pennsylvania—a ship carpenter and a ship joiner from New York state, another ship carpenter from Vermont, and a house carpenter who had come up from Maryland.[9]

Kensington's main industry was weaving, both cotton cloth and, to a lesser extent, woolen. Its output, combined with that of other suburbs like Manayunk and Moyamensing, helped keep Philadelphia County the leading textile producing region of the country down to the Civil War. After the city of Philadelphia had absorbed these suburbs by the consolidation act of 1854, it boasted 260 separate cotton and woolen factories which was more, its champions claimed, than any other city in the world.[10] But most of its weaving was not carried on in these factories. Weaving was basically a cottage industry, based on the putting-out system and the use of handlooms. As early as 1827 the local Society of Weavers boasted, probably with some exaggeration, that 104 warping mills in the region supplied about 4,500 weavers. On the eve of the Civil War Edwin Freedley estimated that 6,000 handloom frames were in use in the county.[11]

Kensington alone had 2,238 weavers when the 1850 census was taken.[12] During the preceding decade some rooms used for cloth weaving and more of those used for carpet weaving had "assumed more of a 'factory' air, and a few really important establishments [had begun] their career."[13] Some large manufacturers put out yarn to as many as 100 weavers each, while many more supplied but half a dozen cottages. Spools of yarn for the journeymen's shuttles were wound either by their own families or by women and children employed by the master. In that case the master passed on the cost of winding to the journeyman at a rate of 75 cents a week, a rate which remained quite constant from the 1820s through the 1840s.[14] For the most part as Edwin T. Freedley observed, "the persons engaged in the production have no practical concern with the ten-hour system, or the factory system, or even with the solar system. They work at such hours as they choose in their own homes, and their industry is mainly regulated by the state of the larder."[15] A starker description by the contemporary novelist, George Lippard, suggested perhaps luridly, but nonetheless accurately, that the "state of the larder" was usually far from good: "Here we behold a house of time-worn brick, there a toppling frame; on every side the crash of looms, urged by weary hands even at this hour, disturbs the silence of the night."[16]

The neighborhood Lippard described surrounded the Nanny Goat Market, storm center of the great riots of 1844. In that neighborhood the census takers of 1850 confirmed the literary images of Lippard and Freedley. They found, for example, an Irish-born master weaver, Alexander Myers, living with his American wife and three small children, as well as a laborer and his wife who performed domestic service. Six Irish weavers with their families tenanted the surrounding buildings. The whole complex was valued at some $3,000.[17] Not far off lived Jacob Hopes, who similarly had come from Ireland early in the 1830s, married an American woman and now boarded seven single men, all weavers and presumably his journeymen.[18] John Lavery, another boss weaver, had lost in the 1844 riots a $2,000 establishment described by a metropolitan newspaper as "a large and handsome brick house with brick back buildings." The journeyman weaver, whose $150 two-story frame house next door was also wrecked, was a tenant as were the weaver residents of the next eight houses burned down the street.[19]

As these few examples suggest, both masters and workmen in the weaving business were predominantly Irish. In fact, 78 percent of the weavers were of Irish birth. In wards three and six (of 1850), where 70 percent of the town's weavers dwelt, 85 per cent of them were Irish. The 5 per cent who were born in America and the 9 per cent born in England seem to have been largely children of Irish immigrants.[20] The ages of the weavers' oldest children born in the United States indicate that the parents came to Kensington in two great waves, one about 1828-33 and the second in the latter half of the forties, after the riot of 1844.[21]

Although the immigrant weavers seem to have been predominantly Roman Catholic, there was a significant Protestant minority among them. The precise division cannot be known because the census takers specified the religion of no one but clergymen. Just to the east of Second Street, the north-south axis of the weaving district, lived many Irish weavers with such names as Montgomery, Campbell, McTaige and Stewart. Though it is always dubious to guess an Irishman's faith by his family name, firmer evidence of Protestantism lies in the presence among these weavers of a Presbyterian minister, a Methodist minister and an Irish-born agent of the American Tract Society. One Presbyterian preacher shared the home of an Irish boss weaver, William Wallace. Two Catholic priests, presumably serving the large St. Michael's Church, were their close neighbors.[22] In a word, Catholics and Protestants were found in almost random dispersal among both boss and journeyman weavers, but almost all were Irish. Their ethnic cohesiveness was epitomized by the case of Bernard Sherry, a master weaver who lost one frame and three brick houses inhabited by his journeymen during the riot. After his buildings had been burned, Sherry was arrested on charges of having armed his workmen to defend them against the nativists.[23]

The ethnic cohesiveness of the weaving community did not preclude sharp economic conflict within it. From the end of the 1820s through the 1840s, the weavers fought a running battle against the constantly recurring efforts of their countrymen-masters to reduce piece rates. When times were hard, as they were in 1833-34 or in 1837, or desperate as they were from 1839 to 1843, the masters claimed the fierce competition of the market compelled them to lower prices for weaving. When times were good, as in the flourishing years of 1835-36, the same masters argued that the high price of cotton threatened to wipe out profits if production costs did not fall. The dilemma of American hand weavers was precisely what Frederick Engels described in England at the same time: "One class of woven goods after another is annexed by the power-loom, and hand-weaving is the last refuge of workers thrown out of employment in other branches, so that the trade is always overcrowded."[24] Well might the Royal Commission on Handloom Weavers of 1838 warn British workers "to flee from the trade, and to beware of leading their children into it, as they would beware of the commission of the most atrocious of crimes."[25] But the supply of weavers stubbornly refused to fall. From the manufacturing towns of Yorkshire to the banks of the Delaware River, the rural poverty of Ireland kept the weaving cottages full from the late 1820s onward.[26]

In 1827 an English emigrant warned weavers of Yorkshire not to expect to improve their lot by coming to America. In Philadelphia, he wrote, a "smart weaver . . . by a fair week's work of 12 hours per day" would do well to acquire gross earnings of $4.50 a week. Some did no better than $4.00.[27] A press statement of master weavers the same year claimed $5.00 as a weekly average for journeymen.[28] There seemed general agreement throughout this period that 100 yards of three shuttle gingham was something of a standard week's work, 120 yards the fruit of an extremely intensive week's application. From the late twenties through the mid-thirties, prices paid to journeymen hovered around 4 cents a yard for this rather common style of cloth. If a weaver had a family, their work at spooling could save the journeyman a charge of 75 cents weekly and possibly, with enough children, earn a pittance more for the household by winding spools for the use of other journeymen who had no children. Customarily part of the worker's pay was given in store goods rather than cash.

Wages were fixed by agreements negotiated each spring and fall between the manufacturers and a committee representing the weavers. Kensington and Moyamensing rates were governed by separate but usually similar scales at least from the mid-1830s on.[29] Often the agreements were reached only after severe strikes, and during the 1830s these conflicts brought the weavers into affiliation with the General Trades' Union of the City and County of Philadelphia, an assembly of delegates from all the organized trades of the area. During the weavers' strike in the fall of 1836 their societies received $1,500 in aid from the Trades' Union.[30] In turn the weavers contributed one of the most prominent leaders of the local workers' movement, John Ferral. To accommodate both immigrants and the native American crafts-men the Trades' Union banned from its midst all "party, political, or religious sectarian" questions. "The followers of Christ acknowledge a time for all things," explained the American-born saddler John Crossin on behalf of the Trades' Union, and "we do the same."[31]

As the depression of 1839-43 deepened, weavers' strikes became increas-ingly violent. The basic gingham scale (which was used as the yardstick throughout this discussion) was cut to 3 cents a yard in 1841, yet scabs were available in abundance especially from the most recent immigrants. From August of 1842 until January of the next year Kensington weavers refused to work at the fall scale offered by their employers. When some workers broke ranks, stalwarts staged parades of 150 to 500 participants through the streets, entered the houses of non-strikers and hurled their unfinished chains into bonfires in the streets. Early in November they dispersed a meeting of their masters by threatening to tear down the house where it was taking place, and two months later a sheriff's posse attempting to arrest some strikers was routed by a charge of over 400 weavers armed with muskets and brick-bats. Three military companies arrived during the night, and in their presence the workers and masters reached agreement on a scale which left hundreds of families living on less than three dollars a week.[32]

A strike in the spring of 1843 won a small raise, which was celebrated by a massive unity parade of Kensington and Moyamensing weavers.[33] That August improving market conditions, optimism over the new tariff and a very effective one-month strike allowed the Kensington weavers to negotiate an enormous raise—to 5¼ cents a yard for the standard gingham. When three of the largest employers refused to accede to the new scale and de-manded that other masters support them in continuing to resist, the em-ployers' conference broke up in a brawl.[34] As the early glimmerings of re-turning prosperity shone over the land, the weavers' incomes actually moved upwards.

The trend did not last long. The following May saw the Kensington weav-ing district gutted by nativist rioters. Ten days after the disturbance, the handloom weavers' committee announced that a number of manufacturers, "willing to take advantage of the then existing circumstances to enrich themselves," had reduced "our wages at a time when it is uncalled for by the markets" and when journeymen could not respond because the authori-ties had banned all meetings. The committee spoke the truth. The basic gingham price had been slashed from 5¼ cents a yard back to 3¼ cents.[35]

The key to the weavers' downfall lay in the fact that no longer did they enjoy the support of the other workmen of Philadelphia. Quite the con-trary; the final defeat had come in the wake of actual physical assault by other workers, for the most part native-born Protestant artisans. The central problem for this study, therefore, is to explain the rift between the weavers and their fellow workmen of Philadelphia County.

During the 1830s all groups of Philadelphia workmen—Protestant and Catholic, native and immigrant, superior craftsmen, outworkers, factory operatives and laborers—had been caught up in an awakening of class solidarity as significant as any in American history. The formation of the General Trades' Union, which included delegates from some 50 organized trade societies by 1836, and the successful general strike for the ten-hour day in 1835 epitomized this movement.[36] With revenues of $400 to $500 a month from its constituent unions, the Trades' Union could boast early in 1836: "Within the last six months more than one half of the Societies in the Union have struck, and no instance is known where a Society has struck, under the sanction of the Union, and failed in that strike."[37] Most significant of of all, these successful strikes were conducted by workers who ranged in status from laborers and factory operatives at one end of the scale to bookbinders and jewelers at the other. Even journeymen cabinet makers (whose primary concerns were to collect debts due them from merchants and to halt competition from auction sales) and butchers and victuallers (struggling to hold down stall rent charged by the city and impede the "shaving" practices of cattle dealers) participated in the Trades' Union.[38]

From the ranks of these diverse groups, the Trades' Union could summon up what a local paper called "one of the largest meetings ever held in this city," conducted "with strict order and propriety" to protest the conviction of striking coal heavers, who were among the poorest but also the most militant of the city's working people. The rally demanded the defeat of Mayor John Swift for "the false imprisonment and unconstitutional bail [he] demanded of the Schuylkill laborers. . . whose only crime consisted in asking 25 cents per day addition to former wages."[39]

Many prominent workingmen plunged into the county's political struggles, for the most part supporting the anti-bank wing of the Democratic Party. Ferral of the weavers, Benjamin Sewell the tanner, William Thompson the carpenter, William English, William Gilmore and Samuel Thompson, all shoemakers, and Edward A. Penniman and Joshua Fletcher of the coachmakers were but some of the Trades' Union leaders who promoted Henry A. Muhlenberg's gubernatorial campaign as an anti-monopoly Democrat, sent their champion Lemuel Paynter to Congress from the Southwark area (the manufacturing suburb to the south of Philadelphia which was the birthplace of the artisans' movement), and helped maintain a consistent Democratic majority of almost two to one in Kensington elections.[40] After the depression struck, they organized mass rallies to support President Van Buren's Independent Treasury scheme, demand resumption of specie payments and suppression of "shin plaster" small notes by banks and dispatched committees to visit each of the city's banks with these demands.[41] Ferral proudly boasted to Senator James Buchanan that "the working classes" had frustrated the efforts of pro-bank "shin plaster democrats" to dominate the local party. He concluded that "all is well with the bone and sinew" who had rededicated the Democratic organization to the "emancipation of our Country from the bondage in which it is at present held by chartered Monopolists."[42]

At the very time Ferral wrote, however, the impact of the depression was relentlessly undermining the working-class cohesiveness which the Trades' Union had built up on both the economic and political fronts. As a prominent Philadelphian confided to his diary in the summer of 1842: "The streets seem deserted, the largest houses are shut up and to rent, there is no business, there is no money, no confidence & little hope, property is sold every day by the sheriff at a 4th of the estimated value of a few years ago, nobody can pay debts, the miseries of poverty are felt by both rich & poor. . . ."[43] In this setting most trade societies collapsed, and the General Trades' Union disintegrated with the evaporation of its once munificent treasury.

With the demise of the Trades' Union, Philadelphia lacked any institution uniting the Catholic weaver, the Methodist shoemaker and the Presbyterian ship carpenter as members of a common working class. Strikes became as uncommon as they were hopeless, except among the handloom weavers. Artisan struggles of other types excited the county. In the spring of 1839, for example, the butchers waged a brilliantly executed campaign against "shaver" cattle dealers. Through great public fanfare they enlisted the support of their impoverished customers behind the butchers' concerted refusal to pay more than 10 cents a hundredweight for live cattle.[44] The next year shoemakers set up a committee to aid their Boston counterparts then being prosecuted in the famous case of *Commonwealth v. Hunt.*[45]

From August to October 1842, a Workingmen's Convention met weekly, organized ward clubs and staged street meetings throughout the county to protest unemployment and "to guard their more indigent brethren against the inclemencies of the coming winter." An Equal Rights Party which was launched by the movement, however, failed abysmally at the polls.[46]

When prominent mechanics convened a series of meetings during January and February of 1839 in an effort to revive their trades movement, laborers, factory operatives and even the struggling weavers were conspicuously absent. An address signed by well known spokesmen of the coach makers, shoemakers, painters, bricklayers, tailors, cabinet makers and others blamed the economic crisis on "corrupt legislation," stressed the theme of self-help and made its chief demand "a system of education which shall teach every child in the Commonwealth his duty and interests as a citizen and freeman." It argued that "the old system of pecuniary benefits through the assistance of Trades' Unions seems to have fallen into disrepute" and criticized the "old Union" for "indiscriminate association of all the Trades without any regard to their assimilation or affinity."[47]

It was precisely by making strikes futile, destroying the Trades' Union beyond even hope of resurrection and stimulating this new emphasis on self-improvement that the depression opened the way for the rise of nativism among the artisans. By magnifying the importance to artisans of the temperance and public education movements, these developments set their aspirations on a collision course with those of Catholic immigrants.

The temperance movement paved the way. Like the stress on education, it involved nothing new to artisan culture. In his eloquent pleas for working-class unity at the founding of the Mechanics Union of Trade Associations in 1827, William Heighton had implored his fellow craftsmen to put aside their "drinking, gaming, and frolicking," and devote themselves to self-education.[48] Almost 40 years before that a commentator describing the gathering of 17,000 Philadelphians, proudly arrayed by trades to celebrate the newly-adopted federal constitution, had attributed their orderliness to their drinking nothing but "American Beer and Cyder," and admonished his readers to "despise spiritous liquors, as *Anti-Federal,* and to consider them as companions to all those vices, that are calculated to dishonor and enslave our country."[49]

The depression cast this traditional artisan virtue in a new light. The hard times made temperance societies with middle-class evangelical leadership ubiquitous in the manufacturing districts, infused a new sense of crusading militancy into their ranks and made them an integral part of artisan life. When the Journeymen House Carpenters prepared their futile strike for a wage increase in March 1839, they appealed publicly for help from the "friends of temperance," arguing that under current wages carpenters "are frequently driven by poverty and care to intemperance, to dispel for a season, the horrid gloom which envelopes their homes," thereby "encompassing their families with misery."[50] The Temperance Society responded with a public letter endorsing the carpenters' demands and calling upon them to make total abstinence a condition of membership in their society.[51] By 1842-43 the temperance societies in almost every ward were supplemented by others organized on trade lines, like the Cordwainers' Beneficial Temperance Association. A new labor-for-labor exchange, The First Co-operative Labor Association of Philadelphia, met in a city temperance house.[52]

In 1838 the movement acquired a new leader of increasing prominence named Lewis C. Levin. This Charleston-born lawyer, described by Alexander McClure as "one of the most brilliant and unscrupulous orators I have ever heard," both lectured for the cause and edited the *Temperance Advocate.*[53] In January 1842, he attracted attention to a new temperance society in the waterfront woodworking district of Kensington, which then had only 15 members, by staging a spectacular bonfire of booze obtained from a converted saloon keeper before the eyes of thousands of spectators. Gathering as much of his audience as would fit into a nearby church, he blamed drunkenness on "the prodigality of the mushroom aristocracy of the country," appealed to the "steady habits of old times" and demanded that the public be allowed to vote on whether taverns should be tolerated in neighborhoods.[54]

It was this demand for popular control of liquor licensing which brought the temperance movement with its new evangelical leadership and artisan base into the political arena.[55] There its impact blended with that of an even more emotionally-charged controversy over reading the Bible in the common schools.

There is no end of irony in the Bible-reading issue, and most of it stems from the fact that two very divergent groups had been involved in the struggle for free public education in Philadelphia in the 1820s and 1830s. One group was the artisans, starting with those involved in the Mechanics' Union of Trade Associations, founded in 1827 with the quest for "equal education" one of its foremost goals. "The original element of *despotism,*" argued one of its reports, "is a MONOPOLY OF TALENT." The republican alternative, it contended, was the extenison of the same education to all citizens "as a matter of right."[56] This theme was repeated at the 1836 Trades' Union mass meeting in defense of the coal heavers. Resolutions adopted there denounced governments grants "to colleges, academies and seminaries, where the children of the wealthy alone are taught, that they may move in the same sphere of life as their parents," while "our children are destined to hereditary bondage, in consequence of the prevailing ignorance of the poorer classes."[57] Similarly the artisans' convention of 1839 demanded a "levelling system. . . of education," in the belief that "intelligence is a passport everywhere."[58] That artisan devotion to education was not simply rhetorical is suggested by a list of the students admitted from the city's common schools to its select Central High School in 1844. Of the 90 students admitted that year, 37 were sons of artisans and four were sons of laborers. Together they almost equalled in number the children of merchants, manufacturers and professional men admitted. Not one weaver's child was on the list.[59]

The other, and ultimately more effective promoter of free public education, was a band of paternalistic merchants and professional men, largely old Federalists, led by Roberts Vaux and Samuel Breck. These men spoke not of "levelling education" to emancipate the working man, but of "universal education" as "a powerful check on vice," to use the words of Governor Wolf's message in support of the Public School Bill which became law in 1834.[60]

Prominent evangelists endorsed this effort. Albert Barnes, the "New School" leader of Philadelphia's First Presbyterian Church, took a comprehensive view of the problem when he warned that "the lower stratum of society. . . that dense and dark mass, the population of alleys and cellars, and garrets—the ignorant, the degraded, the grossly sensual, the idle, the worthless—the refuse of society. . . are not in a condition where revivals of religion can be expected such as I am advocating." The remedy, he suggested, was to elevate "that dark mass" by closing the city's "fountains of poison," placing the Bible in the homes of the poor, providing them "self-denying instruction," and ensuring that "these hordes of wandering and wretched children [are] to be gathered into schools and taught."[61]

More secular objectives for the same crusade were expressed by the Reverend Orville Dewey of Massachusetts in a review of two new elementary school textbooks. Dewey saw "combinations of the employed to procure higher wages" and "political workingmen's parties" as threats to "tear up every social institution by the roots, and leave nothing behind but disorder, waste, and ruin." The remedy for such evils lay in looking "to the very power which has given the impulse to control it. That power, undoubtedly, is education" of the common people. To fulfill its function of preserving social order, education must above all be moral, Dewey concluded. "Conscience," and he repeated, "conscience is our safeguard!"[62]

It was fine to have available such spelling lessons as "Obedience to superiors is requisite in all society; it is consistent with propriety and adds to general convenience,"[63] but what better text for the safeguarding conscience was available than the Bible? The study of the scriptures was seen by these reformers not as peripheral to the purposes of the common schools, but central.

Now every good American Protestant knew that the volume God had written personally was that authorized by King James. To the Roman Catholic clergy, however, that translation was anathema. Its use in classrooms endangered the very souls of Catholic pupils. The dramatic expansion of the common school system in Philadelphia County in the decade following the 1834 act added urgency to the issue. All the while Protestants simply found Catholic objections incomprehensible. "We have never discovered anything in that book, the reading of which we could suppose would injure the morals of either Catholic children or their parents!" wrote one indignant Protestant.[64]

Bishop Francis Patrick Kenrick of Philadelphia fought relentlessly and skillfully to protect his Catholic flock from the Protestant Bible. He realized that news of the burning of King James Bibles by a Catholic missionary priest in a small town in upstate New York and of Bishop John Hughes' call to New York City's Catholics to form a separate political party around the Bible issue had inflamed Philadelphia's Protestant establishment. Consequently Bishop Kenrick issued a discreet but firm public appeal to the Board of Controllers of the Pennsylvania common schools to allow Catholic children to use their own version of the Bible in class and to be excused from other religious instruction. He was partially successful. The Board of Controllers ruled in January 1843, that children whose "parents were conscientiously opposed" might be excused from class during Bible readings.[65]

Agitation over the Bible in schools, like the excitement over liquor licensing, aroused both Catholic and Protestant workingmen with several important consequences. The first was the rise of Democratic politicians in Kensington and similar towns who were closely tied to the Irish weavers, but who defended them on cultural, rather than economic, grounds. Leaders of the stripe of John Ferral, who had fought manufacturers and bankers in the political arena, were shunted aside by men like Hugh Clark, a boss weaver who fought "Puritan fanaticism." Born in Ireland in 1796, Clark came to the United States around 1813 and by 1827 was a member of the masters' Society of Weavers. His brother Patrick was a tavern keeper, and Hugh himself was a police magistrate of such prominence in the Catholic community that Protestant rioters made a point of sacking both of their homes and tavern in 1844. When listed by the census-takers six years later, Hugh was an alderman and manufacturer, the owner of $30,000 of real estate, more than was reported by any other individual in the town. With him lived his 70-year-old mother and his two younger brothers, both weavers. Next door dwelt Patrick, who had replaced his lost tavern with a dyeing establishment valued at $6,700.[66] Here was the political leader of Kensington's Irish weavers, a man who opposed them in a succession of bitter strikes, then mounted the hustings to champion their right to a drink and the consciences of their children.

Second, Democratic artisans, among them some of the party's most consistent anti-monopolists, reacted angrily to the new prominence of Irish ethnic politics in their party. A revolt of the self-styled "Incorruptibles" against Clark's nomination for County Treasurer in 1841 split the Democratic Party and helped defeat Clark in his own home town.[67] Two years later an insurrection was mounted by Thomas Grover, Lemuel Paynter and William D. Kelley, the leaders of the artisan wing of the Democratic Party in Southwark, against the party's nomination of an Irishman for that district's Congressional seat. The result again was victory for the Whigs.[68] The whole Incorruptible movement was remarkably similar to the struggle in Williamsburg (Brooklyn) which the emigre Irish Chartist and land reformer Thomas A. Devyr described in his memoirs. Furiously opposing Catholic sectarian politics in the name of the local Democratic Party's Jacksonian economic program, Devyr found himself denounced by his fellow Irishmen and hailed by the nativists.[69]

Third, the cleavages opened in Democratic ranks by the issues of liquor and schools tempted prominent Whigs to try to strike bargains with Democrats like Clark in order to capture county offices. In fact, nativist publicists charged that Whig lust for such votes lay behind the decision of the Whig-dominated Board of Controllers of the common schools to accede to Bishop Kenrick's demand on the Bible reading question. Whether or not there was any truth in that charge, it is certain that when Morton McMichael ran for sheriff on the Whig ticket in 1843 he received considerable support from Irish Catholics out to avenge their recent defeats at the hands of native Democrats. An open letter in the press from "A NATURALIZED CITIZEN; A DEMOCRAT AND AN IRISHMAN FOREVER" accused the Democratic party of proscribing Irish candidates both in 1841 and in the current Congressional elections in Southwark. The remedy it proposed was for Irishmen to vote Whig so that they could later return to the chastised Democratic fold. "The Whig County Ticket," it claimed, "is made up of known and ardent friends of Ireland, and is headed with the name of Morton McMichael, who, like General Jackson, is the son of Irish parents, and, like him, every inch an Irishman!''[70] Enough Irish voters heeded the advice of "A NAT-URALIZED CITIZEN" that McMichael won the election, carrying even Kensington by almost 200 votes, while the Democrats, as usual, handily won every other office in that town.[71]

Finally, the success of Catholic sectarian politics and the Bishop's partial victory on the school issue account for the overnight mushrooming of the American Republican Party, a political movement to exclude immigrants from the suffrage and to defend the use of the King James Bible in schools. American Republican clubs had been operating in nearby Spring Garden since the end of the 1830s, and for more than a decade itinerant ministers, spellbound by the Romish menace, had been peddling the *Awful Disclosures of Maria Monk* about the county. They had little to show for their pains, though one had been arrested on charges of selling pornography in the guise of anti-Catholic literature. The school controversy, however, had united 94 leading clergymen of the city in a common pledge to strengthen Protestant education and "awaken the attention of the community to the dangers which . . . threaten these United States from the assaults of Romanism.''[72] The American Tract Society took up the battle cry and launched a national crusade to save the nation from the "spiritual despotism" of Rome.[73] The whole Protestant edifice of churches, Bible societies, temperance societies, and missionary agencies was thus interposed against Catholic electoral maneuvers in the name of "non-sectarian politics" at the very moment when those maneuvers were enjoying some success. Lewis Levin stepped over from the temperance movement to take command of the American Republican Party and led it with such skill that within one year it was in full control of the political life of the county.

The meteoric rise of the American Republican movement cannot be understood as a capitalist conspiracy to divide and crush the workers, even though it was portrayed in precisely this way by George Lippard's contemporary novel *The Nazarene,* and it did enable the master weavers to destroy the union of their journeymen. To be sure, it enjoyed widespread but ordinarily tacit sympathy from the old Quaker elite of Philadelphia. Many of them shared the sentiment which Sidney G. Fisher confided to his diary:

This movement of the "native" party is decidedly conservative, because by excluding foreigners so much democracy is excluded, so much of the rabble, so much ignorance & brutality from political power. The natural ally of this party are the Whigs. Their object harmonizes with the instincts & secret wishes & opinions of the Whigs.[74]

Nevertheless, the American Republicans themselves were decidedly not upper class in leadership or following. Levin surrounded himself with out-of-office Whig politicians who opposed their party's 1843 deal with the

Catholics and Democrats of the Incorruptible camp. To their ranks he added an imposing array of minor publishers, attorneys, ministers of the gospel and a few master craftsmen as the leading cadres of his party. Among them were an ex-colonel, C. J. Jack, who sought to prove during the riots that a big city can have its village idiot, and Charles Naylor, a Southwark lawyer and former Whig Congressman from the northern suburbs, whom Fisher described as "partially deranged."[75] Thomas Grover, the wharf builder, and Lemuel Paynter, whom Grover had helped put in Congress a decade earlier as spokesman of Southwark's artisans, were well known but hardly upper class. Only William B. Reed, of all the prominent nativists, had personal ties to the First Families, being a nephew of John Sergeant. But Reed's involvement in bribery scandals connected with the Bank of the United States had not only cost him a Congressional seat; it also left him in disgrace with his fellow gentlemen.[76]

The following these men gathered can be identified from the lists of nativists injured or arrested in the riots and from the rolls of ward club officers printed in their newspaper *Native American.* This enumeration provides almost as many occupations as it does names of individuals, but the trades which appear more than once give a clue to the nature of the rest. They are victualler, butcher, cordwainer, merchant and ship carpenter. All these occupations were not only dominated by native Americans, but were also the traditional trades and crafts of an American seaport.

In Kensington itself, the candidates nominated by the American Republicans for the February elections following the riots (1845) included a tax collector, a carpenter, a blacksmith, a tailor, a carter and a cabinetmaker. In the two wards where the party ran strongest, its candidates were an alderman and former combmaker, two ship carpenters, a chair maker, a brass worker and a victualler.[77] The tightly-knit community of Kensington fishermen not only supplied a candidate for that election, but marched as a body in the American Republicans' grand parade of July 4, 1844.[78]

In short, during 1844 the American Republicans mobilized not only the electoral support but the active participation of Protestant artisans in Kensington, Southwark and other industrial suburbs. Superior tradesmen abounded at the movement's secondary levels of leadership: cabinet makers, ship carpenters, butchers and victuallers, whose occupations had as yet suffered little erosion of traditional status and practices from burgeoning industrializaiton. Their conspicuous support to the top leadership of professional men and small proprietors gave the American Republican clubs an eerie resemblance to a resurrected Sons of Liberty three generations out of date. Less numerous but still evident among the activists were such building tradesmen as carpenters and bricklayers, and such workmen enmeshed in the putting-out system as shoemakers and tailors, who often suffered from the new competitive development of the economy almost as bitterly as the weavers, and who had contributed extraordinary strength to the General Trades' Union of the thirties.[79]

While all these workmen shared the animosity against Roman Catholicism which pervaded Anglo-Saxon culture, it is difficult to determine just how fully they were incorporated into the institutional structure of organized Protestantism. The upper classes of the time tended to scoff that most of the rioters would not know the difference between a Protestant and a Catholic Bible if they were confronted with the two books. Leading evangelists of the age, furthermore, not only disdained to preach to the lower classes, but agreed with Albert Barnes that workingmen were by and large incapable of genuine religious experience.[80] On the other hand, four Protestant churches (Episcopalian, Baptist, Presbyterian and Unitarian) were substantial enough to appear on a Kensington map of 1850, and the census takers of that year were to uncover no fewer than 16 Protestant ministers in town.

There is no way of knowing the nature of the congregations served by each of these preachers, but perhaps some meaningful guess can be made on the basis of the character of the neighborhoods in which they resided. Six of the preachers were found among substantial home-owning tradesmen and small employers near the waterfront, or in one case in the rustic outskirts of the weaving district. One of them did not specify his denomination. The others were a New Light Baptist, an Old Light Baptist, a Presbyterian and two Methodists (one of which was a very young man with very prosperous neighbors). The Episcopalian priest lived among poor laborers and weavers but probably because that was where his large church was situated. A Presbyterian, a Reformed Presbyterian and a Methodist lived among Irish weavers but probably because that was where his large church was situated. A Presbyterian, a Reformed Presbyterian and a Methodist lived among Irish weavers, as has already been pointed out.

The remaining six lived among poorer workmen of various occupations. One was a German who gave no affiliation. Another was an Irish-born Old School Presbyterian. Near him lived a 19-year-old Primitive Methodist, whose father was a Pennsylvania-born carpenter. Two others were Methodists, one Irish and one native Pennsylvanian, both living among shoemakers, tailors and carpenters. The last was William Metcalf, a 70-year-old Bible Christian ("ranting Bryantite") from England who lived in a pocket of native- and English-born workmen in the midst of the largest weaving ward.[81] It is probable that these men represented the world of popular sects or "store front churches," which is as elusive to the historian as it was central to the culture of the working classes.

It appears, then, that Protestantism was a vital force in the ideology of these workingmen. Through its influence they could be attached to the middle-class leadership of a political party whose negative reference group was the Catholic immigrant, provided those leaders draped the movement with the most cherished symbols of artisan culture. Lewis Levin played to the values, the hopes and the anxieties of his audience of artisans with unerring aim. His paper, the *Native American,* displayed Longfellow's *Village Blacksmith* and with equal emphasis acclaimed the continuing "march of improvement.''[82] The evils of the times were attributed to the behavior of the corrupt politician, who had allied himself with foreign-born voters, alien to America's egalitarian traditions and subject in their voting behavior to the discipline of the Roman Catholic church. The American Republicans promised to reintroduce into politics the sense of personal honor once exemplified by the Revolutionary Founding Fathers, to win the ''entire separation of sectarianism from Politics'' and to secure both objectives through ''AN OPEN BIBLE and a PURE BALLOT BOX!''[83]

Kensington soon provided the nativists an ideal battleground for their cause. While Bishop Kenrick tried to soothe Protestant fears with statement after statement denying any desire to deprive Protestant school children of their King James Bible, magistrate Hugh Clark himself authorized a Kensington teacher to omit Bible reading altogether in her overwhelmingly Catholic class. American Republicans responded by dispatching emissaries to the weaving town to demand the culprit's resignation. At first the meetings attracted more Catholic hecklers than Protestant supporters, and two local American Republicans who tried to organize a club in the middle of the weaving district were prevented by their neighbors from holding a meeting.[84] Inspired by their party's triumph in the April elections in New York City, however, the nativists did stage an open air rally addressed by S.R. Cramer, a Philadelphia carpenter and publisher of the *Native American,* on a Friday evening early in May within a block of a Catholic church, only to see the speaker driven from his platform by about a hundred angry Catholics.[85]

The following Monday, May 6, Levin himself accompanied Cramer to the scene of Friday's debacle to avenge the insult. Tensions were already running high when a heavy rain drove the nativists across the street to the shelter of the Nanny Goat Market. There Levin ascended some packing boxes in the midst of Irish shoppers to hold forth on ''the deleterious effects of Popish interference in the elective franchise.'' Hardly had he begun when the marketers assaulted him and his followers with vegetables, fists and bricks. Rallying their forces, the nativists charged the Irish in the streets, then assaulted the Hibernia Hose House and two weavers' cottages from which, they later claimed, they had been fired upon. Gunfire was soon general on both sides; but because the Protestants were in the open and the Irish snipers inside, the heavy casualties were suffered by the nativist side: four badly beaten, seven shot, and a morocco dresser's apprentice, George Shiffler, killed.[86]

By mid-evening both sides had swelled to great crowds, freely shooting at each other. Protestant reinforcements from Philadelphia fought their way north along Second Avenue into the weaving district. Two more nativists, a blind maker and the son of a salt merchant, were killed and an Irish captive severely beaten in a battle which, quite appropriately, found Catholics firing from behind the walls of a seminary while the nativists barricaded themselves across the street in a temperance grocery store.[87]

"Another St. Bartholomew's day is begun in the streets of Philadelphia," editorialized the *Native American* the next day, while Colonel Jack rallied Protestants to march from Philadelphia and Southwark north to Kensington, armed with fife and drum, torch and musket, to exorcise the menace of Popish bigotry. By early afternoon the town was locked in pitched battle. Nativists charged from building to building burning and sacking the homes and back buildings of weavers John Lavery, Matthew Quinn, Barnard Sherry Owen McCulloch, Michael Keenan, Hugh Devlin and John Mellon. Two carpet manufactures and the homes and stock of peddler Patrick McGee and tailor Thomas Sheridan were put to the torch. In all, some 30 buildings were ablaze by the time troops arrived escorting firemen into the town.[88]

On Wednesday, more than 3,000 troops, complete with artillery, placed Kensington under martial law. Sheriff McMichael tried to secure his political future by demanding that the troops shoot no one, save in self-defense, and restrict themselves to guarding the property of the Roman Catholic church. In this setting, bands of nativists, mostly boys, searched Irish homes for arms and beat the owners of houses where weapons were found. Despite the presence of soldiers, Protestants set fire to St. Michael's Church in Kensington and to St. Augustine's Church in Philadelphia along the route north to Kensington, as well as hugh Clark's house and his brother's tavern.[89] Not Until Thursday was the town smoldering quietly, with refugees trudging aimlessly about and small bands of boys looting. Public meetings were banned everywhere in the county, and troops dispersed anything that faintly resembled a demonstration as far away as Southwark and Moyamensing.[90]

The weavers' community had been gutted. General George Cadwalader's successful defense of the city's cathedral and, later in July, of St. Philip's Church in Southwark was to earn him the praise and thanks of Bishop Kenrick; but the army had been unable to protect the cottages or even the lives of the weavers. In fact, it had little will to do so; the soldiers visibly sympathized with the nativists.[91]

Judging from the names of the victims, it seems that the rioters burned the homes of Protestant as well as Catholic weavers. Although American Republican rhetoric identified Roman Catholicism as the enemy, the nativist rioters made the weaving community as a whole their target. Conversely, there is no evidence of participation by Protestant weavers in the American Republican movement before the riot. It is true that the first American Republican shot in the Nanny Goat Market, former constable Patrick Fisher, was a Protestant Irishman and that four years later a weavers' spokesman charged that the riot had been "incited by North of Ireland Orangemen." But the three Irishmen who led the first American Republican club in Kensington were a flour dealer, a rope maker and an undertaker-cabinetmaker.[92] Possibly the common wage struggles and the single union organization of Protestant and Catholic weavers generated a group solidarity which rendered these particular Protestants impervious to the American Republican appeal.

Only as avenging mobs stormed toward their homes did some Protestants understandably begin to post American flags, or better yet, mastheads from the paper *Native American,* in their windows to convert the crowd from angry shouts to loud cheers.[93]

Despite the familiarity of clashes between Orangemen and Catholics to Irishmen on both sides of the Atlantic, it does seem that there were Irish Protestants among that significant minority of workingmen who remained loyal Democrats in defiance of the new trend to sectarian politics. A Protestant lad from County Antrim could write home to his father after the riots that he despised the nativists, was "a Democrat out and out, and takes the platform for the cause against Monarchy and aristocracy."[94] The persistent vitality of the Repeal Association in Philadelphia, in which both Hugh Clark and William D. Kelley participated even though they were on opposite sides of the "Incorruptible" fence at the time, testifies to the resilience of the eighteenth-century Irish heritage of Catholic-Dissenter cooperation against the Anglican Establishment. On the fourth of July 1841, the Repealers had turned out 1,860 participants for a parade led by the Montgomery Hibernia Greens, a rifle company of Protestants which three years later was to find itself brutally attacked by nativists in Southwark.[95] When President Tyler, ostracized from the Whig Party, set out to build a Democratic base, his son Robert became president of the Philadelphia Repeal Association.[96] Consequently, while there were Irish Protestant activists among the American Republicans, it is understandable that the party at times denounced all Irishmen and doubly understandable that Levin sometimes identified the Repeal Association as his main enemy.[97]

Clearly there were other workmen who found the nativist movement unattractive. The Democratic vote throughout the county remained far larger in 1844 than could be accounted for by Catholics alone. Shoemakers, tailors and laborers appear in the rolls of American Republican activists but in numbers far smaller than their proportion of the labor force. Factory operatives are conspicuously absent, though one should study a mill town like Manayunk before passing judgment on their role. Such shoemakers' leaders as Samuel Thompson, William English and William Gilmore, who had entered politics as Democrats in the 1830s, remained Democrats through the forties. Like William D. Kelley and the land reformer-novelist George Lippard, who attributed the riots to a joint conspiracy of Calvinist bankers and Rome to destroy American democracy, these men denounced both sides in the sectarian controversies which raged about them. They were the genuine Locofocos, political foes of capitalists, evangelists and priests alike, and at least some of them still adhered publicly to the Painite Rationalism which had been so widespread among workingmen's leaders in the 1830s. Their working-class following, that minority which was neither nativist nor immigrant, needs and deserves a historical study all its own.[98]

Neither Repealers nor Locofocos, however, could stop American Republican artisans from securing control of local politics in the wake of the Kensington riot. Large numbers of nativists enlisted in the armed citizen guards raised to protect Catholic buldings and police Kensington, a service for which they were highly praised by Major General Patterson. They saw to it that 13 of the 19 men arrested for disturbances in Kensington had unmistakably Irish names and, later in July when Protestants were to fight the army in Southwark, that volunteers en masse refused to turn out.[99]

While the weavers and all others were strictly forbidden by military orders to assemble, General Patterson was persuaded to allow a public meeting of the Washington Temperance Society nine days after the end of the riot. Nine days after the temperance meeting, he permitted a gathering of the American Republicans in the second ward of Kensington itself and sent along troops of the second brigade to protect it. By mid-June all bans had been lifted and a memorial service for eight nativists killed in the riots was held in Kensington's Brickmakers' Methodist Protestant Church. A soiree at the Christian Home Missionary Society of Philadelphia the same evening raised funds for families of the Protestant martyrs.[100] The report of the Grand Jury of the Court of Quarter Sessions investigating the riot placed all the blame on the Catholics, Magistrate Clark and Sheriff McMichael.[101] All the while, American Republican rallies of ever-growing size were being held throughout the county; and Levin trumpeted charges that "persons of wealth" were financing the arming of Catholics with "splendid rifles and warlike munitions" for their "Guy Fawkes plots and infernal machinations." "Burn no churches, even if your fathers were murdered before your eyes," he advised, but defeat the enemy at the polls.[102]

Independence Day provided the occasion for a long heralded manifestation by the nativists of their power and their determination to "sweep the demagogues" from office. Whether the parade numbered the 30,000 participants claimed by the *Native American* or the 4,500 Colonel A.R. Pleasonton noted in his diary, it must have been impressive. The pageantry and symbolism were of the same pattern displayed in artisans' demonstrations from the welcoming of the Federal Constitution in 1788 to the July Fourth processions of trades' unions in the 1830s. All delegations were gaily bedecked, many with their trade insignia. A Temple of Liberty was drawn at the front of the parade, and replicas of Washington, the Declaration of Independence and the Bible were everywhere to be seen. Widows and orphans of the Kensington martyrs held a special place of honor. Even two blacks were allowed to participate in this celebration of Protestant liberties— as water carriers for the other marchers.[103]

The nativists had every reason to be exultant. Despite blistering verbal assaults to which they were subjected by leading spokesmen of both the Whigs and the Democrats, they carried the fall elections in all the manufacturing suburbs. Levin was sent to Congress from Southwark and his colleague J. H. Campbell from the district which included Kensington. One state senate seat and those of the eight county representatives in the state house, all of which had formerly been filled by Democrats, were taken by American Republicans. The county commissioner's office was handily captured by Thomas Grover. Everywhere the pattern of voting was the same. Democratic tallies fell off sharply, and almost all former Whig votes went American Republican.[104] No longer was the commercial city the stronghold of the Whigs and the manufacturing county that of the Democrats, as had long been the case. American Republican endorsement of two Whig candidates, Henry Clay for President and Joseph Markle for Governor, allowed both men to carry with ease the city and county alike.[105]

In local elections the following February the nativists strengthened their political grip on the county. In the five wards of Southwark, all of them once solidly Democratic, the American Republicans' share of the total vote cast ran from a low of 63.2 percent to a high of 71.8 percent. In Kensington, where the Whigs fielded no candidates of their own and native-born Democrats clung to their traditional party in far greater numbers than their Southwark counterparts, the contest was somewhat less one-sided. The fourth ward, and even the fifth, where most of the fighting had taken place, went to the nativists in what their press hailed as a "Waterloo sweep." In the first and third wards American Republican candidates were narrowly defeated (in the former by only two votes). Of special interest is the second ward, situated directly on the line of march from Philadelphia to the Nanny Goat Market. Alderman Boileau of this erstwhile bastion of anti-bank Democrats switched his affiliation from the Democratic to the American Republican party and was handily re-elected.[106]

The route by which the nativists attained this level of political power had involved them in more street fighting, as well as electioneering. The conflict which raged in the vicinity of St. Philip de Neri Church in Southwark between Friday, July 5, and Monday, July 8, took a considerably greater toll of lives, though not of property, than had the riot in Kensington. Southwark was an American Republican stronghold, a community of traditional seaport craftsmen, laborers and sailors. An assault by more than a thousand of its residents on St. Philip's Church, following the rumor that Catholics were caching arms there, precipitated a direct clash between the nativists and the troops. No Catholics were involved in the fighting which ensued. Nativist leaders sought ardently, though in vain, to fend off violence. On the other hand, though soldiers frequently proved reluctant to fire at the crowd and troops of the Markle Rifles actually deserted the church to fraternize with those storming it, their commanders were clearly determined to put a forceful end to rioting once and for all. Generals Patterson and Cadwalader demanded that city officials give them a free hand, not the restraints under which they had served in Kensington; and they got their way.[107]

Although there is not the space here for a narrative of the battle, two aspects of the encounter are of importance. First, the behavior of Philadelphia's social elite showed that while they might have sympathized with the nativists' proclaimed objectives, they were aghast at the mob forces which nativism had unleashed. Even before the southwark riot the *Public Ledger* had drawn the editorial lesson from Kensington that soldiers should not fire *over* the heads of rioters but *at them*. Joseph R. Ingersoll had written to General Cadwalader that "the population of a large town is always excitable," so that a "power must exist to check its first outbreak, and it must be both willing and able to do so effectually. A strong preventive police is cheaper than indemnity for destroyed churches," he argued. Especially in "a country like ours where the people are supreme," there should be a "paid police on a basis which would always be in action—like Sir Robert Peel's men in England."[108]

After the Southwark fighting, scores of the city's "members of the bar, merchants, & men of education & property,"[109] among them Horace Binney, John Sergeant, Joseph R. Ingersoll and Sidney Fisher, met at Evans Tavern and addressed a memorial to the Governor praising the performance of the military forces. "Religion and politics have nothing whatever to do with such men as have been acting in these scenes, nor such men with them," they wrote. "The rioters are men cast off from all respect for law, or for our institutions, and are ready for arson, for murder, for rapine. . . ." To quell such activities, they recommended the quartering of a permanent military regiment in the city.[110]

Secondly, for the mass of Philadelphia's voters, the Southwark battle had cast the American Republicans in a heroic role, as embattled American workmen courageously defending their homes against invading troops. The cannonades of grape shot and the cavalry charges of the soldiers had been answered by three cannons used with considerable success by the citizens. By early Monday morning, when the exhausted troops found themselves at last patrolling empty streets, 15 of their number had been wounded, four more dangerously lacerated and two lay dead. Fallen civilians were estimated by J.H. Lee at 50, though there is little firm evidence to support his guess. Threats of a mob assembling for renewed assault later Monday induced governmental authorities to withdraw the battered troops and allow the American Republican leaders themselves to pacify the town. No one else could control the populace.[111]

The perspective of the next ten years helps one judge the significance of these tumultuous events. The First Families got their uniformed, professional police force, with a permanent military establishment of 1,350 cavalry, infantry and artillery men to stand in reserve.[112] For a full decade, furthermore they fended off a drive led by Morton McMichael, who now allied himself with the nativists, to consolidate the suburbs with the city. Fear that popular demagogues would dominate the larger unit prompted Horace Binney to rally municipal bondholders against the absorption of Kensington and South-wark into Philadelphia until the next nativist upsurge, the Know-Nothings, overwhelmed them.[113]

The handloom weavers were never to recover the wages with which they had entered 1844. Several subsequent strikes, based more in Moyamensing than in Kensington, failed to rescue their trade from the economic obsoles-cence and overcrowding which haunted it in this decade from Pennsylvania to Yorkshire and Silesia.[114] However, in contrast, Hugh Clark, Michael Keenan and other master weavers recovered quickly and progressed to greater fortunes.

The American Republicans' electoral strength began to wither within two years after 1844, as one office after another returned to the Whigs or Demo-crats. But there was no resurgence of class cohesiveness in the political be-havior of workingmen. On election days Protestant and Catholic working-men continued to align themselves not with each other, but with employers of their respective ethnic groups.[115]

Although the economic impact of industrialization was felt in quite dif-ferent ways and involved remarkably different rates of change for factory operatives, outworkers and the many varieties of craftsmen, all these groups shared common interests enough to allow them to act as a class in support of trade union efforts and such political demands as the legal ten hour day. This unity had been the driving force behind the urban radicalism of the 1830s. Quite different was the impact of the ideology of modernization by which a new sense of social order and discipline was imposed on the indus-trializing community. Because major elements of this ideology were trans-mitted through the political demands of evangelical Protestantism, above all liquor licensing and the moral content of public education, the responses of workingmen to modernization varied with their own religious beliefs. No political conflicts of the age touched the daily lives of the people more in-timately than these issues. By their very nature, evangelical demands frag-mented the working class as a political force in ante-bellum Philadelphia and thereby created for historians the illusion of a society lacking in class conflict.

Notes

1. See Liston Pope, *Millhands and Preachers, A Study of Gastonia* (New Haven), E.P. Thompson, "Time, Work-Discipline, and Industrial Capitalism," *Past and Present,* No. 38 (Dec. 1967), 56-97. Lee Benson, *The Concept of Jacksonian Democracy* (Princeton, 1961), is the classic work on "ethnocultural" determinants of American political behavior, but the book shows no awareness of the interaction between those determinants and class relations in the setting of industrialization.

2. U.S. Census Office, *Sixth Census or Enumeration of the Inhabitants of the United States . . . in 1840* (Washington, 1841), 151.

3. U.S. National Archives, 1850 Census Population Schedules, Pennsylvania (microfilm rolls 806-07), 4th ward, dwellings 72, 74, 78 (p. 245); 3d ward, dwellings 621-22 (p. 170), 1071 (p. 205); 5th ward, p. 324. Hereafter these schedules will be cited as 7th Census MSS.

4. Adam Smith, *An Inquiry into the Nature and Causes of the Wealth of Nations* (London, 1822), Book I, chap. 1.

5. See T.W. Dyott, *An Exposition of the System of Moral and Mental Labor Established at the Glass Factory of Dyottville* (Philadelphia, 1833), for a description of this works when it employed about 400 people. The calculation of nativity of glass workers is mine, from 7th Census MSS.

6. All figures are calculated form 7th Census MSS.

7. *Sixth Census,* 151; Sam Bass Warner, Jr., *The Private City: Philadelphia in Three Periods of Its Growth* (Philadelphia, 1968), 51.

8. 7th Census MSS, 2d ward, dwelling 757, p. 106.

9. *Ibid.,* 1st ward, dwelling 682, p. 41.

10. Edwin T. Freedley, *Philadelphia and Its Manufactures* (Philadelphia, 1858), 234, 250-51.

11. Samuel Hazard, ed., *The Register of Pennsylvania,* I (Jan., 1828), 28 (hereinafter cited as *HR*); Freedley, 250-54.

12. My count from 7th Census MSS.

13. Pennsylvania Bureau of Industrial Statistics, *Report,* XVII (1889),. 4D (hereinafter cited as *Pa. Bis*).

14. *HR,* (Jan., 1828), 28; letter of "One Who Knows, and a Weaver" to *Spirit of the Times,* Sept. 13, 1848; "Meeting of the Weavers," Philadelphia *Public Ledger,* March 2, 1845 (hereinafter cited as *PPL*).

15. Freedley, 241-42.

16. George Lippard, *The Nazarene; or, The Last of the Washingtonians, A Revelation of Philadelphia, New York, and Washington, in the Year 1844* (Philadelphia, 1846), 168.

17. 7th Census MSS, 2d ward, dwellings 98-102, pp. 63-64.

18. *Ibid.,* 3d ward, dwelling 1329, p. 231. The date of emigration in this and later cases is guessed from the age of the oldest child born in America.

19. *PPL,* May 11, 1844.

20. My count from 7th Census MSS. Of 2,238 weavers, 1,758 were born in Ireland. Of the weavers not born in Ireland 204 were English, 114 American, and 105 German by birth. The rest were from Scotland (55), France (2), and Switzerland (1). Of the 114 born in the U.S., 33 were clearly sons of Irish immigrants, as were many of those born in England. The 3rd and 6th wards of 1850 were made from the 5th ward of 1844, focal point of the riots, as was the rural 7th ward.

21. A significant but smaller peak of immigration was reached between 1836 and 1838.

22. 7th Census MSS, 6th ward, dwellings 70 (p. 406), 103 (p. 408), 96 (p. 408), 528 (p. 440).

23. *PPL,* May 11, 1844.

24. Frederick Engels, *The Condition of the Working-Class in England in 1844* (translated by Florence Kelley Wischnewetzky, London, 1892), 140.

25. Quoted in Asa Briggs, ed., *Chartist Studies* (London, 1962), 8-9.

26. Engels, 93, 138-40, 183-84; E.P. Thompson, *The Making of the English Working Class* (London, 1963), 296, 431; A. Redford, *Labour Migration in England, 1800-1850* (Manchester, 1964), 144-64. See also K.H. Connell, *The Population of Ireland, 1750-1845* (Oxford, 1950).

27. An Intelligent Emigrant at Philadelphia, *A Letter on the Present State of the Labouring Classes in America* (Bury, 1827), 5-6.

28. *HR,* I (Jan., 1828), 28.

29. Carpet weavers' assemblies of the Knights of Labor continued this practice in Kensington into the 1870s. *See Pa. Bis,* XVII (1899), 18D-19D; Terence V. Powderly, *Thirty Years of Labor, 1859-1889* (Columbus, 1889), 183.

30. John R. Commons, et al., *A Documentary History of American Industrial Society* (Cleveland, 1910), V, 351, 377, 384.

31. *Ibid.,* V, 391.

32. *Pa. Bis,* VIII (1880-81), 266-68.

33. *PPL,* June 6, 1843.

34. Letter of "One Who Knows, and a Weaver" to *Spirit of the Times,* Sept. 13, 1848; *Pa.*

Bis, VIII (1880-81), 269; *PPL,* Aug. 11, 16, 1843. This rate may have been as much as one cent per yard higher than the season's scale in Moyamensing, but a march of weavers from that town to Kensington failed to inspire a sympathy strike there. See *PPL,* Aug. 12, 15, 16, 1843; "Meeting of the Weavers," *ibid.,* March 2, 1845.

35. *PPL,* May 24, 1844; "One Who Knows, and a Weaver" to *Spirit of the Times,* Sept. 13, 1848. In 1848 Freedley was to find the going rate no higher than three cents. Freedley, 254.

36. See Commons, *Documentary History,* V, 325-92; William A. Sullivan, *The Industrial Worker in Pennsylvania, 1800-1840* (Harrisburg, 1955), 133-36; Leonard Bernstein, "The Working People of Philadelphia from Colonial Times to the General Strike of 1835," *Pennsylvania Magazine of History and Biography,* LXXIV (July, 1950), 322-39.

37. Commons, *Documentary History,* V, 390.

38. On the special demands of cabinet makers, see *PPL,* Oct. 15, 1841; Sept. 4, 1843. On those of butchers, see *PPL,* May 9, 1839.

39. *PPL,* Aug. 25, 1836.

40. Bruce G. Laurie, "The Working People of Philadelphia, 1827-1853," unpublished doctoral dissertation (University of Pittsburgh, 1971), 79-90, 253-65; Sullivan, 196-207; Warner, 90-91. On Kensington votes see *PPL,* Oct. 14, 1837; Oct. 12, 1839.

41. *PPL,* April 28, Sept. 8, 1838.

42. John Ferral to James Buchanan, Feb. 19, 1838 (Buchanan Papers, Box 92, Historical Society of Pennsylvania).

43. Sidney G. Fisher, *A Philadelphia Perspective, The Diary of Sidney George Fisher Covering the Years 1834-1871,* edited by Nicholas B. Wainwright (Philadelphia, 1967), 134-35.

44. *PPL,* May 9, 1839.

45. *PPL,* Nov. 21, 1840.

46. *PPL,* Aug. 1, 8, 13, Sept. 16, Oct. 19, 24, 1842.

47. E.A. Penniman, etc., *An Address to the Workingmen of the City and County of Philadelphia* (Philadelphia, 1839), 2, 3. On the mechanics' meetings see John R. Commons, et al., *History of Labour in the United States* (4 vols., New York, 1918-35), I, 469-71.

48. William Heighton, *An Address Delivered Before the Mechanics and Working Classes, Generally of the City and County of Philadelphia* (Philadelphia, 1827), 13. See also Heighton, *An Address to the Members of Trade Societies and to the Working Classes Generally* (Philadelphia, 1827).

49. *American Museum,* IV (July, 1788), 78.

50. *PPL,* March 22, 1839.

51. *PPL,* March 29, 1839.

52. *PPL,* Feb. 21, 1842; Dec. 13, 1843. Artisans supporting Whig candidates had organized their efforts in temperance halls as early as 1838. See the account of the Naylor meeting, *PPL,* Sept. 24, 1838.

53. A.K. McClure, *Old Time Notes of Pennsylvania* 2 vols., Philadelphia, 1905), I, 89. On Levin see *Dictionary of American Biography* (New York, 1937), VI, 200-01 (hereinafter cited as *D.A.B.*).

54. *PPL,* Jan. 24, 1842.

55. For a good discussion of the transition from temperance to prohibition see Joseph Gusfield, *Symbolic Crusade, Status Politics and the American Temperance Movement* (Urbana, Ill., 1963).

56. Report of the Joint Committee on the Common Schools, New York *Daily Sentinel,* Feb. 20, 22, 1830.

57. *PPL,* Aug. 25, 1836.

58. Penniman, 2.

59. *PPL,* July 10, 1844.

60. Warren F. Hewitt, "Samuel Breck and the Pennsyvania School Law of 1834," *Pennsylvania History,* I (April, 1934), 63-75; Joseph J. McCadden, "Roberts Vaux and His Associates in the Pennsylvania Society for the Promotion of Public Schools," *ibid.,* III (Jan., 1936), 1-8; Warner, 111-23. The quotation from Wolf is in Hewitt, 68.

61. Albert Barnes, *Sermons on Revivals* (New York, 1841), 155-57. See also Timothy L. Smith, "Protestant Schooling and American Nationality, 1800-1850," *Journal of American History*, LIII (March, 1967), 679-95.

62. [Orville Dewey], "Popular Education. 1. The Political Class Book . . . by WILLIAM SULLIVAN . . . 2. The Moral Class Book . . . by the SAME . . ." *North American Review* XXXVI (Jan., 1833), 73-99. The quotations are on pp. 81 and 96.

63. B. Brandneth, *A New System for the Instruction of Youth* (New York, 1836), quoted in Ruth Elson, *Guardians of Tradition* (Lincoln, Nebraska, 1964), 102.

64. J.H. Lee, *History of the American Party in Politics: Embracing a Complete History of the Philadelphia Riots in May and July, 1844* (Philadelphia, 1855), 29-30. On the expansion of the schools during 1834-44, see Warner, 117-18. On anti-Catholic bias in school textbooks, see Elson, 47-55, 123-28.

65. Hugh J. Nolan, *The Most Reverend Francis Patrick Kenrick, Third Bishop of Philadelphia, 1830-1851* (Washington, D.C., 1948), 289-96; Ray A. Billington, *The Protestant Crusade, 1800-1860* (New York, 1938), 142-66; Lee, 17-21. On Bishop Hughes in New York see Charles H. Haswell, *Reminiscences of an Octogenarian of the City of New York* (New York, 1897), 372-75; Thomas A. Devyr, *The Odd Book of the Nineteenth Century* (Greenpoint, N.Y., 1882), American Section, 33-38; Anna E. Carroll, *The Great American Battle; Or, The Contest between Christianity and Political Romanism* (New York and Auburn, 1856), *passim*.

66. 7th Census MSS, 3d ward, dwellings 621-22, p. 170; *PPL*, May 11, 1844; *HR*, I (Jan., 1928), 28; letter of "A NATURALIZED CITIZEN: A DEMOCRAT AND AN IRISHMAN FOREVER" to *PPL*, Oct. 7, 1843.

67. *PPL*, Oct. 14, 1841. Plankenton, the Whig candidate, carried Kensington with 852 votes. Clark came second with 821. Faunce, the Incorruptible, got 679 votes.

68. *PPL*, Oct. 12, 1843.

69. Devyr, American Section, 35-38.

70. *PPL*, Oct. 7, 1843. For the American Republicans' accusations of conspiracy between Bishop Kenrick and Whigs on the Board of Controllers, see Lee, 17-21; Billington, 214, n.49.

71. *PPL*, Oct. 12, 1843. Charges of collusion in this election between McMichael and the Catholics were commonplace at the time of the riots. See the *Address of the American Republicans* (Cadwalader Collection, folder May 22-June 29, 1844, Historical Society of Pennsylvania, hereinafter cited as CC); George Cadwalader to J.R. Ingersoll, May 24, 1844 (CC); Grand Jury Report, *PPL*, June 17, 1844.

72. Lee, 31-32; Billington, 182-184. The quotation is from Billington, 183.

73. Clifford S. Griffin, "Religious Benevolence as Social Control, 1815-1860," *Mississippi Valley Historical Review*, XLIV (Dec., 1957), 423-44.

74. Fisher, 177. On the anti-Catholic attitudes of the upper classes, see P. Kenny, "The Anti-Catholic Riots in Philadelphia in 1844," *American Catholic Historical Researches*, XIII (1896), 50-64; Joseph Ripka's testimony, *Journal of the Senate of Pennsylvania* (1838), II, 357-58.

75. On Jack, see his letter to *Native American* (hereinafter cited as *NA*), Aug. 2, 1844. On Naylor see U.S. Congress, 81st Cong., 2d sess., House Doc. 607, *Biographical Directory of the American Congress* (Washington, 1950), 1379; Fisher, 172.

76. *D.A.B.*, VIII, 461-62; McClure, I, 89-91; Fisher, 125.

77. The names of activists are taken from Grand Jury of the County of Philadelphia Minute Book, Sept. 2-Oct. 23, 1844; list of American Republican casualties in *NA, May 7, 1844;* article on May 6 rally, *ibid.;* North Ward officers, *ibid.;* Fifth Ward Southwark officers, *NA*, April 23, 1844; Kensington candidates, *NA*, Feb. 22, 1845. The best source for occupations was McElroy's *Philadelphia Directory* for 1843 and 1844.

78. The candidate was Charles Bakeover. *NA*, Feb. 22, 1845. On the parade, see Lee, 155.

79. It is noteworthy, however, that despite the strength of Methodism and temperance among shoemakers, their most prominent spokesmen in political life, William English, William Gilmore, Israel Young and Samuel Thompson, remained Democrats through the 1840s.

80. This thesis is well argued in Teresa L. Bradley, "The Response of Evangelical Protestant-

ism to the Urban Working Class, 1830-1860," unpublished M.A. paper, University of Pittsburgh History Department Library.

81. 7th Census MSS: 1st ward, J.C. Lyons (O.S. Presbyterian), George W. Brindle (Primitive Methodist); 2d ward, C. Hummel (no denomination), Francis Hoffman (Methodist); 3d ward, William Metcalf (Bible Church), John Shields (Methodist); 4th ward, David Dailey (Methoist), Wiliam Paulin (O.L. Baptist), George Hand (N.L. Baptist); 5th ward, George Chandler (Presbyterian), Alfred Cookman (Methodist), John G. Maxwell (Presbyterian); 6th ward, John G. Wilson (Methodist Protestant), Thomas Flavell (Reformed Presbyterian), Robert Black (Presbyterian); 7th ward, Daniel Gaston (no denomination).

82. See editorial and article on Kensington industry, *NA,* Sept. 16, 1844. Longfellow's poem appeared in *NA,* July 30, 1844.

83. *NA,* Sept. 16, 1844. The argument that immigration depressed American wages was a late-comer to American Republican editorializing. See *NA,* Nov. 29, 1844.

84. Billington, 221-24; Lee, 40-46.

85. Lee, 42-64; *PPL,* May 4, 1844. On the New York elections see Carroll, 264-65; Haswell, 409-10.

86. *PPL,* May 7, 1844; *NA,* May 7, 1844; Lee, 48-65.

87. *PPL,* May 7, 8, 9, 184; *NA,* May 7, 1844; Lee, 63-66.

88. *NA,* May 7, 1844; *PPL,* May 8, 11, 1844; Lee, 71-78.

89. *PPL,* May 9, 1844; Lee, 78-89; Cadwalader notebook, "Suppression of Riots," 8-16, 19, 62-64 (CC); Col. A. R. Pleasonton to Gen. Patterson, May 8, 1844 (CC); Tho. T. Firth to Col. A.R. Pleasonton, May 8, 1844 (CC); Order No. 6, May 9, 1844 (CC).

90. *PPL,* May 9, 11, 1844; Order No. 7, May 10, 1844 (CC).

91. Francis Patrick Kenrick (Bishop) to Brigadier General George Cadwalader, July 29, 1844 (CC). On the behavior of troops, see Brig. Gen. H. Hubbell to Cadwalader, dated "20 minutes to noon" (CC); Col. Pleasonton to Gen. Cadwalader, May 20, 1844, (Cadwalader notebook, 62-64); *PPL,* May 9, 1844; General August Pleasonton Diary, 1838-1844, 422-23 (Historical Society of Pennsylvania); Fisher, 173.

92. On Irish-born American Republicans, see Lee, 54, 71-72. On the Orangemen charge, see "One Who Knows, and a Weaver" to *Spirit of the Times,* Sept. 13, 1848.

93. *PPL,* May 11, 1844. I Moyamensing two leaders of the weavers' union were prominent American Republicans. See Laurie, 269.

94. Robert Smith to James Smith, Aug. 14, 1844 (Record D1828/25, Public Record Office of Northern Ireland).

95. *PPL,* March 13, July 7, 1841; Jan. 21, Feb. 23, 1842. On the fate of the Montgomery Hibernia Greens in Southwark see Capt. John B. Colahan to Gen. Cadwalader, July 11, 1844 (CC). On political collaboration between Ulster Presbyterians and Catholics in Ireland, see Owen Dudley Edwards, *The Sins of Our Fathers: Roots of Conflict in Northern Ireland* (Dublin, 1970), 74-78, 221-24. It is remarkable that religious conflict in Ireland grew more intense in the early 1840s just as it did in America. Still the Orange Lodge of Stewardstown enlisted as a body in the Repeal Association, to the delight of Philadelphia Repealers. *PPI,* Aug. 15, 1843.

96. Fisher, 170-71.

97. Lee, 105.

98. On Kelley, see *NA,* Sept. 16, 1844. On Lippard, see *The Nazarene;* [anon.,] *The Life and Choice Writings of George Lippard* (New York, 1855). For evidence of continuing Rationalist meetings, see notices in *PPI,* Feb. 19, 1842. For the politics of the shoemakers' spokesmen, see Laurie, 253-65. Lee Benson, interestingly, finds Locofocoism in New York most pronounced among voters of old Pennsylvania Scotch-Irish and German stock. Benson. 184.

99. Order No. 19, May 13, 1844 (CC); *PPL,* May 9, 1844; Fisher, 167, 173; Edward Hurst to Alderman Snyder, May 10, 1844 (CC); Grand Jury of the County of Philadelphia Minute Book, Sept. 2-Oct. 23, 1844.

100. Order No. 20, May 14, 1844 (CC); pass slip initialed G.C., May 19, 1844 (CC); Geo. Cadwalader to Gen. Patterson, May 19, 1844 (CC); *PPL,* May 28, 1844; *NA,* June 15, 1844.

101. *PPL,* June 17, 1844. Col. C. J. Jack was charged with embracery for a letter he sent to the Grand Jury. *PPL,* May 30, June 10, 1844.

102. *NA,* June 25, 1844. The quotations are all from Levin editorials in the Philadelphia *Sun,* May 11-13, reproduced in Lee, 104-09.

103. *NA,* July 6, 1844; Pleasonton Diary, 417. For examples of earlier artisans' parades see *American Museum,* IV (July, 1788), 57-78; Frederick Robinson, *An Oration Delivered before the Trades Union of Boston and Vicinity* (Boston, 1834), 32.

104. *PPL,* Oct. 12, 14, 1844. For examples of major party attacks on the American Republicans as instigators of violence, see the speeches of William Seward and William D. Kelley, *NA,* Aug. 10, Sept. 16, 1844. For an excellent summary of the editorial attitudes of Philadelphia newspapers toward American Republicans, see Lee, 103-30.

105. *PPL,* Oct. 12, 14, 1844.

106. Laurie, 266; *NA,* Feb. 22, 1845.

107. Brig. Gen. Geo. Cadwalader to Major General Patterson, July 19, 1844 (draft report in CC); Capt. John B. Colahan to Gen. Cadwalader, July 11, 1844; Colahan to Cadwalader, July 7, 1844 (CC); Pleasonton Diary, 418-24; Col. C.J. Jack to *NA,* Aug. 2, 1844; Geo. Cadwalader to J.R. Ingersoll, May 24, 1844 (CC); Col. Pleasonton to Gen. Cadwalader, May 20, 1844 (Cadwalader notebook, 62-63); Cadwalader notebook, 70-71.

108. *PPL,* May 13, 1844; J.R. Ingersoll to Gen. Cadwalader, May 20, 1844 (CC).

109. Fisher, 174.

110. *United States Gazette,* July 12, 1844; letter of Horace Binney et al., *loc. cit.,* July 11, 1844 (clippings in CC); Fisher, 174.

111. Cadwalader to Patterson, July 19, 1844 (draft report in CC); Lee, 174-77; Fisher, 172-73.

112. Gen. Cadwalader to Select and Common Councils, Sept. 26, 1844 (CC); Ellis P. Oberholtzer, *Philadelphia: A History of the City and Its People* (4 vols., Philadelphia, 1911), II, 496-97.

113. Warner, 152-57; Fisher, 179.

114. See "One Who Knows, and a Weaver" to *Spirit of the Times,* Sept. 13, 1848; Freedley, 254.

115. See David Montgomery, *Beyond Equality: Labor and the Radical Republicans, 1862-1872* (New York, 1967), 42-44 and *passim.*

HERBERT G. GUTMAN

THE OCCUPATIONAL STRUCTURE AND THE ALLEGED SOCIAL MOBILITY OF SLAVES

The following excerpt from Herbert G. Gutman's review of Time on the Cross *by Robert W. Fogel and Stanley L. Engerman is not itself an example of the new economic history so much as it is a devastating critique of what is without doubt the best known and most notorious historical study utilizing the methodology of the new genre. If* Time on the Cross *can be called notorious, it is because of the savage criticisms directed against its methods, assumptions, and conclusions by new economic historians above all, scholars such as Peter Temin, Paul David, and Richard Sutch. Gutman's comments are included here because they are more accessible to the general reader than are those of Fogel and Engerman's fellow cliometricians. As this brief excerpt makes clear,* Time on the Cross *posited an impressive amount of upward mobility on the part of slaves, on the basis of data extracted from private inventories and other primary sources. In demolishing one after another of the assumptions, the misuses of sources, and the statistical errors perpetuated by "F + E," Professor Gutman implicitly reminds us that with the new economic history, as with other things, what finally counts is not the theoretical potentialities of its methodology but how it is used in a particular case; that is, the good sense shown by those using it, the accuracy and the relevancy of the data they employ. As his own study of the black family shows, Gutman himself possesses a wide knowledge of many of the issues dealt with in* Time on the Cross, *a knowledge that perhaps better than anything else safeguards one against uncritical acceptance of exciting conclusions merely because they are based on a new method.*

Herbert G. Gutman, "The World Two Cliometricians Made: A Review Essay of F + E = T/C," *Journal of Negro History,* 50 (January 1975), 111-126. Reprinted by permission of the author.

The Rural Slave Occupational Structure: An Inappropriate Comparison Between the Occupations of Slave Males in 1850 and All Males in 1870

F + E have greatly exaggerated the number of skilled urban slaves and have done the same with the rural slaves and especially those working on plantations, a much more serious error than the misuse of the 1848 Charleston census. Most slaves, after all, did not live in cities. Different kinds of errors, however, have been committed in exaggerating the number of non-field hands and non-common laborers among the rural slaves, errors so severe as to make the entire analysis useless. The errors, incidentally, nearly all bias the evidence "upward" so as to increase greatly the percentage of non-field hands and non-common laborers. These errors then become "evidence" in arguing that enslaved Afro-Americans benefited from the "mobility" opportunities accessible to rural Blacks. Data on the slave rural occupational structure and on how it functioned in the larger incentive and reward system sponsored by profit-hungry owners are scattered throughout the two volumes of T/C but are combined here to do full justice to all the evidence and the arguments flowing form that "evidence." The critical evidence is summarized in pages 38 to 43 of volume one, and these pages rest entirely on Table B.5 in volume two (page 40). The essential data in Table B.5, The Derivation of the Occupational Structure of Adult Male Slaves' on Farms (and Plantations), are printed below:

Slaves Per Plantation	1 Ordinary "Field Hands"	2 Slave Drivers	3 Slave Over-seers	4 Non-Field Craftsmen	5 Non-Field Semi-Skilled	6 Assistant Drivers
1-10	84.6%	0.0%	0.0%	11.9%	3.5%	0.0%
51 or more	70.8%	12.2%	1.6%	11.9%	3.5%	0.0%
All Male Farm Hands	73.7%	6.5%	0.5%	11.9%	3.5%	3.9%

The above table (B.5),—one of the two or three most important in the entire study—appears in volume one in a different form where it is used to compare the adult male occupational distribution among slaves and free persons. That comparison is made in Figure 10, a bar chart entitled "A Comparison between the Occupational Distribution of Adult Male Slaves (about [sic] 1850) and the Occupational Distribuiton of All Adult Males (in 1870)."

It is assumed for the moment that the percentages in Table B.5 are accurate, and Figure Ten—the comparative bar chart—is examined first. (It shall be seen below that there is good reason to deny every percentage reported in Table B.5.) Figure Ten is summarized as follows:

A Comparison between the Occupational Distribution of Adult Male Slaves (about 1850) and the Occupational Distribution of All Adult Males (in 1870)

	Slaves (About 1850)	All Adult Males 1870
Managerial and Professional	7.0%	33.0%
Artisans and Craftsmen	11.9%	11.0%
Semiskilled	7.4%	7.0%
Laborers	73.7%	49.0%

This data can be read in only one way. Although in "about 1850" adult male slaves were mostly laborers and had far less opportunity than free adult males in 1870 to become "managers and professionals," the percentage of adult slaves male artisans and semi-skilled workers hardly differed from the percentage of free males with roughly similar skills. Figure Ten allows F + E to challenge the "conventional wisdom":

While slavery clearly limited the opportunities of bondsmen to acquire skills [sic], the fact remains that over 25 percent of [slave] males were managers, professionals, craftsmen, and semiskilled workers. Thus, the common belief that all slaves were menial laborers is false. Rather than being one undifferentiated mass, slave society produced a complex social hierarchy which was closely related to the occupational pyramid. . . . Neglect of the fact that more than one of every five adult slaves held preferred occupational positions, which involved not only more interesting and less arduous labor but also yielded substantially higher real incomes, has encouraged still another oversight: that is, the failure to recognize the existence of a flexible and exceedingly effective incentive system within the framework of slavery. The notion that slaveowners relied on the lash alone to promote discipline and efficiency is a highly misleading myth. In slave, as in free society, [sic] positive incentives, in the form of material rewards, were a powerful instrument of economic and social control. Although slavery restricted economic and social mobility for blacks, it did not eliminate it.[1]

The utter inappropriateness of a comparison between the slave occupational distribution in "about 1850" and the 1870 adult male occupational distribution is noted first. F + E themselves appear somewhat uncomfortable with their "comparison":

Ideally, we would have preferred to compare the occupational distribution of slaves in 1850 with whites in the same year. However, 1870 is the first year for which an occupational distribution of the labor force is sufficiently detailed to permit a breakdown into the four skill categories used in Figure 10.

Unfortunately, the data needed to separate the occupations of whites from blacks are not available for 1870. This limitation is not as serious as it might seem, since it is unlikely that the occupational distribution of white labor would have been much different from that of all labor in 1870.[2]

Unconvincing and actually quite lame excuses for using the 1870 "data," they also are factually erroneous. Any one familiar with the 1850 and 1860 federal manuscript censuses knows that occupational distributions are available for whites and free blacks. Some historians have used this detailed data; data which can be easily fitted into appropriate "skill categories." One distribution—that for Charleston in 1860—has been used in these pages. It is, furthermore, incorrect to suggest that "the occupational distribution of white labor" hardly differed "from that of all labor in 1870." Manuscript census schedules for that year (or for that matter for 1850, 1860, and 1880) offer decisive evidence in any southern rural or urban area that the occupational distributions of Blacks and whites differed radically. That F + E assert the opposite suggests that such evidence has not been examined in preparing T/C. That, however, is hardly reason to tell readers that this evidence is either inadequately "detailed" or "not available." Comparisons between the white and black occupational structures are badly needed, but not between a distribution in 1870 and one in "about 1850" that counts only slaves. A useful comparison must hold the time factor constant. Important changes in the status of Afro-Americans, after all, took place between 1850 and 1870 which greatly impair any comparison using these two moments in time. The proper comparison is between slaves and non-slaves in either 1850 or 1860. And that comparison should be *regional*—not "national." It will reveal nothing more than the vast occupational differences between slaves and non-slaves.

A small but not insignificant additional caveat about the "skill categories" F + E use for the 1870 occupational distributions is that historians comparing whites and Blacks need much more subtle and complex occupational distinctions than those used in Figure 10. The skill category "managerial and professional," for example, includes "landowning farmers." That is not an appropriate "category"; it homogenizes too many differences. The suggestion that "managers and professionals" were three times more common than "artisans and craftsmen" surely surprises anyone familiar with Gilded Age American society. If F + E are right, that will only be known after we are told how various occupations were assigned to these four "skill" levels. As it stands, the occupational categories used for the 1870 listing are of little analytic use. A Georgia black farmer and former slave who "owned ten acres of land and J. Pierrepont Morgan have been counted together in calculating that "33%" of adult males in 1870 who were either "managers" or "professionals."

The Rural Slave Occupational Structure: Constructing a "Residual Percentage" to Determine the "Number" of Rural Slave Fields Hands and Laborers.

Figure 10 needs to be put aside and so does Table B.5 which is so important to F + E's central thesis. The assertion that "over 25 percent" of slave

males were "managers, professionals, craftsmen, and semi-skilled workers"—
a far-fetched percentage—is the essential statistic from which F + E write
about "a flexible and exceedingly effective incentive system within the framework of slavery." That "percentage"—and no other new empirical data in
T/C—allows them to describe limited but, nevertheless, important slave
"economic and social mobility." F + E break down the rural slave male
occupational structure into six very useful categories: (1) "ordinary 'field
hands'," (2) slave drivers, (3) slave overseers, (4) nonfield craftsmen, (5) nonfield semi-skilled, and (6) assistant drivers. Vexing questions exist about
the percentages assigned each category. Overall, the percentages assigned to
occupational categories two through six are greatly inflated. Column One—
"ordinary 'field hands,' " the most important occupational grouping (73.7%),
is a residual percentage, calculated quite simply. Column One is the difference between the sum of columns two through six subtracted from 100.0%
and, therefore, rests entirely on how the percentages in columns two through
six have been derived. If, for example, the sum of columns two through six
is 10 percent, it means that about 90 percent of rural male slaves were "ordinary 'field hands'." It is important, therefore, to examine closely how the
percentages in columns two through six were assigned. Columns Four ("nonfield craftsmen") and Five ("nonfield semiskilled")—based upon a sample
of probate records—are discussed below. Columns Two (slave drivers), Three
(slave overseers), and Six (slave assistant drivers) are not based upon any
empirical evidence. These are merely speculative and inferential percentages.
They depend upon assumptions, not evidence.

The Rural Slave Occupational Structure: Estimating the Percentage of Slave Drivers on the Basis of a Misused "Conventional Ratio."

Columns Two and Six are wrong: the percentage of adult male drivers
(6.5%) and assistant drivers (3.9%) has been greatly exaggerated. F + E
tell how they arrived at these estimates:

The probate records thus far processed do not provide an adequate basis for determining the proportion of slaves on each plantation who were drivers. Our estimate
of the share of males over 10 who were drivers is based on the conventional ratio of
one driver to every 30 slaves. This ratio was applied to all plantations with 30 or more
slaves. On plantations with 11 to 30 slaves, fractional drivers were computed. . . .
Since virtually all drivers were male, on plantations with 30 or more slaves, one out
of 15, or 6.7 percent of all males, were drivers. . . .[3]

This percentage, however, is based upon an erroneous "conventional ratio."
Citations to studies by Ralph Flanders, Lewis Gray, and William K. Scarborough allow F + E to fix that "conventional ratio." Flanders, however,
fixed that ratio only for the Georgia rice plantations and only for the 1820s.
("In the twenties one driver to every thirty working hands was the customary
division on the seacoast," Flanders wrote.[4] The task system of organizing

labor was more common among rice than cotton planters, and it is too facile to assume that the gang system of labor—common on cotton plantations—had the same "ratio" of drivers as the task system. Flanders' observation, moreover, was not based upon a study of plantation records. He cited two published sources, one describing Georgia plantations in the 1850s. Its author was F. L. Olmsted.) F + E also refer the reader to Scarborough's 1966 study of the plantation overseer. Scarborough wrote:

In general, it is likely that in the rice, sugar, and cotton regions most planters employed an overseer when their total working field hands approached thirty. The figure in the tobacco and grain areas, where slaves were utilized on small farms, was probably closer to twenty. In making generalizations upon this point, it is important to distinguish between the total number of *slaves* and the total number of *field hands*—a distinction usually not made by earlier authorities. (Italics in the original).[5]

In the pages F + E cited, Scarborough never mentioned slave drivers but discussed the ratio of overseers to slaves. F + E apparently failed to see this rather important difference. Moreover, first Flanders and then Scarborough (much more decisively) pointed out that plantation and farm supervisory personnel, slaves among them, were related to the number of field hands (or "working slaves"), not "slaves." Scarborough pointedly criticized earlier historians for failing to make that distinction. F + E repeat the same error in setting a "conventional ratio" ("the conventional ratio of one driver to 30 slaves"), an error that greatly increases the estimated percentage of adult male slave drivers and assistant drivers. Its magnitude can be illustrated by a simple example. "If we define the adult labor force as those who are fifteen years of age or over," write F + E about large plantations, "drivers formed 12.2% of adult males on these large estates." For example, there may be a plantation with 150 slaves, half of them females. Using F + E's estimates, 32 percent were not yet ten years old, and another 13 percent between the ages of 10 and 14. That leaves 44 adult males and 44 adult females. We assume that the plantation had no superannuated slaves, no artisans, no semi-skilled workers, and no domestic servants. All males and females aged 10 years and older labored as field hands. That, of course, greatly exaggerates the size of the group. We also assume that all females and males aged 10 to 14 counted as half-hands. Even if the so-called "conventional ratio" (1:30) is used, this plantation had 2.4 drivers. That means that 5.5 percent—not 12.2 percent—of this plantation's adult males were drivers. The estimate by F + E is slightly more than twice too high. The difference between 12.2 percent and 5.5 percent—that is, 6.7 percent of all adult slave males—needs to be shifted from columns two and six to column one, "ordinary 'field hands'." That increases F + E's residual column one (73.7%) by several percentage points. The percentages are small, but the numbers involved are quite large. If, for example, there were about 800,000 rural adult male slaves in 1850, the F + E estimate puts the number of drivers and assistant drivers at "83,000." The actual number is much closer to 41,600. Adult male slaves competed for far fewer slots as drivers and assistant drivers. That is because there was less "room at the top."[6]

The Rural Slave Occupational Structure: Estimating the Percentage of Slave Overseers on the Basis of Erroneous Assumptions Which Create A Large Class of Unemployed Southern White Overseers in 1860.

According to F + E, slave overseers (Column Three) account for only a tiny percentage of adult black males, 0.05 percent. But a conceptual error has inflated even that small but important percentage. It has long been known that some slaves labored as overseers just as some Blacks owned slaves.[7] But if there were about 800,000 rural adult male slaves in 1850, "some," according to the F + E estimate, becomes 4,000 slave overseers. That *is* a significant number. It, too, is far too large. Let us see why. Using the "Parker-Gallman sample" of cotton plantations, F + E find that surprisingly few had resident white overseers:

Among moderate-size holdings (16 to 50 slaves) less than one out of every six planta-tions used a white overseer. On large slaveholdings (over 50 slaves) only one out of every four owners used white overseers. Even on estates with more than one hun-dred slaves, the proportion with white overseers was just 30 percent, and on many of these the planters were usually in residence.[8]

F + E also report that on 75 percent of large cotton plantations without over-seers "there were no sons or other males who could have assumed the duties of the overseer." An inference of some importance follows: "The conclusion indicated by these findings is startling: On a majority of the large planta-tions, the top nonownership management was black." We leave aside the shift in language from overseer to "top . . . management."[9] Later, in these same pages, F + E describe "a system" which produced "a high-quality class of slave managers." If there were as many as "4,000" slave overseers, it is appropriate to write about them as a class. But this statistic is just an inference. No empirical data exist to support it. David and Temin properly point out:

. . . [Q]uite obviously, there are two unstated premises underlying the inference that the authors draw from these census observations: (1) they assume a large plantation could not be properly run without an overseer in addition to the resident owner, and (2) they suppose the large plantations must have been well run—because they were so efficient. Once the latter presumption is withdrawn, however, this piece of inference unravels along with the rest of the fabric of Fogel and Engerman's argument.[10]

No hard evidence indicates the presence of "a high-quality class of slave managers," and F + E worry unnecessarily about why "so many scholars could have been so badly misled on this issue." In volume II, F + E write:

Some scholars have overestimated the number of free overseers employed in the slave sector because they assumed that all whites listed in the census as overseers worked on slave plantations. However, since the word "overseer" is a synonym for "supervisor," it was used to describe managers in industry as well as in agriculture, on free farms as well as on slave farms, in the North as well as in the South.[11]

How many white overseers were listed in the 1860 federal census? No fewer than 37,883. If their residence patterns had not changed greatly since 1850, about 10 percent lived outside the South. That leaves about 34,000 free white southern overseers in 1860. If we assume (and this surely is greatly exaggerated) that one in three managed free southern farms, free southern factories, and slave southern factories, that still leaves about 22,000 white overseers available to supervise southern plantations. Is that a "large" or a "small" number? Once more, it depends. Scarborough's study helps answer this question. In the sugar, rice, and cotton regions, "most planters employed an overseer when the total number of working field hands approached thirty." In estimating the use of overseers, Scarborough insists, it is essential to "distinguish between the total number of *slaves* and the total number of *field hands.*"

About how many slaves did a planter have to own to hire an overseer? That depends upon the ratio of slave field hands to slaves. About *fifty slaves* were needed to produce a residue of *thirty field hands.*[12] How many slave owners in 1860 owned fifty or more slaves? About ten thousand. After making the above generous allowances, about 23,000 free white *plantation* overseers lived in the South in 1860, more than twice the number needed to manage these large plantations. So far no allowance has been made for slave overseers. It is now assumed that F + E are correct, but that 2,000 (not 4,000 but enough to make for a "class") slaves labored as overseers. That would mean that 8,000 white overseers labored for the owners of fifty or more slaves. And what of the other 13,000? Did they labor for owners of fewer than 50 slaves and, therefore, fewer than 30 field hands? Were many unemployed in 1860? Or had large numbers of whites misrepresented their occupations to the census enumerators? The inference that 0.05 percent of adult male slaves labored as overseers rests on the F + E assumption that "most" planters did not employ white overseers and, therefore, had to employ slave overseers. If that was so, what did most white overseers in the South do for a living in 1860? Rather than answer that question, the 0.05 percent also needs to be put aside. The ante bellum South had slave overseers, but their number was insignificant. They deserve study, but their place in the Southern slave occupational structure and plantation managerial system needs to be measured more carefully first. It is not possible that "within the agricultural sector about 7.0 percent of the [slave] men held managerial posts."[13] That percentage is much closer to 3.0 percent, and nearly all were drivers. There is no reason to ponder over why historians "have been so badly misled on this issue." There is no issue.

The Rural Slave Occupational Structure: The Missing
Rural Southern White and Free Black Artisan.

Columns Four (nonfield craftsmen) and Five (nonfield semiskilled) are based upon much more substantial evidence than columns two, three, and six and come from a little used source, probate records. The authors write:

The share of skilled and semiskilled laborers in nonfield occupations on plantations was determined from a sample of 33 estates, ranging in size from 3 to 98 slaves, retrieved from the probate records. This sample revealed that 15.4 percent of slaves over age 15 were engaged in such occupations. The percentage of skilled slaves was fairly constant over plantation size.[14]

Most of such men were artisans (11.9%). F + E make much of this sample, but there are many difficulties associated with it. We save for the last the biases built into a sample of *artisans* drawn from probate records. "The fact is," F + E write, "that slaves . . . held a large share of the skilled jobs in the countryside."[15] That is not a fact. No one has yet studied the number of rural and village white and free black artisans in the ante bellum South so that estimates ("a large share") of the relative importance of rural slave artisans remain speculative. If slave artisans were as common on plantations as F + E suggest, how, then, is evidence which indicates that profit-hungry planters hired white artisans to do skilled plantation jobs handled? Bennet Barrow, for example, did not own a slave blacksmith. "There is no record," writes his biographer, "of a single major repair job being consigned to a slave."[16] J. C. Sitterson's study of the Bayou LaFourche McCollam plantation reveals that its owners hired carpenters and blacksmiths from the outside—even to build slave cabins.[17] There is, furthermore, some question about the quality of *rural* slave artisanal skills. Did a plantation carpenter or blacksmith share a common skill *level* with an urban slave carpenter and blacksmith? That is a subject which requires much careful study. In 1860, for example, the Charleston slave trader Louis Desaussure advertised the sale of four "good carpenters": Stephen, Scipio, Jack, and Jacob. But Jacob was also described as a "plantation carpenter."[18] What did that distinction mean? There is, finally, some question about the occupations F + E include under the category "non-field semiskilled": "teamsters, coachmen, gardeners, stewards, and house servants." A slave gardener, for example, was usually an elderly male retired from field labor. Is semi-skilled the appropriate skill level for such a person?

The Rural Slave Occupational Structure: Estimating the Size of An
Unknown Sample of Probate Records That Reveal the Distribution
of Slave Artisans.

The general and particular use of probate records by F + E as a source for estimating the percentage of slave artisans in the entire rural male population merits unusually close attention. The size of the sample is considered first: "33 estates, ranging in size form 3 to 98 slaves." That brief summary denies much to the reader: (1) the names of these estates, (2) their location, (3) the dates these probates were filed, (4) whether "3 to 98 slaves" means just adult males or all slaves, including women and children, and (5) the average size of these estates. If it is assumed that the average estate listed fifty slaves, 25 percent of them adult males, the entire sample included about 412 rural slave males, 50 of them "nonfield" craftsmen and 14 of them "nonfield" semi-skilled workers.[20] Can percentages of slave skill distributions based upon so small a sample reveal very much? Is this sample—50 rural artisans and 14 semi-skilled slaves— adequate to indicate the diversity of occupations among rural slaves?

The Rural Slave Occupational Structure: Contrasting Percentages of Black Artisans in a Rural Mississippi County (1880) and in Four Rural Virginia Counties (1865-1866).

The sample size is emphasized because the percentage of artisans found on these 33 estates far exceeds that found in other manuscript records examined by the author and by L. R. Lowrey. It is best to work backward with such data from 1880 to the late ante bellum period. An occupational breakdown which includes all rural Adams, County, Mississippi, adult black males in 1880—nearly three thousand men—shows that 1 percent had artisan skills.[21] Two-thirds of these few artisans were either carpenters or blacksmiths. It might be argued that this is an unfair comparison. It is possible that a large number of rural Adams County slave artisans quit that place upon emancipation. But if that happened, they did not move to nearby Natchez because in 1880 that town had proportionately just as few black artisans as other Southern towns. It also is possible that local white Southern artisans drove the slave artisans from the rural Adams County market following emancipation. Buf if F + E are right and the slaves "held a large share of the skilled jobs in the countryside," that would have been a superhuman task. In 1880, more than 90 percent of rural Adams County residents were Blacks and that county's rural law enforcement officers were still Blacks.

Data closer in time to enslavement reveal a different occupational distribution than in rural Adams County, but one that nevertheless shows a lower percentage of artisans than the F + E sample. Two military population censuses (Montgomery, and York Counties) and two Freedmen's Bureau marriage registers (Goochland and Louisa Counties) indicate that far fewer Virginia slave males had artisanal skills than suggested by the probate sample.[22] These data were collected in either 1865 or 1866. The range of skills among these former slaves was hardly wider than among the rural Adams County Blacks a decade and a half later. Just over half in all four counties were either carpenters or blacksmiths. These censuses and marriage registers were compiled too soon after emancipation to indicate that slave skills had deteriorated—for whatever reasons—as a consequence of emancipation. (The percentage of artisans in York, Goochland, and Louisa Counties is somewhat higher than for the overall black population in 1865-1866 because artisans tended to be older men and these three censuses or marriage registers had too great a number of older men among them to be typical.)

Adult Black Male Occupational Distribution Rural Adams County, Mississippi, 1880

Occupation	Percent
Farmer: Owns Land	6%
Tenant, Sharecropper, Farm Laborer	70%
Non-Farm Laborer	22%
ARTISAN	1%
High Status Occupation	1%
N	2976

Artisans as a Percent of All Adult Males Virginia Counties, 1865-1866

County	Number of Adult Males	Percent Of Artisans
Montgomery County Census	610	6.7%
York County Census	929	8.0%
Goochland County Marriage Register	719	8.3%
Louisa County Marriage Register	1232	8.1%

The Slave Occupational Structure: The Occupations of 20,576 Union Army Kentucky Black Soldiers Contrasted With the F + E Estimates: A "Test of the F + E "Thesis."

The third set of comparative statistics—and by far the most convincing—comes from Kentucky Union Army recruitment records and have been collected by Leslie Rowland Lowrey as part of her on-going major study of Kentucky Blacks during the Civil War. She generously has allowed me to use them in this essay. The information is in Union Army Company Descriptive Rolls (or, when lacking, in Regimental Descriptive Rolls) filed in the National Archives in Record Group 94, Records of the Adjutant General's Office. These military records contain the most complete information yet available on slave occupations. By the Civil War's end, about half (a conservative estimate) of Kentucky's adult male slaves were in the Union Army. They came from all parts of the state. Lowrey has examined records for

20,905 black Kentucky soldiers. Occupations are listed for all but 329 of these men (98.4%).[23] This evidence shows an opposite distribution of slave skills from the one F + E constructed by sampling a few probate records.[24] Of the 20,576 men with listed occupations, all but 527—that is, 97.4 percent—gave as their occupations "farmer" and "laborer." The occupational distribution detailed in the following table also includes for comparison the distribution drawn by F + E primarily from the sampled probate records. As elsewhere, Kentucky slave carpenters and blacksmiths predominated (three out of five) among the artisans.

Occupational Distribution of Kentucky Black Union Army Soldiers Compared to the Occupational Structure of Adult Male Slaves on Farms (Table B.) in Time on the Cross.

| Occupation | Kentucky Black Solders | | F + E |
	Number	Percent	Percent in T/C
Farmer and Laborer	20,039	97.44%	73.7%
Artisan	331	1.61%	11.9%
Servant	99	.48%	
Drayman, Waggoner, Teamster	86	.42%	7.4%
High Status**	11	.05%	7.0%
Total	20,576	100.0%	100.0%

**Among these eleven were five clergymen and three clerks.

(Shoemakers made up the third most common craft, but only twenty-one shoemakers were listed.) The differences in these two occupational distributions are not slight. There is no possible way to reconcile these two sets of data.

It is possible, of course, that slaves with high skill levels—artisans and managers (drivers and overseers) were underrepresented among those Kentucky Blacks who took up arms against the Confederacy. Such men may have retained a loyalty to their owners, a reward their owners gained by allowing them to hold privileged slave status. But if that explains why nearly all black Kentucky soldiers were "farmers" and laborers, such evidence severely damages another proposition put forth in T/C:

While the reward structure created much more room for upward mobility within the slave system than is usually supposed, the scope of opportunity should not be exaggerated. The highest levels of attainment were irrevocably foreclosed to slaves. The entreprenurial talent obviously possessed by bondsmen such as Aham could not be used to catapult them into the stewardship [sic] of great businesses as long as they remained slaves.[25] No slave, regardless of his gifts, could aspire to political position. No man of letters—there were slaves who acquired considerable erudition—

could ever hold an appointment in the faculty of a southern university as long as he was a bondsman. The entreprenurial genius had to settle for lingering in the shadow of the master on whose protection he was dependent. The man of letters could go no further than the position of tutor to the children of a benevolent and enlightened planter. It was on the talented, the upper crust of slave society, that [the?] deprivations of the peculiar institution hung most heavy [sic]. This, perhaps, explains why it was that the first to flee to northern lines as Yankee advances corroded the Rebel positions were not ordinary field hands, but the drivers and the artisans.[26]

F + E make a similar point in volume two. "Slavery," they suggest, "weighed most heavily on the talented."[27] F + E present no evidence that the "first to flee to northern lines" were "the drivers and the artisans." There is none. And the occupations of Kentucky black soldiers—no matter how interpreted—severely damage one or another of the central themes that flow through T/C. If the Kentucky military occupational distribution is an accurate reflection of the Kentucky slave occupational distribution, that is good reason to doubt that slaves worked "hard" to rise within the slave occupational structure. It is known now how little "room" there was "at the top." The "scope of opportunity" was indeed narrow. There was not much economic "pay-off" in working "hard." But if the Kentucky military occupational distribution under-represented the more privileged slaves ("the drivers and the artisans") because they remained loyal to their masters and would not join the Union Army (the Emancipation Proclamation was issued prior to the time Kentucky Blacks could join the army), then there is no way to argue that the "deprivations of the peculiar institution hung most heavy [sic]" on "the talented, the upper crust of slave society." If that was so, the "upper crust" should have been over-represented in the military occupational structure. (Unless one is prepared to argue that joining the Union Army after 1863 was not an expression of profound discontent by an Afro-American slave.) F + E cannot have it both ways.

Notes

1. T/C, I, pp. 40-41.

2. *Ibid.,* II, p. 37.

3. *Ibid.,* II, p. 39.

4. Flanders, *Plantation Slavery in Georgia,* p. 147.

5. W. K. Scarborough, *The Overseer: Plantation Management in the Old South* (1966), pp. 8-9.

6. If the crude assumption in this example is dropped (that all adult men and women were field hands) and we assume that F + E's estimates on the percentage of artisans (11.9%), semi-skilled hands (3.5%), and female field hands (80% of all adult women) are accurate and that about 5% of adult men and women were too old to do field labor, it turns out again using the conventional 1:30 "ratio" that the plantation had 1.95 drivers. That drops even further the percentage of adult male slaves laboring as drivers and assistant drivers. It does down from 12.2 percent to 4.4 percent, a decline of nearly two-thirds. Assuming 800,000 adult male slaves, it drops from 83,000 to 35,200.

7. See, for example, Robert Starobin, "Privileged Bondsmen and the Process of Accommodation: the Role of the Houseservants and Drivers as Seen in Their Own Letters," *Journal of Social History,* V (Fall 1971), pp. 59-65.

8. T/C, I, pp. 200-201, pp. 210-212.

9. T/C, *ibid.*

10. David and Temin, "Slavery: The Progressive Institution,"

11. T/C, II, p. 39, pp. 151-152.

12. This estimate is arrived at as follows. It is assumed that male and female slaves were equal in number, that 32% (the F + E estimate) were under ten years of age, that another 13% (the F + E estimate) were 10 to 14 years of age, that 5% were too old to work in the fields, that 80% of the remaining women (the F + E estimate) labored in the fields, and 85% of the remaining males (the F + E estimate making allowance for artisans, semi-skilled workers, and servants) labored as field hands. On a fifty-slave plantation, that leaves about *27 full field hands.* I have counted women and youths 10 to 14 years as full field hands because, as shall soon be seen, the F + E estimate that 15.4% of adult male slaves labored as either artisans or semi-skilled workers is far too high.

13. T/C, I, p. 39.

14. T/C, II, p. 37.

15. T/C, I, p. 38.

16. Davis, ed., *Flordia Parishes,* p. 35.

17. J. C. Sitterson, "The McCollams: A Planter Family . . .," *Journal of Southern History,* VI (August 1940), p. 350.

18. The advertisement is printed in Bancroft, *Slave Trading in the Old South.*

19. T/C, I, p. 39.

20. I have multiplied 412 by F + E's estimates to get the approximate number of artisans (11.9%) and semiskilled workers (3.5%).

21. This Adams County data are not a sample. It include all adult Blacks listed in the pages of the 1880 federal manuscript census.

22. The 1865-1866 data draw from unpublished records in the Freedmen's Bureau and are further analyzed in my forthcoming study, chapter three.

23. One hundred fourteen men did not have an occupation next to their names, and another 215 were simply described as "slaves."

24. The rolls make no distinction between slaves and free blacks, but the majority listed were slaves. Regiments (and the companies therein) were used for those units known by Lowrey to have been recruited primarily in Kentucky. The descriptive rolls do not give a place of residence, but Lowrey assumed that recruitment at a Kentucky point indicated that the slave or free black had been a Kentucky resident in 1860. Because her work focuses on Kentucky blacks, Lowrey correctly counted only volunteers and drafted men at Kentucky points. No substitutes, wherever they entered the army, were counted. To be acceptable as a substitute, a black had to be ineligible for the Kentucky draft. That meant he had to be under the age of 21 (17 to 20 years old) or from another state which had no draft (that is, a state in rebellion). Large numbers of substitutes were contraband blacks from the Confederate states so that no substitutes were counted in this tally. The resultant undercount of 17-20-year-olds biases the occupational distribution of the *soldiers* upward. Men under 20 years old were less likely to have skills than men over 20 years of age. That means that the percentage of unskilled Kentucky soldiers was greater than that given in the table printed in this text.

When the final calculations appear in Lowrey's completed work, they will be more refined, but the essential outline sketched in these pages should not change much.

This writer has tried without success to think of a reason why Kentucky slaves and free blacks would have misrepresented their occupations to Union Army officers. Some men may have inflated their skills in order to advance more rapidly in the military service. But there is no reason why a slave carpenter would have called himself a slave laborer. It is possible, however, that the recruitment and other officers carelessly listed black occupations.

Lowrey examined records for the following regiments: U.S. Colored Infantry 100, 101, 107, 108, 109, 114, 115, 116, 117, 118, 119, 120, 121, 122, 123, 124, 125; U.S. Cavalry 4 and 5; and U.S. Heavy Artillery 4, 12, and 13. The records for all except four of these regiments appear complete.

25. "The highest annual figure we have been able to uncover for extra earnings by a field hand and in a single year is $309. Aham, the Alabama slave whose sale of peaches, apples, and cotton yielded this sum, had accumulated enough capital over the years so that in 1860, he held notes on loans totaling over $2,400." This example, its origin never given, appears in the paragraph preceding the one quoted in this text.

26. T/C, I, pp. 152-153.

27. T/C, II, p. 118. The evidence cited is Theodore Hershberg's study of a small number of former slaves living in ante bellum Philadelphia. It suggests that in 1838, and again in 1847, the ex-slaves had more wealth than those Philadelphia Afro-Americans born in the North. But Hershberg's study has one serious limitation so far as supporting this F + E argument. Nothing at all is known about the prior occupational status of these former slaves. What if most had been field hands and common slave laborers prior to making it to Philadelphia?

ROBERT W. FOGEL

HOW IMPORTANT WERE RAILROADS TO THE ANTEBELLUM ECONOMY?

Robert W. Fogel's study of American railroads is an interesting example of the new economic history. Analytical rather than descriptive, its purpose was to test the validity of Walt W. Rostow's thesis that railroads played a vital and indispensable part in the "takeoff" stage that supposedly transformed the American economy in the two decades after 1843. Relying on comprehensive aggregate data and statistical samples rather than the partial and not necessarily representative evidence that had been the stock in trade of earlier economic historians, Fogel devised an ingenious approach for testing the takeoff thesis. In a sense he created a nineteenth-century America without railroads and sought to discover how goods and persons would have been moved in their absence, as well as how the products consumed in the manufacture of railroads and their rolling stock would have been otherwise used in an economic world without the "iron horse." In the section that follows Fogel attempts to show that, in contradiction to Rostow's assertion, the growth of the antebellum iron, coal, and lumber industries did not depend heavily on the consumption by railroads of their products. It should be kept in mind that the data underlying Fogel's argument can be read and interpreted differently than they are by him.

From Robert William Fogel, *Railroads and American Economic Growth: Essays in American Econometric History* (Johns Hopkins University Press, 1964), 129-146. Copyright © 1964, by Johns Hopkins University Press.

Railroads and the Leading Sectors Thesis

One of the most interesting aspects of [Walt W.] Rostow's stages-of-growth theory is the concept of leading sectors and particularly the proposition that the American "take-off" was triggered by the railroad, the rapid expansion of which generated a series of "secondary" growth sectors. "The development of railways," Rostow writes, "has led on to the development of modern coal, iron and engineering industries. In many countries the growth of modern basic industrial sectors can be traced in the most direct way to the requirements for building and, especially, for maintaining substantial railway systems."[1]

Is there, in the American case, an actual historical counterpart to Rostow's generalization? To what extent can the rapid growth of American manufacturing and the concomitant increase in the manufacturing share of commodity output during the "take-off" years be attributed to the railroad's consumption of manufactured goods? In answering these questions data bearing on five industries will be examined. The industries are coal, iron, machinery (the three emphasized by Rostow), transportation equipment, and lumber.[2]

Some objection might be raised to so limited a focus. For while it is true that railroads did not directly consume large amounts of the output of other industries, Rostow has suggested that the repercussions of the consumption of the primary growth sector may "have to be tracked many stages back into the economy."[3] It might be argued that if such a line of analysis were followed, the number of industries in which a substantial proportion of output was indirectly used for railroad construction would exceed the five selected. However, an attempt to find the total demand for goods required by a given industry by summing the successive increments of demand generated at receding stages of the production results in series with terms which rapidly approach zero. Suppose, for example, that railroads did not directly consume chemicals but that the iron industry consumed 10 per cent of the output of the chemical industry. Suppose also that railroads purchased 10 per cent of the output of the iron industry. Then the error involved in neglecting the second stage demand for chemicals—the output of chemicals consumed in the production of railroad iron—would amount to 1 per cent of chemical production. Quite clearly, if none of the other industries from which the railroads made large direct purchases used significant amounts of chemicals, the error involved in neglecting the tertiary and subsequent stages of demand would be negligible. Thus, if it is found that the railroad's direct and second stage demand for the output of given industries was small, it is unlikely that the track-back suggested by Rostow would significantly alter the relevant conclusions.

THE IRON INDUSTRY

No industry in nineteenth-century America is said to have leaned more heavily on railroads as a market than the iron industry. This dependency has been referred to by many historians. However, the fact that 1,000,000 tons of rails were produced in 1872 (about 35 per cent of the weight of pig iron production) and that 1,461,000 tons of steel rails (75 per cent of all rolled steel) were turned out in 1882 is irrelevant here.[4] The issue posed by the designation of the railroad as a "primary growth sector" cannot be resolved by citing, as Rostow does, evidence which suggests that rails may have dominated iron production in the post-Civil War era.[5] The point at issue is the share of the output of the iron industry consumed by railroads between 1843 and 1860; it is the extent to which the growth of the iron industry *during the "take-off" years* can be attributed to railroads.

Column 1 of Table 1 reveals that amount of domestic crude iron consumed in the production of the final products of the domestic iron industry more than trebled between 1840 and 1860, although this growth was uneven. After an initial decline, consumption of domestic crude iron rose steadily from 1842 through 1847, reaching a peak of nearly 900,000 tons in the latter year. The increase in the five-year period was over 230 per cent. Following 1847, the industry's consumption of domestic crude iron declined steadily until 1851 when it stood at 58 per cent of the previous peak. The industry recovered during the next two years and consumption hovered at about 900,000 tons from 1853 through 1858. The final two years of the period show a new rise of about 30 per cent over the level prevailing in 1858.

If the 20 years from 1840 through 1859 are broken into four quinquennia, corresponding to Gallman's time periods, one finds that the second quinquennium was the most important with respect to the rise in crude iron consumption (see Table 1). The average annual consumption of that quinquennium was 775,000 tons, 99 per cent above the average of the previous five years. Average consumption in the third quinquennium fell slightly below, and in the fourth quinquennium it rose somewhat above, the level achieved in the second one. Thus during the years 1845-49 the iron industry appears to have ascended a plateau on which it remained for the most of the rest of the "take-off" years.

Table 1 also reveals that the amount of domestic crude iron consumed by domestic firms in manufacturing the iron products used in the construction and maintenance of railroads constituted only a minor part of total consumption. Far from dominating the iron industry, crude iron used in the domestic production of rails averages less than 12 per cent of the total over the 21-year period. All the other forms of iron used by railroads raised the share to an average of only 17 per cent.[6] While it is true that in the final six years of the period the railroad's share rose to 25.4 per cent, more sig-

Table 1. The Consumption of Domestic Iron by Railroads, 1849-1860 (in thousands of net tons)

	1	2	3	4	5	6	7	8
	Domestic crude iron consumed by the domestic iron industry	Domestic crude iron used for the domestic production of rails	Domestic crude iron used in rail fastening	Domestic crude iron used in locomotives	Domestic crude iron used in freight, passenger and baggage cars	Railroad consumption of domestic crude iron sum of Cols. 2, 3, 4, 5	Share of domestic crude iron consumed by iron industry going into rails Col. 2 ÷ Col. 1	Share of domestic crude iron consumed by the iron industry going into all railroad construction and maintenance Col. 6 ÷ Col. 1
1. 1840	394	5	6	1	5	17	1.3	4.3
2. 1841	317	20	7	0	4	31	6.3	9.8
3. 1842	267	29	7	1	8	45	10.9	16.9
4. 1843	412	13	5	1	7	26	3.2	6.3
5. 1844	558	9	4	2	13	28	1.6	5.0
6. 1845	661	31	6	2	16	55	4.7	8.3
7. 1846	790	48	7	4	25	84	6.1	10.6
8. 1847	881	58	8	4	23	93	6.6	10.6
9. 1848	809	54	10	2	10	76	6.7	9.4
10. 1849	733	42	13	3	15	73	5.7	10.0
11. 1850	574	44	15	3	18	80	7.7	13.9
12. 1851	502	47	16	5	24	92	9.4	18.3
13. 1852	651	58	20	5	24	107	8.9	16.4
14. 1853	864	84	23	6	31	144	9.7	16.7
15. 1854	802	102	23	7	31	163	12.7	20.3
16. 1855	869	143	22	5	24	194	16.5	22.3
17. 1856	989	196	28	7	33	264	19.8	26.7
18. 1857	932	172	27	9	38	246	18.5	26.4
19. 1858	868	168	27	4	18	217	19.4	25.0
20. 1859	1,036	198	24	10	38	270	19.1	26.1
21. 1860	1,146	206	25	12	46	289	18.0	25.2
				Period Averages				
22. 1840-44	390	15	6	1	7	29	3.8	7.4
23. 1845-49	775	47	9	3	18	76	6.1	9.8

24. 1850-54	679	67	19	5	26	117	9.9	17.2
25. 1855-59	939	175	26	7	30	238	18.6	25.3
26. 1855-60	973	181	26	8	33	247	18.6	25.4
27. 1840-49	582	31	7	2	13	53	5.3	9.1
28. 1850-59	809	121	23	6	28	178	15.0	22.0
29. 1850-60	839	129	23	7	30	188	15.4	22.4
30. 1840-60	717	82	15	4	21	124	11.4	17.3

Sources and Notes:

Column 3. According to data in Henry S. Tanner, *A Description of the Canals and Railroads of the United States* (New York, 1840), fastenings on roads with heavy plate or edge rails averaged 18.36 net tons per track-mile in 1840. Those laid with light plate averaged 3.52 tons. In 1840 a little less than 54 per cent of roads were laid with light plate and the rest were laid with heavy rails (L. Klein, "Railroads in the United States," *Journal of the Franklin Institute*, Vol. 30 [1840], pp. 89-102, 227-30, 301-7). These proportions indicate that the average weight of fastenings on roads in 1840 was 10.8 tons per track-mile. Bell put the average weight of fastenings in the United States in the post-Civil War period at 6.4 tons per track-mile (Sir I. Lowthian Bell, *The Iron Trade of the United Kingdom Compared with That of the Other Chief Iron-Making Nations* [London, 1886], p. 143).

It was assumed that the average weight of fastenings declined linearly from 10.8 tons in 1840 to 6.5 tons per track-mile in 1860. The weight of fastenings was multiplied by 1.125 to obtain a crude iron equivalent on the assumption that half of the fastenings were made from wrought iron and half from cast iron.

The number of track-miles laid each year was taken from Table 5.8 in original book.

Track-miles multiplied by the average amount of crude iron required for a track-mile of fastenings yielded the total crude iron requirement in each year. The amount of domestically produced crude iron consumed in fastenings was found by multiplying the entries in the last series by the corresponding entries for the share of crude iron consumed by the domestic iron industry that was domestically produced.

Column 4. The number of locomotives produced in each year was taken to be equal to the number produced by the Baldwin Locomotive Works multiplied by the ratio of national production in the census year of 1859-60 to a weighted average of the Baldwin production in 1859 and 1860. *Eighth Census, Manufacturing*, p. clxxxix; *History of the Baldwin Locomotive Works, 1831-1923* (n.p., n.p., n.d.), p. 182.

The average weight of locomotives was assumed to have increased linearly from 12 to 27 tons over 1840-60 on the basis of the weights given in *ibid*, pp. 24, 35; cf. Ringwalt, *Development, passim*; *Tenth Census, Manufacturing*, pp. 661-662; and Stephen Roper, *Handbook of the Locomotive* (Philadelphia, 1874), p. 126.

In 1880, 90 per cent of a locomotive by weight was iron (*Tenth Census of Manufacturing*, p. 662). This factor was applied to all the years from 1840-60. The proportion of iron in locomotives was probably less during the ante-bellum era, especially during the earlier years when considerable amounts of lumber were still used in the construction of the locomotive frame.

Table 1 Continued

The total weight of locomotives produced in a given year multiplied by 1.0125 (on the assumption that half of the iron in locomotives was wrought and half was cast) yielded the amount of crude iron required for locomotives. This was dividing between domestically produced crude and imported crude in proportion to the share of total crude iron consumed by the domestic iron industry that was domestically produced in the corresponding years.

Column 5. Data contained in Ringwalt, *Development*, p. 338, and *Eighth Census, Manufacturing*, p. clxxxv, indicate that the amount of iron in the "first class," eight-wheeled freight car of 1886 was approximately 8,000 pounds, of which 6,500 pounds was in the trucks (including the wheels). Cast iron represented about 74 per cent of the total; the remainder was primarily wrought iron. Hence the indicated amount of crude iron per car is 4.262 net tons.

A sample of 29 roads drawn from H. V. Poor, *History of Railroads and Canals of the United States of America* (New York, 1860), revealed that the average number of freight cars per locomotive in 1859 was 15.92. However, since the ratio increased over time, one would expect dF/dL to be larger than F/L (where F = the number of freight cars and L = the number of locomotives). A linear regression was fitted to the sample data. The first derivative of the equation was $dF/dL = 23.09$. The number of freight cars constructed each year was estimated by multiplying the estimated number of locomotives produced each year by 23.09. (This value of dF/dL is very close to the first derivative of a second degree equation forced through the origin and fitted to data in *Poor's Manual of Railroads* on the aggregate number of freight cars and locomotives in the United States over the years 1871-95. In this case $dF/dL = 23.82 + 0.00056 2L$. Since L varied between 56 and 517 over the years 1840-60, dF/dL only varied between 23.85 and 24.11.)

The tons of crude iron required for freight cars in each year was thus the estimated number of cars produced each year multiplied by 4.262 net tons. The total requirement was again divided between domestically produced crude and imported crude in proportion to the share of total crude iron consumed by the domestic iron industry was domestically produced in each year.

The procedure followed in estimating the domestic crude iron consumed in passenger and baggage cars was similar to that employed for freight cars. According to data cited by Ringwalt, (*Development*, pp. 338-39), there were 9,449 pounds of iron in the standard passenger car built for the Pennsylvania Railroad in 1876. This figure was turned into a crude iron equivalent by multiplying it by 1.091. The conversion factor was obtained in the manner indicated for freight cars. The resulting figure, 5,155 net tons per passenger (or baggage) car, probably overstates the average amount of crude iron consumed for such cars during 1840-60. Passenger cars were generally larger and used more iron after the Civil War than before it. However the data needed for an adjustment have not been located.

The number of passenger and baggage cars was obtained in the manner indicated for freight cars, the relevant derivative being $dP/dL = 1.673$, where P stands for passenger and baggage cars. (The derivative obtained by fitting a second degree equation forced through the origin to data on national totals over the years 1871-95 as contained in *Poor's Manual* was $dP/dL = 0.9214 + 0.0000026L$. Consequently, the use of 1.673 as the marginal rate may lead to an over-statement of the production of passenger and baggage cars.)

Column 7. This is index I.

Lines may not add across because of rounding.

nificant for this discussion is the fact that during the quinquennium ending in 1849, railroad consumption of domestic crude iron was just 10 per cent of the total. Even if there had been no production of rails or railroad equipment whatsoever, the domestic crude iron consumed by the iron industry would have reached an average of 700,000 tons in the second quinquennium. The rise over the previous quinquennium would still have been 338,000 tons— an increase of 94 per cent as opposed to the 99 per cent rise that took place with the railroads. Clearly railroad consumption of iron had little effect on the rate of growth of the industry during the crucial first decade of Rostow's "take-off" period; the new high level of production attained by the iron industry during 1845-49 did not depend on the railroad market.

The strongest statement that can be made in support of Rostow's thesis is that the demand for railroad iron played an increasingly important role during the fifties in maintaining the *previous* level of production when the demand for other items sagged. Otherwise one could just as well argue that nails rather than rails triggered the 1845-49 leap in iron production. Indeed, in 1849 the domestic production of nails probably exceeded that of rails by over 100 per cent.[7] Whatever role rail production might have played in growth of the iron and steel industry during the seventies and eighties, the construction and maintenance of railroads in the "take-off" did more to build up the British than the American industry. From 1840 through 1860 only 40 per cent of the rails required by the United States were supplied by domestic industry. The rest of the demand was satisfied in the English Market.[8]

COAL

The direct demand for coal by the railroad during the two decades ending in 1860 was negligible. Coal had been used to fire the vertical boilers of some of the early engines, but first attempts to use mineral fuel on locomotives with horizontal boilers failed due to the serious damage caused by "the destructive effects of a coal fire." While the pace of experimentation increased during the fifties, few coal burners were in regular service at the end of the decade.[9] In later decades the switch to coal became more rapid. By 1921 locomotives consumed about one-quarter of the annual output of coal.[10] But this was more than half a century after the close of the "take-off." Wood was the fuel that powered the land leviathan prior to 1860.

If the analysis is pushed back to the second stage of demand, the picture changes slightly. The iron industry was a major consumer of coal during the "take-off" years. Approximately 2.5 tons of coal were required to produce 1 ton of pig iron and another 2.5 tons were needed to turn the crude metal into a rail.[11] Over the 21 years from 1840 through 1860, some 1,372,000 tons of pig iron were transformed into rails.[12] At the specified rate, this transformation required 6,860,000 tons of coal. Another 579,000 tons of rails

Table 2. The Consumption of Lumber by Railroads, 1840-1860 (in thousands of feet B.M.)

	1	2	3	4	5
	Total lumber production	Wood used for ties	Ties supplied by mills Col. 2 × 07683	Lumber consumed by cars	Total mill-produced lumber consumed by railroads Col. 3 + Col. 4
1. 1840	1,982,800	79,734	6,126	6,945	13,071
2. 1841	2,361,600	105,377	8,096	6,200	14,296
3. 1842	2,740,400	87,899	6,753	10,790	17,543
4, 1843	3,119,200	56,005	4,304	9,292	13,596
5. 1844	3,498,000	56,516	4,342	16,977	21,319
6. 1845	3,876,800	73,738	5,665	20,823	26,488
7. 1846	4,255,600	87,516	6,724	32,473	39,197
8. 1847	4,634,400	114,945	8,831	30,125	38,956
9. 1848	5,013,200	157,428	12,095	15,491	27,586
10. 1849	5,392,000	230,273	17,692	23,181	40,873
11. 1850	5,655,700	270,969	20,819	28,627	49,446
12. 1851	5,919,400	299,291	22,995	38,672	61,667
13. 1852	6,183,100	376,729	28,944	37,799	66,743
14. 1853	6,466,800	417,298	32,061	46,362	78,423
15. 1854	6,710,500	446,257	34,286	47,849	82,135
16. 1855	6,974,200	417,043	32,041	36,314	68,355
17. 1856	7,237,900	519,230	39,892	45,617	85,509
18. 1857	7,501,600	500.987	38,491	50,948	89,439
19. 1858	7,765,300	528,926	40,637	25,540	66,177
20. 1859	8,029,000	498,308	38,285	54,036	92,321
21. 1860	8,501,654	519,358	39,902	64,085	103,987
22. Totals	113,799,154	5,843,827	448,981	648,146	1,097,127

23. Total Col. 2 + total of Col. 4 as a per cent of
  (total of Col. 1 + total of Col. 2) 5.426
24. Total of Col. 3 as a per cent of total of Col. 1 .... 0.395
25. Total of Col. 4 as a per cent of total of Col. 1 .... 0.570
26. Total of Col. 5 as a per cent of total of Col. 1 .... 0.964

Sources and Notes:
  Column 1. The census year figures are taken from U.S.D.A., *Yearbook of Agriculture, 1933* (Washington, 1933), p. 748. The other entries are linear interpolations.
  Column 2. According to Tratman, the largest ties required 127,575 board feet per mile of

were rerolled and, at a rate of 2.5 tons of fuel per ton of reworked rail, rerolling required an additional 1,448,000 tons of coal.[13] The manufacture of the iron used in fastenings, locomotives, and cars involved still another 4,335,000 tons of coal.[14] All told, railroads consumed 12,643,000 tons of coal from 1840-60 through purchases of rail and other products made of iron. Over the same period total coal production was 211,680,000 tons.[15] Thus coal consumed by railroads through consumption of iron products represented only 5.97 per cent of the coal produced during the "take-off." Even this low figure is biased upwards, since the calculation is based on the assumption that all pig iron was produced with coal. Yet as late as 1860, 30 per cent of domestic pig iron still spilled from charcoal furnaces.[16]

LUMBER

As a consumer of goods, railroads exercised even less influence on the development of the modern lumber industry than on the expansion of coal production—this despite the huge quantities of wood used by the railroads as fuel and in the construction of track. The paradox is partly explained by the fact that wood used as fuel in the fire boxes of railroad engines was not lumber. Chopping trees into fire wood was as distinct from the manufacture of boards and planks as the picking of cotton was from the manufacture of cloth. While the railroad's fuel requirements served to swell the output of forest products, it did not provide a market for the output of the nation's saw and planing mills.

A similar consideration is involved in connection with the railroad's consumption of cross ties. According to E. E. R. Tratman, the author of the

Table 2 Continued

track (E. E. Russel Tratman, *Railway Track and Track Work* [3rd ed.; New York, 1909], pp. 32, 40). . . .

Column 3. *Census of Manufactures, 1890,* Part III, p. 620; *Historical Statistics* (1960), p. 427; Tratman, *Railway Track,* p. 32. According to Tratman, about 2,700 ties were required for each new track mile constructed and replacements ran at the rate of about 250 ties for each mile of old track. At the end of 1888 there were 191,376 miles of track in existence. Hence at Tratman's rate, about 47,844,000 ties were required for replacements during the census year of 1889. Approximately 8,775 miles of new track wre built in the census year (this figure is a weighted average of construction in 1889 and in 1890), requiring another 23,693,000 ties, for a total of 71,537,000 ties. However, mills produced only 5,496,174 ties or 0.07683 of the requirement. The column entries were obtained by multiplying the entries in Column 2 by the last figure. This procedure overstates the purchases from mills during the "take-off" years because the size of ties, the number used per mile of track, and probably also the proportion purchased from mills, increased over time.

Column 4. According to Ringwalt, *Development,* pp. 338-339, there were 4,474 feet of lumber in a "first class," 1886 freight car and 12,340 feet in the 1876 passenger cars built by the Pennsylvania Railroad. These figures, multiplied by the corresponding series on passenger and freight cars described in the notes to Table 1, yielded the desired estimates of lumber consumed in the construction of cars. Since cars were generally smaller during 1840-60 than in 1876 or 1886, the resulting series probably overstates lumber consumption.

leading manual on track construction at the turn of the twentieth century, the largest ties then in general use were 7x9 inches by 9 feet. Approximately 2,700 ties were laid per mile of track.[17] Hence, railroads required a maximum of 127,575 feet of wood, board measure, for each mile of track. Taking account of both the ties needed for new construction and for replacement, Column 2 of Table 2 indicates that railroads required a total of 5,844,000,000 feet B.M. in ties over the 21 years from 1840 through 1860. Only a small proportion, however, of this amount was supplied by lumber mills. Throughout the nineteenth century railroad men believed that ties hewed by axe would resist decay better than sawed ties.[18] Thus as late as 1889, only 7.68 per cent of all ties were produced by lumber mills.[19] Applying this ratio to the 1840-60 output of ties, one finds that, at most, lumber mills supplied 449,000,000 feet B.M. during the 21-year period. This was less than one-half of 1 per cent of all lumber production. When the lumber required for car construction is included, the figure rises by half a percentage point to 0.96 per cent. Indeed, even if all the ties that were required by the railroad were arbitrarily lumped into the category of mill products, railroad consumption of lumber over the 21-year period would still have constituted only 5.43 per cent of the estimated total production. The relatively modest position of railroads in the market for lumber products emphasizes the large volume of the consumption of lumber by other sectors of the economy.

TRANSPORTATION EQUIPMENT

Perhaps the most surprising aspect of the impact of railroad construction and maintenance on the markets of manufacturing industries is the relatively small share of the output of the transportation equipment industry accounted for by railroads. Historians have stressed the rapid progress of the railroad during the decade of the fifties. From 1850 through 1860 some 26,300 miles of new track were laid. During the same time about 3,800 locomotives, 6,400 passenger and baggage cars, and 88,600 freight cars were constructed.[20] Yet value added in the construction of railroad equipment in 1859 was only $12,000,000 or 25.4 per cent of value added by all transportation equipment (see Table 3). During the the years leading up to the Civil War, the rapid progress of the railroad captured the American mind. But popular reaction is not always a sound basis for evaluating the strategic significance of economic events. In 1859 the dollar value of the output of vehicles drawn by animals was still almost twice as great as the output of equipment for the celebrated iron horse.

MACHINERY (OTHER THAN TRANSPORTATION EQUIPMENT)

The relatively small share of the output of the iron, coal, lumber, and transportation equipment industries accounted for by the railroad pur-

Table 3. Value Added in 1859 by Industries Supplying Transportation Equipment for Steam Railroads

Industry	Value added
1. Locomotive engines and repairing	$ 2,454,946
2. Springs	1,024,142
3. Cars, construction and repairing by firms other than steam railroads	2,461,269
4. Cars, construction and repairing by steam railroads	5,371,087
5. Car wheels	753,150
6. Axles	86,372
7. Car brakes	7,800
8. Car linings	12,193
9. Total	12,170,959
10. Value added by all transportation equipment in 1859	47,827,000
11. Line 9 as a per cent of line 10	25.4

Sources and Notes:

All lines except lines 4 and 10 were taken directly from the *Census of Manufacturing, 1860*. Line 4 was estimated by multiplying the figure in line 3 by the 1889 ratio of value added in the construction of cars by steam railroads to the value added in the construction of cars by firms other than steam railroads as contained in the *Census of Manufacturing, 1890*.

Line 10 is from Gallman, "Value Added," p. 357.

chases suggests that the railroad was also a relatively small consumer of machinery. This possibility is supported by Table 4 which indicates that the locomotive and car construction industries utilized machinery requiring only 11,500 horsepower. Assuming that the output of machinery in 1859 was distributed among the various industries in proportion to the distribution of horsepower, the railroad directly consumed less than 1 per cent of machine production. Again, the situation does not change appreciably when indirect purchases form industries at more remote levels of production are considered. If the share of machinery consumed by the lumber, iron, and machine industries attributable to the railroad is added to that of transportation equipment, the railroad would have still accounted for only 6 per cent of machine production in 1859 (see Table 4).

MANUFACTURING AS A WHOLE

Table 5 shows that the value added in the manufacturing of those goods which railroads purchased, directly and indirectly, from the transportation equipment, iron, lumber, and machinery industries amounted to only $22,500,000 or 2.76 per cent of all value added in manufacturing. Thus if, in the absence of railroads, there had been no increase in the demand for these goods by other forms of transportation, value added in manufacturing

Table 4. An Estimate of the Proportion of Value Added in the Production of Machinery Attributable to Railroads, 1859

	1	2	3	4	5	6	7
Industry	Horsepower used in 1900	Number of workers in 1900	Horsepower per worker in 1900 Col. 1 ÷ Col. 2	Number of workers in 1860	Estimated horsepower in 1860 Col. 3 × Col. 4	Proportion of output attributable to railroads	Horsepower attributable to railroads in 1859 Col. 5 × Col. 6
1. Locomotives	29,806	24,806	1.20156	4,174	5,015	1.0	5,015
2. Lumber	1,889,050	378,840	4.98641	75,595	376,948	0.01180	4,448
3. Iron and steel rolling mills	1,164,035	183,023	6.36005	22,014	140,010	0.41638	58,297
4. Iron and steel blast furnaces	50,965	39,241	12.89378	15,927	205,350	0.08422	17,295
5. Railroad cars	134,117	210,105	0.63833	10,116	6,457	1.0	6,457
6. Machinery	818,441	528,390	1.54893	63,078	97,703	0.06092	5,952

7. Horsepower used in manufacturing attributable to railroads in 1859 (sum of Col. 7)................. 97,464
8. Total horsepower used in manufacturing in 1859............. 1,600,000
9. Proportion of total horsepower used in manufacturing in 1860 attributable to railroads (line 7 ÷ line 8) 0.06092
10. Value added in the production of machinery attributable to railroads in 1859 (line 9 × $54,117,000) $3,297,000

Sources and Notes:

Columns 1 and 2, Line 1. The figures are for 1904 and are taken from *Thirteenth Census, Manufacturing*, VIII, 612. Line 2. *Thirteenth Census, Manufacturing*, X, 488. Lines 3, 4, and 5. *Twelfth Census, Manufacturing*, X, 80, 84, 88, 272, 274, Line 6. The figures are for 1904. The industries included under the heading of machinery are those designated in Gallman, "Value Added," pp. 357–58. The source is *Thirteenth Census, Manufacturing*, VII, 552, 584, 590, 632. Column 4, Line 5. The number of workers in "Cars construction and repairing by steam railroads" was determined by multiplying the figure in Table 3, line 4, by the ratio of workers to value added for "Cars, construction and repairing by firms other than steam railroads," as taken from the *Eighth Census, Manufacturing*. Lines 1–4, 6. *Eighth Census, Manufacturing*. Cf. note to Columns 1 and 2, line 6, of this table.

Column 5. The figures in this column probably overstate estimated horsepower used in the specified firms in 1860. For manufacturing as a whole, the horsepower per worker was 1.64 in 1900 but only 1.23 in 1860. Carroll R. Daugherty, "An Index of the Installation of Machinery in the United States Since 1850." *Harvard Business Review*, VI (April, 1928), 283; Gallman, "Commodity Production," p. 30; *Historical Statistics* (1960), p. 74.

Column 6, Line 2. The entry is a weighted average of the share of lumber used in ties and in the construction of cars for the years 1859 and 1860. The weights are 0.5833 and 0.4167. Table 2, lines 20 and 21 of Columns 1 and 5. Line 3. The following equation was computed from state production data on rolled iron given in *Census of Manufacturing, 1860*, p. clxxxiii:

$$V = 17.61R + 29.19B$$
$$(5.57) \qquad (5.52)$$

where V is the value added in rolling all iron, R is the gross tonnage of rails rolled, and B is the tonnage of all other rolled iron. The coefficient of R is the average amount of value added in dollars per gross ton of rail; the coefficient of B is the average amount of value added in dollars per ton of all other rolled iron. Total value added in the production of rails then is equal to $17.61 multiplied by the census figure for the production of rails. The value added in the rolling of the wrought iron used for fastenings, locomotives, and cars is equal to $29.19 multiplied by the tonnage of this iron (as computed in Table 1). The sum of the two products divided by value added in the production of all rolled iron (as computed from the equation) is the estimated proportion of the output of rolling mills consumed by railroads. Line 4. The coefficient is the sum of the additional domestic pig iron used for rails plus all domestic crude iron used in other iron products by railroads divided by the total production of pig iron. Both the numerator and denominator are a weighted average of the entries for the years 1859 and 1860. . . . Table 1, lines 20 and 21 of Columns 3, 4, and 5. Line 6. This coefficient was obtained iteratively; i.e., by making the ratio of the sum of Column 7 divided by line 8 equal to the coefficient. In other words the coefficient includes machinery required to produce the machines used for the production of the railroad goods in the first five industries.

Line 8. Daugherty, "An Index," p. 283.
Line 10. Gallman, "Value Added," p. 357.

would have declined to $792,000,000. But then the market provided by the *non-railroad* demand for manufactured commodities would still have resulted in a 230 per cent rise in the output of manufacturing over the years from 1840 to 1859—as opposed to an increase of 240 per cent with the railroad market.[21]

Of course, this calculation is based on a consideration of direct and indirect purchases by railroads in only four of the 18 industries into which Gallman divides manufacturing. And even here the repercussions of railroad consumption are tracked back through just two or three stages of productive activity. While no attempt will be made to arrive at detailed estimates of the share of the products of other manufacturing industries consumed by railroads, it is possible to estimate the aggregate amount of the neglected items (in terms of value added). The estimate pivots around the fact that the value added in manufacturing all of the goods consumed in the construction of a railroad must be less than the cost of construction. The procedure will be to deduct from an estimate of the total cost of railroad construction in 1859 purchases of labor and other non-manufactured items as well as those manufactured items already taken into account. The residual will be an estimate of the total value of the neglected items which railroads purchased from

Table 5. Value Added in Manufacturing Attributable to Railroad Consumption of Manufactured Goods, 1859

Industry	1 Value added in 1859 (dollars)	2 Proportion of output purchased by railroads	3 Value added in 1859 attributable to railroads (dollars) Col. 1 × *Col. 2*
1. Transportation equipment	42,827,000	0.25450	12,171,000
2. Machinery	54,117,000	0.06092	3,297,000
3. Rolled iron	12,646,000	0.41638	5,266,000
4. Pig iron	8,577,000	0.08422	722,000
5. Lumber	90,755,000	0.01180	1,071,000
6. Total of Column 3			22,527,000
7. Value added by all manufacturing in 1859			814,888,000
8. Line 6 as a per cent of line 7			2.76

Sources and Notes:
    Column 1, Lines 1, 2, 5: Gallman, "Value Added," p. 357. Lines 3, 4: *Census of Manufacturing, 1860,* p. clxxxiii.
    Column 2. Tables 2-4.
    Line 7. Gallman, "Value Added," p. 357.

manufacturing. The residual multiplied by a suitable ratio of value added to value of the final product will yield the desired estimate.

Over the decade from 1850 through 1860 the average cost of new railroads, including equipment, etc., was $38,416 per mile.[22] At this rate, the estimated total cost of the construction of the 2,118 miles of new road built during the census year of 1859-60 was $8,365,000.[23] Of this amount at least 50 per cent appears to represent the cost of the labor required for grading, track laying, and the erection of structures; the purchase of other services (engineering, surveying, legal); interest charges; land; and the cost of non-manufactured commodities (e.g., forest products).[24] Consequently, the total cost of the manufactured materials purchased by railroads was probably less than $40,683,000.

To obtain the value of the neglected items one must subtract from this figure the items which have already been taken into account. One of the items previously considered is locomotives, the 1859 value of which was $4,867,000.[25] A second deduction must be made for the value of all cars manufactured by firms other than railroads, $4,303,000, and for 56.75 per cent of the value of the product of the car shops of steam railroads, $4,510,000— the remaining 43.25 per cent represent the repair and maintenance of existing rolling stock.[26] Previous account has also been taken of the rails used in new construction which amounted to approximately $5,843,000.[27]

Deduction of the sum of these items from $40,683,000 leaves a residual of $21,160,000. This residual probably overstates the value of the neglected purchases from manufacturing since, in addition to the other upward biases, it still includes the value of spikes, rail chairs, and similar items of iron which were taken into account in the calculation shown in Table 5. Multiplying the residual by the ratio of value added to the value of all manufactured goods in 1859, one obtains $9,585,000 as the value added in the manufacturing of the neglected items.[28] No addition need be made to this figure for manufactured goods used in the maintenance of track and equipment since these items are covered by Table 5.

Consequently, the total amount of the value added in manufacturing the goods purchased from that sector in 1859 was probably less than $32,112,000, or 3.94 per cent of the figure for all manufacturing. It would be wrong, however, to interpret $32,112,000 as a measure of the amount by which railroad purchases increased the market for manufactured goods. In the absence of railroads there would have been a considerable increase in the consumption of wagon and water transportation services. To determine the incremental contribution of railroad purchases to the market of each particular industry as well as to manufacturing as a whole, it is necessary to subtract from railroad purchases the increase in the purchases of corresponding items that would have been made by other forms of transportation. The incremental contribution of railroad purchases to the market for various manufactured goods is still to be determined—but it is clearly smaller than the limited amount of railroad purchases already derived.

Notes

1. W. W. Rostow, *The Stages of Economic Growth* (Cambridge, Mass., 1960), p. 55.

2. The industrial classification followed here is that contained in Gallman, "Value Added," pp. 357-58.

3. Rostow, *Stages,* p. 52.

4. A.I.S.A., *Annual Report, 1883,* pp. 23, 28, 41. The use of tons of rails produced divided by tons of pig iron production as an index of the position of rails in the market for iron leads to a large upward bias.

5. Walt W. Rostow, ed., Leading Sectors and the Take-off," *The Economics of Take-off into Sustained Growth* (New York, 1963), p. 5.

6. An index based on value added would make the railroad share substantially smaller.

7. Approximately 30,300 net tons of nails were produced in Pennsylvania in 1849 (Charles E. Smith, "The Manufacture of Iron in Pennsylvania," *Merchants' Magazine,* vol. 25 [Nov., 1851], p. 578). The national tonnage (88,800) was obtained by multiplying 30,300 by the 1856 ratio of U.S. to Pennsylvania production as given in J. P. Lesley, *The Iron Manufacturer's Guide to the Furnaces, Forges and Rolling Mills of the United States* (New York, 1859), p. 758; hereafter referred to as Lesley, *Guide.*

8. Table 5.15 of the original book.

9. John L. Ringwalt, *Development of Transportation Systems in the United States* (Philadelphia, 1888), pp. 135, 161-162. Albert Fishlow states that the problem of the firebox was not solved until 1854. He points to estimates that put the total number of coal burning locomotives in early 1859 at between 250 and 400. Albert Fishlow, *The Economic Contribution of American Railroads Before the Civil War* (Unpublished doctoral dissertation, Harvard University, 1963), pp. 180, 183.

10. *Historical Statistics* (1960), pp. 356, 359, 436.

11. Benjamin F. French, *History of the Rise and Progress of the Non Trade of the United States from 1821 to 1857* (New York, 1858), pp. 69,100-102, 152.

12. Table 5.15 of the original book.

13. *Ibid.* The rate of fuel consumption used here is probably too high because old rails did not have to be puddled, and because some of the pig in new rails was imported.

14. Table 1, Columns 3, 4, 5. This calculation is based on the assumptions that the items shown in Columns 3-5 were domestically produced, and that all of the crude iron was rolled from domestic pig. Undoubtedly some of the crude iron was scrap and some was imported pig. There was also a considerable amount of cast iron used in locomotives and cars. Consequently the figure given in the text overstates the amount of coal required for the specified items.

15. *Historical Statists* (1960), pp. 357, 360.

16. A.I.S.A., *Annual Report, 1877,* p. 16.

17. See note to Column 2 of Table 2.

18. E. E. Russel Tratman, *Railway Track and Track Work* (3rd ed.; New York, 1909), pp. 32-40.

19. See note to Column 3 of Table 2.

20. The derivation of these estimates is discussed in the notes to Table 1.

21. Gallman, "Value Added," p. 357. In calculating the rate of growth of manufacturing output in the absence of railroads, the value added in the manufacture of commodities consumed by railroads has been deducted from the figure for all value added in manufacturing only for the year 1859. If a similar reduction wre made for 1839, the resulting rate of growth would, of course, be higher than 230 per cent.

22. U.S. Census Office, *Preliminary Report of the Eighth Census* (Washington, 1862), p. 231. According to data in Poor, *History,* the average cost of constructing roads in the New England and Middle Atlantic states in 1859 was $38,835 per mile. E. R. Wicker, "Railroad Investment Before the Civil War," Conference on Income and Wealth, *Trends,* p. 516.

23. The mileage is a weighted average of the entries for 1859 and 1860.

24. The ratio is based on an examination of the listed construction costs of various railroads built during the 1850's and 1860's. In the case of the Illinois Central, for example, only 33.3 per cent ($6,863,000) of the total expenditures on the road, as listed in an 1856 report, was for rails, fastenings, rolling stock, machinery, furniture, and other equipment. While this figure included the purchase of some services (insurance and transportation charges), most of the $6,863,000 represented payments to the manufacturing sector. On the other hand, 47.5 per cent ($9,978,000) of the total expenditure was for construction activities in which labor was virtually the only cost (grading, construction of the superstructure), the purchase of non-manufactured materials (ties), the purchase of services (engineering, advertising), promotional expenses (interest, charter expenses), and the purchase of land. The final 19.2 per cent ($3,954,000) was for the erection of buildings and structures (terminals, engine houses, bridges, fencing) in which labor and other service charges probably represented over half of the total cost. *American Railroad Journal,* Vol. 30 (April 19, 1856), p. 250; cf. *ibid.,* Vol. 30 (March 8, 1856), p. 148; *ibid.,* Vol. 27 (February 25, 1854), pp. 123-26, 215-16; *Annual Report of the State Engineer and Surveyor of the State of New York in Relation to Railroad Reports, 1850-1861* (Albany, 1851-62), *passim*; U.S. Congress, Senate, *Reports of the Government Directors of the Union Pacific Railroad Company,* Exec. Doc. No. 69, 49th Cong., 1st Sess. (Sr. No. 2336), p. 54; Wicker, "Railroad Investment," pp. 521-22.

25. *Census of Manufacturing, 1860,* p. clxxxix.

26. The value of the product of car shops not connected with railroads is taken from *ibid.,* p. 734. The value of the product of railroad car shops was determined by multiplying the 1859 figure for non-railroad shops by the 1889 ratio of the value of the product of the rail to the value of the product of non-rail shops (car shops of steam railroads not only built and repaired cars but also repaired engines). It was assumed that the per cent of the value of the product of rail shops which represented new construction was the same in 1859 as in 1900 (*Census of Manufacturing, 1900,* Part IV, pp. 278, 279).

27. A weighted average of the A.I.S.A. data for 1859 and 1860 indicates that 200,000 net tons of domestic rails were produced in 1859. The average price of rails was $54.83 per net ton, indicating a total value of $10,966,000. This figure was divided between new construction and replacement in proportion to the ratio of the track-miles of new construction to the track-miles of replacements. *Tables* 5.8 and 5.15 in original book; A.I.S.A., *Annual Report, 1878,* p. 47.

28. *Census of Manufacturing, 1860,* p. 742.

Part Three: POLITICS

RICHARD H. BROWN

THE MISSOURI CRISIS, SLAVERY, AND THE POLITICS OF JACKSONIANISM

*Although Richard H. Brown's essay focuses to a large
extent on events that antedated Andrew Jackson's
years in the White House, it offers an interpretation
that throws interesting light on party politics for the
third of a century between the Missouri Compromise of
1820-1821 and the Dred Scott decision in 1857. Brown's
is a realistic appraisal in the sense that it urges us to pay
less attention to personal and individual factors, such as
the role of ambition or that of the notorious Peggy
Eaton affair, in dividing Van Buren and Calhoun, and
more attention to large underlying realities. The
particular reality stressed in Mr. Brown's argument
is the South's determination both to keep slavery
removed from the agenda of national government and
to have the Presidency occupied by men who accepted
this principle. Brown holds that the forging of the
New York-Virginia alliance by Martin Van Buren and
Thomas Ritchie, explained by some contemporaries in
terms of the restoration of "Old Republicanism," was
actually concerned with achieving this central objective
of the South. It might be argued that Brown's analysis
attributes too much influence to this single factor,
explaining a great variety of the political developments
of the second quarter of the nineteenth century by
reference to it. While he does not agree with all of its
judgments, the editor finds that Brown's thesis is well
and tightly argued, offering a useful point of departure
in our never ending search for greater insight into
antebellum politics.*

Richard H. Brown, "The Missouri Crisis, Slavery, and the Politics of Jacksonianism,"
South Atlantic Quarterly, 65 (Winter 1966), 55-72. Copyright © 1966, by Duke University Press.

From the inaguration of Washington until the Civil War the South was in
the saddle of national politics. This is the central fact in American political
history to 1860. To it there are no exceptions, not even in that period when
the "common man" stormed the ramparts of government under the banner
of Andrew Jackson. In Jackson's day the chief agent of Southern power
was a Northern man with Southern principles, Martin Van Buren of New
York. It was he who put together the party coalition which Andrew Jackson
led to power. That coalition had its wellsprings in the dramatic crisis over
slavery in Missouri, the first great public airing of the slavery question in
ante bellum America.

I

More than anything else, what made Southern dominance in national
politics possible was a basic homogeneity in the Southern electorate. In the
early nineteenth century, to be sure, the South was far from monolithic.
In terms of economic interest and social classes it was scarcely more homogeneous than the North. But under the diversity of interests which characterized
Southern life in most respects there ran one single compelling idea which
virtually united all Southerners, and which governed their participation in
national affairs. This was that the institution of slavery should not be dealt
with from outside the South. Whatever the merits of the institution—and
Southerners violently disagreed about this, never more than in the 1820's—
the presence of the slave was a fact too critical, too sensitive, too perilous
for all of Southern society to be dealt with by those not directly affected.
Slavery must remain a Southern question. In the ante bellum period a southern
politician of whatever party forgot this at his peril. A Northern politician
might perceive it to his profit. There had been, Martin Van Buren noted
with satisfaction late in life, a "remarkable consistency in the political positions" of Southern public men. With characteristic insouciance the Little
Magician attributed this consistency to the natural superiority of republican
principles which led them to win out in a region relatively untainted by the
monied interest. But his partisan friend Rufus King, Van Buren admitted,
ascribed it to the "black strap" of Southern slavery.

The insistence that slavery was uniquely a Southern concern, not to be
touched by outsiders, had been from the outset a *sine qua non* for Southern
participation in national politics. It underlay the Constitution and its creation of a government of limited powers, without which Southern participation would have been unthinkable. And when in the 1790's Jefferson and
Madison perceived that a constitution was only the first step in guaranteeing
Southern security, because a constitution meant what those who governed
under it said it meant, it led to the creation of the first national political
party to protect that Constitution against change by interpretation. The
party which they constructed converted a Southern minority into a national

majority through alliance with congenial interests outside the South. Organically, it represented an alliance between New York and Virginia, pulling between them Pennsylvania, and after them North Carolina, Georgia, and (at first) Kentucky and Tennessee, all states strongly subject to Virginia's influence. At bottom it rested on the support of people who lived on that rich belt of fertile farmland which stretched from the Great Lakes across upstate New York and Pennsylvania, southward through the Southern piedmont into Georgia, entirely oblivious of the Mason-Dixon line. North as well as South, it was an area of prosperous, well-settled small farms. More farmers than capitalists, its residents wanted little from government but to be let alone. Resting his party on them, Jefferson had found a formula for national politics which at the same time was a formula for Southern preeminence. It would hold good to the Civil War.

So long as the Federalists remained an effective opposition, Jefferson's party worked as a party should. It maintained its identity in relation to the opposition by a moderate and pragmatic advocacy of strict construction of the Constitution. Because it had competition, it could maintain discipline. It responded to its constituent elements because it depended on them for support. But eventually its very success was its undoing. After 1815, stirred by the nationalism of the postwar era, and with the Federalists in decline, the Republicans took up Federalist positions on a number of the great public issues of the day, sweeping all before them as they did. The Federalists gave up the ghost. In the Era of Good Feelings which followed, everybody began to call himself a Republican, and a new theory of party amalgamation preached the doctrine that party division was bad and that a one-party system best served the national interest. Only gradually did it become apparent that in victory the Republican party had lost its identity—and its usefulness. As the party of the whole nation it ceased to be responsive to any particular elements in its constituency. It ceased to be responsive to the South.

When it did, and because it did, it invited the Missouri crisis of 1819-1820, and that crisis in turn revealed the basis for a possible configuration of national parties which eventually would divide the nation free against slave. As John Quincy Adams put it, the crisis had revealed "the basis for a new organization of parties . . . here was a new party ready formed, . . . terrible to the whole Union, but portentously terrible to the South—threatening in its progress the emancipation of all their slaves, threatening in its immediate effect that Southern domination which has swayed the Union for the last twenty years." Because it did so, Jefferson, in equally famous phrase, "considered it at once as the knell of the Union."

Adams and Jefferson were not alone in perceiving the significance of what had happened. Scarcely a contemporary missed the point. Historians quote them by the dozens as prophets—but usually *only* as prophets. In fact the Missouri crisis gave rise not to prophecy alone, but to action. It led to an urgent and finally successful attempt to revive the old Jeffersonian party

and with it the Jeffersonian formula for Southern pre-eminence. The re-
suscitation of that party would be the most important story in American
politics in the decades which followed.

II

In Jefferson's day the tie between slavery, strict construction of the Constitution, and the Republican party was implicit, not explicit. After Missouri
it was explicit, and commented upon time and again in both public and
private discussion. Perceptive Southerners saw (1) that unless effective
means were taken to quiet discussion of the question, slavery might be used
at any time in the future to force the South into a permanent minority in the
Union, endangering all its interests; and (2) that if the loose constitutional
construction of the day were allowed to prevail, the time might come when
the government would be held to have the power to deal with slavery. Vital
to preventing both of these—to keeping the slavery question quiet and to
gaining a reassertion of strict construction principles—was the re-establish-
ment of conditions which would make the party in power responsive once
again to the South.

Not only did the Missouri crisis make these matters clear, but it shaped
the conditions which would govern what followed. In the South it gave
marked impetus to a reaction against the nationalism and amalgamationism
of postwar Republicanism and handed the offensive to a hardy band of Old
Republican politicans who had been crying in the wilderness since 1816. In
the early 1820's the struggle between Old Republicans and New would be
the stuff of Southern politics, and on the strength of the new imperatives to
which the Missouri conflict gave rise the Old Republicans would carry off
the victory in state after Southern state, providing thereby a base of power
on which a new strict construction party could be reared.

For precisely the same reason that it gave the offensive to the Old Republicans of the South—because it portrayed the tie between slavery and
party in starkest form—the Missouri crisis put Northern Old Republicans
on the defense. Doing so, it handed the keys to national party success thereafter to whatever Northern leader could surmount charges of being pro-
Southern and command the necessary Northern votes to bring the party to
power. For that reason Thomas Jefferson's formula for national politics
would become, when resurrected, Martin Van Buren's formula for national
politics. What has long been recognized as happening to the Democratic
party in the forties and fifties happened in fact in 1820. After Missouri and
down to the Civil War the revised formula for Southern pre-eminence would
involve the elevation to the presidency of Southerners who were predominantly Westerns in the public eye, or of Northern men with Southern principles.

Because they shaped the context of what was to come, the reactions to the
Missouri crisis in the two citadels of Old Republican power, Richmond and

Albany, were significant. Each cast its light ahead. As the donnybrook mounted in Congress in the winter of 1820, the Virginia capital was reported to be as "agitated as if affected by all the Volcanic Eruptions of Vesuvius." At the heart of the clamor were the Old Republicans of the Richmond Junto, particularly Thomas Ritchie's famous *Enquirer,* which spoke for the Junto and had been for years the most influential newspaper in the South. Associates of Jefferson, architects of Southern power, the Old Republicans were not long in perceiving the political implications of the crisis. Conviction grew in their minds that the point of Northern agitation was not Missouri at all but to use slavery as an anvil on which to forge a new party which would carry either Rufus King or DeWitt Clinton of New York to the presidency and force the South from power forever. But what excited them even more was the enormity of the price of peace which alone seemed likely to avert the disaster. This was the so-called Thomas Proviso, amending the Missouri bill to draw the ill-fated 36°30′ line across the Louisiana Purchase, prohibiting slavery in the territory to the north, giving up the lion's share to freedom.

No sooner had the proviso been introduced in Congress than the temper of the Old Republicans boiled over, and with prescient glances to the future they leapt to the attack. Ritchie challenged the constitutionality of the proviso at once in the *Enquirer,* a quarter century before Calhoun would work out the subtle dialectic of a Southern legal position. Nathaniel Macon agreed. "To compromise is to acknowledge the right of Congress to interfere and to legislate on the subject," he wrote; "this would be acknowledging too much." Equally important was the fact that, by prohibiting slavery in most of the West, the proviso forecast a course of national development ultimately intolerable to the South because, as Spencer Roane put it to Monroe, Southerners could not consent to be "dammed up in a land of Slaves." As the debates thundered to their climax, Ritchie in two separate editorials predicted that if the proviso passed, the South must in due time have Texas. "If we are cooped up on the north," he wrote with grim prophecy, "we must have elbow room to the west."

When finally the Southern Old Republicans tacitly consented to the Missouri Compromise, it was therefore not so much a measure of illusion about what the South had given up, as of how desperately necessary they felt peace to be. They had yielded not so much in the spirit of a bargain as in the spirit of a man caught in a holdup, who yields his fortune rather than risk his life in the hope that he may live to see a better day and perhaps even to get his fortune back. As Ritchie summed it up when news of the settlement reached Richmond, "Instead of joy, we scarcely ever recollect to have tasted of a bitterer cup." That they tasted it at all was because of the manipulative genius of Henry Clay, who managed to bring up the separate parts of the compromise separately in the House, enabling the Old Republicans to provide him his margin of victory on the closely contested Missouri bill while they saved their pride by voting to the end against the Thomas Proviso. They had not bound themselves by their votes to the proviso, as Ritchie warned they should not. If it was cold comfort for the moment, it was potent with significance for the future.

In fact, the vote on the proviso illuminated an important division in Southern sentiment. Thirty-seven slave state congressmen opposed it, while thirty-nine voted for it. On the surface the line of division ran along the Appalachian crest and the Potomac, pointing out seemingly a distinction in interest between the South Atlantic states on the one hand and those in the Southwest and mid-Atlantic regions on the other—between those states most characteristically Southern and those which in 1820 were essentially more Western or Northern in outlook. More fundamental, within each section it divided Southerners between those who were more sensitive to the relationshp of slavery to politics and those who were less so; between those who thought the party formula for Southern pre-eminence and defense important and those who thought parties outmoded; between particularists and postwar Republican nationalists; between the proponents of an old Republican polity and the proponents of a new one as defined in the years of postwar exuberance; between those closest to Jefferson, such as the Richmond Junto and Macon, and those closest to Monroe, such as Calhoun. It was a division which prefigured Southern political struggles of the twenties. When two years later 70 per cent of those congressmen from the South Atlantic states who had opposed the Thomas Proviso returned to the next Congress, compared to 39 per cent of those who had supported it, it was a measure of the resurgence of Old Republicanism. Two years after that, in the chaotic presidential election of 1824, the Southerners who had opposed the proviso were the Southerners who sought to sustain the party caucus as a method of nominating in a vain attempt to restore old party discipline. Four years after that they marched back to power at last under the banner of Andrew Jackson, restoring to effectiveness in so doing a political system intended to make future Missouri crises impossible, and committed in due time to rectify the Thomas Proviso.

Equally important to the reaction in Richmond was what went on in Albany. There command of the state's Old Republicans was in the hands of the Bucktails, a group of which State Senator Martin Van Buren, at thirty-eight, was already master spirit. Opposed to the Bucktails was Governor DeWitt Clinton, an erstwhile Republican who drew a good deal of his support from former Federalists. With the Bucktails committed to the old Virginia-New York alliance, the Missouri question offered Clinton a heaven-sent opportunity; indeed there were those who suspected the ambitious governor of playing God himself and helping to precipitate the crisis. Whether or not this was true, Clinton tried desperately while the storm was raging in Washington to get a commitment from the Bucktails which would stamp them as proslavery, but the Bucktails acted cautiously. When a large meeting was called in Albany to indorse the prohibition of slavery in Missouri, Van Buren found it convenient to be off on circuit. When the Clintonians whipped a resolution indorsing the restriction through the legislature, not a Bucktail raised a voice in dissent. But for all their caution against public commitment it was generally understood both in Washington and New York that the Bucktails were anxious for peace, and that they supported the corporal's guard of Northern Republicans in congress who, retreating finally from the Missouri prohibition, made peace possible. Several of the Bucktail newspapers said as much, and despite the lack of public commitment on the part of party leaders, more than one Clintonian newspaper would brand them the "Slave Ticket" in the legislative elections which followed.

In private, Van Buren left no doubt where he stood, or where he meant to go once the storm had passed. No sooner had the compromise been adopted in Washington than the Little Magician got off a letter to his friendly rival Rufus King, promising at "some future day" to give that veteran Federalist his own views on the expediency of making slavery a party question, and remarking meanwhile that notwithstanding the strong public interest in the Missouri question, "the excitement which exists in regard to it, or which is likely to arise from it, is not so great as you suppose." It was a singularly important assessment of Northern public opinion for a politician who had fallen heir to a tattered Southern alliance, and in it King apprehensively saw the panorama of forty years of national politics stretching before him:

The inveteracy of party feelings in the Eastern States [he wrote a friend], the hopes of influence and distinction by taking part in favor of the slave States, which call themselves, and are spoken of by others as the truly republican States and the peculiar friends of liberty, will keep alive & sustain a body considerably numerous, and who will have sufficient influence, to preserve to the slave States their disproportionate, I might say exclusive, dominance over the Union.

Twenty months after that, in the late fall of 1821, Van Buren set off for Washington as a newly elected United States senator. With his party having taken the measure of Clinton in the meantime, he carried with him into the lion's den of presidential politics effective command of the thirty-six uncommitted electoral votes of New York. If he would be the most disinterested statesman in all the land, he could not avoid for long the responsibility that went with that power. It was an opportunity to be used for large purposes or small, as a man might choose, and the Little Magician lost no time in indicating his intended course. Within weeks of his arrival he was pulling the strings of the New York delegation in the House to bring about return of the speakership to the slave states, from whom it had been wrested by a straight sectional vote upon Clay's retirement the year before. The new speaker was P. P. Barbour of Virginia, a leader of the Old Republican reaction in the South. Three months after that Van Buren was on his way to Richmond to plan the resurrection of the Old Republican Party.

That he should do so was partly for reasons of personal ambition, partly because the Bucktails after years of frustrating struggle with Clinton had their own clear reasons for wanting to redraw party lines. Beyond this there would appear to be the simple fact that Van Buren believed implicitly in the whole system of republican polity as Thomas Jefferson had staked it out. Committed to the principle of the least possible government, the Republican party was the defender of that republican liberty which was the sole political concern of the disinterested agrarian constituency for which, through life, Van Buren saw himself as a spokesman, and which constituted the majority of Americans. That majority was strongest where it was purest, least subject to the corrupting power of money. That was in the South. Slavery was a lesser issue than republicanism. Nor was it by any means clear in 1820 that agitation was the best way to deal with it. For while some who were nominally Old Republicans, such as Senator William Smith of South Carolina, were beginning to argue that slavery was a positive good, it was generally true that no men in America were more honestly committed to the notion that the institution was wrong than those men of Jeffersonian conscience who were the Old Republicans of the South. Eleven years later, in 1831, some of them would mount in the Virginia legislature the last great effort south of the Mason-Dixon line to abolish slavery. It required no very extended rationalization to argue in 1820 that the whole perplexing question would be best left in their hands, even if in fact the North had the right to take it up. Particularly was this true when, as Van Buren put it, the motives of those in the North who sought to take it up were "rather [more] political than philanthropical." Because he believed as he did, Van Buren's efforts to revive party distinctions and restore the Old Republican Party were to be more than a mere matter of machinations with politicians, looking toward the making of the Democratic party. He looked to Southern power, and he would quiet the slavery question if he could. He was dealing with the root principle of the whole structure of ante bellum politics.

III

In the long history of the American presidency no election appears quite so formless as that of 1824. With no competing party to force unity on the Republicans' candidates who could not command the party nomination were free to defy it. They did so, charging that "King Caucus" was undemocratic. Eventually no fewer than four candidates competed down to the wire, each a Republican, every many for himself. Because they divided the electoral votes between them, none came close to a majority, and the election went to the House of Representatives. There, with the help of Henry Clay, John Quincy Adams outpolled the popular Andrew Jackson and the caucus nominee, William H. Crawford of Georgia, and carried off the prize.

Historians, viewing that election, look at King Caucus too much through the eyes of its opponents, who stated that the caucus represented an in-group of political officeholders attached to Crawford and anxious to preserve their own political power. In fact it was the Old Republicans who organized the caucus, not so much to sustain Crawford and preserve power as to revive the Virginia-New York party and regain power. They took up Crawford unenthusiastically because he came closest to the Old Republican pattern, and because he alone of all the candidates could hope to carry Virginia. They took up the caucus at the behest of Van Buren after two years of searching for a method of nominating which would command the support of all, because four years after Missouri the only hope of winning New York for a Southern candidate was to present him, however unpopularly, as the official party nominee.

Hidden in the currents and crosscurrents of that campaign was the reiterated issue of party versus amalgamation. Behind it, in turn, were repeated pleas by Old Republican presses, North and South alike, that unless genuine Republicans agreed on a method of choosing a candidate the division must be along sectional lines, in which case a Federalist or proto-Federalist might sneak into the White House. Behind it too was the repeated warning that party organization alone would make democracy work. Without it, the Old Republicans correctly prophesied, the election would end up in the House of Representatives, subject to the worst kind of political intrigue, and with the votes of the smallest states the equals of those of populous Virginia and New York.

When the caucus failed it was because amalgamation had destroyed the levers which made party discipline possible. Exhortation could not restore them. Meantime the issue of democracy had been turned against the advocates of party, because in key states like New York and North Carolina they tried to use the power of the party organizations for Crawford, bucking more popular candidates such as Jackson and Adams. It was a bogus issue. The real issue was whether a party was necessary to make democracy work, and because they were more nearly right than their opponents about this, and the election in the House shortly proved it, the Old Republicans would recover quickly after 1824, after Crawford and the caucus issue were politically dead. Let circumstances limit the number of candidates, and tie up party and democracy on the same side, and the results would be different another time.

In the campaign of 1824 and the years immediately following, the slavery issue was never far below the surface. The Denmark Vesey conspiracy for an insurreciton in Charleston (now a subject of controversy among historians) was to contemporaries a grim reminder of the Missouri debates, and it was attributed publicly to Rufus King's speeches on the Missouri question. In 1823-1824 some Southerners suspected that an attempt by Secretary of

State Adams to conclude a slave trade convention with Great Britain was an attempt to reap the benefit of Northern anti-slavery sentiment; and some, notably Representative John Floyd of Virginia, sought to turn the tables on Adams by attacking him for allegedly ceding Texas to Spain in the Florida treaty, thus ceding what Floyd called "two slaveholding states" and costing "the Southern interest" four Senators.

Old Republicans made no bones about their concern over the issue, or their fear that it might be turned against them. In the summer of 1823 an illuminating editorial debate broke out between the New York *American,* which spoke the thoughts of the old Federalists in New York, and the Richmond *Enquirer.* So vehemently had the *American* picked up a report of a plan to revise the Illinois constitution to admit slavery that Ritchie charged its editors with reviving the slave question to put New York into the lap of the "Universal Yankee Nation" and to put the South under the "ban of the Empire." "Call it the Missouri question, the Illinois question, what you please; it was the *Slave question,*" Ritchie shrilled, which the *American* was seeking to get up for political purposes. Shortly, the Albany *Argus* got into the argument. The *Argus,* which got its signals from Van Buren and spoke the thoughts of New York's Old Republicans, charged the *American* with trying to revive the slave question to "abrogate the old party distinctions" and "organize new ones, founded in the territorial prejudices of the people." "The more general question of the North and South," the *Argus* warned, "will be urged to the uttermost, by those who can never triumph when they meet the democracy of the country, openly, and with the hostility they bear towards it." Over and over the debate rang out the argument that the attempt to revive party distinctions was an attempt to allay sectional prejudices, and by the time the debate was over only the most obtuse citizen could have missed the point.

Nor was the election of Adams destined to calm Southern fears on issues having to do with slavery. A series of incidents early in 1825 suggested that the New Englander's election had made anti-slavery advocates more bold, and Southern tempers grew shorter in the summer of 1825 than they had been at any time since Missouri. One of the incidents was a reported argument before the Supreme Court in the case of the South Carolina Negro Seaman's Act by Attorney General William Wirt, stating that slavery was "inconsistent with the laws of God and nature." A second was a resolution offered in the Senate a scant nine days after Adams' election by Rufus King, proposing to turn the proceeds from the sale of western lands to the emancipation and export of slaves, through the agency of the American Colonization Society. In the same week the New Jersey legislature proposed a system of foreign colonization which "would, in due time, effect the entire emancipation of the slaves in our country." John Floyd enclosed a copy of the New Jersey resolution to Claiborne Gooch, Ritchie's silent partner on the *Enquirer,* with salient warning:

Long before this manifestation I have believed, connected with the Missouri question, would come up the general question of slavery, upon the principles avowed by Rufus King in the Senate . . .

If this indication is well received, who can tell, after the elevation of Mr. A. to the presidency—that he, of Missouri effort, or DeWitt C. or some such aspirant, may not, for the sake of that office, fan this flame—to array the non-slaveholding States against the Slaveholding states, and finally quiet our clamor or opposition, by the application of the slaves knife to our throats. Think of this much, and often.

Meantime, the New York *Commercial Advertiser* expressed publicly the hope that Adams' administration would introduce "a new era, when the northern, eastern, and non-slaveholding states, will assume an attitude in the Union, proportionate to their moral and physical power." Ritchie responded hotly in an editorial asking what the designs of such a combination would be against the "southern and *slave-holding* states." Soon in Georgia the Old Republican Governor George M. Troup, at the instigation of Senator John M. Berrien, put before the legislature a request for resolutions stating slavery to be exclusively within the control of the states and asking that the federal government "abstain from intermeddling." In May there was another violent editorial exchange between the New York *American* and the *Enquirer,* growing out of an *American* editorial which attacked the "slave press" and taunted the South with the comment that "the sceptre has departed from Judah, and those who have long ruled must be content to obey." Ritchie picked up the taunt as a challenge to the South, admitting that slavery was evil but insisting pointedly that the South had "too much at stake" to allow decisions on the matter by men ignorant of Southern "habits, manners, and forms of society." Ultimately, the Virginian concluded belligerently, Southern defense would be found in the traditional mechanisms of national politics: "Mr. John Adams the 2d is now upon his trial, [and] his friends consult as little his own interest as the public good, by conjuring up these prejudices against the *Slave people.* Should they persevere in their misguided policy, it will require no prophet to foretell that the son will share the fate of his father."

With the slavery issue thus drawn taut, the Old Republicans recovered quickly from the setback of 1824. Calhoun's inveterate foe William Smith was returned to the Senate from South Carolina, completing for the moment an Old Republican sweep of the South Atlantic states begun in 1821, a sweep which put Calhoun's political career in jeopardy and forced the Carolinian, now vice president, to break with Adams. For the Old Republicans, moreover, Adams made an infinitely better target than Monroe. The high-toned nationalism of the New Englander, combined with popular revulsion to the alleged bargain which secured his election, put the kiss of death on amalgamation as a political theory. The stage was set, under more favorable circumstances, for the Old Republicans to try again.

IV

For all the illuminating insights into Jacksonianism to which Americans have been treated in recent years, Jacksonian politics are still interpreted in Victorian terms, along classic lines descended from an early biographer of Jackson, James Parton, who recorded them one hundred years ago. To the Victorians, it is perhaps not too much to say, most of history could be ultimately attributed either to whores or to the unbridled pursuit of ambition. It was a simple view of history, and the Jacksonians got both barrels, one through the beguiling story of Peggy Eaton, the other through the notion of a sterile and essentially meaningless struggle for the succession between Van Buren and Calhoun. As Parton quaintly put it, "the political history of the United States, for the last thirty years, dates from the moment when the soft hand of Mr. Van Buren touched Mrs. Eaton's knocker."

When finally it rode to power, the Jacksonian party was made up of two clearly discernible and distinct wings. One comprised the original Jacksonians, those who had supported him in 1824 when he ran on his own, bereft, like all the rest, of party, and nearly of allies. As measured in that election this strength was predominantly in the West. It spilled over into a few states east of the mountains, most notably Pennsylvania, where the chaos of the existing political structure enabled Jackson as military hero to ride roughshod over all the rest. But this was all. The Western vote, especially when shared with Clay, amounted in electoral terms to little. Even with the votes of the Carolinas, thrown to him gratuitously by Calhoun and counting onequarter of his total, he was far short of an electoral majority. To get even this much he had been formally before the public for two years, and all his considerable natural appeal as a Westerner and a hero had gone into the bargain.

After 1824 Jackson found himself the candidate of a combined opposition. The concrete measure of difference between defeat in 1824 and victory in 1828 was the Old Republican strength of the South Atlantic states and New York, brought to the Jackson camp carefully tended and carefully drilled by Van Buren. Nearly equal in size to the original Jackson following, they constituted a political faction far older, far more permanent, far more purposeful, far better led, and in the long run far more important. Their purposes were set forth by Van Buren in a notable letter to Ritchie in January, 1827, proposing support of the old hero. Such support, as the New Yorker put it, would be "the best and probably the only practicable mode of concentrating the entire vote of the opposition & of effecting what is of still greater importance, the substantial reorganization of the Old Republican Party." It would "restore a better state of things, by combining Genl Jackson's personal popularity with the portion of old party feeling yet remaining." It would aid Republicans of the North and middle states "by substituting *party principle* for *personal preference* as one of the leading points in

the contest. . . . Instead of the question being between a northern and Southern man, it would be whether or not the ties, which have hitherto bound
together a great political party should be severed." Most important, its
effects would be highly salutary for the South:

We must always have party distinctions and the old ones are the best of which the
nature of the case admits. Political combinations between the inhabitants of the different states are unavoidable & the most natural & beneficial to the country is that
between the planters of the South and the plain Republicans of the north. The country has once flourished under a party thus constituted & may again. It would take
longer than our lives (even if it were practicable) to create new party feelings to keep
those masses together. If the old ones are suppressed, geographical divisions founded
on local interests or, what is worse prejudices between free and slave holding states
will inevitably take their place. Party attachment in former times furnished a complete antidote for sectional prejudices by producing counteracting feelings. It was
not until that defence had been broken down that the clamour agt. Southern Influence
and African Slavery could be made effectual in the North. . . . Formerly, attacks
upon Southern Republicans were regarded by those of the north as assaults upon
their political brethren & resented accordingly. This all powerful sympathy has been
much weakened, if not, destroyed by the amalgamating policy . . . it can & ought to
be revived.

Lastly, Van Buren noted, a Jackson administration brought to power by
the "concerted effort of a political party, holding in the main, to certain
tenets & opposed to certain prevailing principles" would be a far different
thing from one brought to power by the popularity of a military hero alone.
An administration brought to power by Old Republican votes would be
governed by Old Republican principles. Van Buren would make himself the
guarantor of that.

Because the Jacksonian Party was what it was, Jacksonian policy was
what it was, and Jacksonian politics as well. Because the administration
rested on an Old Republican alliance which bridged the Mason-Dixon line
and linked New York with the Old South, the two most important steps in
the development of Jacksonian policy were the veto of the Maysville Road
bill and the veto of the bill to recharter the Bank of the United States. Whatever the social and economic consequences of each, they were in their origins
political measures, designed to solidify and hold together the Old Republican
party; and they were predicated, each of them, on a strict construction of
the Constitution. And, too, because its political base was what it was, the
one great question of public policy which nearly brought the administration
to disaster, one with which it could not deal and never did, was the tariff.

No less important, it was the structure of the Jackson party which gave
meaning to—and dictated the course of—that struggle between Van Buren
and Calhoun which bulks so large in the politics of the Jackson years. It was
far more than an empty struggle for the succession. Its essence was competition between two conflicting ideas as to how best to protect Southern se-

curity in the Union, and thus, inferentially, how to preserve the Union itself. One of those ideas was the old Jeffersonian idea, resuscitated by Van Buren, sustained by the Jackson party and by the Democratic party until the Civil War. It was that Southern security rested ultimately on the maintenance in national office of a political party which would be responsive to the South because dependent on it for election. A political answer, not a doctrinaire one, it was product of the practical, pragmatic, and thoroughly political minds of Thomas Jefferson and Martin Van Buren. It depended for its success on the winning of national elections by a party which would maintain its identity in relation to the opposition as a states' rights—strict construction party, but which would at the same time be moderate, flexible, pragmatic in tone, able to win support in the North as well as the South if it would serve its purpose.

Counter to this was the proposition developed by John C. Calhoun. Last of the Southern nationalists, Calhoun had held to his position through 1824, long after the Old Republicans had routed Southern nationalism in every state but his own. In the mid-twenties, with his own political strength at rock bottom, his hold slipping even in South Carolina, Calhoun made his portentous switch from Nationalist to Sectionalist, squaring the two in his own mind with the development of a counter theory to that of the Jeffersonians. This was that Southern security was dependent in the last analysis on the maintenance of an effective Southern power to veto anything it didn't like—thus nullification—and that failing, on the right to secede. In contrast to the political and moderate remedy of the Old Republicans, this was a constitutional remedy, product of the brilliant legal, doctrinaire, and essentially nonpolitical mind of the great Carolinian.

That Van Buren won out over Calhoun in the Jackson years had nothing to do fundamentally with Mrs. Eaton or with a long chronicle of personal intrigue. It had everything to do with the fact that the Old Republican moderates controlled the South, all but South Carolina, almost that, in the twenties. While Calhoun brought only South Carolina and some personal support in Congress to the Jackson fold, Van Buren brought all the rest of the South, and New York as well. The fact was not lost on Jackson or his Tennessee friends, either before his election or after. Van Buren's triumph over Calhoun was won not on Washington backstairs after 1829 but on the Southern hustings in the early twenties. Two years before it came to power the Jackson party was already, in fact, a Jackson-Van Buren party.

V

There were postscripts, too, which harked back to the structure of the Jackson party, to the Missouri question, and to the political prophecies of Thomas Ritchie, woven into the very fabric of the party by the skilled political weaver from New York. First of these was that the Jackson party, the issue once raised, was committed to Texas. When in 1844 a new drumfire of antislavery sentiment in the North made it impossible for Van Buren to honor that commitment, Ritchie and Van Buren, after nearly a quarter century of fruitful political teamwork, would part ompany, and Van Buren would give up leadership of the party he had created. After 1844 the party of the Jeffersonian formula sustained itself in the face of the rising slavery issue by giving vent to its expansionist tendencies; and the Northern man with Southern principles who replaced Van Buren was in fact a Northwestern man with Southern principles, Stephen A. Douglas of Illinois. It was to be Douglas, governed by the irresistible logic of the party structure, who carried through Congress finally, in 1854, the repeal of the Missouri Compromise. And when three years after that the Supreme Court in the Dred Scott decision held the Thomas Proviso of the Missouri Compromise unconstitutional, as Ritchie and Nathaniel Macon had said it was thirty-seven years before, who were the judges who comprised the majority? Of six, one had been appointed in 1846 by "Young Hickory" James K. Polk, a second in 1853 by the next successful Democrat, Franklin Pierce. The four others were James M. Wayne of Georgia, coadjutor of Van Buren's Georgia lieutenant John Forsyth, appointed to the court by Jackson in 1835; Roger B. Taney of Maryland, appointed by Jackson in 1836; John Catron, Van Buren campaign manager in Tennessee, appointed by Jackson in 1837; and Peter V. Daniel of Virginia, long-time member of the Richmond Junto, confidante of Thomas Ritchie, appointed in 1841 by Van Buren.

MAJOR L. WILSON

WHAT WHIGS AND JACKSONIAN DEMOCRATS MEANT BY FREEDOM

The editor must confess that when he first read the chapter that follows he considered it almost perversely wrongheaded. He still disagrees with its author's approach to politics, as with its particular readings of major party politicians' statements and writings. My own tendency is to focus on the behavior or actions of the major parties, while viewing their public utterances largely as rhetoric, calculated to put self-serving policies in the best light, the better to separate the citizenry from their vote. Mr. Wilson, on the other hand, not only takes the speeches of party leaders most seriously—as indeed they must be taken—but he regards these statements both as reflections of and clues to the innermost political feelings of those who made them. It is no doubt Wilson's conviction that public pronouncements are of central importance that explains his patient and detailed treatment of the ideas contained in them. His judgment that the Whig concept of freedom emphasized order and qualitative improvement, in contrast to the Democratic emphasis on quantitative improvement or spatial expansion, is arguable but it is also interesting and original. (Skeptics will of course insist that the Jacksonians merely sought to put in the loftiest terms a crude policy of territorial aggrandizement.)

From the nullification controversy to the outbreak of the Mexican War the initiative and shape to the national debate came from the ideology of Jacksonian Democracy. By the end of the 1830s the newly established *Democratic*

Pages 94 to 119 taken from *Space, Time, and Freedom* by Major L. Wilson, reprinted by permission of the publisher, Greenwood Press, Inc.

Review gave systematic expression to this position. Taking as its motto, "The world is governed too much," the review pleaded for a larger freedom from the force of past prescriptions and from the coercion of present institutions. Through the workings of the "voluntary principle," it rather supposed, individual "floating atoms" would naturally create and sustain an order "far more perfect and harmonious" than any the "fostering hand" of a paternalistic government might ever devise. In his war on the Second Bank of the United States, President Jackson manifested this idea of larger liberty and generated, as well, a more pervasive spirit of hostility to all forms of government monopoly and privilege. Equality of opportunity for freemen to pursue their several interests in the present, it was claimed, would automatically promote the good of the whole nation and make more manifest its glorious destiny. Of special interest here was the impulse in the Jacksonian outlook to rapid expansion and, with it, the tendency in its spokesmen to make more explicit the idea of freedom as a function of open and unsettled spaces. The floor of the growing empire of freemen, the *Democratic Review* thus exulted, would be "a hemisphere," and its roof would be "the firmament of the star-studded heavens."[1] At last a happy and progressive nation would vindicate the universal truth of its idea of freedom from control.

Fuller analysis of three points will serve to illuminate the course of the national debate from the nullification crisis in the early 1830s to the end of the following decade. A close look will first be given to the way Daniel Webster and John Quincy Adams defended the American System in the crisis against what they reckoned to be the iconoclasm of President Jackson. Secondly, it will be shown how, in a dialectical fashion, many Jacksonians argued for manifest destiny as the true alternative to the American System. Finally, consideration will be given to the clear, but ineffectual, opposition posed by Whig spokesmen in the 1840s to the imperatives of national expansion.

The response of Webster and Adams to the dismantling of the American System during the nullification crisis reveals a good deal about the thrust of Jacksonian Democracy. By their support of the Force Bill, both affirmed the integrity of the Union against the threat of the nullifiers. But they equally opposed the President's other compromise tactic, namely, that of lowering the tariff and undoing with his veto its related policies. While agreeing with Jackson that liberty and the Union were not so easily separated, they conceived of freedom within the Union in a far different way. Both remained identified with a corporate view of social man within the process of time. By its dual emphasis on the good of order from the past and on improvement to be realized through some degree of planning for the future, this corporate concept served to place in sharper relief the Jacksonian impulse to a larger liberty for individuals in the present and a manifest destiny of expansion for the nation.[2]

Throughout the nullification controversy, to consider Webster first of all, the Massachusetts Senator stressed the order of Union as the highest good. It was an "absolute and vital necessity to our welfare," he told the Senate in reply to Robert Y. Hayne. Later public addresses developed more fully the theme of its "transcendent value," while the speech against Calhoun on the Force Bill brought into fullest form his legal argument for the Union as an end in itself.[3]

In its highest function Webster conceived of the Union under the Constitution as essentially religious in character. It gave stable form to liberty, as he had observed earlier, and thus enabled each generation of freemen to relate itself meaningfully in "the great chain of being." Primal chaos, in such a view, was the only alternative. The emotional appeal and choice of symbols in his reply to Hayne made this very clear. By using a chain, a temple, or a constellation as a symbol Webster dramatized the awful possibility that the snapping of any link, the collapse of a single column, or the bolting of any one star would involve the whole in ruin. Nullification led to secession, he warned, and secession from the "happy constellation" of Union could not stop until all had descended, "star after star, into obscurity and night."[4] The practical import of Hayne's position, as he changed the figure, brought the nation to "the precipice of disunion" and threatened a fatal plunge to "the depths of the abyss below." Repelled by the very thought of disunion, he chose "not to penetrate the veil" to see what might lie hidden in "the dark recess behind."[5]

Less emotion marked Webster's later speeches after the confrontation with Hayne, for popular approval assured him that the Union was safe. But the attribute of order remained central in his thought about the destiny of the Union and the ways freemen pursued happiness within it. In regard to economic policies, as a consequence, he defended the status quo against Jackson's efforts to dismantle the American System. Many of the time hailed the end of the debt as a propitius opportunity for putting the country on a new course. Webster, alarmed rather by the "morbid sort of fervor" on the subject in some quarters, wanted to cling to the existing policies. "The duty of the Government, at the present moment," he said with reference to the tariff, "would seem to be to preserve, not to destroy; to maintain the position which it has assumed. . . ." As a spokesman for the earlier free trade interests in New England, he had long opposed government aid to industry. With considerable capital in his section now diverted into manufacturing, he argued for protection as the "settled course of public policy."[6]

Personal and sectional interests also helped to inspire his protest against Jackson's veto of the bill for rechartering the Second Bank of the United States. "This message," he declared ominously, "calls us to the contemplation of a future, which little resembles the past." In answer to the constitutional scruples of the President he cited the authority of usage and precedent, of the nation's acquiescence in a national bank for forty years. He deplored as well the dislocation which the end of the bank would cause in an economy adapted to its powerful and benign influences. But the greatest alarm was produced by the iconoclastic spirit of the day, he confessed, by the "un-accountable disposition to destroy the most useful and most approved insti-tutions of the Government."[7]

As he looked to the future, then, Webster adduced no new system of poli-cies to shape the destinies of the country. He wanted its course to unfold in a more organic fashion under the steady direction of past policies. What-ever changes were to be made, he supposed, should reflect the new and imperious needs of the time. His votes for western improvements and for special pre-emption laws provided a case in point and illustrated as well his ability to transcend narrow sectional interests. The government was less a planner of the future, in his way of thinking, than an agency to comprehend new interests and to harmonize them all. "The interests of all must be con-sulted, and reconciled, and provided for, so far as possible," he explained, "that all may perceive the benefits of a united government." His earlier reluctance to place the great interests of the country under the patronage of government had arisen from the professed belief that harmony could come only where all were left alone. Now Webster accepted the statesman's task as a more positive and creative one. His earlier fears that freedom for most people would be doomed in an industrial age likewise gave way to the hope that laborers under the protection of the government might also acquire "a stake in the welfare of that community."[8]

A recent student, taking note of the conversion by 1828 from a negative to a more active concept of government, has concluded that Webster was essentially a player of roles.[9] The Massachusetts Senator sought, in any case, to conserve what he took to be the realities of developing national unity. While the tariff and related policies already reflected the facts of interde-pendence, he rejoiced that one effect of those polices would be to create even stronger ties of mutual interest. Retrospectively, indeed, he imputed that same purpose to the Founding Fathers. Consolidation had been, he affirmed, "the very end of the constitution." As the bonds of Union grew stronger, he believed that a fuller "national character" would continue to emerge out of the disparate elements. Nor did this process rule out mod-erate growth for the Union across territory already in its possession. He would "bring the interests of these new States into the Union," he told a New York audience in 1831, "and incorporate them more closely in the family compact."[10] But Webster did anticipate here his later opposition to new territorial acquisitions, for he assumed that there were geographical limits to the development of a homogeneous nation. The destiny of the Union thus involved in large measure the realization of the existing elements of solidarity.

Freedom for each generation caught up in this process had about it a distinctly historical quality. Webster made this clear in the way he vindicated the right of the numerical majority to rule. The will of the numerical majority truly expressed the will of the nation as a whole, he explained, but only when it operated within the framework of the Constitution, the prescriptions of the past, and ultimately the interpretations of the courts. Without the judiciary, Webster ever argued, the Union would cease to exist. In contrast to Jackson's predilection for "mere majorities," he thought the Union of freemen rested on the collected will of all generations. In larger perspective, he deemed freedom in America to be in the family line of English liberties gained and disciplined through the centuries. The American Revolution, in this light, represented a supremely conservative act. Freedom was hence to be regarded less a universal impulse in man than a social product of time, with a history and a pedigree of its own. It was, he explained, "our established, dear-bought, peculiar American liberty."[11]

In two aspects of his formal thought about the Union Webster managed, by taking liberties with the contract theory, to conserve the new national order. He professed to believe, it was true, that the Union was "artificial and founded on agreement." By the way he thought of the parties to the agreement and of the time when it was made, however, he apparently took new ground.[12] Accepting as a literal fact the preamble phrase, "We the people," he insisted that the Constitution had been formed by the people as a whole and not by several peoples separately organized before 1787, that the Union was older than the Constitution. With the First Continental Congress in 1774, Webster rather noted at one point, the people constituted themselves "in some measure, and to some national purposes," a body politic. But the agreement in this case could not have been a very conscious one, for none could possibly have realized the full consequences of the act. In effect, he read back into the period before 1787 that sense of nationality which had subsequently developed. It was, in any case, good patriotic pedagogy, if not good history. In praise of Webster for teaching "the citizens in general what their relation to the Federal government is," an admirer could only express surprise that no one had thought of it sooner.[13]

In the way he conceived of the nature of the constitutional agreement, Webster diverged even more from the contract school. He deemed the Constitution to be, not a continuing agreement among freemen, but an executed contract. In the same sense that a law "is not the agreement, but something created by the agreement," he said the Constitution was not itself a compact "but its result." Ratification by the people terminated agreement and gave to the document the force of a supreme law. "The compact is executed, and the end designed by it attained. Henceforth, the fruit of the agreement exists, but the agreement itself is merged in its own accomplishment," he concluded.[14] Webster had earlier argued before the Supreme Court that the Dartmouth College charter was of this nature. As an irreversible grant it had brought a private corporation into existence and stamped it with perpetuity. The Constitution in like fashion had created the corporate Union with "a will of its own" and the "powers and faculties to execute its own purposes."[15]

This view of the constitutional agreement as a self-liquidating one did provoke considerable criticism, yet it served Webster's purpose well. It gave legal form to his view of the Union as a grand instrument of order comprehending all generations. It savored as well the historical sentiment of love for the "constitution as it is" and the "union as it is."[16] With the paradoxical stance of a conservative, Webster deemed the Union very firm in its own self-defense, yet fragile in the face of experimentation or radical change. No matter how grand its future prospects, he never forgot that the Union was a unique product of human hands and ever required the solicitude of the statesman. He would thus be disposed to resist any substantial reform, even with regard to what many reckoned the unequal provision for the three-fifths representation of slaves. The Union of freemen was an absolute in the first instance, not because it was strong enough to stand any shock, but because the shock of its dissolution would reduce the life of the nation to nothing. As the advance of larger liberty deepened the rift in the corporate outlook. Webster's position pointed at last to what one student of the 1850s called the "doctrine of institutions." Much of this can be seen in his summary definition of the Union:

The Union is not a temporary partnership of States. It is the association of the people, under a constitution of Government, uniting their power, joining together their highest interests, cementing their present enjoyments, and blending, in one indivisible mass, all their hopes for the future. Whatsoever is steadfast in just political principles, whatsoever is permanent in the structure of human society, whatsoever there is which can derive an enduring character from being founded on deep laid principles of constitutional liberty, and on the broad foundations of the public will— all these unite to entitle this instrument to be regarded as a permanent constitution of Government.[17]

While Webster revered the order from the past, John Quincy Adams valued most highly the prospect of qualitative progress for the nation in the future. "The Constitution itself," he said in 1833, "is but one great organized engine of improvement—physical, moral, political." Assuming that freedom in America had already been attained and ordered, he looked to the fruitful consequences of its full sway. Liberty here meant the power of men, freed from the irrational trammels of the past, to work out their own destinies. "It is the purpose for which intellectual power was given to man by his Maker," he exclaimed. Hopefully, the dominion of mind and the arts of peace were in process of replacing the reign of prejudice, exploitation, and war.[18] By taking thought, he believed, men could truly advance toward a higher stage of civilization. While holding progress to be a law of man's nature, he did not suppose it to be a self-fulfilling one. It rather prescribed the joint and sustained effort of freemen.

Basic in Adams' thinking was the assumption that happiness for the individual necessarily required the improvement of the whole community. The pursuit of happiness was a collective and cumulative enterprise, in the very nature of things, for social progress created ever-widening opportunties for self-realization. In its social and economic aspects, the ideal community possesed a relatively stable and compacted population, a balance of rural and urban elements, and great variety in its occupations. Such a milieu gave scope to the diversity of talents and interests in men, thus conducing "to their own elevation in the scale of being." Against the agrarian rhetoric and rampant individualism of the day Adams pleaded for a more collective mastery over the forces of nature. The task would also require time and the cooperation of oncoming generations. Freemen in any one age would find fulfillment through their participation in the long-range goal of building a better common life. Freedom here involved far more than the mere absence of social or political constraint. It was less a quantitative function of open space than a qualitative function of time. The Union in this sense was at once a positive means for progressive improvement and a teleological ideal to be more fully realized. It was in its grand prospective dimensions "an union of all classes, conditions, and occupations of men; an union coextensive with our territorial dominions; an union for successive ages, without limitation of time."[19]

Because the full measure of the Union's grandeur lay in the future, Adams professed to see the impending retirement of the national debt as a truly rare opportunity. It was given to his age, he supposed, to become the greatest link in the chain of the corporate Union. In a very significant figure he compared the American people to the children of Israel. After a similar travail of forty years, his own nation could at last "survey from the top of Pisgah the happy and promised land" reserved by Providence for its reward and use. By retiring the old debt his generation participated with the Founding Fathers in the glory of gaining freedom. By diverting more of the unencumbered resources of the country to the improvement of the nation's estate, his age might thereby incorporate future generations more fully in the grand pursuit of happiness.[20] Webster lamented the end of the debt as another bond of Union and order set loose, and Jackson welcomed it as an opportunity to gain freedom from the policy determinations of the past. Adams hailed it as the occasion for doing something positive and constructive with the freedom it allowed.

The policies to be adopted or retained at such a moment were thus of unusual importance. Adams appreciated, no less than Webster, the role of the government in harmonizing the interests of the country. But he brought to the defense of the American System of policies against the iconoclasm of Jackson a much greater spirit of system. He wanted the government to direct in an active and selfconscious way the course of the country. He saw in the protective tariff a way to continue the diversification of pursuits and in the National Bank a salutary means to stimulate yet control the development of the country. Much of his opposition to the policy of Indian removal arose from the fear that too rapid a settlement of the West would create imbalance in the national community. In part for the same reason he resisted the numerous proposals for the speedy disposal of the public lands. With the continued revenues from these lands, moreover, Adams wanted to finance the key feature in his system, namely, a vastly expanded program of internal improvements. Carefully planned roads and canals would give direction to the development of industry and trade within the country. They would also serve to enhance the value of public lands and hence the amount of revenue available to the government for promoting the arts and sciences.[21] Though favoring for these purposes direct appropriations by the central government, Adams also supported the plan of Henry Clay for distributing land revenues to the states. In either case, orderly progress and enrichment of the nation through time remained the goal.

It is in this context that the distinctive response Adams made to the nullification crisis can be most clearly seen. With a predilection for order, Webster expended the greatest effort in supporting the Force Bill. Because Adams looked to the progressive improvement of the nation, he spent a greater part of his energy in opposing Jackson's second tactic of compromise, that of dismembering the American System.[22] The Fourth Annual Message of the President, he bitterly noted, displayed a "speculative aversion to control" which would reduce to a "simple machine" the corporate instrument of government at the disposal of freemen. "It is the adoption for the future of a system of policy directly opposite to that with which the administration of Washington laid the foundations of the social existence of the great community—our National and Federal Union." Since much of the Union's true meaning lay in what it might in time become, the destruction of policies for that purpose would "untie the ligaments of the Union." Adams especially deplored the President's disposition to throw away the treasure of western lands. "The American Union as a moral person in the family of nations," he later observed, "is to live from hand to mouth, to cast away, instead of using for the improvement of its own condition, the bounties of Providence, and to raise to the summit of power a succession of Presidents the consummation of whose glory will be to growl and snarl with impotent fury against a money broker's shop, to rivet into perpetuity the clanking chain of the Slave, and to waste in boundless bribery to the West the invaluable inheritance of the Public Lands."[23]

Adams attributed the downfall of the American System to planters and plain republicans, or, in cruder polemical terms, to "the nullifiers of the South and the land robbers of the West." He supposed that the "Sable Genius" of the South had been chiefly responsibile.[24] As he looked to the future, moreover, it seemed to present a permanent obstacle to his hopes for the progressive improvement of the nation. Consequently in the bitterness of the moment, he defined the political force of the evil genius in terms which gained wider currency later on as that of the slave power. Because of the added weight of three-fifths representation and the sectional solidarity that the peculiar institution forged, a small and declining minority of slave-holders were able to suborn plain republicans in the North and effectively rule the destinies of the nation. In the same spirit Adams felt compelled to surrender the optimistic premise in his corporate outlook which held that the positive actions of the government could produce through time a greater degree of harmony and consensus. He was now bold to declare, to the contrary, that an irreconcilable conflict of interests and ultimately of principles obtained within the Union:

It cannot be denied that in a community spreading over a large extent of territory, and politically founded upon the principles proclaimed in the declaration of independence, but differing so widely in the elements of their social condition, that the inhabitants of one-half the territory are wholly free, and those of the other half divided into masters and slaves, deep, if not irreconcilable collisions of interest must abound. The question whether such a community can exist under one common Government, is a subject of profound, philosophical speculation in theory. Whether it can continue long to exist, is a question to be solved only by the experiment now making by the people of this Union, under that national compact, the constitution of the United States.[25]

The political prescription for dividing the enemies of the American System, however, threatened its advocates with a profound dilemma. As if in anticipation of the later Free-Soil movement, Adams seemed ready to enlist the plain republicans of the North in a crusade against the slave power. The real enemies of freemen were not presumed monopolists or a moneyed aristocracy, he protested, but the small minority of southern slaveholders who sought "to rob the free workingmen of the North of the wages of his labor, to take money from his pocket and put it into the southern owner of machinery." But success in removing the slave power obstacle in this way could not assure that corporate direction to national life would be resumed. The majority of Americans might rather remain as they were before—perversely present-minded in their outlook. "Democracy has no forefathers, it looks to no posterity," Adams once complained, "it is swallowed up in the present, and thinks of nothing but itself." The sum of its philosophy of freedom from government control, he elsewhere noted with contempt, was "comprised in the maxim of leaving money in the pockets of the people."[26] If Webster's penchant for order pointed to a "doctrine of institutions" by the 1850s, the progressive emphasis represented by Adams would tend to become absorbed into the Free-Soil crusade. The rift in the corporate outlook between the elements of past order and future improvement would then be complete and, as a fateful consequence, the vision of the nation within the process of time substantially lost to the political dialogue.

Until the end of the 1840s, however, this corporate vision remained as a real, if not always effective, foil to the affirmations of larger liberty in Jacksonian Democracy. It found lodging in the Whig party and, however chastened by the democratic spirit of the day, its spokesmen still invoked the essential idea of the earlier American System to conquer space. This meant, in their terms, giving some degree of direction to the nation's course across the continent in order to realize a more solid order and enrichment of the common life.[27]

In the dialectic of debate, many of the triumphant Jacksonians clearly embraced the policy of manifest destiny. The fundamentally timeless concept of freedom involved in their outlook provided an ample basis for this alternative course of the nation. Freedom from the prescriptions of the past and the prospects of future control, as staked out in the nullification crisis, meant essentially a freedom in the eternal present. As a political good it was not an entity pointing beyond itself to progressive development through time. It was rather a quantity to be possessed and enjoyed in its entirety at the time and to be reproduced in each successive generation. For the Union of freemen, as a consequence, the future would be a continuation of the present: its destiny would simply be more of the same. Not until 1843 did Jackson hit upon the felicitous phrase, "extending the area of freedom," but the substance of the notion inhered in his thought all along. In contrast to the Whiggish predilection for qualitative development through time, he sponsored the goal of quantitative progress across space.[28]

Classic expression of this view came from two ardent disciples of Jackson. In describing "the great nation of Futurity," it was true, John L. O'Sullivan hinted at qualitative change. But other phrases betrayed the notion of freedom as a function of space and not of time. "We are entering its *untrodden space,*" he said of the *"expansive"* future, "with the truths of God in our minds, beneficent objects in our hearts, and with a clear conscience unsullied by the past." In like spirit, Representative Alexander Duncan of Ohio thought that the expansion of the nation necessarily meant the aggrandizement of freedom. World without end, as he stated the matter in 1845, the nation's true destiny had "the love of liberty for its means, liberty itself for its own reward, and the spread of free principles and republican institutions for its end."[29]

By 1848 it must have seemed to many that the manifest destiny of the country was happily in the process of being fulfilled. With the Independent Treasury, President Martin Van Buren had completed the task of divorcing federal revenue from the private banking system. The effort by the Whigs in 1842 to re-establish the American System was undone four years later by the Walker Tariff, a renewal of the Independent Treasury, and vetoes by President James K. Polk of measures for internal improvement. The flag of the nation was, in the meantime, advancing to the Pacific with the annexation of Texas, undisputed control of Oregon south of the 49th parallel, and the acquisition of New Mexico and California. With his last annual message to Congress, Polk hopefully pronounced the epitaph of the American System and suggested the desirability of further acquisitions. In good earnest, then,

Americans were answering the call made earlier by Representative Chessel-
den Ellis of New York for "filling up the grand outlines of a territory intended for the possession and destiny of the American race—an outline
drawn by the Creator himself."[30]

Further analysis of manifest destiny will reveal more fully the workings of
the concept of freedom in the eternal present. For Jacksonians who regarded
the people as "the great social residuum after alien elements have been removed," the chief task of the statesman was to isolate and banish the enemies
of freedom. On the domestic level, moneyed aristocrats were thought to
comprise the chief enemy. Their quest for special privileges threatened to
destroy the equality of pursuits, corrupt the government, and commit the
nation to the evils of time. "Legislation has been the fruitful parent of nine-
tenths of all the evil, moral and physical, by which mankind has been af-
flicted," the *Democratic Review* declared. By his war on the Second Bank
of the United States, Senator Thomas Morris of Ohio claimed, President
Jackson had purged the evils of the past and thereby become "the second
father of his country." Representative David Wilmot of Pennsylvania,
looking to the future, warned anew that "the lords of the spindle" sought
with a high tariff to enslave the factory workers: "True independence consists
in freedom from restraints," he affirmed, "untrammeled to all things not
morally wrong."[31] Another saw in internal improvements a threat to freedom, for one generation might so easily run up the debt and become the
"mortgagers of posterity." Horace Greeley denounced the Jacksonian
politics of conflict as a species of "social war" and bitterly disclaimed the
label of "aristocrat" for those favoring positive legislation by the government. But his protests merely served to underscore the impulse to larger
liberty, to essential freedom from direction and control.[32]

The spread of freemen across the unsettled spaces of the country was, in
this view, a practicable way to keep liberty from being lost in the toils of
time. The "speedy settlement" of the public lands, Jackson had declared in
his Fourth Annual Message, "constitutes the true interest of the Republic."
Along with the removal of the Indians farther west, his call to end federal
control over the land amounted to a domestic policy for extending the area
of freedom within the existing boundaries of the Union. Because he supposed that "personal liberty is incompatible with a crowded population,"
Representative Duncan of Ohio thus joined others in opposing all efforts to
revive the American System of policies.[33] In a somewhat "primitivist" vein
Senator Lewis Linn of Missouri likewise condemned the "high state of civilization" which involved a compacted population, refinements for a few, and
great corporations "enabling one set of men to lord it over another." The
"rigorous morals and stern virtue of a republic," argued another partisan,
comprised the true alternative to overcivilization. The "rough carol" of a
Mississippi boatman or the sound of an ax, he explained, were "better
guaranties for the stability and perpetuity of our republican institutions"
than the trill of a cavalier or the songs of the gondoliers.[34]

The praises President Polk sang to the federative nature of the Union also expressed the predilection for timeless freedom. The Union of essentially self-governing state communities was suited to indefinite expansion, he exulted, because the decentralization of power enabled it to comprehend what it did not control. Freemen, going forth to settle new areas without direction from the center, could yet be integrated into the Union at the time of statehood. The very nature of the Union made expansion possible, and expansion in turn strengthened the Union for extending the area of freedom still farther. A policy of consolidation, by contrast, would presumably commit the nation in time and wreck the Union. "It may well be argued," Polk said in his Inaugural Address, "whether it would not be in greater danger of overthrow if our present population were confined to the comparatively narrow limits of the original thirteen states." Empty space had spared the Union the possible evils of time, and the continued expansion across the continent would enable it to reproduce this unchanging essence in the future.[35]

But the advocates of manifest destiny looked beyond the need for a rapid settlement of the empty spaces already in the Union. Since growth was "the normal state" of the young nation, Joseph J. McDowell of Ohio urged the House to support a policy of new territorial acquisitions. It constituted "the condition of our political existence," John A. McClernand of Illinois likewise argued. One of the most ardent of expansionists, John L. O'Sullivan, professed to see in every new acre of territory "an additional guaranty" for the "free development of our yearly multiplying millions." It would enable each new generation to move out to open space and reproduce the miracle of federative freedom from control. With a different view of the nature of freedom, many Whigs thought the existing boundaries sufficient, but the concept of freedom as a function of space made Representative John Reynolds of Illinois anxious to enlarge the homestead of the nation for the benefit of posterity. "This great Republic was not created for the few people who were in it at the Revolution," he warned, "nor for the few who are *now* in it, in comparison to the hundreds of millions of souls who will hereafter exist in it." Added space, in other terms, assured the freedom for each generation to recreate the essentials of the Union, to participate in the act of "extended genesis."[36]

To most partisan observers, Great Britain, by the early 1840s, appeared to be the chief external enemy to the natural and peaceful growth of American freedom. In geopolitical terms, Representative Duncan of Ohio feared, the nation was in danger of being "circumnavigated by British power" on the continent and surrounding islands. "We cannot bear that Great Britain should have a Canedy on our west as she has on the north," Jackson thus argued in behalf of annexing Texas. In like fashion McClernand of Illinois displayed "several beautifully colored maps" in the House to show how a cordon of British power stretching from Canada through Oregon and California to Mexico and the Caribbean posed a deadly peril. Senator Lewis Cass of Michigan invoked anew the law of growth. The nation's course must be onward across the continent, he warned, or else "we shall find ourselves in the decrepitude of age, before we have passed the period of manhood."[37]

But far more was thought to be involved in the emnity of the nation's ancient foe than merely stopping its outward expansion. Sam Houston of Texas advised the Senate in a speech opposing compromise over Oregon that, because of her hatred for free institutions, Great Britain actually sought to drive the nation back "within the limits of the good old thirteen States" and possibly destroy its existence altogether. One concession would lead to another, Houston predicted, until freemen were ousted "from every outpost of the Republic." It would be much better, Cass agreed, to fight for the first rather than the last inch of territory. Accepting in an aggressive way the terms of conflict defined by the external enemy of freedom, Stephen A. Douglas of Illinois vowed "to drive Great Britain and the last vestiges of royal authority from the continent of North America, and extend the limits of the republic from ocean to ocean."If the unsettled continent of the New World was to become all one thing or all another, he wanted to make it the exclusive province of freedom. A full decade before Abraham Lincoln formulated the idea of the "house divided" within the nation between slavery and freedom, the advocates of manifest destiny similarly found an irrepressible conflict in the New World between "monarchy and freedom."[38]

War to remove an obstacle to national growth would help to secure freedom for the future. To freemen in the present, moreover, war might prove very attractive as a moral equivalent, if not moral superior, to peace. Because "personal enfranchisement" was the essence of nationality in the Jacksonian view, little in the way of common purposes and common discipline remained to objectify and sustain the sense of community.[39] For negative liberals, as a consequence, a crusade against the enemies of freedom might very well serve to revive and strengthen the subjective bonds of national unity. It would in this sense fulfill the Jeffersonian prescription for a revolution in each generation. It was in this way that Jackson's dismemberment of the American System, no less than the "revolution of 1800," constituted a national revival.

War against the external enemies of freedom could promote the same end. "It was a maxim of the venerable Macon," Houston thus remarked, "that war was necessary to such a government as ours at least once in every thirty years." By calling on the people to "pay a price for their freedom," it provided a means for recreating and regenerating the first principles of the nation. If "the seeds of Democracy were cast into the earth by the hand of the Revolution," Representative Andrew Kennedy of Indiana explained, then the tree of liberty needed to be "occasionally moistened by the blood of the patriot." In a negative way, the *Democratic Review* noted, war would discipline turbulent spirits and enable other individuals to transcend the "selfishness and mediocrity" which ever threatened to overtake a country of free individuals. "It would only be in such a conflict that the sinews and strength of freemen could be fully displayed," Representative McClernand stated more positively, "That the moral sublimity of republicanism would loom forth as a phoenix from the smoke and thunders of war." The two earlier contests with Britain, Cass agreed, had pushed the country forward "in character and position" in the world.[40] President Polk made the same claim for the Mexican War. A fuller sense of national identity would also come from the knowledge that, as Representative McDowell put it, a victory by republican arms might spark "a great moral explosion" for liberating Europe from the thralldom of priestcraft and kings. "Young America" was here beginning to contemplate more aggressive means for fulfilling the mission of freedom.[41]

Whigs confronted the affirmations of manifest destiny with a more positive appreciation of the qualitative dimensions of time. Webster, standing "as in the full gaze of our ancestors and our posterity," called for his generation in 1838 to think of itself as part of a larger corporate whole. In this perspective a contributor to the *Whig Review* could deplore the mad hostility Jacksonians were showing toward everything established. "It is high time for us to have settled something," he insisted, "to be ready to take something for granted." In opposition to the impulses for freedom in an eternal present, he protested that "this everlasting beginning will be the ruin of us." Looking to the future, Senator Albert S. White of Indiana likewise condemned the Democrats for their reluctance to commit the nation to a positive course. "Is this Confederated Government," he asked in 1841, "a mere machine to run in an endless cycle of inanity?" Governor William H. Seward of New York explicitly dismissed as a "specious theory" the Jeffersonian ideal of essential autonomy for each generation in the pursuit of happiness. The great resources of the country impressed him rather with the peculiarly collective and cumulative nature of the nation's destiny. While working within the context of "causes anterior to his own existence," Seward wanted his generation to define the nation's course by a set of policies whose consequences would be as "distant as its dissolution."[42]

The Whigs, who deemed order as the highest good, expressed the strongest opposition to a policy of territorial aggrandizement. A rapid settlement of the western lands already placed enough strain upon the corporate Union, Representative Joseph R. Ingersoll of Pennsylvania protested, because "a want of nationality" generally characterized the people from the newest states in the Union. To acquire even more territory and strange peoples would surely wreck the delicate task of building up a homogeneous nation. "What has the rock of Plymouth or the settlement of Jamestown," he asked, "to do with Texas or the Rio del Norte?" Another spokesman complained that "we shall not know ourselves or know our country." In explaining his opposition to further acquisitions. Webster confessed that the theme of his entire career had been to make Americans "*one people*, one in interest one in character, and one in political feeling." Departure from this goal would "break it all up," he lamented, and make a "deformed monster" of the Union. Its very existence no less than its nature was ultimately at stake. "There must be some limit to the extent of our territory," Webster declared in the debate over the annexation of Texas, "if we would make our institutions permanent."[43]

A resumption of domestic policies for building a "more substantial Union," according to Representative Robert C. Winthrop of Massachusetts, constituted the best alternative to indefinite expansion. A good life for the nation could be achieved, he thought, within "the old and ample homestead which our fathers bequeathed us." Henry Clay agreed that the American System alone could bring to the people "additional security to their liberties and the Union." Consistent support of its policies by the nation would, another explained, "knit together its various sections by the indissoluble bonds of a common interest and affection." A greater sense of nationality, "a fixed and decided national character," would then emerge. The appearance in the files of the *Whig Review* of an organic theory of Union to challenge the "fiction of a social compact" also underlined this urgency for order. Society was based on a contract, to be sure, but it was at first an unconscious contract rising up from the absolute moral and physical needs of man as a social being. "The aim of this contract, nay, its very essence is nationality," so the reasoning went, "the union of as many as can be bound by the ties of kindred, country, language, and a common destiny."[44] This concept of nationality obviously stood in sharp contrast to that of the Jacksonians. Whereas the latter sponsored a larger liberty for individuals from the determinations of time as the Union progressed across space, the party of order here wanted to set bounds to the Union and to thicken and make irreversible the elements of unity within.

A second group of Whigs, comprising in Seward's terms "the party of hope, of progress, and of civilization," responded to the manifest destiny of Jacksonians in a way that revealed their desire for qualitative improvement of the nation through time. "We have a great country," Representative Luther Severance of Maine argued, "which I think it is our manifest destiny to improve." Few in this group absoutely opposed the further enlargement of national boundaries, but they were anxious to build up the country as it spread out across space. Mastery over the continent, one observed, "must be the supremacy of man over nature as *man*." While enlarging the bounds of the nation they were for "expanding and cultivating all the powers and capacities of man considered as a social being."[45] In the name of "a complete man" essentially free from time, one Jacksonian railed against that high degree of specialization which reduced the individual to "a supplementary being" of society. But Whigs answered that only from "a fixed center of thought," provided in a well developed society, could the individual discover his true talents and realize the fullness of his being.

Thus might "the great ends of government be realized," Representative Jacob Collamer of Vermont noted, which would "make us a homogeneous people, all elevated and adorned with a taste and refinement becoming the members of a *glorious republic.*" Henry C. Carey summarized this position well. "The highest civilization is marked by the most perfect individuality and the gratest tendency to union," he said in 1848.[46]

As positive liberals, some of the Whigs also hoped that a policy of internal improvement might provide a moral equivalent to war. Horace Mann and Abraham Lincoln clearly analyzed the problem. The spirit of restlessness across the land in the 1840s reflected, in Mann's view, the "unexampled energies" set loose as the nation became liberated from the force of "traditional feelings of respect for established authority." Nor was the young Lincoln altogether sure that this spirit of the eternal present would be able to impose upon itself a new discipline or control. It evinced a destructive urge to tear down and reproduce the primal drama of the fathers, he rather supposed, and not a corporate impulse to build "story to story" upon their work.[47]

But Seward was more hopeful that freemen could, by constructive and positive means, "constantly renovate and regenerate society." He clearly perceived that "action is the condition of our existence" and that action could be directed by the government "to pursuits consistent with public order and conducive to the general welfare." He revered the fathers in the first instance not as heroes who destroyed enemies of freedom, but as freemen of one generation who made great sacrifices to enrich the life of the larger corporate whole. "The principle of internal improvement derives its existence," he thus observed, "from the generous impulses of the Revolutionary age." Only with the "arts of peace," Representative George Perkins Marsh of Vermont agreed, could freemen express their nationality in the highest form. Progress was then to be measured by the fuller realization of the "dormant power" of the national mind and not by victory over trumped-up foes of freedom. "What would the money, already expended in killing those miserable Mexicans," Andrew Stewart of Pennsylvania bitterly asked in the House, "have done for the improvement of our country?"[48]

In their own terms of order and improvement, however, the Whigs had failed. While advocating a policy of "internal improvement," as Winthrop put it, they saw the nation following instead a course of "external aggrandizement."[49] The Jacksonian impulse to a larger liberty for men in time was here accompanied by the rapid spread of freemen across the spaces of the continent. A new contest with Great Britain was averted, but war came with Mexico and in its train the annexation, of a vast territory westward to the Pacific. Even more fatefully, as it turned out, came a profound sectional controversy over the fruits of manifest destiny. The Free-Soil demand of the Wilmot Proviso in 1846 to prohibit slavery in the new territory soon generated the terms of a new national debate which brought to an end the old dialogue over the destiny of the nation in space and time. Elemental conflict between freedom and slavery for the right to shape the future now tended to replace the older concern for the shape which the future ought to have. In the ranks of Free Soil, as a consequence, the champions of manifest destiny would soon find an adversary far stronger than the Whigs had proved to be.

Notes

1. "Introduction," *Democratic Review,* I (October, 1837), 7; "The Great Nation of Futurity," *ibid.,* VI (November, 1839), 427. See also Arieli, *Individualism and Nationalism in American Ideology,* 179-206.

2. The sections of this chapter on the thought of Webster and Adams during the nullification controversy first appeared in an article by the present author, " 'Liberty and Union': An Analysis of Three Concepts Involved in the Nullification Controversy," *Journal of Southern History,* XXXIII (August, 1967), 331-55. Copyright 1967 by the Southern Historical Historical Association. Reprinted by permission of the Managing Editor.

3. *Register of Debates,* 21 Cong., I Sess., 38 (January 20, 1830); Public Dinner at New York, March 10, 1831, Webster, *Writings and Speeches,* II, 45; *Register of Debates,* 22 Cong., 2 Sess., 553-87 (February 16, 1833).

4. First Settlement of New England, December 22, 1820, Webster, *Writings and Speeches,* I, 182; *Register of Debates,* 21 Cong., I Sess., 38 (January 20, 1830).

5. *Ibid.,* 80 (January 20, 1830).

6. *Ibid.,* 38, 69 (January 20, 27, 1830). Representative Rufus Choate likewise invoked a conservative stricture against the "original perfect freedom" which Jackson and others assumed in destroying the policy of protection. "You have put your hand to the plough," he protested, "and how can you turn back?" *Ibid.,* 22 Cong., I Sess., 3516 (June 13, 1832).

7. *Ibid.,* 1240, 1222 (July 11, 1832).

8. Public Dinner at New York, March 10, 1831, Webster, *Writings and Speeches,* II, 57; Reception at Buffalo, June, 1833, *ibid.,* 134.

9. Richard N. Current, *Daniel Webster and the Rise of National Conservatism* (Boston: Little, Brown, 1955), 184-93. Clarence Mondale has, in a like vein, analyzed Webster's changing rhetoric in "Daniel Webster and Technology," *American Quarterly,* XIV (Spring, 1962), 37-47.

10. *Register of Debates,* 21 Cong., I Sess., 68 (January 27, 1830); Public Dinner at New York, March 10, 1831, Webster, *Writings and Speeches,* II, 46, 57-58. Webster's open attitude toward the West is dealt with in Peter J. Parish, "Daniel Webster, New England, and the West," *Journal of American History,* LIV (December, 1967), 524-49. For a fuller analysis of the balance of sectional interests and the importance of "national character" in Webster's concept of nationalism, see Robert F. Dalzell, Jr., *Daniel Webster and the Trial of American Nationalism, 1843-1852* (Boston: Houghton Mifflin, 1973).

11. *Register of Debates,* 22 Cong., 2 Sess., 576, 554 (February 16, 1833). Webster exemplified here the English historical element that went into the composite national idea of freedom analyzed so well in Kohn, *American Nationalism,* 1-37.

12. Andrew C. McLaughlin, "Social Compact and Constitutional Construction," *American Historical Review,* V (April, 1900), 470; Charles Warren, *The Making of the Constitution* (Boston: Little, Brown, 1937), 394-95; Charles E. Merriam, *A History of American Political Theories* (New York: Macmillan, 1924), 252-90.

13. *Register of Debates,* 22 Cong., 2 Sess., 556 (February 16, 1833); William Sullivan to Webster, March 23, 1830, Webster, *Writings and Speeches,* XVII, 497.

14. *Register of Debates,* 22 Cong., 2 Sess., 564 (February 16, 1833). This reflected a consensus among such legal nationalists as Nathan Dane, Joseph Story, and James Kent. See

Elizabeth Kelly Bauer, *Commentaries on the Constitution, 1790-1860* (New York: Columbia University Press, 1952), 219-26.

15. Dartmouth College Case, March 10, 1818, Webster, *Writings and Speeches,* X, 194-233; *Register of Debates,* 22 Cong., 2 Sess., 564 (February 16, 1833).

16. *Ibid.,* 21 Cong., I Sess., 62 (January 27, 1830). Criticism of Webster's concept of the "executed contract" came even from John Quincy Adams, who otherwise shared the belief that the Union was founded by the people as a whole. Webster had "hung his cause upon a broken hinge," Adams noted, for "all constitutional government is a compact." Charles Francis Adams (ed.), *Memoirs of John Quincy Adams,* VIII, 526 (February 16, 1833). For a contemporary critique of Webster's position see Alexander H. Everett, "The Union and the States," *North American Review,* XX-XVII (July, 1833), 190-249.

17. *Register of Debates,* 22 Cong., 2 Sess., 571 (February 16, 1833). The preoccupation with order to be found in the "doctrine of institutions" is dealt with in Fredrickson, *The Inner Civil War,* 23-36.

18. Report of the Committee on Manufactures, *Register of Debates,* 22 Cong., 2 Sess., Appendix, 45 (February 28, 1833); Report on Manufactures, *ibid.,* I Sess., Appendix, 85 (May 23, 1832). Works pertaining to Adams and the idea of progress have already been cited in Note 28 of Chapter 3.

19. *Ibid.,* 2 Sess., Appendix, 46, 59 (February 28, 1833).

20. *Ibid.,* I Sess., Appendix, 80 (May 23, 1832).

21. *Ibid.,* 79-92 (May 23, 1832); Charles Francis Adams (ed.), *Memoirs of John Quincy Adams,* VIII, 229 (May 22, 1830).

22. This is not to say, however, that Adams was indifferent to the integrity of the Union or the threat of the nullifiers. He voted without hesitation for the Force Bill in 1833, while his Fourth-of-July Address in Quincy two years earlier anticipated many of the constitutional arguments Jackson used in his Proclamation Bemis, *John Quincy Adams and the Union,* 269, 233-36.

23. *Register of Debates,* 22 Cong., 2 Sess., Appendix, 46, 49, 59 (February 28, 1833); Adams to Charles W. Upham, February 2, 1837, cited in Bemis, *John Quincy Adams and the Union,* 151.

24. Charles Francis Adams (ed.), *Memoirs of John Quincy Adams, VIII, 503 (December* 5, 1832); Adams to Upham, February 2, 1837, Bemis, *John Quincy Adams and the Union,* 151.

25. *Register of Debates,* 22 Cong., 2 Sess., Appendix, 53, 41-61 (February 28, 1833). This quote and the fuller analysis of the slave power came from his minority report of the Committee of Manufactures. He considered it at once the epitaph of the American System and a clarion call to awaken the people. Bemis, *John Quincy Aams and the Union,* 270-72; Charles Francis Adams (ed.), *Memoirs of John Quincy Adams,* VIII, 537 (March 12, 1833).

26. *Rgister of Debates,* 22 Cong., 2 Sess., Appendix, 59 (February 28, 1833); Charles Francis Adams (ed.), *Memoirs of John Quincy Adams,* VIII, 433 (December 11, 1831); 519 (January 9, 1833). "The great difficulty," Justice Joseph Story had similarly discovered in 1831, "is to make the mass of the people see their true interests." Cited in Nagel, *One Nation Indivisible,* 51.

27. Lynn L. Marshall has well demonstrated the undemocratic elements in the make-up of the Whig party in "The Strange Stillbirth of the Whig Party," *American Historical Review,* LXXII (January, 1967), 445-68. In contrast to the tendency of the consensus historians to stress the similarities between Whig and Democrat, Charles Grier Sellers has set forth their differences in "Who Were the Southern Whigs?" *ibid.,* LIX (January, 1954), 335-46. Though his purpose was somewhat different, Glyndon G. Van Deusen achieved much of the same effect in "Some Aspects of Whig Thought and Theory in the Jacksonian Period," *ibid.,* LXIII (January, 1958), 305-22.

28. Jackson's phrase appeared in a letter to Aaron V. Brown, February 9, 1843, Bassett (ed.), *Correspondence of Jackson,* VI, 201. Though considerably altered from the original, the remainder of this chapter dealing with the debate over manifest destiny is drawn from an

article by the present author, "The Concept of Time and the Political Dialogue in the United States, 1828-1848," *American Quarterly,* XIX (Winter, 1967), 619-44. Copyright 1967, Trustees of the University of Pennsylvania.

29. *Democratic Review,* VI (November, 1839), 427. *Italics* added. *Congressional Globe,* 28 Cong., 2 Sess., Appendix, 178 (January 29, 1845).

30. *Ibid.,* 138 (January 28, 1845). Albert K. Weinberg overstated the case when he argued that the ideals of democracy and expansionism did not become linked together until the 1840s and only then as a defensive effort to forestall the encroachments of Europe in North America. *Manifest Destiny: A Study of Nationalist Expansionism in American History* (Baltimore: Johns Hopkins Press, 1935), 109. The tendency toward a spatial, atemporal concept of freedom lodged in Jacksonian thought, it would rather seem, made expansionism one of its essential attributes. Frederick Merk discovered something of this in his analysis of the federative nature of the Union. *Manifest Destiny and Mission in American History,* 24-60. The argument of the present study also gains support from Ward, *Andrew Jackson: Symbol for an Age,* 133-49. A good bibliographical essay can be found in Norman A. Graebner (ed.), *Manifest Destiny* (Indianapolis: Bobbs Merrill, 1968), *lxxiv-lxxxii.* The distinction Graebner made in another work, *Empire on the Pacific: A Study in American Continental Expansion* (New York: Ronald Press, 1955), between the goal of acquiring Pacific ports and of annexing new territory is a valid one, but it should not be pushed too far. The mission of regenerating benighted Asia by means of commerce on the Pacific was, in the minds of many at the time, an integral part of the "westward course of empire" which also included new territorial acquisitions.

31. Meyers, *The Jacksonian Persuasion,* 15; *Congressional Globe,* 24 Cong., I Sess., Appendix, 340 (April 29, 1836); *Democratic Review,* I October, 1837), 6; *Congressional Globe,* 29 Cong., I Sess., Appendix, 769 (July 1, 1846).

32. *Democratic Review,* XXI (October, 1847), 332; Greeley cited in *Whig Review,* IV (July, 1846), 30.

33. Fourth Annual Message, December 4, 1832, Richardson (comp.), *Messages and Papers,* II, 1164; *Congressional Globe,* 28 Cong., 2 Sess., Appendix, 178 (January 29, 1845).

34. *Ibid.,* 27 Cong., 3 Sess., Appendix, 154 (January 26, 1843); *Democratic Review,* XXI (November, 1847), 425. The dichotomy of "primitivism" and "civilization" first used extensively by Henry Nash Smith in *Virgin Land,* has been qualified in two later studies. Leo Marx developed the concept of pastoralism" in *The Machine in the Garden: Technology and the Pastoral Ideal in America* (New York: Oxford University Press, 1964, 3-11); John William Ward, the idea of "cultivated nature" in *Andrew Jackson: Symbol for an Age,* 30-45.

35. Inaugural Address, March 4, 1845, Richardson (comp.), *Messages and Papers,* V, 2230. For a very penetrating analysis of this matter see William T. Hutchinson, "Unite to Divide, Divide to Unite: The Shaping of American Federalism," *Mississippi Valley Historical Review,* XLVI (June, 1959), 3-18. Background for the ideas and policies in Polk's "continental vision" can be found in Charles Grier Sellers, *James K. Polk: Continentalist, 1843-1846* (Princeton: Princeton University Press, 1966), 213-66.

36. *Congressional Globe,* 29 Cong., I Sess., Appendix, 76 (January 5, 1846); 2 Sess., Appendix, 104 (January 15, 1817); *Democratic Review,* XVII (July, 1845), 5; *Congressional Globe,* 27 Cong., 3 Sess., Appendix, III (January 30, 1843). A very good analysis of the idea of "extended genesis" appears in Max Lerner, *America as a Civilization: Life and Thought in the United States Today* (New York: Simon and Schuster, 1957), 35-39. Nor did the experience of re-creation necessarily require the initial settlement of new territories by Americans. It could also be realized as the force of freedom served to regenerate neighboring areas settled or to draw them into the Union by its "gravitational pull." Weinberg, *Manifest Destiny,* 160-89, 224-51.

37. *Congressional Globe,* 28 Cong., 2 Sess., Appendix, 178 (January 29, 1845); Jackson to Francis P. Blair, May 11, 1844, Bassett (ed.), *Correspondence of Jackson,* VI, 286; *Congressional Globe,* 29 Cong., I Sess., Apendix, 278 (January 8, 1846); 427 (March 30, 1846).

38. *Ibid.,* 639 (April 15, 1846); 45 (December 15, 1845); 28 Cong., 2 Sess., Appendix, 68 (January 6, 1845). In a speech on the Oregon question Senator Daniel Dickinson of New York used the terms, "monarchy and freedom," to define the ideology of conflict on the continent. *Ibid.,* 29 Cong., I Sess., Appendix, 327 (February 24, 1846).

39. *Democratic Review,* VI (November, 1839), 427.

40. *Congressional Globe,* 29 Cong., I Sess., Appendix, 640 (April 15, 1846); 211 (January 10, 1846); *Democratic Review,* XVI (June, 1845), 532; *Congressional Globe,* 29 Cong., 1 Sess., 276 (January 8, 1846); 430 (March 30, 1846).

41. Fourth Annual Message, December 5, 1848, Richardson (comp.), *Messages and Papers,* VI, 2481-82; *Congressional Globe,* 29 Cong., I Sess., Appendix, 76 (January 5, 1846); Merle Curti, "Young America," *American Historical Review,* XXXII (October, 1926), 34-55.

42. Second Speech on the Sub-Treasury, March 12, 1838, Webster, *Writings and Speeches,* VIII, 237; *Whig Review,* IV (July, 1846), 30; *Congressional Globe,* 26 Cong., 2 Sess., Appendix, 78 (January 19, 1841); Annual Message to New York Legislature, January 7, 1840, George E. Baker (ed.), *The Works of William H. Seward* (5 vols., New York: Redfield, 1853-1884), II, 240, 241.

43. *Congressional Globe,* 28 Cong., 2 Sess., Appendix, 56 (January 4, 1845); *Whig Review,* VII (May, 1848), 440; Objects of the Mexican War, March 23, 1848, Webster, *Writings and Speeches,* X, 32; The Admission of Texas, December 22, 1845, *ibid.,* IX, 56.

44. River and Harbor Improvements, March 12, 1846, Winthrop, *Addresses and Speeches on Various Occasions* (4 vols., Boston: Little, Brown, 1852-1886), I, 500; Clay to James F. Babcock and others, December 17, 1844, Colton (ed.), *Private Correspondence of Clay,* 515; *Whig Review,* I (January, 1845), 3.2; II (October, 1845), 447; IX (March, 1849), 225. Clay, like many other Whigs at the time, privately found much to commend in the Native American movement. Clay to John S. Littell, November 17, 1846, Colton (ed.), *Private Correspondence of Clay,* 536.

45. Mass Meetings of Whigs in Auburn, February 22, 1844, Baker (ed.), *Works of Seward,* III, 245; *Congressional Globe,* 29 Cong., I Sess., Appendix, 490 (March 13, 1846); *Whig Review,* VII (February, 1848), 149; III (June, 1846), 616.

46. *Democratic Review,* XVIII (January, 1846), 13; *Whig Review,* I (April, 1845), 423; *Congressional Globe,* 30 Cong., I Sess., Appendix, 217 (February 1, 1848); Hency C. Carey, *The Past, the Present, and the Future* (Philadelphia: Carey and Hart, 1848), 416.

47. "The Necessity of Education in a Republic," 1838, Mrs Mary Mann (ed.), *Life and Works of Horace Mann* (5 vols., Boston: Walker, Fuller, 1865-1868), II, 150, 168; Address Before the Young Men's Lyceum of Springfield, Illinois, January 27, 1838, Basler (ed.), *Collected Works of Lincoln,* I, 114. Harry V. Jaffa provided a very stimulating analysis of this matter in *Crisis of the House Divided,* 183-232.

48. To the Whigs of Orleans, May 13, 1844, Baker (ed.), *Works of Seward,* III, 395; Annual Message to the New York legislature, January 1, 1839, *ibid.,* 205; Annual Message, January 7, 1840, *ibid.,* 242; *Congressional Globe,* 29 Cong., I Sess., Appendix, 1012, 1013 (June 30, 1846); 2 Sess., Appendix, 373 (February 13, 1847).

49. *Ibid.,* 29 Cong., I Sess., Appendix, 483 (March 12, 1846).

HERBERT ERSHKOWITZ
AND WILLIAM G. SHADE

CONSENSUS OR CONFLICT?
POLITICAL BEHAVIOR IN THE STATE
LEGISLATURES DURING THE
JACKSONIAN ERA

Some of the most ringing historical generalizations ever written have been aimed at the demolition of straw men. If the belief that some "consensus" and other historians have viewed the major parties of the Jacksonian era as mere electoral machines concerned only with winning and holding office is not a straw man it is very close to being one. It is this belief that Ershkowitz and Shade test on the state level, primarily by examining the roll calls in six states on matters affecting corporations, banks, currency, internal improvements, what the authors call "humanitarian reform," and economic reform. They discover that in states in every geographical section Whigs and Democrats usually acted in opposition to each other, the members of each party voting as though they belonged to a bloc. The usefulness of this essay derives from its substantial data base drawn from a number of possibly representative states. Of course the problem with roll call evidence—as with other forms of aggregate data—is that by itself it does not explain complex behavior, in this case voting behavior, throwing no light on the motives and factors responsible for the behavior (voting) patterns it discloses. The authors of this article, aware of the limitation of their method, make no grandiose claims for it. They perform the useful service

Originally published in the *Journal of American History*, LVIII (Dec. 1971), 591-621. Reprinted with the permission of the copyright holder, the Organization of American Historians.

*of puncturing the simpleminded belief that major parties
can be so intent on office that their legislative behavior
betrays neither pattern nor reason.*

In *The Age of Jackson,* Arthur M. Schlesinger, Jr., fashioned a brilliant interpretation of party battles in the Jacksonian era.[1] Utilizing the work of progressive historians and his own research, he depicted a dynamic struggle between "conservative" and "liberal" forces representing the interest of certain economic groups, acting through the Whig and Democratic parties. Subsequently, students of the period have challenged many aspects of Schlesinger's work, but a bitter debate continues between those who, like Schlesinger, stress social cleavage and ideological differences,[2] and those who emphasize an ideological consensus. The latter agree with Richard McCormick who said, "American parties are above all electoral machines, engaged in nominating and electing candidates, rather than, as Edmund Burke put it, being a body of men united for promoting by their joint endeavours the national interest upon some particular principle in which they are all agreed. . . .'"[3] Although studies of congressional voting behavior show clear differences between the parties,[4] the "electoral machine" hypothesis finds its main support in the "variegated . . . practice on the state and local level."[5] To test this hypothesis the authors of this essay examined legislative behavior of Whigs and Democrats in six geographically disbursed states—New Hampshire, Pennsylvania, Ohio, New Jersey, Virginia, and Missouri between 1833 and 1843.[6] While any conclusions derived must remain tentative, this study indicates that the "electoral machine" hypothesis does not provide an adequate explanation of the nature of the party system of the Jacksonian era.

Jacksonian America was a nation on the move, restless and optimistic with an eye toward the main chance. Nearly every foreign observer noted the all-pervasive activity directed primarily toward the accumulation of wealth. "Here one lives hundredfold more than elsewhere," Michel Chevalier wrote, "here all is circulation, motion and boiling agitation. Experiment follows experiment; enterprise follows enterprise.'"[7] It was not the "marvellous grandeur of some undertakings" which most astonished Alexis de Tocqueville, but rather "the innumerable multitude of small ones."[8] America's business was business, and most Americans delighted in the risks of enterprise. "There are no bounds among us to the restless desire to be better off . . . ," noted a writer in the *American Review;* "No man in America is contented to be poor, or expects to continue so.'"[9]

The "flush times" of the 1830s, however, gave way to the chaos and disorder of the early 1840s; questions concerning economic policy dominated legislative sessions and gave rise to popular excitement and partisan conflict. Because state legislatures granted corporate charters, discussions relating to this power not only occupied the greatest part of legislative sessions but also led to some of the bitterest controversies of the period. The economic advantages of incorporation accounted for many of the pressures put on legislatures by both the public and lobbyists, while the impersonal nature of these "soulless beings" gave a moralistic quality to opponents' arguments.[10]

Table 1 is based on votes on incorporation in several state legislatures. It includes divisions on individual charters and on attempts to restrict the effectiveness of corporations.[11] Although most charters were granted without roll calls, the ballots that do exist reveal support or disapproval of the incorporation principle. Efforts to strip the corporation of its most valuable and most morally suspect feature, limited liability, are indicative of hostility to corporations. In general, a legislator favoring corporations voted for individual charters and limited liability and against legislative repeal of charters once granted.[12]

On only four of the forty-nine votes tabulated did a higher percentage of Democrats than Whigs favor corporations. Democratic opposition seldom equalled Whig sanction of corporations. Few Whigs ever voted against incorporation or showed hostility to limited liability, especially after 1836 when 80 to 100 percent unity on the subject was common. Although Democratic cohesion on the issue increased as party lines hardened after 1836, usually enough Democrats broke with their party to defeat anti-corporation measures.[14]

This tendency should not obscure the general Democratic animosity toward incorporation measures. On only twelve of forty-nine ballots did as much as 50 percent of the party support pro-corporation legislation. Pro-corporation Democrats seldom represented more than 20 percent of their party. Opposition to the corporate form was not a prerequisite for becoming a Democratic legislator, but Democratic lawmakers apparently were usually opposed to corporations. Democrats were reluctant to create corporations not only for private business but also for nonprofit associations, including religious, charitable, and fraternal organizations. On only two of ten occasions did a higher percentage of Democrats than Whigs vote to grant a charter to a nonprofit association (see Table 2).

Banking was a second area of political controversy during the Jacksonian era. Early unpleasant experiences with financial institutions and alarm over the consequences a "paper aristocracy" posed for a republican society led many Americans to be hostile to banks. Jackson's "war" with the Bank of the United States inspired local assaults on banks with significant effects on state politics.

Banking questions before 1837 centered on requests by entrepreneurs for charters, appeals by older institutions for increases in capital, and efforts to create general laws to which all new banks would conform. After 1837 legislators discussed the suspension of specie payments, the problems arising out of bank failures, and the elimination of all banks of issue. During the 1830s and 1840s the Democratic party became as clearly opposed to state banks as it

Table 1. Percentage of Democratic and Whig Legislators Favoring the Use of Incorporation for Business Enterprises[13]

State	1833 D	1833 W	1834 D	1834 W	1835 D	1835 W	1836 D	1836 W	1837 D	1837 W	1838 D	1838 W	1839 D	1839 W	1840 D	1840 W	1841 D	1841 W	1842 D	1842 W
New Jersey	73	63			52	81	41	75	00	96	00	93	53	61			13	75	18	74
					31	100	60	81	00	90	00	96	25	59						
							58	66	12	85			56	61						
Pennsylvania					58	47			61	59	31	66					27	89	42	96
									37	100							05	90	04	100
									63	100										
New Hampshire									12	53	03	91	05	96	20	96			00	100
													09	84	13	88				
Ohio	49	65	48	95	15	57	24	91	04	78										
					26	74	14	100												
					39	61	42	100												
Missouri											44	47			17	100				
Virginia	60	71											14	82					43	94
	50	49																	66	85

Table 2. Percentage of Whig and Democratic Legislators Favorable to the Incorporation of Nonprofit Organizations[15]

State	Democrats	Whigs
Pennsylvania	16	60
New Hampshire	26	97
	68	100
Ohio	15	77
	74	74
	52	20
Missouri	61	87
	51	93
	03	65
Virginia	04	39

had formerly been to the Bank of the United States.[16] Democrats favored state audits of bank records, inclusion of the right to amend in bank charters, and removal of limited liability.[17] After 1837, when most banks in the country suspended specie payments because of a shortage of gold and silver, Democratic legislators harassed these financial institutions by demanding that the suspended banks resume specie payments before reopening.[18] With worsening economic conditions and declining party fortunes, the majority of Democrats came by the mid-1840s to favor the elimination of banking corporations.[19]

The ballots of Whig and Democratic legislators voting in favor of individual bank charters and against restrict banking laws reveal a consistent Whig predisposition toward incorporation of financial institutions and against encumbering these charters with hostile amendments (see Table 3). On fifty of fifty-five roll call votes, a greater percentage of Whigs than Democrats favored banks. In fact, on thirty-nine occasions over 80 percent of the Whigs accepted their party's position on the question. Only twice were a majority of Whigs in opposition even to chartering an individual bank. Democratic unity, as observed on the question of corporation, was less complete. Generally, 20 to 40 percent of the Jackson-Van Buren forces did not sustain their party's repugnance toward banks; on sixteen ballots, a majority of Democrats held pro-banking sentiments. These divisions meant that an alliance between Whigs and Democratic "softs" dominated most legislative sessions and frustrated the radical opponents of banks. But Demo-

Table 3. Percentage of Party Voting Yes on Legislation Favorable to Banking Interests in the States, 1833-1842[21]

State	1833		1834		1835		1836		1837		1838		1839		1840		1841		1842	
	D	W	D	W	D	W	D	W	D	W	D	W	D	W	D	W	D	W	D	W
New Jersey	71	50					48	100	00	100	05	89					11	94		
							33	74									26	100		
							31	94												
Pennsylvania			50	42	84	54	39	86	09	88							00	100	55	60
					48	82	49	100											00	89
							43	81												
New Hampshire			65	75	77	87					20	97							20	87
			76	89	28	34														
Ohio	38	91	35	86	53	04	41	93	03	100	34	69					00	92	57	66
	52	83	50	68			10	97	00	97	39	87							43	100
																			44	100
Missouri					66	50	66	66							00	100				
							57	44							06	90				
															08	67				
Virginia			13	50	52	81	47	95					28	98			39	82		
													34	95			16	90		
													11	91			28	93		

cratic unity increased substantially after 1837 as party organization matured and opposition to banks became a test of party orthodoxy.

Closely connected to attitudes on banking were views on currency. During the presidencies of Andrew Jackson and Martin Van Buren, currency questions were intimately tied to the attack on the Bank of the Untied States and the establishment of the independent subtreasury system. Although his position was at times clouded in rhetoric, Jackson favored the use of specie and opposed inflating the currency with bank notes.[20] Following his lead most Democratic legislators opposed wide-scale use of paper currency and advocated either eliminating small bills—generally under five dollars—or even prohibiting note issue completely and returning to the "Constitutional currency" of gold and silver. If successful, the Democratic effort to eliminate or limit "monied situations" would have further drastically reduced the currency in circulation.

Greater party unity among both Democrrats and Whigs existed on monetary questions than on either the corporation or banking (see Table 4). Between 75 and 100 percent of Jackson's party voted to restrict the circulation of small notes, while their opponents usually resisted such legislation by even larger margins. Democratic cohesion indicates the symbolic value of this issue for their party, especially after 1835. When in power, the Democrats, because so few of them voted with the Whigs on this question, either limited the circulation of small bills or abolished bank paper entirely.[23] However, such victories were usually sort-lived; the Whigs annulled these laws upon regaining power.[24]

Internal improvement questions also consistently appeared in the legislative debates of the 1830s. Discussions of railroads, canals, and turnpikes seemed at times almost the chief preoccupation of the period. The main disputes arose over whether to build these improvements; and if so whether they should be publicly or privately financed.[25] All the states under consideration, except New Jersey, used both public and private funds to construct their turnpikes, canals, and railroads. New Jersey relied solely on chartered private corporations for its internal improvements, although the state owned stock in the Camden and Amboy Railroad and the Delaware and Raritan Canal.[26]

There were few differences between the parties on the issue of internal improvements (see Table 5). Of the thirty-one legislative ballots recorded on state aid to internal improvements, Whigs gave a higher percentage of their votes to such appropriations on eighteen occasions. But their edge over the Democrats vanishes upon a closer examination. Only a few percentage points separated the two parties, and on nineteen ballots over 50 percent of the Democrats favored state aid. On only three ballots did either party vote unanimously for or against a canal or railroad bill. Greater variation developed within the parties than between them.

Party alignment on charters for internal improvement corporations indicates approximately the same result (see Table 6). Despite their aversion

Table 4. Percentage of Party Voting to Limit the Circulation of Small Bills within the States, 1833-1842[22]

State	1833		1834		1835		1836		1837		1838		1839		1840		1841		1842	
	D	W	D	W	D	W	D	W	D	W	D	W	D	W	D	W	D	W	D	W
New Jersey									100	07										
Pennsylvania			43 / 13	33 / 26					47	82	47	29					98	09	94	03
New Hampshire									82	02	99	00					90	00	84	02
Ohio	56	44			86	00	97	23	100	03	97	03								
Missouri											96 / 77	00 / 06							71	00
Virginia							86	16			57	41					100	00	59 / 68	00 / 02

Table 5. Percentage of Party Voting for Internal Improvement Bills within the States, 1833-1842[27]

State	1833		1834		1835		1836		1837		1838		1839		1840		1841	
	D	W	D	W	D	W	D	W	D	W	D	W	D	W	D	W	D	W
Pennsylvania			43	39			70	63			54	94					22	71
			66	56			79	63	37	90	30	66						
							48	55										
New Hampshire													33	83				
Ohio					38	90			73	57	51	65						
					94	19			52	63								
Missouri							68	00			42	63			29	100		
											60	100						
Virginia	51	40	40	57	60	57	64	59			54	49	37	54				
	54	48	49	60	59	40	62	63			56	69	56	39				

Table 6. Party Vote Favorable to the Incorporation of Internal Improvement Enterprises[30]

	1833		1834		1835		1836		1837		1838		1839		1840		1841		1842	
	D	W	D	W	D	W	D	W	D	W	D	W	D	W	D	W	D	W	D	W
New Jersey					55	12							63	59						
Pennsylvania					65	33	49	96									42	89	52	100
					100	50	63	65												
New Hampshire													16	93	83	06				
Ohio					40	86			61	51										
Missouri											64	29								
Virginia	46	58	41	80																

to using the corporate form for industrial, financial, and nonprofit institutions, Democrats were even more willing than Whigs to charter transportation corporations. On nine of fifteen ballots, a higher percentage of Democrats than Whigs inclined toward such institutions. Voting patterns on internal improvements appear to have been affected by intrastate rivalries and local needs rather than partisan consideration. In fact, party leaders often avoided taking positions on these questions, and Whigs joined Democrats from the same area in passing these bills (see Table 6).[28]

If economic acquisitiveness and fights over economic matters dominated the Jacksonian era, the period also witnessed agitation for and the enactment of a wide range of political and social reforms. Although Ralph Waldo Emerson later associated this "great activity of thought and experimenting" with the middle and upper classes in New England, he wrote in 1841 that "in the history of the world the doctrine of Reform had never such scope as at the present hour."[29] Groups outside the arena of partisan conflict often carried on the agitation for reform, but many such issues came before the state legislatures. Tables 7 through 9 are concerned with eight major areas of reform. Not every state discussed all these measures; few came up for votes in either Virginia or Missouri, the only two slave states examined.

Reform broke down into two categories: humanitarian and economic. If their votes in the legislature are any indication, Whigs were more interested in humanitarian reform and more closely connected to the reform movements of the day than were their Democratic rivals. In twenty-three of twenty-six votes on humanitarian issues—militia reform, abolition of capital punishment, temperance, and establishment of new prisons and asylums—a greater percentage of Whigs than Democrats advocated reform. On economic reform, the situation was more complex. Fewer Whigs than Democrats supported stay laws and laws to end imprisonment for debt on thirteen of nineteen ballots, but these votes, particularly on the latter issue, do not reveal clear-cut party differences.

Their positions on education further portray Whig and Democratic views on social reform (see Table 8). The struggle for educational reform involved largely the creation of common schools with partial state support. Although a number of Democrats played important roles in educational reform, notably Governors George Wolf of Pennsylvania and Peter Vroom of New Jersey, the Whigs were the education party in the legislatures. Not only did a higher percentage of Whig legislators favor education on thirteen of the fourteen ballots but also they presented greater unity on the issue.

The party votes on slavery and matters related to the position of blacks in the society confirm the connection between Whigs and the humanitarian movements (see Table 9). Increasingly after 1837, questions pertaining to the Negro, abolitionism, and slavery came before northern legislatures. These ranged from major national issues, such as annexation of Texas and nullification of the fugitive slave law, to state matters, such as prohibition of miscegenation. On every occasion, a higher percentage of Whigs voted the antislavery, pro-Negro position than did Democrats. In fact in only one case—an 1837 resolution in the New Hampshire legislature to accept petitions favoring abolition of slavery in Washington—did more than 50 percent of the Whigs abandon their antislavery stance.[33] The Whig susceptibility to antislavery measures in northern legislatures may indicate why that party was so vulnerable to the antislavery movements of the late 1840s and 1850s (see Table 9).

Although the economic situation and geogrpahy of the six states under discussion varied greatly, they maintained an amazing consistency both in the problems their legislatures discussed and in the positions the political

Table 7. Percentage of Party Voting on Social Reforms, 1833-1843[31]

	Penn.		N.J.		N.H.		Ohio		Mo.		Va.	
	D	W	D	W	D	W	D	W	D	W	D	W
Militia Reform	36	68	40	58	43	46	33	68				
					45	25	09	72				
					46	82	35	41				
Abolish Capital Punishment			38	80	59	23	17	38				
			79	88			39	75				
							34	61				
Temperance					24	52	49	73				
	22	100					64	87				
	49	76										
	23	66										
Prison and Asylum Reform	65	100	58	83	85	05	07	68				
			43	41	15	77						
			31	93	40	71						
Abolish Imprisonment for Debt			18	86	68	32	69	69	53	94	53	26
	43	45	53	21					81	43		
	61	46	100	74					62	28		
									39	52		
Relief for Debtor	76	41					100	03	33	17	52	53
							89	19			55	33
							95	11				

parties maintained on these issues. From this examination of legislative behavior, it appears that, although there were deviations from party position, one could generally differentiate a Democrat from a Whig. The typical legislative supporter of Jackson and Van Buren opposed corporations, banks, and paper currency, while showing little disposition toward humanitarian reform. His Whig counterpart supported corporations, banks, paper money, and reform. While a perfect correlation between party loyalty and voting behavior did not exist, the patterns are consistent enough to warrant the conclusion that the Whig and Democratic parties were more than national combinations of ambitious politicians united to promote a common presidential aspirant and to divide the spoils of office. Deviations from party voting norms declined after 1836 so that by 1840 from 80 to 100 percent of the Democrats and Whigs adhered to the dominant views of their own party. Because of the usual supposition that the Whig party was simply a heterogeneous alliance of politicians opposed to Jackson, the high level of unity which that party maintained throughout the whole period is somewhat surprising. Further research on *all* roll calls in these legislatures during this decade would be necessary to show the cohesion of state parties, but it seems

Table 8. Percentage of Party Voting for Bills Favorable to a Public Supported Education[32]

State	Democrats	Whigs
New Jersey	47	80
	44	64
Pennsylvania	64	76
	63	65
	65	69
New Hampshire	41	89
Ohio	37	63
	53	87
	46	54
	70	48
Missouri	48	92
	22	59
Virginia	40	77
	29	44

Table 9. Percentage of Party Voting for Pro-Negro and Antislavery Legislation[34]

State	1834 D	1834 W	1835 D	1835 W	1836 D	1836 W	1837 D	1837 W	1838 D	1838 W	1839 D	1839 W	1840 D	1840 W	1841 D	1841 W	1842 D	1842 W
Pennsylvania							00	83			(35) 18	63	(36) 16	86	02	52	18	96
							16	85					05	66				
Ohio	00	95					00	56	08	51							22	96
							00	51	00	66							54	81
New Hampshire							12	49	06	94	03	94	07	97			02	91
									04	99								

safe to assume that on the major issues of the period Democrats and Whigs in the state legislatures, like their counterparts in Congress, took distinct and contrasting positions.

Those who conceive of parties in the Jacksonian era as simple electoral machines also assert that these parties were part of an ideological consensus, varying little in their basic beliefs. This is, of course, a matter of emphasis. Consensus and conflict coexist in all political communities. Recent studies of contemporary parties insist that regardless of a large measure of consensus, basic dissimilarities in partisan "attitude structures" or "belief systems" do exist.[35] Attention to legislative behavior helps the historian cut through political rhetoric and clarify the areas of diversity in outlook and perspective that characterized the parties of the Jacksonian era.

Neither the struggle between "liberals" and "conservatives" so cogently sketched by Schlesinger nor the denial of real conflict embodied in many "consensus" interpretations adequately explains the patterns of partisan behavior in the state legislatures. An examination of arguments in the public press and the extended debates in the state constitutional conventions of the period shows elements of both conflict and consensus. The parties shared a general ideology, a democratized version of the liberal republicanism fashioned in the Revolutionary struggle.[36] But within the bounds of this broad ideological perspective, Whigs and Democrats disagreed over the proper role of government in securing liberal republican ends and in shaping American culture. Their legislative behavior illustrates the dimensions of this conflict. The parties' contrasting views can be briefly sketched in relation to the above issues.

The Whig legislators derived their support for economic expansion through the use of corporations and credit from their conception of republican society as a commonwealth of interrelated interests and their belief that government should encourage the development of society.[37] Legislation directly benefitting one section of society indirectly served all other segments of the community. "Agricultural, commercial, manufacturing and mechanical labor are linked together by a strong common interest," wrote Ohio Governor Joseph Vance, "and he who shall undertake to sever either branch of business from the other strikes a blow at the prosperity of the whole."[38]

Whigs viewed corporations as quasi-communal agencies for furthering the public interest. Charters issued to industrial corporations aided not only the manufacturer but also improved the position of the laborer and the farmer by creating additional jobs, increasing the demand for agricultural products, raising the economic level of all groups, and expanding the realm of economic opportunity. The limited liability provision in corporate charters protected the small as well as the large investor's personal property should the corporation in which he owned shares fail. Rather than serving the interests of the wealthy, who could always profitably employ their excess capital and afford occasional losses, the limited liability provision tended to increase the number of shareholders among the middle class and acted as a force to democratize the economy.[39]

The Whigs used similar arguments to defend banks and the "credit system." They viewed credit and currency as dynamic elements in economic growth and a source of general prosperity. Bank paper supplied the necessary supplement to limited amounts of specie while bank credit made capital available for both private and public improvements and encouraged the spirit of enterprise. But Whigs also reasoned that banks fostered opportunity as well as enterprise by giving to the honest and industrious "who have not been favored by an inheritance of wealth . . . a power to wield capital, not often possessed even by our wealthiest individuals." Democratic attempts to destroy the "credit system" could only contract the currency, reducing wages, property values, and farm prices while making the payment of taxes more burdensome.[40] Further, Democratic policy discouraged enterprise and "made the rich richer and the poor poorer" by depriving the latter of the means to alter their situation. Only cooperation between government and private enterprise and expansion of the "credit system" could encourage economic growth and enhance individual opportunity.

The northern Whigs' response to humanitarian reform was also related to their commonwealth concept of society and their emphasis on the role of government in encouraging socially beneficial behavior and individual opportunity. The balance of social and individual implications was clear in the movements for temperance and educational reform. According to Jonathan Kittredge, a New Hampshire temperance advocate, the drunkard "is useless, and worse than useless; he is a pest to all around him."[41] The sober man made a more productive worker, a better father, and a more responsible citizen. Certainly no democratic republic could be built upon self-indulgence; and "It was ridiculous to talk of the 'will of the sovereign people,' when intoxicated citizens were taken to the polls, and legislators were not ashamed to parade their inebriety while discussing important public measures."[42] In such a society ignorance was as dangerous as intoxication. Widespread education became essential, once political power passed into the hands of the masses. As the major Ohio Whig paper noted: "Other nations have hereditary sovereigns, and one of the most important duties of their governments is to take care of the education of the heir to their throne; these children all about your streets, who cannot even speak your language, are your future sovereigns."[43] At the same time Whigs emphasized that a statewide educational system, open to the poor as well as the rich, would insure that "those of our people who begin at the bottom of the ladder may get to the top."[44] For Whigs social reform meant using the government to foster intelligence and enterprise, to expand individual opportunity, and also to shape the culture by defining and building moral character.[45]

The emphasis on reform highlights a contrast between northern Whigs and their southern allies as well as their Democratic opponents.[46] Whigs in both sections manifested the desire to shape the society's economic future, but it was only one aspect of the Yankee Whigs' efforts to mold the entire culture. It seems clear from their behavior that Yankee Whigs wished to legislate morality and to use the state to set the moral norms of the society. In sharp contrast to their Democratic opponents who retained the earlier conception of the relation of virtue to a republic, northern Whigs believed that "forms of government are instituted for the protection and fostering of virtue, and are valuable only as they accomplish this. . . ."[47] The southern Whigs' unwillingness to join in the movements for humanitarian reform reveals a deep fissure in the Whig party which could be covered only so long as these issues remained local matters.

Democratic legislative behavior indicates quite different preconceptions about government and society.[48] Less optimistic than their Whig counterparts, and more fearful of concentrations of power, Democrats emphasized limited government to insure individual liberty rather than create opportunity. The classic statement of this view is in the first issue of the *United States Magazine, and Democratic Review*:

The best government is that which governs least. No human depositories can, with safety, be trusted with the power of legislation upon the general interests of society so as to operate directly or indirectly on the industry and property of the community. Such power must be perpetually liable to the most pernicious abuse, from the natural imperfection, both in wisdom of judgment and purity of purpose, of all human legislation, exposed constantly to the pressure of partial interests; interests which, at the same time that they are essentially selfish and tyrannical, are ever vigilant, persevering, and subtle in all the arts of deception and corruption.[49]

Most of the humanitarian reforms of the age, from temperance to abolition, were looked upon as meddlesome interferences with individual liberty and personal property.[50] For example, Democrats attacked public education as a dangerous governmental interference with parents' control over their children and as subversive to freedom of religion.[51]

The concern for individual liberty and the distrust of governmental tinkering also animated Democratic economic views. Although there were many facets to their economic thought, Democrats pictured the economy as a static "zero-sum" game in which certain groups—usually with the aid of corrupt government—enriched themselves at the expense of others. In sharp contrast to the Whig emphasis on community, the Jacksonians described a "politics of conflict."[52] Corporations illustrated the evils of government interference by giving advantages to privileged individuals while removing the moral restraints of personal responsibility.[53] "All Bank charters, all laws conferring special privileges, with all acts of incorporation, for purposes of private gain, are monopolies, in as much as they are calculated to enhance the power of wealth, produce inequalities among the people and to subvert liberty," a Trenton newspaper maintained.[54]

Hostility toward corporations focused primarily upon banks. Democrats denied that credit and paper money served any important function because they did not increase the "real" wealth of the country. In fact, they had the opposite effect. An inflated money supply tended to drive the only "real" currency out of the country leading to economic depression.[55] The paper issued by banks had no "intrinsic" value and was merely a subterfuge through which the "paper aristocracy" siphoned real wealth from the producing classes. Banks upset the "natural and just laws" of the distribution of wealth, created a dangerous "artificial inequality of fortune," and debased the morals of the young.[56] The "paper aristocracy" became at once a foe of liberty more powerful than European nobility and the single most important danger to the republic.[57] To Thomas Hart Benton the effect of the "credit system" was nothing short of apocalyptic: "Rome had her Pharsalia— Greece her Chaeronea—and many barbarian kingdoms have given immorality to the spot on which they expired; and shall this great republic be subjected to extinction on the contingencies of trade and banking?"[58] The movement toward deflation and hard money was an attempt to stabilize the economy by removing government interference with the "natural" currency and eliminating special privilege in order to allow free reign for individual liberty in the economic sphere.

On questions involving manufacturing and benevolent corporations, banks and currency, and social reform, the different patterns of legislative behavior described above reflected the contrasting ideological perspectives of the parties. What of those issues on which Whigs and Democrats voted together? Close examination shows that most often such instances were the product of convergence of different ideological strains or local interests rather than an indication of the basic similarities of the parties.

Four major factions developed in the New Jersey legislature during the early struggles over internal improvements. The Joint Companies through the ownership of the Delaware and Raritan Canal and Camden and Amboy Railroad not only had a monopoly of all transportation between New York City and Philadelphia but also the privilege of vetoing any other projected routes in the area.[59] This powerful monopoly was chartered by a Democratic legislature in 1830 and included several prominent Democrats on its board of directors. It was generally supported by the followers of Jackson, especially those from central Jersey.[60] Allied with them were a number of Whigs who defended the rights of the company to maintain a monopoly over transportation in the New York-Philadelphia corridor because they generally defended as sacrosanct any corporate privilege. Opposition to the Joint Companies came from Democrats appalled by their party's support for a dangerous "monster" and from Whigs who either sought to embarrass their opponents and gain political capital from the issue or who were involved in the promotion of rival railroads.[61]

Similarly votes in Ohio in the mid-1830s on banks sometimes brought together divergent elements. In the 1833-1834 session of the Ohio legislature a state bank was proposed and defeated. In the same session legislators chartered a number of local banks and registered their opinion on the Bank of the United States. A comparison of these votes shows that the coalition which defeated the proposed state bank was made up of Whig advocates of a national bank, backers of local banks from both parties, and "hard money" Democrats who opposed banks of any kind.[62]

Finally, the struggle against imprisonment for debt brought together different social groups with contrasting motives. The movement in Pennsylvania "reflected a mingling of the ideologies produced by both business development and the advancing democratic movement."[63] Entrepreneurs seeking to encourage enterprise and workingmen defending their own interests joined with humanitarians who decried the loss of productive energies represented by the imprisoned debtor. Such situations reveal the limits of roll call analysis, but in no way contradict the basic dissimilarity between the parties of the Jacksonian era.

Advocates of the "electoral machine" view, particularly McCormick, have added measurably to an understanding of the Jacksonian party system. But once having discredited the progressive view, they perceived only chaos ordered by self-serving politicians. To develop a new approach to the period, historians must begin with concrete patterns of political behavior and then describe the "attitude structures" or "ideologies" which rationalized that behavior. This essay suggests that the dissimilarities of the major parties on the national level were, with only modest alterations, reflected in the behavior and thought of state party leaders. Certainly there were sectional splits and party unity was never perfect, but this study indicates that the two major parties in the Jacksonian era represented contrasting belief systems and differed about more than the spoils of office.

Notes

1. Arthur M. Schlesinger, Jr., *The Age of Jackson* (Boston, 1945).

2. For example, see Marvin Meyers, *The Jacksonian Persuasion: Politics and Belief* (Stanford, 1957); Charles Sellers, *James K. Polk* (2 vols., Princeton, 1957, 1966); Lee Benson, *The Concept of Jacksonian Democracy: New York As A Test Case* (Princeton, 1961); Donald B. Cole, "The Presidential Election of 1832 in New Hampshire," *Historical New Hampshire,* XXI (Winter 1966), 33-50; John Vollmer Mering, *The Whig Party in Missouri* (Columbia, 1967); Frank Otto Gatell, "Money and Party in Jacksonian America: A Quantitative Look at New York City's Men of Quality," *Political Science Quarterly,* LXXXII (June 1967), 235-52. These studies sharply disagree over the content of party principles and the socio-economic groups represented by Whigs and Democrats.

3. Richard P. McCormick, *The Second American Party System: Party Formation in the Jacksonian Era* (Chapel Hill, 1966), 4. See also Philip Shriver Klein, *Pennsylvania Politics 1817-1832: A Game without Rules* (Philadelphia, 1940); Thomas Payne Govan, *Nicholas Biddle: Nationalist and Public Banker 1786-1844* (Chicago, 1959); Lonnie J. White, *Politics on the Southwestern Fronteir: Arkansas Territory, 1819-1836* (Memphis, 1964); Roy F. Nichols, *The Invention of the American Political Parties* (New York, 1967); Edward Pessen, *Jacksonian America: Society, Personality, and Politics* (Homewood, Ill., 1969).

4. Joel H. Silbey, *The Shrine of Party: Congressional Voting Behavior 1841-1852* (Pittsburgh, 1967); Thomas B. Alexander, *Sectional Stress and Party Strength: A Study of Roll-Call Voting Patterns in the United States House of Representatives, 1836-1860* (Nashville, 1967).

5. Pessen, *Jacksonian America,* 234. Edward Pessen is speaking about the Whigs. General comments in this book and in Edward Pessen, *Most Uncommon Jacksonians: The Radical Leaders of the Early Labor Movement* (Albany, 1967), have caused the authors to number him among the advocates of the "electoral machine" view.

6. The choice of these states requires a methodological note. The major source for this article is the microfilm publication of the Library of Congress, "The Early State Records." (For a description of the materials available in this series, see William Sumner Jenkins and Lillian A. Hamrick, eds., *A Guide to the Microfilm Collection of Early State Records: Prepared by the Library of Congress in Association with the University of North Carolina* [Washington, 1950]). As not all the states that existed during the Jacksonian era were included in this series, the selection process was narrowed, eliminating, for example, two of the most interesting commonwealths, Massachusetts and New York. (The "Early State Records" does not include the Pennsylvania legislative data, but since these were available from other sources, they were included in the study.) Other states were eliminated because of the nature of their legislative journals. No uniformity existed among the journals. They varied from sketchy outlines of the debates containing but a few roll call votes to very extensive accounts. Where not enough information existed, or where the records were so voluminous as to make them unworkable, they were eliminated. In Tennessee, for example, up to 1,000 roll call votes were taken in a single year, making anything but a computerized study impossible. In one case, that of Rhode Island, the debates are in manuscript form, making their use extremely difficult in this project. Another limitation on the use of some of the state debates was the lack of a roll call vote which clearly differentiated the two parties. Representatives were not listed by party. In order to tabulate the votes, it was necessary to find a clear issue in which the Democrats voted one way and the Whigs another. In several states, the parties regularly debated some symbolic national question to indicate these party lines such as resolutions supporting Jackson's policies toward the Bank of the United States, or instructing the senators from the state to expunge from the Senate journal that body's 1834 censure of Jackson, or even urging Congress to return a fine Jackson paid during the War of 1812. Where such roll call votes were missing it was impossible to distinguish between the two parties as was the case with most Louisiana and North Carolina sessions. The six states used in this study were thus selected from those remaining to give as wide a geographic representation as possible—New Hampshire in New England, New Jersey and Pennsylvania in the middle states, Virginia in the South, Ohio in the Northwest, and Missouri in the Southwest. The journals of the lower houses were used because the lower houses were larger than the upper houses and provided a better base to allow for contrast between the parties.

7. Michel Chevalier, *Society, Manners and Politics in the United States: Being a Series of Letters on North America,* John William Ward, ed. (Garden City, 1961), 299.

8. Alexis de Tocqueville, *Democracy in America,* Phillips Bradley, ed. (2 vols., New York, 1954), II, 166.

9. "Influence of the Trading Spirit upon the Social and Moral Life of America," *American Review: A Whig Journal of Politics, Literature, Art and Science,* I (Jan. 1845), 95.

10. Marvin Meyers brilliantly analyzes the moralitic quality of Jacksonian rhetoric in *Jacksonian Persuasion.*

11. The votes recorded on these pages represent a small fraction of the roll calls taken during these legislative sessions. For example, of 289 votes taken at the 1837 meeting of the Ohio legislature only twenty were used. A number of votes were eliminated because so little information was given about a bill that it was impossible to discover what the vote meant. Moreover, during the course of a yearly session, the lawmaking bodies discussed only a few substantive issues. Most debates dealt with private matters, such as requests for divorces, or were on procedural matters, such as the time set for the House to meet. The votes examined in detail were

on topics which transcended state lines and were discussed in all the states during the 1833-1843 era, such as the corporation, banking, and internal improvements. In cases where there was more than one vote on a single bill, the authors of this essay used the most revealing ballot, which was not always the final motion for passage. On occasion, this vote occurred on an amendment, such as the repeated efforts to eliminate the limited liability clause from corporate charters. Once such a resolution passed or failed, the final vote was a formality. Often issues were discussed a number of times during a single legislative session, while at other times few of these issues were discussed. In order not to give undue weight in these tables to one legislative session in which a number of roll calls were taken on the same question, the maximum number of votes listed at any one session was three. The other votes were checked to ensure that they did not vary substantially from the ones used.

12. Attacks on limited liability were made by either amending the charters of individual corporations omitting this feature or by writing general incorporation bills without this provision. The stockholder in such instances might be held liable for all the debts of the company out of his own property or for a proportion of the debts based upon the percentage of stock held. He might even be liable for these debts up to one year after disposing of his stock. The passage of general corporation laws was less important in many cases than the type of laws passed. These could be phrased liberally, granting wide powers to the institutions incorporated under them or be quite narrow by restricting its powers and by making stockholders individually liable. *Journal of the House of Delegates of the Commonwealth of Virginia, Begun and Held at the Capitol, in the City of Richmond, on Monday the Second Day of December, One Thousand Eight Hundred and Thirty-three* (Richmond, 1833), 55; *Journal of the House of Representatives of the State of Ohio; Being the First Session of the Fortieth General Assembly, Begun and Held in the City of Columbus, Monday, December 6, 1841, and in the Fortieth Year of Said State* (Columbus, 1841), 35; *Journal of the House of Representatives of the State of New Hampshire, at their Session Holden at the Capitol in Concord Commencing Wednesday, June 5, 1839. Published By Authority* (Concord, 1839), 176-97. Extremely useful on the corporation during these years is John W. Cadman, Jr., *The Corporation in New Jersey: Business and Politics 1791-1875* (Cambridge, Mass., 1949), 3-110.

13. *Votes and Proceedings of the Fifty-Eighth General Assembly of the State of New Jersey, at a Session Begun at Trenton, on the Twenty-Second Day of October, One Thousand Eight Hundred and Thirty-Three* (New Brunswick, 1834), 328; *Votes and Proceedings of the Sixtieth General Assembly of the State of New Jersey, at a Session Begun at Trenton, on the Twenty-Seventh Day of October, One Thousand Eight Hundred and Thirty-Five* (Freehold, 1836), 130; *Votes and Proceedings of the Sixty-First General Assembly of the State of New Jersey, at a Session Begun at Trenton, on the Twenty-Fifth Day of October, One Thousand Eight Hundred and Thirty-Six* (Belvidere, 1837), 549, 572, 251; *Votes and Proceedings of the Sixty-Second General Assembly of the State of New Jersey, at a Session Begun at Trenton, on the Twenty-Fourth day of October, One Thousand Eight Hundred and Thirty-Seven* (Newark, 1838), 577, 609, 353; *Votes and Proceedings of the Sixty-Third General Assembly of the State of New Jersey, at a Session Begun at Trenton, on the Twenty-Third Day of October, One Thousand Eight Hundred and Thirty-Eight* (Newark, 1839), 324, 408; *Votes and Proceedings of the Sixty-Fourth General Assembly of the State of New Jersey, at a Session Begun at Trenton, on the Twenty-Second Day of October, One Thousand Eight Hundred and Thirty-Nine* (Belvidere, 1840), 258, 280, 478; *Votes and Proceedings of the Sixty-Sixth General Assembly of the State of New Jersey, at a Session Begun at Trenton, on the Twenty-Sixth Day of October, One Thousand Eight Hundred and Forty-One* (Trenton, 1842), 367; *Votes and Proceedings of the Sixty-Seventh General Assembly of the State of New Jersey, at a Session Begun at Trenton, on the Twenty-Fifty Day of October, One Thousand Eight Hundred and Forty-Two* (Trenton, 1843), 475; *Journal of the Forty-sixth House of Representatives of the Commonwealth of Pennsylvania, Commenced at Harrisburg, Tuesday, the First of December, in the Year of Our Lord One Thousand Eight Hudnred and Thirty-Five, and of the Commonwealth the Sixtieth* (2 vols., Harrisburg, 1835-1836), I, 577-78; *Journal of the Forty-Eighth House of Representa-*

tives of the Commonwealth of Pennsylvania, Commenced at Harrisburg, Tuesday, the Fifth of December, in the Year of Our Lord One Thousand Eight Hundred and Thirty-Eight, and of the Commonwealth the Sixty-Third (2 vols., Harrisburg, 1838-1839), I, 587; Journal of the Fifty-First House of Representatives of the Commonwealth of Pennsylvania: Commenced at Harrisburg, Tuesday the Fifth Day of January, in the Year of Our Lord One Thousand Eight Hundred and Forty-One, and of the Commonwealth the Sixty-Fifth (2 vols., Harrisburg, 1841), I, 287, 397; Journal of the Fifty-Second House of Representatives of the Commonwealth of Pennsylvania: Commenced at Harrisburg, Tuesday, The Fourth of January, in the Year of Our Lord One Thousand Eight Hundred and Forty-Two, and of the Commonwealth the Sixty-Sixth (2 vols., Harrisburg, 1842), I, 196, 331-33; Journal of the House of Representatives, of the State of New Hampshire, at Their Session Holden at the Capitol in Concord, Commencing Wednesday, June 7, 1837. Published by Authority (Concord, 1837), 147-49; Journal of the House of Representatives, of the State of New Hampshire, at Their Session Holden at the Capitol in Concord, Commencing Wednesday, June 6, 1838. Published by Authority (Concord, 1838), 196-99; Journal of the House of Representatives, of the State of New Hampshire, at Their Session Holden at the Capitol in Concord, Commencing Wednesday, June 5, 1839. Published by Authority (Concord, 1839), 276-77, 211-13; Journal of the House of Representatives, of the State of New Hampshire, at Their Session Holden at the Capitol in Concord, Commencing Wednesday, November 18, 1840. Published by Authority (Concord, 1841), 156-58, 190-93; Journal of the House of Representatives of the State of New Hampshire, at Their Session Holden at the Capitol in Concord, Commencing Wednesday, November 2, 1842. Published by Authority (Concord, 1843), 26; Journal of the House of Representatives of the State of Ohio; Being the First Session of the Thirty-Second General Assembly: Begun and Held in the Town of Columbus, Monday, December 2, 1833, and in the Thirty-Second Year of Said State (Columbus, 1833), 480; Journal of the House of Representatives, of the State of Ohio; Being the First Session of the Thirty-Third General Assembly: Begun and Held in the City of Columbus, Monday, December 1, 1834, and in the Thirty-Third Year of Said State (Columbus, 1834), 141; Journal of the House of Representatives of the State of Ohio; Being the First Session of the Thirty-Fourth General Assembly, Begun and Held in the City of Columbus, Monday, December 7, 1835, and in the Thirty-Fourth Year of Said State (Columbus, 1835), 419, 477, 836; Journal of the House of Representatives, of the State of Ohio; Being the First Session of the Thirty-Fifth General Assembly, Begun and Held in the City of Columbus, Monday, December 5, 1836 and in the Thirty-Fifth Year of Said State (Columbus, 1836), 177, 308, 400; Journal of the House of Representatives, of the State of Ohio; Being the First Session of the Thirty-Sixth General Assembly, Begun and Held in the City of Columbus, Monday, December 4, 1837, and in the Thirty-Sixth Year of Said State (Columbus, 1837-1838), 722; Journal of the House of Representatives of the State of Missouri, at the First Session of the Tenth General Assembly, Begun and Held at the City of Jefferson, on Monday, the Nineteenth Day of November, in the Year of Our Lord, One Thousand Eight Hundred and Thirty-Eight (n.p., 1839), 340; Journal of the House of Representatives, of the State of Missouri, at the First Session of the Eleventh General Assembly, Begun and Held at the City of Jefferson, On Monday, the Sixteenth Day of November, in the Year of Our Lord, One Thousand Eight Hundred and Forty (Jackson, Mo., 1841), 261; Journal of the House of Representatives, of the State of Missouri, at the First Session of the Twelfth General Assembly, Begun and Held at the City of Jefferson, on Monday, the Twenty-First Day of November, in the Year of Our Lord, One Thousand Eight Hundred and Forty-Two (Jefferson City, 1843), 409, 306; Journal of the House of Delegates of the Commonwealth of Virginia, Begun and Held at the Capitol., in the City of Richmond, on Monday, the Second Day of December, One Thousand Eight Hundred and Thrity-Three (Richmond, 1833), 55-56, 81; Journal of the House of Delegates of the Commonwealth of Virginia, Begun and Held at the Capitol, in the City of Richmond, on Monday, the Seventh Day of January, One Thousand Eight Hundred and Thirty-Nine (Richmond, 1839), 41.

14. The consequence of this lack of unity can be observed more clearly when the percentage

figures are broken down into the actual vote. Examples of this pattern occurred in Missouri in 1841 and New Jersey in 1836. In Missouri seven of forty-one Democrats joined all forty Whigs to defeat an amendment to a turnpike charter which gave the legislature the privilege of repealing it whenever this action was considered in the public interest. In New Jersey the Totowa Manufacturing Company was chartered when nine of twenty-nine Democrats joined the fifteen members of the opposition in voting for the bill. *Journal of the House of Representatives . . . Missouri . . . November, One Thousand Eight Hundred and Forty-two*, 261; *Votes . . . of the General Assembly of . . . New Jersey . . . October, One Thousand Eight Hundred, Thirty-five*, 130.

15. *Journal of the . . . House of Representatives . . . of Pennsylvania . . . January . . . One Thousand Eight Hundred and Forty-One . . .* , I, 610; *Journal of the House of Representatives of . . . New Hampshire . . .* , June 6, 1838, p. 177; *Journal of the House of Representatives . . . of New Hampshire . . . June 3, 1840*, p. 255; *Journal of the House of Representatives . . . of Ohio . . . December 4, 1837 . . .* , 37; *Journal of the House of Representatives of the State of Ohio; Being the First Session of the Fortieth General Assembly, Held in the City of Columbus, and Commencing Monday, December 6, 1841* (Columbus, 1841), 624; *Journal of the House of Representatives of the State of Ohio; Being the First Session of the Forty-First General Assembly, Held in the City of Columbus, Commencing on Monday, December 5, 1842* (Columbus, 1842), 416; *Journal of the House of Representatives of . . . Missouri . . . November, One Thousand Eight Hundred and Forty*, 196; *Journal of the House of Representatives of . . . Missouri . . . November, One Thousand Eight Hundred and Forty-Two*, 397, 399; *Journal of the House of Delegates of the Commonwealth of Virginia, Begun and Held at the Capitol, in the City of Richmond, on Monday, the Sixth Day of December, One Thousand Eight Hundred and Forty-One* (Richmond, 1841), 70.

16. James Roger Sharp, *The Jacksonians and the Banks* (New York, 1970); William Gerald Shade, *Banks or No Banks: The Money Issue in Western Politics, 1837-1865* (Detroit, 1971); Erling Arthur Erickson, "Banks and Politics Before the Civil War: The Case of Iowa, 1836-1865" (doctoral dissertation, University of Iowa, 1967); and Rodney O. Davis, "Partisanship in Jacksonian State Politics: Party Divisions in the Illinois Legislature, 1834-1841," Robert P. Swierenga, ed., *Quantification in American History: Theory and Research* (New York, 1970), 157-60.

17. *Journal of the House of Representatives . . . of Ohio . . . December 5, 1836 . . .* , 362; *Journal of the House of Representatives of . . . New Hampshrie . . . June 6, 1838*, pp. 246-48; *Journal of the House of Delegates of Virginia . . . January, One Thousand Eight Hundred and Thirty-Nine*, 157; *Journal of the House of Representatives . . . of Pennsylvania . . . January . . . One Thousand Eight Hundred and Forty-One . . .* , I, 640.

18. *Votes . . . of the . . . General Assembly of . . . New Jersey . . . October, One Thousand Eight Hundred and Thirty-Seven*, 333; *Journal of the House of Representatives . . . of Pennsylvania . . . December . . . One Thousand Eight Hundred and Thirty-Seven . . .* , I, 69; *Journal of the House of Delegates of . . . Virginia . . . December, One Thousand Eight Hundred and Thirty-Nine*, 17; *Journal of the House of Representatives . . . of Ohio . . . December 5, 1842*, p. 125; *Journal of the House of Delegates of . . . Virginia . . . December, One Thousand Eight Hundred and Forty-One*, 228.

19. "Constitutional Reform," *United States Magazine, and Democratic Review*, XIII (Dec. 1843), 563-76; "The Progress of Constitutional Reform in the United States," *ibid.*, XVIII (April and June 1846), 243-56, 403-20; "The New-York Constitutional Convention," *ibid.* XIX (Nov. 1846), 339-48; "Constitutional Government," *ibid.*, XX (March 1847), 195-204; "Constitutional Reform," *ibid.*, XXIX (July 1851), 3-18.

20. Jackson's views during these years are expressed in his correspondence with Moses Dawson, a leading opponent of banks in Ohio. See John J. Whealen, ed., "The Jackson-Dawson Correspondence," *Bulletin of the Historical and Philosophical Society of Ohio*, 16 (Jan. 1958), 3-30.

21. *Votes . . . of the General Assembly of . . . New Jersey . . . October, One Thousand Eight Hundred and Thirty-Three*, 540; *Votes . . . of the . . . General Assembly of . . . New Jersey . . . October, One Thousand Eight Hundred and Thirty-Five*, 405; *Votes . . . of the General Assembly of . . . New Jersey . . . October, One Thousand Eight Hundred and Thirty-Six*, 184, 201, 240; *Votes . . . of the . . . General Assembly of New Jersey . . . October, One Thousand Eight Hundred and Thirty-Seven*, 333; *Votes . . . of the . . . General Assembly of . . . New Jersey . . . October, One Thousand Eight Hundred and Thirty-Eight*, 466; *Journal of the Forty-Fifth House of Representatives of the Commonwealth of Pennsylvania, Commenced at Harrisburg, Tuesday, the Second of December, in the Year of Our Lord One Thousand Eight Hundred and Thirty-Four, and of the Commonwealth the Fifty-Ninth* (2 vols., Harrisburg, 1834-1835), I, 799; *Journal of the . . . House of Representatives . . . at Pennsylvania . . . December, . . . One Thousand Eight Hundred and Thirty-Five . . .* , I, 951, 281; *Journal of the Forty-Seventh House of Representatives of the Commonwealth of Pennsylvania, Commenced at Harrisburg, Tuesday, the Sixth of December, in the Year of Our Lord One Thousand Eight Hundred and Thirty-Six, and of the Commonwealth the Sixty-First* (2 vols., Harrisburg, 1836-1837), I, 517, 503-04, 917; *Journal of the . . . House of Representatives . . . of Pennsylvania . . . December . . . One Thousand Eight Hundred and Thirty-Seven . . .* , I, 69; *Journal of the . . . House of Representatives . . . of Pennsylvania . . . January . . . One Thousand Eight Hundred and Forty-One . . .* , I, 86, 640; *Journal of the . . . House of Representatives . . . of Pennsylvania . . . January . . . One Thousand Eight Hundred and Forty-Two . . .* , I, 576, 277; *Journal of the House of Representatives, of the State of New Hampshire, at Their Session, Holden at the Capitol in Concord, Commencing Wednesday, June 4, 1834. Published by Authority* (Concord, 1834), 162-63, 163-64; *Journal of the House of Representatives . . . New Hampshire . . . June 6, 1838,* pp. 246-48; *Journal of the House of Representatives of . . . New Hampshire . . . November 1, 1842,* pp. 314-17; *Journal of the House of Representatives . . . of Ohio . . . December 2, 1833 . . .* , 550, 501; *Journal of the House of Representatives . . . of Ohio . . . December 1, 1834 . . .* , 143, 216; *Journal of the House of Representatives . . . of Ohio . . . December 7, 1835 . . .* , 617; *Journal of the House of Representatives . . . of Ohio . . . December 5, 1836 . . .* , 362, 288; *Journal of the House of Representatives . . . of Ohio . . . December 4, 1837 . . .* , 230, 422; *Journal of the House of Representatives of the State of Ohio; Being the First Session of the Thirty-Seventh General Assembly, Begun and Held in the City of Columbus, Monday, December 3, 1838, and in the Thirty-Seventh Year of Said State* (Columbus, 1838), 619, 677;; *Journal of the House of Representatives . . . of Ohio . . . December 6, 1841 . . .* , 554; *Journal of the House of Representatives . . . of Ohio . . . December 5, 1842 . . .* , 125, 299, 284; *Journal of the House of Representatives of the State of Missouri, at The First Session of the Eighth General Assembly, Begun and Held at the City of Jefferson, on Monday, the Seventh Day of November, in the Year of Our Lord, One Thousand Eight Hundred and Thirty-Four* (Fayette, 1835), 255; *Journal of the House of Representatives, of the State of Missouri, at The First Session of the Ninth General Assembly, Begun and Held at the City of Jefferson, On the Twenty-First Day of November, in the Year of Our Lord, One Thousand Eight Hundred and Thirty-Six* (Bowling-Green, 1837), 315, 312; *Journal of the House of Representatives of . . . Missouri . . . November . . . One Thousand Eight Hundred and Forty*, 337-338, 103, 152; *Journal of the House of Delegates of the Commonwealth of Virginia, Begun and Held at the Capitol, in the City of Richmond, on Monday, the First Day of December, One Thousand Eight Hundred and Thirty-Four* (Richmond, 1834), 168; *Journal of the House of Delegates of the Commonwealth of Virginia, Begun and Held at the Capitol, in the City of Richmond on Monday, the Seventh Day of December, One Thousand Eight Hundred and Thirty-Five* (Richmond, 1835), 143; *Journal of the House of Delegates of the Commonwealth of Virginia, Begun and Held at the Capitol, in the City of Richmond, on Monday the Sixth Day of December, One Thousand Eight Hundred and Thirty-Six* (Richmond, 1836), 181; *Journal of the House of Delegates of the Commonwealth of Virginia, Begun and Held at the Capitol, in the City of Richmond, on Monday, the Second Day of*

December, One Thousand Eight Hundred and Thirty-Nine (Richmond, 1839), 132, 17, 157; *Journal of the House of Delegates of . . . Virginia . . . December, One Thousand Eight Hundred and Forty-One,* 160, 228.

22. Votes . . . of the . . . *General Assembly of . . . New Jersey . . . October, One Thousand Eight Hundred and Thirty-Seven,* 175; *Journal of the . . . House of Representatives . . . of Pennsylvania . . . December . . . One Thousand Eight Hundred and Thirty-Four . . .,* I, 795, 155; *Journal of the . . . House of Representatives . . . of Pennsylvania . . . December . . . One Thousand Eight Hundred and Thirty-Seven . . .,* I, 607; *Journal of the House of Representatives . . . of Pennsylvania. . . . January . . . One Thousand Eight Hundred and Forty-One . . .,* I, 192; *Journal of the . . . House of Representatives . . . of Pennsylvania . . . January . . . One Thousand Eight Hundred and Forty-Two . . .,* I, 930; *Journal of the House of Representatives of . . . New Hampshire . . . June 7, 1837,* p. 234; *Journal of the House of Representatives of . . . New Hampshire . . . June 6, 1838,* p. 180; *Journal of the House of Representatives, of the State of New Hampshire, at Their Session Holden at the Capitol in Concord, Commencing Wednesday, June 2, 1841. Published by Authority* (Concord, 1841), 250-53; *Journal of the House of Representatives, of New Hampshire . . . November 2, 1841,* p. 360-62; *Journal of the House of Representatives . . . of Ohio . . . December 2, 1833 . . . ,* 479-80; *Journal of the House of Representatives . . . of Ohio . . . December 7, 1835 . . . ,* 712; *Journal of the House of Representatives . . . of Ohio . . . December 5, 1836 . . . ,* 255; *Journal of the House of Representatives . . . of Ohio . . . December 4, 1837 . . . ,* 659; *Journal of the House of Representatives . . . of Ohio . . . December 3, 1838 . . . ,* 164; *Journal of the House of Representatives, of . . . Missouri . . . November, One Thousand Eight Hundred and Thirty-Eight,* 376, 197; *Journal of the House of Representatives of . . . Missouri . . . November, One Thousand Eight Hundred and Forty-Two,* 533; *Journal of the House of Delegates of . . . Virginia . . . December, One Thousand Eight Hundred and Thirty-Six,* 132; *Journal of the House of Delegates of the Commonwealth of Virginia, Begun and Held at the Capitol, in the City of Richmond, On Monday, the First Day of January, One Thousand Eight Hundred Thirty-Eight* (Richmond, 1838), 196; *Journal of the House of Delegates of . . . Virginia . . . December, One Thousand Eight Hundred and Forty-One,* 32; *Journal of the House of Delegates of the Commonwealth of Virginia, Begun and Held at the Capitol, in the City of Richmond, On Monday, the Fifth Day of December, One Thousand Eight Hundred and Forty-Two* (Richmond, 1842), 35-36.

23. *Journal of the House of Delegates of . . . Virginia . . . December, One Thousand Eight Hundred and Thirty-Six,* 132; *Journal of the . . . House of Representatives . . . of Pennsylvania . . . January . . . One Thousand Eight Hundred and Forty-One . . . ,* I, 192; *Journal of the House of Representatives of . . . New Hampshire . . . June 6, 1838,* p. 180; *Journal of the House of Representatives . . . of Ohio . . . December 7, 1835 . . . ,* 712; *Journal of the House of Representatives of . . . Missouri . . . November, One Thousand Eight Hundred and Thirty-Eight,* 376.

24. *Journal of the House of Delegates of . . . Virginia . . . December, One Thousand Eight Hundred and Forty-One,* 32; *Journal of the House of Representatives . . . of Ohio . . . December 4, 1837 . . . ,* 659.

25. Carter Goodrich, *Government Promotion of American Canals and Railroads 1800-1890* (New York, 1960), 51-120; Louis Hartz, *Economic Policy and Democratic Thought: Pennsylvania, 1776-1860* (Cambridge, Mass., 1948); Carter Goodrich, "The Virginia System of Mixed Enterprise: A Study of State Planning of Internal Improvements," *Political Science Quarterly,* LXIV (Sept. 1949), 335-87; James Neal Primm, *Economic Policy in the Development of a Western State: Missouri 1820-1860* (Cambridge, 1954); Harry N. Scheiber, *Ohio Canal Era: A Case Study of Government and the Economy, 1820-1861* (Athens, O., 1969).

26. H. Jerome Crammer, "Improvements Without Public Funds: The New Jersey Canals," Carter Goodrich, ed., *Canals and American Economic Development* (New York, 1961), 115-66.

27. *Journal of the . . . House of Representatives . . . of Pennsylvania . . . December . . . One Thousand Eight Hundred and Thirty-Four . . . ,* I, 724-25, 351; *Journal of the . . . House of Representatives . . . of Pennsylvania . . . December . . . One Thousand Eight*

Hundred and Thirty Six . . . , I, 1053, 901-02, 942; Journal of the . . . House of Representatives . . . of Pennsylvania . . . December . . . One Thousand Eight Hundred and Thirty-Seven . . . , I, 1087; Journal of the . . . House of Representatives . . . of Pennsylvania . . . December . . . One Thousand Eight Hundred and Thirty-Eight . . . , I, 607, 772; Journal of the . . . House of Representatives . . . of Pennsylvania . . . January . . . One Thousand Eight Hundred and Forty-Two . . . , I, 807; Journal of the House of Representatives of . . . New Hampshrie . . . June 5, 1839, p. 315; Journal of the House of Representatives . . . of Ohio . . . December 7, 1835 . . . , 642, 699; Journal of the House of Representatives . . . of Ohio . . . December 4, 1837 . . . , 716, 317-18; Journal of the House of Representatives . . . of Ohio . . . December 3, 1838 . . . , 753; Journal of the House of Representatives of . . . Missouri . . . November, One Thousand Eight Hundred and Thirty-Six, 357; Journal of the House of Representatives of . . . Missouri . . . November, One Thousand Eight Hundred and Thirty-Eight, 266, 253; Journal of the House of Representatives of . . . Missouri . . . November, One Thousand Eight Hundred and Forty, 288; Journal of the House of Delegates of . . . Virginia . . . December, One Thousand Eight Hundred and Thirty-Three, 210-11, 57; Journal of the House of Delegates of . . . Virginia . . . December, One Thousand Eight Hundred and Thirty-Four, 198, 70; Journal of the House of Delegates of . . . Virginia . . . December, One Thousand Eight Hundred and Thirty-Six, 302, 220; Journal of the House of Delegates of . . . Virginia . . . January, One Thousand Eight Hundred and Thirty-Eight, 145; Journal of the House of Delegates of . . . Virginia . . . January, One Thousand Eight Hundred and Thirty-Nine, 198, 122.

28. Herbert Ershkowitz, "New Jersey Politics during the Era of Andrew Jackson, 1820-1837" (doctoral dissertation, New York Unviersity, 1965), 26-27, 159-62; Scheiber, Ohio Canal Era, 109-10; Harry N. Scheiber, "Urban Rivalry and Internal Improvements in the Old Northwest, 1820-1860," Ohio History, 71 (Oct. 1962), 227-39, 289-92.

29. Edward Waldo Emerson, ed., The Complete Works of Ralph Waldo Emerson With a Biographical Introduction and Notes: Nature Addresses and Lectures (Boston, 1903), 228; Edward Waldo Emerson, ed., The Complete Works of Ralph Waldo Emerson With a Biographical Introduction and Notes: Essays (Boston, 1903), 251.

30. Votes . . . of the General Assembly of . . . New Jersey . . . October, One Thousand Eight Hundred and Thirty-Five, 132-133; Votes . . . of the . . . General Assembly of New Jersey . . . October, One Thousand Eight Hundred and Thirty-Nine, 483; Journal of the . . . House of Representatives . . . of Pennsylvania . . . December, One Thousand Eight Hundred and Thirty-Five . . . , I, 919, 942; Journal of the . . . House of Representatives . . . of Pennsylvania . . . December, One Thousand Eight Hundred and Thirty-Six . . . , I, 401-565; Journal of the . . . House of Representatives . . . of Pennsylvania . . . January, One Thousand Eight Hundred and Forty-One . . . , I, 355; Journal of the . . . House of Representatives . . . of Pennsylvania . . . January, One Thousand Eight Hudnred and Forty-Two . . . , I, 543; Journal of the House of Representatives . . . New Hampshire . . . June 5, 1839, p. 291; Journal of the House of Representatives of . . . New Hampshire . . . November 18, 1840, p. 250; Journal of the House of Representatives . . . of Ohio . . . December 7, 1835 . . . , 644; Journal of the House of Representatives . . . of Ohio . . . December 4, 1837 . . . , 446; Journal of the House of Representatives . . . of Missouri . . . November . . . , One Thousand Eight Hundred and Thirty-Eight, 374; Journal of the House of Delegates of . . . Virginia . . . December, One Thousand Eight Hundred and Thirty-Three, 212; Journal of the House of Delegates of . . . Virginia . . . December, One Thousand Eight Hundred and Thirty-Five, 164.

31. Militia Reform: Journal of the . . . House of Representatives . . . of Pennsylvania . . . January . . . One Thousand Eight Hundred and Forty-Two . . . , I, 813; Votes and Proceedings of the Fifty-Sixth General Assembly of the State of New Jersey, at a Session Begun at Trenton, on the Twenty-Sixth Day of October, One Thousand Eight Hundred and Thirty-One (Trenton, 1832), 273; Journal of the House of Representatives of . . . New Hampshire . . . June 4, 1834, pp. 160-61; Journal of the House of Representatives of the State of New Hampshire, at Their Session, Holden at the Capitol in Concord, Commencing Wednesday, November 21, 1832. Published by Authority (Concord, 1833), 165-66; Journal of the House

of Representatives of . . . New Hampshire . . . June 1, 1842, pp. 198-99; *Journal of the House of Representatives . . . of Ohio . . . December 2, 1833 . . . ,* 285; *Journal of the House of Representatives . . . of Ohio . . . December 5, 1836 . . . ,* 414; *Journal of the House of Representatives . . . of Ohio . . . December 5, 1842 . . . ,* 251. Capital Punishment: *Votes . . . of the . . . General Assembly of . . . New Jersey . . . October, One Thousand Eight Hundred and Thirty-Seven,* 561; *Votes . . . of the . . . General Assembly of . . . New Jersey . . . October, One Thousand Eight Hundred and Thirty-Three,* 519-20; *Journal of the House of Representatives of . . . New Hampshire . . . June 1, 1842,* pp. 284-86; *Journal of the House of Representatives . . . of Ohio . . . December 1, 1834 . . . ,* 153; *Journal of the House of Representatives . . . of Ohio . . . December 3, 1838 . . . ,* 118-19, 527. Temperance: *Journal of the . . . House of Representatives . . . of Pennsylvania . . . December . . . One Thousand Eight Hundred and Thirty-Eight . . . ,* I, 151; *Journal of the . . . House of Representatives . . . of Pennsylvania . . . December . . . One Thousand Eight Hundred and Thirty-Six . . . ,* I, 549; *Journal of the . . . House of Representatives . . . of Pennsylvania . . . December . . . One Thousand Eight Hundred and Thirty-Five . . . ,* I, 972; *Journal of the House of Representatives of . . . New Hampshire . . . June 7, 1837,* pp. 96-99; *Journal of the House of Representatives . . . of Ohio . . . December 3, 1838 . . . ,* 182, 273. Imprisonment for Debt: *Journal of the . . . House of Representatives . . . of Pennsylvania . . . January . . . One Thousand Eight Hundred and Forty-Two . . . ,* I, 958; *Journal of the . . . House of Representatives . . . of Pennsylvania . . . January . . . One Thousand Eight Hundred and Thirty-Four . . . ,* I, 390; *Votes and Proceedings of the Fifty-Ninth General Assembly of the State of New Jersey, at a Session Begun at Trenton, on the Twenty-Third Day of October One Thousand Eight Hundred and Thirty-Four* (Freehold, 1835), 425-36; *Journal of the House of Representatives of . . . New Hampshire . . . June 5, 1839,* pp. 308-10; *Journal of the House of Representatives . . . of Ohio . . . December 4, 1837 . . . ,* 752; *Journal of the House of Representatives of . . . Missouri . . . November, One Thousand Eight Hundred and Thirty-Four,* 445; *Journal of the House of Representatives of . . . Missouri . . . November, One Thousand Eight Hundred and Forty-Two,* 296, 294; *Journal of the House of Representatives of . . . Missouri . . . November, One Thousand Eight Hundred and Forty,* 339; *Journal of the House of Delegates of . . . Virginia . . . December, One Thousand Eight Hundred and Forty-Two,* 137. Debtor Relief: *Journal of the . . . House of Representatives . . . of Pennsylvania . . . January . . . One Thousand Eight Hundred and Forty-Two . . . ,* I, 820; *Journal of the House of Representatives . . . of Ohio . . . December 4, 1837 . . . ,* 778; *Journal of the House of Representatives . . . of Ohio . . . December 5, 1842 . . . ,* 97, 127; *Journal of the House of Representatives of . . . Missouri . . . November, One Thousand Eight Hundred and Forty-Two,* 153; *Journal of the House of Delegates of . . . Virginia . . . December, One Thousand Eight Hundred and Forty-One,* 246; *Journal of the House of Delegates of . . . Virginia . . . December, One Thousand Eight Hundred and Forty-Two,* 119. Prison and Asylum Reform: *Journal of the . . . House of Representatives . . . of Pennsylvania . . . December . . . One Thousand Eight Hudnred and Thirty-Eight . . . ,* I, 1308; *Votes . . . of the . . . General Assembly of . . . New Jersey . . . October, One Thousand Eight Hundred and Thirty-one,* 225-56; *Votes . . . of the . . . General Assembly of . . . New Jersey . . . October, One Thousand Eight Hundred and Thirty-Eight,* 575; *Journal of the House of Representatives . . . of Ohio . . . December 4, 1837 . . . ,* 440; *Journal of the House of Representatives of . . . New Hampshire . . . November 21, 1832,* pp. 152-53, 128-29; *Journal of the House of Representatives of the State of New Hampshire, At Their Session Holden at the Capitol in Concord, Commencing Wednesday, June 3, 1840. Published in Conformity to Law* (Concord, 1840), 158.

32. *Votes . . . of the General Assembly of . . . New Jersey . . . October, One Thousand Eight Hundred and Thirty-Six,* 662; *Votes . . . of the . . . General Assembly of New Jersey . . . October, One Thousand Eight Hundred and Thirty-Seven,* 529-30; *Journal of the . . . House of Representatives . . . of Pennsylvania . . . December . . . One Thousand Eight Hundred and Thirty-Seven . . . ,* I, 697; *Journal of the . . . House of Representatives . . . of*

Pennsylvania . . . December . . . One Thousand Eight Hundred and Thirty-Four . . . , I, 884, 889; *Journal of the House of Representatives of . . . New Hampshire . . . June 12, 1841,* pp. 93-96; *Journal of the House of Representatives . . . of Ohio . . . December 4, 1837 . . . ,* 510; *Journal of the House of Representatives . . . of Ohio . . . December 5, 1836 . . . ,* 689, 407; *Journal of the House of Representatives . . . of Ohio . . . December 7, 1835 . . . ,* 576; *Journal of the House of Representatives of . . . Missouri . . . November, One Thousand Eight Hundred and Thirty-Six,* 215; *Journal of the House of Representatives of . . . Missouri . . . November, One Thousand Eight Hundred and Thirty-Four,* 299; *Journal of the House of Delegates of . . . Virginia . . . December, One Thousand Eight Hundred and Forty-One,* 220; *Journal of the House of Delegates of . . . Virginia . . . December, One Thousand Eight Hundred and Thirty-Four,* 218.

33. There is some evidence that Whig votes on antislavery questions were part of a strategy that avoided connection with the abolitionists while attempting not to antagonize them. William Sloan to William Seward, Dec. 5, 1838, Simon Gratz Collection (Historical Society of Pennsylvania).

34. *Journal of the . . . House of Representatives . . . of Pennsylvania . . . December . . . One Thousand Eight Hundred and Thirty-Five . . . ,* I, 1207; *Journal of the . . . House of Representatives . . . of Pennsylvania . . . December . . . One Thousand Eight Hundred and Thirty-Six . . . ,* I, 386, 556; *Journal of the . . . House of Representatives . . . of Pennsylvania . . . December . . . One Thousand Eight Hundred and Thirty-Seven . . . ,* I, 236, 331, 1111; *Journal of the . . . House of Representatives . . . of Pennsylvania . . . January . . . One Thousand Eight Hundred and Forty-One . . . ,* I, 193; *Journal of the . . . House of Representatives . . . of Pennsylvania . . . January . . . One Thousand Eight Hundred and Forty-Two . . . ,* I, 1017; *Journal of the House of Representatives . . . of Ohio . . . December 1, 1834 . . . ,* 202; *Journal of the House of Representatives . . . of Ohio . . . December 4, 1837 . . . ,* 526, 696; *Journal of the House of Representatives . . . of Ohio . . . December 3, 1838 . . . ,* 422, 233; *Journal of the House of Representatives . . . of Ohio . . . December 5, 1842 . . . ,* 34, 227; *Journal of the House of Representatives . . . New Hampshire . . . June 7, 1837,* pp. 241-44; *Journal of the House of Representatives . . . New Hampshire . . . June 6, 1838,* pp. 50, 274; *Journal of the House of Representatives . . . New Hampshire . . . June 5, 1839,* pp. 300-02; *Journal of the House of Representatives . . . New Hampshire . . . Nov. 18, 1840,* pp. 335-38; *Journal of the House of Representatives . . . New Hampshire . . . June 12, 1841,* pp. 266-67.

35. Herbert McClosky, Paul J. Hoffmann, and Rosemary O'Hara, "Issue Conflict and Consensus among Party Leaders and Followers," *American Political Science Review,* LIV (June 1960), 406-27; Herbert McClosky, "Consensus and Ideology in American Politics," *American Political Science Review,* LXVIII (June 1964), 361-79; Philip E. Converse, "The Nature of Belief Systems in Mass Publics," David E. Apter, ed., *Ideology and Discontent* (New York, 1964), 206-61.

36. See Bernard Bailyn, *The Ideological Origins of the American Revolution* (Cambridge, Mass., 1967); Gordon S. Wood, *The Creation of the American Republic 1776-1787* (Chapel Hill, 1969); Meyers, *Jacksonian Persuasion*; and Bayrd Still, "State Constitutional Development in the United States, 1829-1851" (doctoral dissertation, University of Wisconsin, 1933).

37. The best discussions of Whig attitudes are: Glyndon G. Van Deusen, "Some Aspects of Whig Thought and Theory in the Jacksonian Period," *American Historical Review,* LXIII (Jan. 1958), 305-22; Major L. Wilson, "The Concept of Time and the Political Dialogue in the United States, 1828-48," *American Quarterly,* XIX (Winter 1967), 619-44; Benson, *Concept of Jacksonian Democracy,* 86-109, 216-53.

38. *Documents Including Messages and Other Communications Made to the Thirty-Sixth General Assembly of the State of Ohio* (Columbus, 1838), 24.

39. *Documents Including Messages and Other Communications Made to the Thirty-Seventh General Assembly of the State of Ohio* (Columbus, 1839), 7.

40. "Report of the Minority of the Standing Committee on Banks and Currency, March 11,

1841," *Journal of the Senate . . . of Ohio . . . December 8, 1840,* Appendix, 2-15. This was the report of the Whig members of the committee.

41. Quoted in Alice Felt Tyler, *Freedom's Ferment: Phases of American Social History to 1860* (Minneapolis, 1944), 330.

42. John Allen Krout, *The Origins of Prohibition* (New York, 1925), 299-300.

43. *Ohio State Journal,* Jan. 13, 1836.

44. New Jersey Writers Project, *Proceedings of the New Jersey State Constitutional Convention of 1844* (Trenton, 1942), 403. See also Stephen Simpson, *The Working Man's Manual: A New Theory of Political Economy on the Principle of Production the Source of Wealth; Including an Enquiry into the Principles of Public Credit, Currency, the Wages of Labour, the Production of Wealth, the Distribution of Wealth, Consumption of Wealth, Popular Education, And The Elements of Social Government in General, as They Appear Open to the Scrutiny of Common Sense and the Philosophy of the Age* (Philadelphia, 1831).

45. The cultural bias of such reform is detailed in Clifford S. Griffin, *Their Brothers' Keepers: Moral Stewardship in the United States, 1800-1865* (New Brunswick, 1960); Joseph R. Gusfield, *Symboic Crusade: Status Politics and the American Temperance Movement* (Urbana, 1963); and Michael B. Katz, *The Irony of Early School Reform: Educational Innovation in Mid-Nineteenth Century Massachusetts* (Cambridge, Mass., 1968).

46. The evangelical, Yankee Protestant element among the northern Whigs was as important as slavery in determining this difference. On this group among the northern Whigs, see Benson, *Concept of Jacksonian Democracy,* 165-207; Ronald P. Formisano, "The Social Basis of American Voting Behavior Wayne County, Michigan, 1837-1852, As a Test Case" (doctoral dissertation, Wayne State University, 1966); Ronald P. Formisano, "Political Character, Anti-Partyism, and the Second Party System," *American Quarterly,* XXI (Winter 1970), 683-709.

47. "Opinions of the Council of Three: Political Bigotry—Conservatism—Radicalism," *American Review: A Whig Journal of Politics, Literature, Art and Science,* VI (Sept. 1847), 242. See also John R. Howe, Jr., "Republican Thought and the Political Violence of the 1790s," *American Quarterly,* XIX (Summer 1967), 147-65.

48. Meyers, *Jacksonian Persuasion*; Wilson, "The Concept of Time and the Political Dialogue"; John William Ward, "Jacksonian Democratic Thought: 'A Natural Charter of Privilege,' " Stanley Coben and Lorman Ratner, eds., *The Development of An American Culture* (Englewood Cliffs, 1970), 44-63. Much of Arthur M. Schlesinger's discussion of Democratic thought in *The Age of Jackson* remains useful, but the book must be used with care.

49. "Introduction: The Democratic Principle—The Importance of Its Assertion, and Application to Our Political System and Literature," *United States Magazine, and Democratic Review,* I (Oct.-Dec. 1837), 6.

50. Wiley E. Hodges, "The Theoretical Basis for Anti-Governmentalism in Virginia, 1789-1836," *Journal of Politics,* 9 (Aug. 1947), 325-54, details this relation between property and liberty. See also C. B. MacPherson, *The Political Theory of Possessive Individualism: Hobbes to Locke* (Oxford, 1962).

51. *Proceedings of the New Jersey State Constitutional Convention,* 346.

52. Wilson, "The Concept of Time and the Political Dialogue," 634.

53. *Proceedings of the New Jersey State Constitutional Convention,* 361, 312, 325, 537, 541; *Proceedings and Debates of the Convention of the Commonwealth of Pennsylvania To Propose Amendments to the Constitution* (14 vols., Harrisburg, 1837-1839), V, 473-78. 490-96 511-12, VI, 58-63, 82-85, VIII, 52-56, 72, XIV, 16-20.

54. Trenton (New Jersey) *Emporium and True American,* March 28, 1835.

55. Annual Message of the Governor, December 3, 1839, *Documents Including Messages and Other Communications Made to the Thirty-Eighth General Assembly of the State of Ohio* (Columbus, 1840), 7-8. The Jacksonian view of the role of banks in causing depressions is treated in William Gerald Shade, "The Politics of Free Banking in the Old Northwest, 1837-1863" (doctoral dissertation, Wayne State University, 1966), 45-74; Harry E. Miller, *Banking*

Theories in the United States before 1860 (Cambridge, Mass., 1927), 55-70, 187-208.

56. William M. Gouge, *A Short History of Paper Money and Banking in the United States, Including an Account of Provincial and Continental Paper Money to Which is Prefixed An Inquiry into the Principles of the System with Considerations of Its Effects on Morals and Happiness The Whole Intended as a Plain Exposition of the Way in which Paper Money and Money Corporations, Affect the Interests of Different Portions of the Community* (Philadelphia, 1833). William Gouge's arguments were extended in the *Journal of Banking* which was published in Philadelphia in 1841 and 1842. See also Benjamin G. Rader, "William M. Gouge: Jacksonian Economic Theorist," *Pennsylvania History,* XXX (Oct. 1963), 443-53.

57. The most radical example of this attitude was the contention of Benjamin Tappan, an Ohio Jacksonian, that banks were a greater danger to "free principles" than slavery. Benjamin Tappan to Lewis Tappan, Sept. 17, 1844, Benjamin Tappan Papers (Ohio Historical Society).

58. Thomas Hart Benton, *Thirty Years' View; or, A History of the Working of the American Government for Thirty Years, from 1820 to 1850* (2 vols., New York, 1854-1856), II, 60.

59. *Acts Incorporating the Delaware and Raritan Canal Company, the Camden and Amboy Railroad and Transportation Company, and the New Jersey Transportation Company, with the General Supplements and Resolutions Thereto* (Trenton, 1849).

60. The Delaware Canal Company and the Camden and Amboy Railroad were created in 1830 and consolidated in 1831 before the general Democratic attack on the corporation. Democratic responsibility for this corporation came, however, after the leaders of that party were frustrated in their efforts to have the canal constructed by the state. Democrats included on the board of directors of the Joint Companies were Senator Garret D. Wall, future Senator Robert F. Stockton, Congressman James Parker, and Federal District Attorney James S. Green. Stockton to Peter Vroom, Dec. 13, 1835, Peter Vroom Papers (Rutgers University Library); Newark *New Jersey Eagle,* Jan. 27, 1832.

61. H. Jerome Cranmer, "The New Jersey Canals: State Policy and Private Enterprise" (doctoral dissertation, Columbia University, 1955); Ershkowitz, "New Jersey Politics," 232, passim; Burlington *Observer,* Feb. 20, 1836; Elizabethtown *New Jersey Journal,* Feb. 9, 1836; Robert Thompson, *Transportation Combines and Pressure Politics in New Jersey, 1833-36, Reprinted from the Proceedings of the New Jersey Historical Society* (n.p., 1939). Scheiber, *Ohio Canal Era,* 88-119, 355-56; and Wiley E. Hodges, "Pro-Governmentalism in Virginia, 1789-1836: A Pragmatic Liberal Pattern in the Political Heritage," *Journal of Politics,* 25 (May 1963), 333-60, discuss the different groups supporting internal improvements in those states.

62. Harold E. Davis, "Economic Basis of Ohio Politics, 1820-1840," *Ohio State Archaeological and Historical Quarterly,* XLVII (Oct. 1938), 311-14; Francis P. Weisenburger, *The History of the State of Ohio: The Passing of the Fronteir, 1825-1850* (Columbus, 1941), 277-85; *Journal of the House of Representatives . . . of Ohio . . . December 3, 1833 . . . ,* 253, 490, 503, 505-06, 509, 517, 534, 559, 646-47, 666, 681, 684, 685, 688, 689; *Journal of the Senate . . . of Ohio . . . December 3, 1833 . . . ,* 252, 454, 466-67, 531, 553, 684-85, 709, 710, 722, 747, 751.

63. Hartz, *Economic Policy and Democratic Thought,* 219-27; Frank T. Carlton, "Abolition of Imprisonment Debt in the United States," *Yale Review,* 17 Nov. 1908), 339-44; William A. Sullivan, *The Industrial Worker in Pennsylvania 1800-1840* (Harrisburg, 1955), 164, 209-15; Benson, *Concept of Jacksonian Democracy,* 44-46; Robert J. Rayback, *Millard Fillmore: Biography of a President* (Buffalo, 1959), 37-39; Walter Hugins, *Jacksonian Democracy and the Working Class: A Study of the New York Workingmen's Movement 1829-1837* (Stanford, 1960), 136-38, 145-46. Edwin T. Randall, "Imprisonment for Debt in America: Fact and Fiction," *Mississippi Valley Historical Review,* XXXIX (June 1952), 89-102, suggests the need for a reassessment of the entire matter.

EDWARD PESSEN

WHO GOVERNED THE NATION'S CITIES IN THE "ERA OF THE COMMON MAN"?

A premise of the article that follows is that politics and important political issues are not confined to the national and state levels. In an era when urban communities attained unprecedented financial, commercial, social, and intellectual importance, the politics of cities and towns similarly became increasingly significant. Major party rhetoric was less flamboyant and less often heard from on the municipal level, perhaps because it rang more hollow in such a context. Whigs and Democrats in urban milieus acted not like great opposing political blocs but like the similarly well-situated property owners in fact they were. Quantitative evidence indicates that a socioeconomic elite invariably occupied the mayor's office and held an inordinate number of seats in councils and boards of aldermen. Impressive if less than comprehensive data on the policies and enactments of local governments large and small, in every section of the country, indicate that the propertied acted politically to serve the interests of the propertied. While the proportion of large wealthholders in local government declined by mid-century, their influence seems to have remained intact; certainly local ordinances continued to reflect the interests above all of the property owning classes.

Those who possess property and carry on the business of the country, can look forward only to living under a government over which they have no influence. . . .

SIDNEY GEORGE FISHER[1]

The more affluent classes of society are . . . directly removed from the direction of political affairs in the United States. . . .

ALEXIS DE TOCQUEVIILLE[2]

Reprinted with permission from the *Political Science Quarterly*, 87 (December 1972), pp. 591-614.

The second quarter of the nineteenth century has long been known as the Era of the Common Man, largely because of the supposedly great political power commanded by persons of little or no property. The astute French visitor Michel Chevalier, observing that poor men in most states had the right to vote, concluded that in the United States the propertyless masses "rule[d] the capitalists, merchants, and manufacturers,"[3] It was widely assumed that democratization of the suffrage had made rich men politically impotent in America.

This essay tests the accuracy of that assumption. It examines the policies pursued by government in the period and considers the wealth and standing of officeholders of the time in New York City, Brooklyn, Philadelphia, and Boston. Both factors are important in any inquiry into the extent of plutocratic influence on politics. Political actions must be considered in order to determine the power of a select number of political actors, for it is conceivable that a small group, such as the rich, could have had disproportionate representation in government and yet have had little influence over it. The obverse is also possible: great influence could have been wielded by a small clique barely, if at all, represented. An influential modern theory, in fact, holds that the mid-twentieth century American city is ruled precisely by covert elites outside government.[4]

A leading urban historian has recently complained that "historians of the Jacksonian era have yet to undertake the kind of systematic quantitative studies of urban [political] leadership" that would carry the modern discussion beyond impressionism.[5] Actually, modern scholars have investigated the backgrounds and occupations of officials in a number of towns and small cities in different parts of the country.[6] The discussion here of large northeastern cities of great wealth and population complements the earlier studies and should help bring us closer to a coherent overview of urban politics and power in the antebellum decades.

In his well known study of New Haven, Robert A. Dahl asks the question, "who governs?" and answers: the commercial and professional patriciate before 1842, a new class of industrial entrepreneurs for the rest of the nineteenth century.[7] Dahl's generalizations are based primarily on the occupations of the mayors and the family backgrounds of several of them. I have investigated not only mayors but recorders, trustees, aldermen, assistant aldermen, and select and common councilmen for the period 1825-50, and I have considered the wealth and status as well as the occupations of these officeholders. Using occupation as the sole criterion, the practice in a number of recent studies of colonial officials, can be misleading. There were merchants and merchants, some conducting modest storefront operations, others sending cargoes to the far corners of the earth. Men listed in directories as artisans have turned out to have been large entrepreneurs. Wealth *and* occupation provide a surer clue to economic standing than does occupation alone.[8]

I have also chosen to take into consideration that elusive intangible, status. Every one of the great cities had an elite, a group of notables distinct from—if containing many members of—the rich, which whom they are so often bracketed. The elite of a city typically numbered several hundred families of great prestige, many of them eminent since the seventeenth century but a surprising number whose renown dated from the middle or late eighteenth century. These families moved in a restricted social orbit, maintaining exclusive relationships, both formal and informal, attending the same dinner parties and balls, active in the same clubs and voluntary associations, living in residential enclaves populated by their own sort, marrying by a rule of social endogamy, usually although not invariably possessessing great wealth.[9] The question is to what extent did such socioeconomic elites meet Dahl's definition of a ruling elite: "a minority of individuals whose preferences regularly prevail in cases of difference . . . on key political issues."[10]

I

In order to discern changing trends in the period, I have divided the second quarter of the nineteenth century in two, with 1837 the middle year. Insofar as the data were available, the tables on occupations record average percentages based on almost every year from 1825 to 1850 rather than randomly selected years, reducing the risk that the generalizations about the era might be based on an unrepresentative or atypical sample.

Throughout the period, there is no discernible change in the kind of men who sat in the mayor's office; they were almost invariably merchants or lawyers. Philadelphians rarely chose other than attorneys; New York City

Table 1. Occupations of Mayors, 1825-50 (in per cent)[a]

Occupation	NYC	Brooklyn[b]	Boston	Philadelphia
merchants	72	50	60	5-10
merchant/manufacturers		10		
lawyers	20	20	32	90-95
officials		15		
publishers	4			
wholesale grocers		5		
artisans-manufacturers	4		8	

[a]In this and in the tables that follow, repeaters, or men reelected in the annual municipal elections that were the norm, are treated as new officeholders for each subsequent term. Treating a man elected a number of times as though he were one officeholder is misleading; men of high-status occupation typically were reelected more often than were those of less prestige.

[b]Includes the years prior to 1834 when Brooklyn was a village whose chief officer was the "president."

favored merchants. Brooklyn and Boston elected first the one, then the other. These were unusually wealthy men of relatively high status. In the early 1830s, a "master builder," Charles A. Wells, managed to be chosen mayor of Boston, sandwiched between such eminences as Harrison Gray Otis and Theodore Lyman Jr. Wells was no ordinary mechanic, however, since his assessed wealth placed him among the richest one per cent of taxpayers, the lofty plateau of wealth occupied by most mayors of the periods.

Elite representation in political office varied in the four cities. The wealthy Philadelphians who occupied the mayor's office, for the most part, did not belong to the city's greatest families; George M. Dallas, mayor in the late 1820s, was very much the exception. Boston was another story. In the first part of the period, Josiah Quincy, Harrison Gray Otis, and Theodore Lyman Jr., eminences all, were mayors, while Quincy's son and Samuel A. Eliot occupied the office for half of the second period. Brooklyn's diverse elite of old Dutch families and later migrants from New England and elsewhere were represented in the office by the very rich General Jeremiah Johnson in the late 1830s and the highly successful lawyers and men of affairs Henry C. Murphy and Edward Copland in the 1840s. New York City had a distinctive pattern. For most of the period before 1837, mayors came from such esteemed families as the Bownes and the Lawrences, two great Long Island lines that had long intermarried. Philip Hone, mayor in 1826, was an example of the new elite—wealthy, active in a great variety of exclusive and socially purposive organizations, and near the center of a social world inhabited by great figures in commerce, the professions, and the city's lore. In the 1840s such mayors as James Harper, the publisher, William F. Havemeyer, the sugar merchant, and Caleb Woodhull, the attorney, were representatives of the prestige of relatively recent achievement rather than of distinguished family.

The backgrounds of municipal legislators were more diverse. During the period 1825-37, the occupational distribution for each city was unique. Lawyers constituted 25 per cent of Philadelphia's select council, for example, while they constituted only 10 per cent of the trustees of Brooklyn village and of the chartered city of Brooklyn. In very few cases was an occupation represented by precisely the same proportion of officeholders in more than one city, and yet the overall configurations were not markedly dissimilar. Merchants, corporate and financial officials, and varied types of businessmen comprised more than half the governing bodies—when Philadelphia's "gentlemen" category, composed in large part of retired merchants, is included. One-fifth of New York City's aldermen and not quite 15 per cent of the two houses of Boston's legislature were lawyers. The number of manufacturers typically hovered around the 5 per cent mark, while the percentage of retail storekeepers, some of them quite wealthy, ranged from 5 per cent in Boston to almost 15 per cent in New York City. Craftsmen or artisans made up 10 per cent of the Philadelphia common council and closer to 5 per cent in the other cities. Unskilled laborers, who together with journeymen mechanics constituted roughly three-fifths of urban populations, were not to be found in office. The occupations of common men were barely visible in the politics of the first part of the era which bears their name.

Wealth was inordinately represented in office in the years before 1838. For the entire quarter-century, mayors almost without exception belonged to the upper one per cent of taxpayers.[11] In the years before 1838, 75 per cent of Brooklyn's trustees and aldermen, who can be identified, were rich. For the other cities, the rate of representation by men of wealth was not as great,

Table 2. Occupations of City Councils and Boards of Aldermen 1825-37 (in per cent)[a]

Occupation	NYC	Brooklyn	Boston Aldermen	Council	Philadelphia[b] Select Council	Common Council
merchants	28	34	43	32	26	28
"gentlemen"					16	9
bankers, insurance company executives, brokers	2		6	4	6	
businessmen, publishers	13	2	17	14	4	5
owners of yards, buildings, wharves, builders, shipbuilders	4	10	4	6		4
manufacturers	3	13	3	4	10	4
attorneys	20	10	11	15	25	11
physicians	3		3	2		5
officials, military & naval officers, ship captains	1	2	3	3	1	3
engineers, accountants, printers	1	2		1		
grocers, distillers, butchers, bakers, druggists, retailers	14	16	3	6	7	13
artisan-entrepreneurs	6		1	7	1	7
artisans, mechanics	6	8	3	7	3	10
farmers		2				

[a]Because fractions have been dropped, not all columns sum to 100.
[b]The period covered for Philadelphia extends to 1840.

and in two of them it declined significantly if not drastically between 1825 and 1838. In Philadelphia, three out of four select councilmen were rich men, both at the beginning and the end of the 1830s, while the proportion actually rose in the common council during that decade, going from about one-third to three-fifths. The rich constituted slightly more than 50 per cent of Boston's aldermen, a body of eight, in the 1830s as they had in the 1820s but in the common council, a more plebian body six times as large, the percentage of rich dropped from 42 to 22 per cent. And in New York, where rich men had comprised two-thirds of the aldermen in 1826, the proportion fell to one-half in 1831 an to about three-eighths in 1837.

Some members of the elite served in local legislatures, but not many. Members of several great commercial families sat in the Philadelphia council: Eyres, Masseys, and Wetherills, next to Duanes, Bories, Lippincotts, Rawles, and Merediths, whose status was perhaps higher. New York City had Motts, Schieffelins, Nevinses, Roosevelts, Bensons, Van Schaicks; Brooklyn had Van Nostrands, Thornes, Furmans, Hickses, Hegemans, Polhemuses, and Bergens; and Boston had Lorings, Grays, Lowells, Everetts, Shaws, Reveres, Winthrops, Prescotts, and Peabodys. In the second part of the period, ending at mid-century, elite representation held fairly firm in Boston as it did in Brooklyn: Crowinshields, Bigelows, Coolidges, Gardners, Cushings, and Frothinghams stepped in to serve the former city, while Ryersons, Boerums, Leffertses, and Van Voorhises took office in Brooklyn. There was a slight falling off in Philadelphia, despite the appearance in the councils of Gilpins, Brecks, Bartons, Binneys, and the great merchant Thomas Pym Cope. In New York City, Caleb Woodhull and Gouverneur Ogden alone served to replace the men of eminent families who had departed the board of aldermen and assistant aldermen in the 1840s.

The occupations of councilmen shifted during the 1840s in a noticeably plebeian direction. The pattern was not entirely consistent, however, Although the numbers of merchants and lawyers fell sharply in New York and slightly in Boston, the proportion rose in Philadelphia and Brooklyn. While manufacturers became more numerous, the "entrepreneurial pattern" of New Haven was hardly matched in the great northeastern cities, since nowhere did the group comprise more than, roughly, one-tenth of elected officials. The most significant change was the increase in artisans. By 1850, skilled workers made up more than one-tenth of the aldermen of New York City and of the "lower houses" of Boston and Philadelphia. These changes, while significant, did not quite produce the proletarianization of city government. The occupations of officeholders at mid-century remained unrepresentative of how most city residents earned their livelihoods. The distortion between governors and governed had lessened, however.

The proportion of rich men in urban councils also declined during the 1840s. Whereas in 1846, 83 per cent of Philadelphia's select council and 60 per cent of the common council were members of wealthy families, by 1850 only one-half the members of the former body and 15 per cent of the latter were from rich families. At five-year intervals between 1838 and 1848 the percentage of rich men in Boston's common council declined from 29 per cent to 25 per cent and finally to 17 per cent. The falling off in New York City between 1838-50 was from 38 per cent to 25 per cent. Brooklyn too became less of a "plutocracy" during the decade, although in 1850, one-half of the aldermen who can be identified remained among the richest men in the community. Although their numbers diminished significantly during the 1840s, rich men at mid-century continued to be inordinately represented in urban government.

Table 3. Occupations of City Councils and Boards of Aldermen 1838-50 (in per cent)[a]

Occupation	NYC	Brooklyn	Boston Aldermen	Council	Philadelphia[b] Select Council	Common Council
merchants	15	42	28	29	42	37
"gentlemen"					4	4
bankers, insurance company executives, brokers	3		1	6		1
businessmen, publishers	18	4	21	16	5	1
owners of yards, buildings, wharves, builders, shipbuilders	6	14	4	6		
manufacturers	9	7	7	3	3	13
attorneys	11	13	13	5	28	13
physicians	1		1	1		2
officials, military & naval officers, ship captains	4		3	4		3
engineers, accountants, printers	1			4		
grocers, distillers, butchers, bakers, druggists, retailers	14	18	1	6	16	15
artisan-entrepreneurs	7	1	13	8	2	2
artisans, mechanics	10	1	8	10	2	9
laborers, farmers						

[a] Because fractions have been dropped, not all columns summ to 100.
[b] The period covered for Philadelphia is 1840-50.

II

What accounted for the disproportionate involvement of wealthy men in antebellum urban government, on the one hand, and the perceptible diminution of this involvement with the passage of time, on the other? One explanation for the preponderance of the well-to-do is the amazing extent of "horizontal mobility" among the poor. In addition to barring them from political participation because they could not meet residence requirements, the inordinate footlooseness of the poor appears to have produced in them a lack of concern for community affairs most unlike the feelings of the more stable and substantial elements in the community.[12]

Moreover, neither particular electoral reforms, such as broadening the suffrage, nor general changes in the provisions of city charters appears to have had very much to do either with the undue representation of rich men in city councils throughout the era or the falling off of their direct participation in the 1840s. Before 1854, councilmen in Philadelphia were chosen in general elections that made possible the selection of men concentrated in high-value residential districts. In Boston, New York City, and Brooklyn, councilmen were elected in separate ward elections.[13] Most of these wards were inhabited primarily by men of little property. Yet the social and economic standing of elected officials was quite similar, whether they were elected from a general ticket or in a series of separate contests.

Poor men of little property had won the right to vote *before* the beginning of the period. By 1822, New York City male residents who were "five dollar taxpayers" were eligible to vote for councilmen. After its incorporation as a city, the same year, Boston granted the vote to all taxpayers. While this system did bar transients and men of no property whatever, it nevertheless enfranchised a voting population composed predominantly of poor men. By the late 1830s, all white Philadelphia males of 21 were granted the vote in local elections; the taxpayer qualification that had prevailed earlier, based on the charter of 1790, has been appraised by scholars as approximating universal manhood suffrage. The wealthy men elected to office in the late 1820s and 1830s were elected by relatively poor voters. The decrease in the number of wealthy councilmen during the 1840s was due to other things than a change in the socioeconomic composition of the electorates. What was true of antebellum Natchez became increasingly true of antebellum New York City, Brooklyn, Philadelphia, and Boston: "The situation was not that rich men tried for office and were defeated: very few of them even offered as candidates."[14] Those who did "offer" were rarely of the group I have elsewhere called the "richest of the rich." Thomas Pym Cope and Robert Gould Shaw, the latter a great merchant of Boston, were exceptions.

In the 1830s, the election of the mayor was transferred from the council to the people in Philadelphia, Brooklyn, and New York City. And yet, as we have seen, mayors elected by the people were of as high status and were as wealthy as mayors elected by the council. The mayor's office carried with it a yearly salary that ranged from $2,000 to $3,000 and perquisites worth several times as much.[15] Philip Hone's comment on New York City's council—"where there is much to do and no pay . . ."—applied equally to the councils of the other cities.[16] The comparatively good salary of the one office and the nonexistent salary of the other appear to explain little about who offered themselves as candidates. According to the argument made in that era by the British Chartists—a variation on a critique dating back to Roman antiquity—offices without salary would invariably be filled by the rich, who alone could afford to hold them. Yet richer men ran for the well-salaried mayoralty than for the nonsalaried council. As a matter of fact, poor men could serve on antebellum city councils because they seldom met; typically, meetings were held from one to four times a month and, even more important, at night, after working hours. Poor men did not hold office, however, not because it was impossible for them to attend, but because they were not nominated. The diminishing representation of the rich and the eminent suggests that membership in the council exerted no irresistible pull on these men.

The mayoralty held greater appeal because combined with the greater prestige of the office was a potential power that for all the inherent weaknesses of the office permitted a man of force and stature such as Josiah Quincy to place his own imprint on it. But what attraction could the city council or board of aldermen hold for great figures in view of the slight part played by any one member in the performance of its tasks and the limited and prosaic nature of these tasks?

After he completed his term as mayor, Philip Hone showed no interest in sitting on the council. When a crisis arose in the winter of 1828-29, however, Hone did agree to preside over a meeting of the third ward, "to adopt measures to relieve the distress of the poor in the present inclement season."[17] Let an issue of critical importance arise and the very rich and the eminent displayed a lively interest in political participation. In 1829, perhaps one-half of New York City's 28 aldermen were rich men, with only 3 worth at least the $100,000 that placed them among the super rich. Possibly 7 or 8 were among the city's socioeconomic elite. Yet when meetings were called and delegates elected that spring to attend a convention that would consider the vitally important matter of changes in the city charter, Hone and a large number of other notables participated. Despite the fact that delegates to a planning meeting were elected by ward, 60 per cent of those elected were wealthy men, most of them of prominent family. The rich and the eminent comprised 80 per cent of the 70 convention delegates elected, five from each ward. Lambert Suydam, Evert Bancker, Peter Augustus Jay, Garret Storm, Robert Bogardus, Effingham Schieffelin, John Hone, Stephen Allen, John Bradhurst, Cornelius Schuyler, M. M. Quackenboss, Philip Hone, and dozens of other men of high status were elected. According to Hone's diary entry, what moved him to action was not the prospect of public activity: he had more than enough of such diversions. Rather, he had "an apprehension that the mistaken zeal of some persons concerned might lead to violent and indiscreet measures."[18]

Not that the duties of urban government were unimportant. Modern historians may find it hard to write dramatic accounts of the problems of police and fire protection, water supply, public health, garbage disposal, poor relief, regulation of markets, street maintenance and lighting, harbors and wharves, building codes, tax assessments, and tax collection. These were nonetheless significant responsibilities. No doubt the ineffable blandness of much urban history derives from the routine and neutral quality of so much of what municipal government did, useful as it was to persons of whatever status. And yet, for all the undramatic character of these problems, the particular manner of treating them could and did reflect conflicts of interest. Whether the city chose to improve harbors or to keep working-class districts clean depended on whether preponderant influence as well as representation was possessed by the urban rich and business classes. For, influence and power are manifested, above all, in the actions of government.

III

Detailed and comprehensive modern studies of municipal governments' policies and enactments in the antebellum period remain to be done. There is, however, substantial evidence available, and its burden is fairly clear. Antebellum cities were governed largely by the propertied for the propertied. Municipal budgets were minuscule largely because wealthy taxpayers were known to be unwilling to pay more. Wealth was notoriously underassessed because rich men insisted that it be.[19] Public outdoor and indoor relief was administered by well-to-do guardians, its scope limited by the parsimony of the great taxpayers, the attendant dissemination of conservative social doctrine reflective of their values.[20] What government did not do is as instructive as what it did do; detailed itemizations of municipal expenditures reveal much. Comparatively little money was allotted to social services. Social inequities and pervasive misery were not simply dealt with in a niggardly way; they were treated as the wages of sin and of individual fault. In Boston, far more money was spent on street repairs and sewers. Street improvements were a matter of broad public interest, to be sure, yet most contemporaries agreed that prosperous districts got the first, the most, and the best attention.[21]

The history of each city contains numerous examples of the special sensitivity municipal governments showed their wealthiest constituents. In New York City, valuable real estate in the form of wharves and "water grants" was leased on easy terms or sold cheaply to members of the Astor, Lorillard, Lenox, Schermerhorn, Havemeyer, Roosevelt, Colden, Bowne, and Goelet families. And aldermen subsequently granted special rights solicited by wealthy owners or lessees.[22] In Brooklyn, opposition by merchants to the special assessment necessary to finance a proposed sewer system on a major thoroughfare succeeded in blocking the project. Mayor Henry C. Murphy, high-minded member of Brooklyn's elite, complained in the 1840s that the city's legislators were indifferent to health problems in poor sections.[23] Unhappy because their city's per capita public expenditures on poor relief in the mid-1820s were almost double the New York City rate, Philadelphia's leaders succeeded, in part by a "more careful screening of applicants," in reducing total costs over the next two decades despite a doubling in the city's population.[24] During the same period, the city's businessmen and politicians lobbied for and helped finance the transportation improvements likely to promote their business prospects.[25] In Boston, men like Harrison Gray Otis cut back expenditures for a proposed expansion of the sewer system, since, "living on well-drained Beacon Hill," they saw little purpose in it. A mayor such as Josiah Quincy was more public spirited and gets higher marks than Otis from a modern historian of Boston. Yet to both mayors, the city was "primarily a place of business, a port, a market and financial capital."[26] In Boston as in New York City, police expenditures were minimal and service pitifully incompetent when men of substance felt no need for better. The professionalization of police services and the high costs it entailed were delayed until lower-class ethnic riots and disorders posed a threat to the life and property of the privileged.[27]

Rich men and their interests did not invariably prevail. For one thing, the rich were not a monolithic class; nor did they conceive of themselves as such. The wealthy had diverse interests. The opposition of many property owners to an expensive improvement of Faneuil Hall, for example, did not stop Quincy from going ahead with it. Otis was compelled by "public demand" to maintain street cleaning operations he wanted to cut back. What is of interest is how often rich men won. A contemporary New Yorker explained their success in realistic terms: "Nearly every alderman has in some degree owed his success to the personal efforts and influence of "backers,' who must be recompensed for their services. This recompense sometimes consists in a return of political assistance. . . ."[28] It is more likely that the relatively substantial men who predominated in city government dealt with issues from the viewpoint of the property owners they themselves were. Until demonstrated otherwise, it appears more sensible to understand them to have been men honestly acting out their conviction that the prosperity of the city depended on the prosperity of its most successful residents, rather than to regard them as politically corrupt.

Whatever the reasons, wealthy men do appear to have had great power in urban government, their influence over local affairs far transcending their small numbers. While the super rich rarely sought office during the era, the presence in city councils and mayors' offices of substantial numbers of large property owners meant that the viewpoints and socioeconomic interests of wealth would have direct representation in government. That such representation declined in the 1840s is no sure sign that the influence of the rich suffered a similar diminution. Men of status, as Robert Zemsky has shown for colonial Massachusetts, need not be a majority in order to dominate.[29] Certainly the pattern of municipal legislation and policy does not suggest that the plebeian interest was more vigorously promoted in the latter part of the period.

There is no way of proving whether covert elites dominated antebellum cities in the way that Floyd Hunter has suggested they control the modern American city. For even if we stumbled across evidence the equivalent of Hunter's, in which some very influential men stated flatly that a given number of named individuals "ran the city," we would have no grounds for accepting such an assertion as authoritative. Robert Dahl has argued that, whatever the merits of Hunter's thesis—and Dahl grants it few—it is not applicable to antebellum New Haven, which was overtly controlled by a commercial and professional patriciate.[30] New York City, Brooklyn, Boston, and Philadelphia before 1850 were hardly governed by the kind of patriciate of old families that ostensibly ruled New Haven. The elite of the great northeastern cities governed, rather, the hundreds of voluntary associations that complemented and in some cases surpassed in importance the work of municipal political bodies. Politics was left to men of wealth but not the greatest wealth and to a sprinkling of elite family representatives, a combination that appears to have been sufficient to assure men of substance, whether they were of the social elite or not, that local governments not only would pose no threat but would be sympathetic to their interests.

IV

Discussions of politics in what historians continue to call the Jacksonian Era usually assign a central role to the major parties. Certainly Democrats and Whigs competed vigorously for local offices. Occasionally contests between them became so hot that Whig and Democratic voters cracked one another's heads, most notably in New York City's local elections of 1834. Councilmen representing the one party or the other were not indifferent to their parties. At one point, Brooklyn Democrats voted against the continuation of the comptroller's office largely because Whigs had created the post.[31] Since rich men overwhelmingly preferred the Whigs to the Democrats,[32] it might seem that the wealthy men influential in local government can be equally well understood if they are treated as Whigs in local government. A recent study of antebellum Boston does precisely that, reporting that "the Common Council, Board of Aldermen, and other city posts were often filled by [wealthy] Whigs. . . ."[33] Assuredly wealthy Whigs often filled municipal posts in the other cities as well. The question is, is the behavior of such men serving in municipal offices better explained by their membership in the Whig party or by the fact of their wealth and standing.

The issues confronting local Whig and Democratic councilmen bore little relation to the matters agitating Martin Van Buren and Daniel Webster in Washington or David Henshaw and William H. Seward in state capitals. James points out that national party alignments meant little in the city politics of antebellum Natchez; the same was true for the great northeastern cities.[34] Many of the rich men who sat in local legislatures were Democrats. Whigs were great winners in Boston elections during the 1830s and 1840s, while in New York City they were more often losers. Yet the socioeconomic composition of New York City's legislature was no more plebeian than Boston's. In Philadelphia, leading Democratic officeholders and political figures, such as Benjamin Richards, Richard Vaux, George Wharton, Henry D. Gilpin, were men of wealth. In Brooklyn, most of the Democratic candidates for council were local merchants and large property holders, as, for that matter, they were in a number of other cities. There is little evidence that the national party preferences of wealthy Democrats in municipal office led them to support policies and expenditures that were either distinctively Democratic or inimical to the interests of large property owners.[35]

Philip Hone so detested the Democrats that from the 1830s on he would not call the party by its rightful name. Yet he maintained close personal relations and often cooperated politically with such elitest "locofocos" as John Treat Irving, Stephen Allen, Walter Bowne, and Jonathan Coddington.[36] Evidence of similar cooperation in the other cities suggests that class attachments counted for more than party differences in determining the political— as it did the social—behavior of rich men.[37]

V

Some perspective on early nineteenth century urban politics can be had by examining the earlier political tradition. Men of wealth understood the significance of political power; as William Bingham, the fabled accumulator of Philadelphia, wrote: "The interests of commerce, as connected with politics, are so striking, that it is difficult to separate one form the other." From this it followed that political leaders should come, as an early eighteenth-century author had written, from "families of distinction, education, and substance."[38] Practice, whether early or late in the colonial era, lived up to this theory. Modern studies of such towns as Salem and Kent reveal that both in the seventeenth and eighteenth centuries. political leadership correlated with wealth. Salem merchants, perhaps one-seventh the number of artisans, outnumbered artisans in government by five to one, as "political power fell in disproportionate share to men of wealth." As for Kent, the rule was clear: the higher the position, the wealthier its occupant. If the mass of officeholders were an economic cut above nonofficeholders, the town leaders "tend[ed] to be among the wealthiest men" of the community.[39]

Of particular interest are the earlier patterns in the four cities that have been considered in this essay. In his classic study of colonial urban society,

Carl Bridenbaugh found that "the commercial, political, and social leadership of [all] the towns was in [the] hands" of a small commercial aristocracy.[40] Detailed investigations of each of the great northeastern cities tend to confirm the validity of Bridenbaugh's generalizations. A small, wealthy, largely Quaker oligarchy controlled the government of colonial Philadelphia.[41] Before 1776, property requirements confined the vote to the wealthiest 2 per cent of the population, yet the liberalization of the suffrage that followed the Revolution produced no great change in the social character of local officeholders. According to Sam Bass Warner, at the end of the eighteenth century, "the wealthy presided over a municipal regime of little government" whose power was confined to "the management of the markets and the holding of the Recorder's Court." Bridenbaugh had noted that such power was not insignificant in the minds of the wealthy merchants who controlled it, since it enabled them to "throttle economic competition from below."[42] Regardless of the breadth of their voting constituencies or the scope of their powers, the men who were mayors, aldermen, or members of the common council early and late in the eighteenth century were predominantly of the great families of Philadelphia. Both before and after 1750, the city was ruled by Willings, Shippens, Biddles, Mifflins, Morrises, Hopkinsons, Chews, Cadwaladers, Binghams, Duchés, Powels, Emlens, and Tilghmans.[43]

The politics of colonial Boston have not been as thoroughly examined by modern researchers as the politics of its two great commercial rivals. Recent studies of related themes do nothing to weaken Bridenbaugh's earlier conclusion that Boston too was dominated by a commercial "aristocracy."[44] Lists of officers of Brooklyn and the neighboring village of Flatbush reveal that the old Dutch families of the eighteenth century also ruled in the nineteenth. Lotts, Boerums, Vanderveers, Wyckoffs, Couwenhovens, Rapelyes, Strykers, Hegemans, Leffertses, and Gerritsons were the supervisors, treasurers, and chief clerks of the town.

Two recent detailed studies of the socioeconomic status of New York City councilmen and other officials reveal that the same pattern applied to New York from 1689 to 1815.[45] All during the colonial period, a disproportionate number of councilmen were from the upper occupational strata—merchants, lawyers, large landowners. From 1689 to 1733, 44 per cent of the identifiable councilmen were of the "occupational elite," while the remaining 56 per cent were of the "middle occupational range"—carpenters, bolters, bakers, innkeepers. Between 1733 and the outbreak of the Revolution, the proportion of councilmen from the occupational elite rose to slightly more than 50 per cent. There was also a rise in the status of officeholders, as measured by religious affiliations, occupations, and previous offices held by their fathers. Skipping over the war years, when the city was controlled by the British, to 1784-1800, the data show slight changes occurred in the occupations and status of officeholders. Forty-seven per cent of the council were of "upper occupational groups," as were 57 per cent of the aldermen.[46] In the generation or one-third of a century after the Revolution, "mechanics" made up one-half of the city's elected officials, with merchants and lawyers equally dividing the other half. These mechanics were hardly ordinary working men, however, since their median wealth almost matched that of the merchants, and a "significant portion" of them were bank and insurance company directors. Measured by a variety of criteria, New York City's officeholders "constituted an elite."[47] As they did in Philadelphia, property restrictions on voting doubtless played an important part in accounting for the disproportionate representation of upper-class New Yorkers in colonial city government; yet even after the post-Revolutionary suffrage liberalization, only a tiny fragment of the eligible voting population cast ballots in the "charter elections" of the late eighteenth and early nineteenth centuries.[48]

The role of tradition should not be discounted in attempting to explain the socioeconomic standing of nineteenth-century urban officeholders. The eighteenth-century "habit" of electing merchants and lawyers of high status and mechanics, whose wealth and backgrounds indicate they are better classified as entrepreneurs than as workingmen, continued to be followed in the nineteenth century. The enlarged, increasingly plebeian electorate of the later time continued to look for leadership from among men of substance, as the election returns from poor wards often indicate.[49]

VI

The great political influence exercised by substantial property owners in the second quarter of the nineteenth century was evidently not a phenomenon confined to the great cities of the northeastern seaboard. Small towns elsewhere in the northeast, in the south, and in the west exhibit similar patterns. Along the "urban frontier," in the youthful cities, "the mercantile class presided over urban affairs." In Cincinnati, after the democratization of the suffrage in 1827, as before, wealthy bankers, merchants, and lawyers controlled government in a city marked by an "indisputable connection between the policies of the City Council and the interests of the wealthier inhabitants." Natchez's selectmen "usually came of two bourgeois categories, young lawyers . . . and the 'rising entrepreneurs.'" Despite its democratic suffrage, Natchez was dominated by a small upper crust. Aldermen in Springfield, Massachusetts in 1850 were primarily lawyers, bankers, business men and merchants, manufacturers, and builders. Representation by artisans and workmen, who had constituted slightly more than 30 per cent of the total, shrank to 6 per cent over the next two decades as the town's economic development brought it closer to the character of its great neighbors in the antebellum period.[50]

In contrast to the beliefs expressed by Chevalier, Tocqueville, and Sidney George Fisher, the "more affluent classes" and "those who carried on the business of the country" had a great deal of influence over the government of the nation's cities during the second quarter of the nineteenth century. The political scientist Norton E. Long has written that American government "places its fundamental politics out of the reach of its formal politics."[51] Men of property had so direct a control over the government of the antebellum community as to place the "fundamental politics" well within the reach of the "formal politics." In view of the power and influence they commanded over the economic, social, and political life of antebellum cities, the rich appear to have been a true "governing class."[52] Despite his possession of the suffrage, the common man had little influence, let alone power, in the nation's cities during the era named in his honor.

Notes

1. Diary of Sidney George Fisher, entry of Dec. 1, 1839, Historical Society of Pennsylvania, Philadelphia.

2. Alexis de Tocqueville, *Democracy in America* (New York, 1954), I, 192.

3. Michel Chevalier, *Society, Manners, and Politics in the United States* (Boston, 1839).

4. See Floyd Hunter, *Community Power Structure: A Study of Decision Makers* (Chapel Hill, 1953).

5. Sam Bass Warner, *The Private City: Philadelphia in Three Phases of Its Growth* (Boston, 1968), 80.

6. Robert A. Dahl, *Who Governs? Democracy and Power in an American City* (New Haven, 1961); D. Clayton James, *Antebellum Natchez* (Baton Rouge, 1968); Kenneth W. Wheeler, *To Wear a City's Crown: The Beginnings of Urban Growth in Texas, 1836-1865* (Cambridge, Mass., 1968); Michael H. Frisch, "The Community Elite and the Emergence of Urban Politics: Springfield, Massachusetts, 1840-1880," in Stephan Thernstrom and Richard Sennett, eds., *Nineteenth-Century Cities: Essays in the New Urban History* (New Haven, 1969), 277-96; Michael Fitzgibbon Holt, *Forging a Majority: The Formation of the Republican Party in Pittsburgh, 1848-1860* (New Haven, 1970), chap. 1; Michael B. Katz, "Patterns of Inequality, Wealth, and Power," unpublished paper given at the annual meeting of the Organizaiton of American Historians, Apr. 19, 1971, New Orleans; and Daniel Aaron, "Cincinnati, 1818-1838: A Study of Attitudes in the Urban West" (Ph.D. diss., Harvard University, 1942).

7. Dahl, *Who Governs?, passim.*

8. Edward Pessen, "The Occupations of the Antebellum Rich: A Misleading Clue to the Sources and Extent of Their Wealth," *Historical Methods Newsletter,* V (1972), 49-52.

9. It is of course impossible to fix precisely the "membership" of the elite, a group whose nature discourages quantitative efforts to weigh the relative significance of the diverse components that enter into its social makeup. My list is drawn from the memberships of the great social clubs of the era, such as the Philadelphia Club, the Somerset Club in Boston, the Union Clubs in New York City and Brooklyn; the families that figure prominently in the diaries kept by such men as Philip Hone, Gabriel Furman, Samuel Breck, and Sidney George Fisher; persons treated as having lofty status in contemporary memoirs or nineteenth-century local histories written by reliable authors. Given the elusive and subjective character of elite status, the mere attribution of such status by competent authorities is itself a suggestion that the rating may be warranted. For so objective a condition as wealth, on the other hand, contemporary attributions are no help at all. For a fuller discussion of the matter see Edward Pessen, "At the Conjunction of History and Sociology: The Lifestyle of Antebellum Elites," paper delivered at the American Historical Association meeting, New Orleans, December 1972.

10. Robert A. Dahl, "A Critique of the Ruling Elite Model," *American Political Science Review,* LII (1958), 464.

11. Unless otherwise indicated in the text, the "rich" for each city but Philadelphia are the families that were among the wealthiest one per cent of taxpayers. Boston's rich were isolated from the annual *List of Persons, Copartnerships, and Corporations who were Taxed twenty-five Dollars and Upwards in the City of Boston,* published by the city's board of assessors during the era. For the New York City and Brooklyn lists and how they were constructed, see Edward Pessen, "The Wealthiest New Yorkers of the Jacksonian Era: A New List," *New-York Historical Society Quarterly,* LIV (1970), 145-72; and Pessen, "A Social and Economic Portrait of Jacksonian Brooklyn: Inequality, Social Immobility, and Class Distinction in the Nation's Seventh City," *ibid.,* LV (1971), 318-53. The list of Philadelphia rich is drawn from *Memoirs and Auto-Biography of Some of the Wealthy Citizens of Philadelphia* (Philadelphia, 1846); there is some question as to the comprehensiveness and the accuracy of the wealth estimates made by this source. For a discussion of its usefulness, nevertheless, as a clue to Philadelphia wealth, see Edward Pessen, "The Egalitarian Myth and the American Social Reality: Wealth, Mobility, and Equality in the 'Era of the Common Man,'" *American Historical Review,* LXXVI (1971), 995-96, n. 18.

12. Peter R. Knights, *The Plain People of Boston: 1830-1860 A Study in City Growth* (New York, 1971); Michael B. Katz, 5; Robert Doherty, "Property Distribution in Jacksonian America," Unpublished paper read at the annual meeting of the OAH, Apr. 19, 1971, New Orleans; Stuart Blumin, "The Restless Citizen: Vertical Mobility, Migration, and Social Participation in Mid-Nineteenth Century America," A 1970 unpublished version of a paper presented at the Conference on Social Science Concepts in American Political History, Oct. 24, 1969, Brockport, N. Y.; Stephan Thernstrom and Peter R. Knights, "Men in Motion: Some Data and Speculations about Urban Population Mobility in Nineteenth-Century America," *Journal of Interdisciplinary History,* I (1970), 29-30.

13. The discussion of electoral and other provisions of city charters is based primarily on facts drawn from the following sources: Edward P. Allinson and Boies Penrose, *Philadelphia 1681-1887: A History of Municipal Development* (Philadelphia, 1887); Eli K. Price, *The History of the Consolidation of the City of Philadelphia* (Philadelphia, 1873); James McKellar Bugbee, "Boston Under the Mayors, 1822-1880," in Justin Winsor, ed., *The Memorial History of Boston* (Boston, 1894); Josiah Quincy, *A Municipal History of the Town and City of Boston* (Boston, 1852); Henry H. Sprague, *City Government in Boston, Its Rise and Development* (Boston, 1890); John Koren, *Boston, 1822 to 1922: The Story of Its Government and Principal Activities During One Hundred Years* (Boston, 1923); Arthur W. MacMahon, *The Statutory Sources of New York City Government* (New York, 1923); Sidney I. Pomerantz, *New York An American City 1783-1803: A Study of Urban Life* (New York, 1938); Frederick Shaw, *History of the New York City Legislature* (New York, 1954); Ralph Foster Weld, *Brooklyn Village 1816-1834* (New York, 1938); and Henry R. Stiles, *Civil, Political, Professional and Ecclesiastical History and Commercial and Industrial Record of the County of Kings and the City of Brooklyn New York from 1683 to 1884* (New York, 1884).

14. James, 91.

15. Martha Lamb and Mrs. Burton Harrison, *History of the City of New York* (New York, 1877-96), III, 471.

16. Diary of Philip Hone, New York Historical Society, New York City, XX, 419.

17. *Ibid.,* I, 240.

18. *Ibid.,* II, 27, 31, 66-67.

19. For detailed documentation of this point, see Pessen, "The Egalitarian Myth," 998, n. 23; and Pessen, "The Wealthiest New Yorkers," 150-51, nn. 8-9.

20. See letter of Samuel A. Eliot to the mayors of New York City, Philadelphia, and Baltimore, New York City Board of Aldermen, City Clerk Filed Papers, Location 2990.

21. Raymond A. Mohl, *Poverty in New York, 1783-1825* (New York, 1971), 72, *passim;* Benjamin J. Klebaner, "The Home Relief Controversy in Philadelphia, 1782-1861," *Pennsylvania Magazine of History and Biography,* LXXVIII (1954), 403-23; Charles Huse, *Financial History of Boston* (Boston, 1916), 12-13, appendix; Roger Lane, *Policing the City: Boston 1822-1885* (Cambridge, Mass., 1967), 11-13; and Jacob Judd, "A City's Streets: A Case Study of Brooklyn, 1834-1855," *Journal of Long Island History,* IX (1969), 32-43.

22. *List of Real Estate Belonging to the Corporation of the City of New York* (New York, 1838); *Proceedings of the Board of Aldermen, 1832-1833,* IV, 416-18; Gustavus Myers, *History of the Great American Fortunes* (Chicago, 1909), I, 148-50.

23. Jacob Judd, "The History of Brooklyn, 1934-1855: Political and Administrative Aspects" (Ph.D. diss., New York University, 1959), 128.

24. Klebaner, 405, 420-21.

25. Warner, 79.

26. Lane, 26-27.

27. James F. Richardson, "The Struggle to Establish a London-Style Police Force for New York City," *New York Historical Society Quarterly,* XLIX (1965), 175-98; Lane, *passim.*; Jacob Judd, "Policing the City of Brooklyn in the 1840s and 1850s," *Journal of Long Island History,* VI (1966), 13-22.

28. [William A. Brewer], *A Few Thoughts for Tax Payers and Voters* (New York, 1853), 74.

29. Robert M. Zemsky, "Power, Influence, and Status: Leadership Patterns in the Massachusetts Assembly, 1740-1755," *William and Mary Quarterly,* XXVI (1969), 502-20.

30. Dahl, *Who Governs?,* 62-66, 117. See also Nelson W. Polsby, *Community Power and Political Theory* (New Haven, 1963), for a vigorous critique of the Hunter thesis.

31. Judd, "History of Brooklyn."

32. Frank Otto Gatell, "Money and Party in Jacksonian America: A Quantitative Look at New York City's Men of Quality," *Political Science Quarterly,* LXXXI (1967), 235-52.

33. Robert Rich, " 'A Wilderness of Whigs': The Wealthy Men of Boston," *Journal of Social History,* IV (1971), 266.

34. James, 94.

35. Judd, "History of Brooklyn," 81; Warner, 82, 92; Joseph J. McCadden, "Roberts Vaux and His Associates in the Pennsylvania Society for the Promotion of Public Schools," *Pennsylvania History,* III (1936), 10; Dahl, *Who Governs?,* 12, 18-19; John V. Mering, *The Whig Party in Missouri* (Columbia, Mo., 1967), 72, 83-84; *New England Historical and Genealogical Register,* XL (1888), 141; Ralph D. Gray, "Henry D. Gilpin, A Pennsylvania Jacksonian," *Pennsylvania History,* XXXVII (1970), 340-51.

36. Diary of Philip Hone, XIV, 30-31, *passim.*

37. According to Robert Rich, eminent Bostonians who became Democrats lost their "elect status." His documentation for this assertion is a libel suit brought against the Democratic publicist George Bancroft by Daniel Webster, and a later reminiscence cited in the twentieth century; Rich, 268. Actually, bearers of Boston names of greater repute than Bancroft's managed to retain both their unusual Democratic affiliation and the elite status earned by their families before them. Most of the sources cited in n. 35 above give evidence of the insignificance of major party labels in the affairs of urban government. My impression is also based on my reading of the legislative histories recorded by local governments during the era.

38. Samuel Fisk, *The Character of the Candidate for Civil Government* . . . (Boston, 1731), 40, cited in Zemsky, 520; William Bingham to W. and J. Willink, cited in Margaret L. Brown, "William Bingham, Eighteenth Century Magnate," *Pennsylvania Magazine of History and Biography,* LXI (1937), 388.

39. Charles S. Grant, *Democracy in the Connecticut Frontier Town of Kent* (New York, 1961), 150-51; Donald Warner Koch, "Income Distribution and Political Structure in Seventeenth-Century Salem, Massachusetts," *Essex Institute Historical Collections,* CV (1969), 60-66.

40. Carl Bridenbaugh, *Cities in the Wilderness: The First Century of Urban Life in America* New York, 1938), 478-79.

41. Frederic B. Tolles, *Meeting House and Counting House: The Quaker Merchants of Colonial Philadelphia, 1682-1763* (Chapel Hill, 1948), 117.

42. Carl and Jessica Bridenbaugh, *Rebels and Gentlemen: Philadelphia in the Age of Franklin* (New York, 1942), 13; Sam Bass Warner, 9; Bridenbaugh, *Cities in the Wilderness,* 362; Tolles, 43, 117-19; E. Digby Baltzell, *Philadelphia Gentlemen: The Making of a National Upper Class* (New York, 1958), 79; Struthers Burt, *Philadelphia, Holy Experiment* (London, n.d.), 261.

43. *The Minutes of the Common Council of the City of Philadelphia, 1704 to 1776* (Philadelphia, 1847).

44. Bridenbaugh, *Cities in the Wilderness,* 479, *passim.* See also Zemsky; James A. Henretta, "Economic Development and Social Structure in Colonial Boston," *William and Mary Quarterly,* XXII (1965), 79-92.

45. Bruce M. Wilkenfeld, "The New York City Common Council, 1689-1800," *New York History,* LII (1971), 249-74, examines the occupations and a few indices of "status." Edmund Willis, "Social Origins of Political Leadership in New York City from the Revolution to 1815" (Ph.D. diss., University of California, 1967), is an extraordinarily broad-gauged quantitative study that considers ten significant criteria.

46. Wilkenfeld, 256-57, 263-73.

47. Willis, 280, 167, 171, 333.

48. Pomerantz is masterful on changing voting requirements.

49. Professor Ira M. Leonard of Southern Connecticut State College, who is engaged in a study of New York City politics at mid-century, advises me that the "elite" appear to have tried to reassert in the 1850s the kind of direct influence they had exercised in the 1820s and 1830s.

50. Frisch, 282, 284-85; James, 92-94; Aaron, 113; Richard C. Wade, *The Urban Frontier* (Chicago, 1959), 209. Michael B. Katz has shown that in the small town of Hamilton, Ontario, a similar pattern prevailed in which "the wealthy monopolozed local political offices" at mid-century: "the connection between wealth and political power was clear"; Katz, 9.

51. Norton E. Long, "Political Science and the City," in Leo F. Schnore, ed., *Social Science and the City: A Survey of Urban Research* (New York, 1968), 247.

52. William Domhoff defines a "governing class" as a "social upper class which owns a disproportionate amount of a country's wealth, receives a disproportionate amount of a country's yearly income, and contributes a disproportionate number of its members to the controlling institutions and key decision-making groups of the country"; Domhoff, *Who Rules America?* (New York, 1967), 5. Domhoff's definition is unsatisfactory, since what is "disproportionate" is not necessarily substantial or decisive. And, as Polsby has noted, a "disproportionate number" does not automatically act in its own "interest." A more precise and at the same time a bolder definition is required, one that indicates more clearly the kind or amount of disproportionate influence a "governing class" exercises.

Part Four: REFORM

AILEEN S. KRADITOR

GARRISON'S POLITICAL TACTICS REEVALUATED

A reform impulse seemed to sweep over the American people in the 1830s and 1840s, manifesting itself in hundreds of organizations, some national, others local, dedicated to the extinction or the amelioration of every form of social evil. The central reform—whether from the standpoint of its moral dimension, the numbers it enrolled, or its importance—was abolition. And at the center of the antislavery movement, at least in the consciousness of his contemporaries, stood William Lloyd Garrison. Their knowledge of Garrison's great moral zeal has led many modern scholars to join the critics of his own time in denouncing him as a rigid zealot incapable of making the compromises that a truly effective leader of antislavery was required to make. In the following essay Aileen Kraditor forcefully challenges this negative appraisal of Garrisonian tactics, particularly as they related to the Liberty party. Garrison's opposition to the new antislavery party of the early 1840s had been often interpreted as an example of his unbending animus toward practical political action. Kraditor makes a good case that the Garrisonians were opposed rather to impractical political action, in this instance the formation of a third party that would, on the one hand, not have any real chance of electing great numbers of its candidates or significantly affecting governmental policy and on the other hand make it easier for the major parties to resist abolitionist pressures that otherwise might have developed from within their ranks.

From *Means and Ends in American Abolitionism,* by Aileen S. Kraditor. Copyright © 1967, 1968 by Aileen S. Kraditor. Reprinted by permission of Pantheon Books, a Division of Random House, Inc. Pages 158-168, 173-177.

The failure to distinguish between Garrison's opinions as a nonresistant and the tactics he thought the abolitionist movement (as a coalition of adherents of many philosophies) ought to pursue has led to an understandable confusion among historians who discuss his views on political tactics. Noting his repudiation of all forceful government and, after 1842, his denunciation of the United States Constitution, they have dismissed his advocacy of certain types of political action as evidence of muddy thinking and have paid too little attention to the theory underlying that advocacy.[1]

The starting point for his discussion of political action was his conception of the abolitionist movement as a broad coalition. Just as he would not exclude from the AASS [American Anti-slavery Society] any abolitionist whose philosophy differed from his, so he could, without prescribing modes of action, theorize about the sort of political tactics proper for an abolitionist who shared little with him but the principles of the society's constitution—the sinfulness of slavery and the duty of immediate emancipation. Given the average abolitionist's acceptance of the United States government and the propriety of voting, what types of political action, Garrison might ask, were inconsistent with that abolitionist's principles? Second, which among those tactics was the most effective way of fighting slavery in the political field?

Garrison's answers to the first question coincided with those of the majority of political abolitionists. That is, the abolitionist could with propriety adopt the "scattering" policy, meaning he could cast a write-in vote for an individual not on the ballot, demonstrate his dissatisfaciton with all the regular nominees; in a thoroughly abolitionized district, these scattering votes could, he thought, represent enough strength to force concessions from the regular parties at the next election. The same effect could be produced by temporary nominations by abolitionists. Or, the abolitionist could work actively as part of a pressure group to force a major party to take acceptable positions and nominate antislavery candidates on the local level, while he would of course refuse to vote for its presidential candidates as long as they were acceptable to the party's Southern wing. Eventually, many abolitionized local parties might force a change in the party's national character. The scattering policy could be combined with this second mode of action.[2] Still another possibility was for the abolitionist to join with others to organize a third party. Garrison and most of his group never condemned the Liberty party as wrong in principle. They condemned it when they answered the second question, that concerning the effectiveness of each of the tactics that were in principle acceptable.

We admit [wrote Garrison] that the *mode* of political action, to be pursued by abolitionists, is not strictly a question of principle, but rather one of sound expediency. We have never opposed the formation of a third party as a measure inherently wrong, but have always contended that the abolitionists have as clear and indisputable right to band themselves together politically for the attainment of their great object, as those of their fellow-citizens who call themselves whigs or democrats. . . . But every reflecting mind may easily perceive, that to disregard the dictates of sound expediency may often prove as injurious to an enterprise as to violate principle. It is solely on this ground that we oppose what is called the "liberty party." We believe it is highly inexpedient, and therefore not the best mode to advance the anti-slavery cause.[3]

Since Garrison the nonresistant opposed all parties on principle so long as the government was based on force, he could not prefer one party to another or condemn one more than another on any but expedient grounds. It would also follow that to the abolitionist who was not a nonresistant there could, he believed, be no principled objection to a third party.

The disagreements on political tactics between the radicals and Liberty-men, then, hinged, in Garrison's opinion, on the question of expediency, not principle. They agreed that the two parties were corrupt and the servants of the slave power, but they proposed different ways of reforming them. According to the radicals, the parties were corrupt because the people were. Only a reformed public opinion could reform the parties in any meaningful, lasting way. Who, they asked, would join the third party? Committed abolitionists. Would they be more useful there or in their old parties? If their task was to convert the masses of voters, they would be more effective if they remained where those masses were.[4] In an abolitionized district both parties would have to make concessions to keep their own abolitionist members from defecting, and a third party, by withdrawing those members from both major parties, would permit them to continue to ignore the interests of the slave. But if abolitionists adopted the scattering policy and demonstrated their refusal to vote for unacceptable candidates and their willingness to cross party lines to vote for abolitionists despite differences on other issues that separated the parties, they could constitute a real balance of power between them.[5] A third party would be a less effective instrument for influencing public opinion than agitation by the AASS and by abolitionists voting as individuals. And once public opinion had been converted, the major parties would, for the sake of votes, reflect the change in their platforms and nominations, and a third party would be unnecessary.[6] This argument was urged whether the third party was of the one-idea or broad-platform type.

The fullest exposition of the Garrisonian theory is in an imaginary dialogue, by Lydia Maria Child, between "A" and "B." In response to "A's" inquiry about the position of the AASS on political action, "B" explains:

[It] stands on precisely the same principles that it did the first year of its formation. Its object was to change public opinion on the subject of slavery, by the persevering utterance of truth. This change they expected would show itself in a thousand different forms:—such as conflict and separation in churches; new arrangements in colleges and schools; new customs in stages and cars; and new modifications of policy in the political parties of the day. The business of anti-slavery was, and is, to purify the *fountain,* whence all these streams flow; if it turns aside to take charge of any *one* of the streams, however important, it is obvious enough that the whole work must retrograde; for, if the fountain be not kept pure, no one of the streams will flow with clear water. But just so sure as the fountain is taken proper care of, the character of all the streams *must* be influenced thereby. We might form ourselves into a railroad society, to furnish cars with the same conveniences for all complexions; but we feel that we are doing a far more effectual work, so as to change popular opinion, that there will be no *need* of a separate train of cars. We might expend all our funds and energies in establishing abolition colleges; but we feel sure that we have the power in our hands to abolitionize *all* colleges.

In answer to a later question, "B" contends that before the Liberty party was organized, both parties in Massachusetts were afraid of abolitionists and hence willing to grant their requests; this is no longer so. "A": But those legislators were not genuine abolitionists, or they would not have refused concessions once the pressure was removed.

B: Those men, let me tell you, did the work of sound anti-slavery; and in doing it, got imbued more or less with anti-slavery sentiment, in spite of themselves. The machinery of a third political party may send into Congress, or the halls of State legislation, a few individuals, who are anti-slavery to the back-bone. But could one Alvan Stewart do as much for our cause in Congress, as twenty of Joshua R. Giddings? Fifty men, who have a strong motive for obliging the abolitionists, could surely do more for our cause, in such a position, than merely two or three radical abolitionists. I too want to see all our legislators anti-slavery; but when that time comes, there will most obviously be no need of a distinct abolition party; and in order to bring about that time, we must diligently exert moral influence to sway *all* parties. . . .

And why, continues "B," assume that the Liberty party will be comprised of more disinterested men? Many are joining it who never were abolitionists. In one county, Democrats join temporarily, to defeat a Whig; in another county, Whigs join to defeat a Democrat. Are these recruits more reliable than major-party legislators who are willing to give abolitionists what they ask? Many Libertymen are sincere abolitionists, but "by the natural laws of attraction, their party will draw around them the selfish and the ambitious." If party machinery is so mischievous, asks "A, how can you work with Whigs and Democrats? "B: By adhering closely to moral influence, we work *through* both parties, but not *with* them. They do our work; we do not *theirs.* We are simply the atmosphere that makes the quicksilver rise or fall."

Later "A" remarks that the South dreads antislavery at the ballot box more than anywhere else, and "B" replies:

I never doubted that political action would be a powerful engine for the overthrow of slavery.—The only question between you and the American Society seems to be, whether the speediest and most extensive political effect would be produced by the *old* scheme of holding the balance between the two parties; or the *new* scheme of forming a distinct party. I apprehend what the slaveholders would like least of all things, would be to see *both* the great political parties consider it for their interest to nominate abolitionists; and this *would* be the case if anti-slavery voters would only be consistent and firm.

"A": But they will not be consistent and firm; under the old plan they always turned aside to vote for a Harrison or a Van Buren. "B": If that is so, will the Liberty party keep them from doing so? Will a two-thirds abolitionized Democrat, who has joined to defeat a Whig, vote Liberty when his ballot is needed by his own party? An antislavery member of an old party will be more reliable if his party interests coincide with his abolitionism and if his work as an abolitionist will mean an increase in the number of antislavery votes for his own party. But you remove that stimulus when you organize a separate party: you force him to give up his party position on all issues besides slavery. And the success of such a third party would be its undoing, for if it gains enough power to influence legislation in a state, one Libertyman will be protariff and another antitariff, and they will be swallowed by their former parties again. "A" suggests that perhaps these lawmakers will be willing to sacrifice those other considerations for the sake of antislavery. In that case, "B" replies, their constituents will complain that their other interests are neglected and will vote the legislators out of office. And so we have come back to moral influence as the legitimate work of an abolitionist. But, asks "A," can we not exert moral influence and work for the Liberty party at the same time? "B": In practice, things have not worked out that way; Libertymen now talk scornfully of moral influence. "A": But now that the Liberty party exists, should we not vote for its candidates? "B": "That is the bait that has hooked half their numbers. . . . *Moral* influence dies under *party* action."[7]

The radicals decried what they believed was the tendency of some to exaggerate the significance of legal enactments; when William Goodell, for example, argued that slavery was the creature of law and that its abolition was "nothing more nor less than the repeal of these slave laws," they replied that slavery was "the creature of avarice and love of domination" and was "only *sanctified* and regulated" by law.[8] Wrote Rogers of New Hampshire.

The best and utmost that political movements—the constitutions, enactments, and decisions could effect for the slave, is to translate him into that anomaly in a *christian republic,* called a "free nigger." New Hampshire has thus transmuted him by the magic force of its politics. What is the liberty of a New Hampshrie emancipated colored man? It barely qualifies him to pass muster as a candidate for the mercy of the Colonization Society. . . . New York has abolished slavery by *law;* yet it is as much as a colored man's life is worth to live in her cities. . . . Slavery has been *legally* abolished in half the states of the Union, and the best they can do for the fugitive slave is to give him race ground to Canada before the Southern bloodhounds and for the freed man of color is to let in upon him the gray hounds of colonization.[9]

Garrison and those who thought like him insisted that to abolish the law would be useless without transformation of the spirit that the law reflected.[10]

The advocates of a third party, wrote Oliver Johnson, have betrayed a degree of impatience with the progress of the cause. They should note that in England the abolitionists continued to hold the balance of power without organizing their own party, until they won. It may be replied, he continued, that the parties in the United States are more subservient to the slave power than they were in England. True, he conceded, but that merely proves that the people here are more corrupted by slavery than were the English; and will a third party counteract that corruption and purify their hearts?

All attempts to abolish slavery by legislation before the people of the country are converted to anti-slavery principles must of necessity be unsuccessful. A political party is not needed as a means of converting the people, and when they *are* converted, such a party will of course be unnecessary. When we say that efforts to abolish slavery by legislation must for the present be necessarily unsuccessful, we do not mean to intimate that such efforts should not constantly and vigorously be made; but only that the want of success should be attributed to the right cause, and not lead to the adoption of a measure which is at best of doubtful utility.[11]

The Libertymen mistook "the right cause" when they contended that the major parties were incorrigibly proslavery and from that contention deduced the need for a third party. The fundamental principles of both parties, said the Garrisonians, were laudable. The Democratic creed preached liberty, reform, and equal rights; the Whig creed, stability, supremacy of law, and security of property; between them the rights of the people and the interests of property were championed. If not for the slave power, temporarily dominating and perverting both, abolitionists who accepted the legitimacy of the government could adhere to one or the other without violating their anti-slavery principles. Abolitionist agitation, then, must aim to bring both parties back to their own principles, to make the leaders of both act consistently with their own professions.[12] Expecting less from organized political action than did the Libertymen, Garrison could not see a political party, regardless of what it called itself, as the insurance of an office-holder's fidelity to the cause. That role he assigned to unorganized (but infinitely more coercive) public opinion.

Running through all the tactical thinking of Garrison and his followers is an emphasis on what today would be called "building a constituency." Their political theory may be seen as a part of their general theory of agitation, a corollary of which was their conception of the AASS itself as no more than a propaganda center, from which abolitionists with a wide variety of philosophies and affiliations would go, armed with agitational weapons to use in whatever parties, churches, or other organizations they chose to belong to. Without public opinion on its side, the movement could accomplish nothing; with public opinion, it could transform all organizations dependent on public opinion into tactical weapons for the cause.

Garrison did not see political action as a way of achieving his goals by parliamentary means. Those goals were far too radical—far too subversive of the fundamental arrangements of American society—to be realized by the vote of a few hundred men, including slaveholders and their allies, in the Capitol in Washington, even if a majority of them had been willing to so vote, which was inconceivable. It would, therefore, be an oversimplification to say that he refused to engage in political action because such action would represent participation in a government whose legitimacy he, as a nonresistant, denied, although this purely abstract formulation was sufficient for the "ultraists" whose spokesman he was. But what of the principles that should, in Garrison's opinion, guide the tactics of those abolitionists who did not repudiate the coercive United States government? One gets the impression from his writings on the subject that he at least sensed the practical danger that other radicals throughout American history have sometimes encountered: that *ad hoc* alliances for partial ends may under certain circumstances strengthen the hegemony of the enemy by legitimizing the institutions, and the ideological justifications of those institutions, by means of which the enemy exercises his hegemony. The radical who recognizes this danger (or who at least senses it, as I think Garrison did) may form such alliances, but on his own terms, with explicit safeguards against his participation being used to foster illusions that political action is more than a temporary tactic for very limited purposes; he will, that is, make it clear that he is using the political machinery and that it is not using him. It is in the light of Garrison's partial insight into this principle that we should interpret his insistence, as against the Libertymen, that the major parties were redeemable; they were redeemable not as parties but as the politically organized constituencies among which nonradical abolitionists could agitate for abolition.

In view of the radicals' opposition to the third party and their belief that the major parties were redeemable, it is understandable that abolitionists who refused to leave their old parties found more common ground with them than with the Libertymen. And since most abolitionists were Whigs, the Libertymen discovered a convenient weapon against both adversaries: the accusation that Whigs and nonresistants had formed an alliance against the Liberty party. The Libertymen themselves recognized that Garrison never, as an abolitionist, condemned voting per se; they asserted that he was inconsistent when he, a nonresistant, advised voters to vote for abolitionists regardless of party label. That assertion constitutes an implicit admission that his policy was not proscriptive, that he did not consider abolitionists who accepted the legitimacy of political action spurious abolitionists. Liberty-men knew they had no reason to fear he would persuade many abolitionists to stay away from the polls. Their real grievance against him was therefore not his antipolitical philosophy as a nonresistant but his anti-third-party position as an abolitionist.[14] That his nonresistance was used as a red herring is suggested by the argument, heavily relied on during the factional struggles, that nonresistance must be officially repudiated because its absurdity and radicalism would alienate most potential supporters. It would follow that after the society had split, the radical remnant, isolated from the more con-servative body of abolitionists, would exert negligible influence. Yet while the Liberty party was struggling to attract the support of anti-slavery Whigs and Democrats, it directed its principal polemics against the nonresistants, ostensibly to prevent them from exerting influence against political action of any sort. And the AASS and the Massachusetts Anti-Slavery Society re-tained the allegiance of thousands of Whig voters in New England who, if the Liberty party's public fears had had substance, would have fought the Garrisonian influence as vehemently as did the Libertymen.[15] Clearly, the real issue was not political action versus nonresistance but third-party politi-cal action versus independent political action. Equally clearly, the real threat was not Garrison's influence for nonresistance, which was small, but his influence for independent (non-Liberty party) political action, which was considerable.

In fact, it is difficult to draw a line between the nonresistants and some major-party abolitionists before the mid-1840s, so far as political tactics are concerned. The independent Whig David Lee Child adhered to the Gar-risonian faction in that period; the same is true of George Bradburn, who broke with that faction when he left the Whig for the Liberty party in 1844.[16] Gamaliel Bailey, Birney's successor as editor of *The Philanthropist* (Cin-cinnati), was certainly no disciple of Garrison, but as long as he opposed the Liberty party his articles were freely reprinted and praised in *The Liberator*.[17] One such article was an editorial in which Bailey observed that abolitionists were a small minority in the free states. If they constituted a majority there would be no need for a third party, because they could force the major parties to nominate suitable candidates. No minority could bring about any legis-lated action against slavery; hence the advocates of a new party must act on the assumption that this measure was the best way to obtain a majority. Now, a new party could not hold out to its adherents the hope of office or political advancement; nor could it threaten to defeat any lawmaker. Unable to succeed by appealing to motives of self-interest, it must operate by moral means—argument, persuasion. Was the third-party scheme the best way to carry on propaganda? No, declared Bailey, quite the opposite. As long as a major party saw that abolitionists did not threaten it as a party, that they said nothing about its doctrines, that they insisted that their cause could be supported by all people without interfering with either party's essential interests, that they asked only that it be true to its own stated principles, it would not war upon them. Let the parties have the offices and prestige, he advised. Our present policy removes as far as possible "every obstacle between those parties and the force of our arguments."

If the larger portion of our fellow countrymen are so corrupted and unprincipled, that they cannot, by any *moral* means we have been accustomed to use, be induced to act on our principles, surely, beyond all doubt, it is visionary to expect to reform them by a political organization, too feeble to bestow political rewards, or inflict political punishment.[18]

Garrison could agree with every one of these statements. "The politics of a people,' he wrote, "will always be shaped by its morals, as the vane on the steeple is ever indicating in what direction the wind blows."[19]

Notes

1. See Thomas, *The Liberator: William Lloyd Garrison,* pp. 275-76, 285-88, 325-26. Merrill, *Against Wind and Tide,* has an extremely brief summary, without comment. One would not learn from Barnes, *The Anti-Slavery Impulse, or Filler, The Crusade against Slavery,* that Garrison even had a theory of political action. See also Dumond, ed., "Introduction," *Birney Letters,* I, ix.

2. One or more of these points may be found in each of the following (as well as in many more documents in the same period): "To the Abolitionists of Massachusetts," by Francis Jackson and Amos A. Phelps, for the board of managers of the Massachusetts Anti-Slavery Society, *The Liberator,* August 10, 1838; Oliver Johnson, "Hear Both Sides," *ibid.,* September 14, 1838; [Oliver Johnson?], "Anti-Slavery Political Party," *ibid.,* June 26, 1840; E[dmund] Q[uincy], "Liberty Party," *ibid.,* September 22, 1843; resolutions presented by Garrison for the business committee, reported in "The Twelfth Annual Meeting of the Massachusetts Anti-Slavery Society," *ibid.,* February 2, 1844; "Extracts from the Twelfth Annual Report of the Managers of the Massachusetts Anti-Slavery Society for 1844," *ibid.,* March 22, 1844.

3. " 'Dying Away'—Another Richmond in the Field—Political Action," *ibid.,* October 1, 1841. (Thomas, *The Liberator: William Lloyd Garrison,* pp. 325-26, cites this statement to prove that Garrison did oppose the Liberty party on principle, but he quotes it in an 1843—1844 context, showing Garrison's alleged reaction to the increasing strength of the Liberty party, and he comments, "Such statements fooled no one. . . ." Yet by October 1841, such successes as the party was to enjoy were in the future. According to Fladeland, *Birney,* p. 188, about one tenth of eligible voters in antislavery societies voted for Birney in 1840.) See also resolution passed at the AASS convention in 1842, reported in *The Liberator,* May 27, 1842. Such statements appeared from time to time in that paper throughout the active life of the Liberty party. Those written by Edmund Quincy in the mid-1840s, when he was editor pro tem. in Garrison's absence, stressed the alleged recreancy of Birney and other Liberty leaders as reason for opposing the party, whereas Garrison most often emphasized arguments against third-partyism per se. In emphasizing their theoretical differences I do not mean to deny that animus influenced their thinking. Historians have dealt at more than adequate length on that motive, and since in my opinion the animus does not fully account for the views expressed, the theories deserve attention on their merits. The conviction that party politics [were] corrupting caused Mrs. Child to assert that abstention from it was a question of principle. Thirty-partyism was more corrupting than agitation within the two major parties, she wrote, since it required closer contact with party machinery (see "The Third Party," *ibid.,* July 9, 1841). The difference

between her position and Garrison's was, however, largely one of terminology. Abby Kelley shared Mrs. Child's view. See James S. Gibbons to Elizabeth Pease, January 31, 1842, Anti-Slavery Letters, BPL.

4. This may seem inconsistent with the come-outer principle defended by Garrisonians (especially Maria Weston Chapman), who stressed the educational value of bearing witness to an ideal by ostentatiously withdrawing from institutions that trampled on it. Again it should be pointed out that these tactical suggestions were intended to apply only to those abolitionists who did not subscribe to nonresistance, come-outerism, and other aspects of Garrison's radical creed, those who believed in working within the framework of the United States government.

5. See two editorials by Garrison, "Gerrit Smith on Political Action" and "The Licence Law—Political Action," *The Liberator,* January 31 and February 21, 1840.

6. See "To the Abolitionists of Massachusetts," *ibid.,* August 10, 1838; [Oliver Johnson?], Anti-Slavery Political Party," *ibid.,* June 26, 1840; L[ydia] M. C[hild], "Talk about Political Party," reprinted from *The National Anti-Slavery Standard* in *The Liberator,* August 5, 1842; E[dmund] Q[uincy], "Liberty Party," *ibid.,* September 22, 1843.

7. Talk about Political Party," *ibid.,* August 5, 1842. In the issue of September 2, Garrison endorsed "B's" position and defended Mrs. Child's article from the ridicule by Beriah Green in a letter from Green printed in an upstate New York paper.

8. Goodell, "Political Action against Slavery," No. 2, *ibid.,* August 31, 1838; resolution passed at New-England Anti-Slavery Convention, *ibid.,* June 7, 1839.

9. Quoted in Robert Adams, "Nathaniel Peabody Rogers: 1794-1846," *New England Quarterly,* XX (September 1947), 372. See also an 1847 speech by Frederick Douglass, in Philip S. Foner, ed., *The Life and Writings of Frederick Douglass,* I (New York, 1950), 278.

10. Senator Thomas Morris, wrote Garrison, "assumes that 'political action is necessary to produce moral reformation in a nation.' This is to reverse the order of events. Moral reformation is necessary to produce an enlightened, conscientious, impartial political action. A man must first be abolitionized before he will be able or willing to burst the shackles of party, and give his vote for the slave. . . ." *The Liberator,* August 16, 1839.

11. [Oliver Johnson?], "Anti-Slavery Political Party," *ibid.,* June 26, 1840. An earlier part of that editorial warrants quotation: "We are confident that our opinion upon this point is not the result of our peculiar views of the inherent character of government, but of a careful estimate of all the considerations which should have weight with a person who regards it not only right in itself, but a duty, to exercise the elective franchise. That slavery in our country will eventually be abolished by law, (so far as it can be done by such means,) unless the views of the people in relation to government shall undergo a speedy and almost miraculous change, and that every consideration of expediency and duty must naturally operate to induce abolitionists, who vote, to carry out their principles by consistent and persevering political action, is what we fully believe. We urge no arguments, on the antislavery platform, to dissuade men from voting. The question is not, whether the ballot-box is not an important instrumentality, which should be wielded by every voter for the promotion of the cause of humanity and freedom; nor whether anti-slavery voters are not under the most sacred obligations to bestow their suffrages upon men who have given unequivocal evidence of their fidelity to the principles of impartial justice; but it is, whether the desired object can be most speedily and effectually accomplished by an organized and independent political party, or by the modes of action hitherto pursued, modified somewhat, perhaps, in the light of past experience. It does not follow, that he who opposes the plan of independent nominations must therefore stay away from the polls, or vote for the pro-slavery candidates of the present parties." And he went on to argue for the scattering policy.

12. "To the Abolitionists of Massachusetts," *ibid.,* August 10, 1838. See also Johnson's article cited in note 11 above; Garrison, " 'Dying Away'—Another Richmond in the Field—Political Action," *ibid.,* October 1, 1841; E[dmund] Q[uincy], "Liberty Party," *ibid.,* September 22, 1843; Garrison, "The Liberty Party . . . ," *ibid.,* March 12, 1847.

13. See especially [William Goodell], "Circular. *To the Abolitionists of New-York who believe it wrong and absurd to retain a connexion with the* PROSLAVERY PARTIES, *com-*

monly called WHIG *and* DEMOCRATIC," reprinted from the Cazenovia (New York) *Abolitionist* in *The Liberator,* November 4, 1842.

14. See Goodell, *Slavery and Anti-Slavery,* pp. 518-19. Nonresistants, he wrote, comprised less than one percent of the Massachusetts Society's membership and numbered no more than 100 or 200 in all New England in 1841-1842 and even fewer elsewhere. In the same passage Goodell argued that there was a practical alliance between the Democratic and Whig abolitionists and the nonresistants against the Liberty party.

15. Their vehemence sometimes bordered on the vitriolic, exceeding anything written by Garrison, although his screeds have been emphasized by historians. See, for example, *The True History of the Late Division in the Anti-Slavery Societies,* Being Part of the Second Annual Report of the Executive Committee of the Massachusetts Abolition Society [led by Libertymen] (Boston, 1841) (the part on political action is pp. 22-26); Goodell's Circular, cited in note 13 above; "The American Anti-Slavery Society," by the Rev. C. T. Torrey, reprinted from *The Tocsin of Liberty* in *The Liberator,* November 4, 1842; "A Hundred Conventions," reprinted from *The Herkimer Journal* in *The Liberator,* August 4, 1843.

16. See his letter *ibid.,* August 16, 1844. It should be added that Samuel E. Sewall, a Libertyman, was a Garrisonian also and that loyalty to that group does not by itself indicate concurrence with the views of Garrison. In the cases of Child and Bradburn, however, I believe that two motives were present: first, belief in the "broad platform" policy of AASS organization and opposition to proscriptionism, and second, agreement with Garrison on political tactics (and, incidentally, women's rights). See *ibid.,* March 5, 1841, for Garrison's comment on Bradburn, then a member of the Massachusetts House of Representatives from Nantucket. Reprinting a letter to the editor of *The Boston Atlas* praising Bradburn, Garrison wrote that it should be read by "the editor of the Friend of Man [Goodell], and all others who insist that no man can be a true abolitionist who is elected to office by the whig or democratic party."

17. For his low opinion of Garrison, see Bailey to Birney, October 14, 1837, and April 18, 1840, *Birney Letters,* I, 428, 556-57. In an editorial reprinted in *The Liberator,* December 6, 1839. Bailey wrote that many of his views on third party coincided with those expressed in a recent address by the Massachusetts Anti-Slavery Society's board of managers. Bailey supported Harrison in 1840, but his views on issues other than slavery coincided with those of the Democrats. See Bailey to Birney, February 21, 1840, and March 3, 1840, *Birney Letters,* I, 531-32, 535-38.

18. "A Separate Political Organization," reprinted in *The Liberator,* December 6, 1839. In an article reprinted *ibid.,* July 17, 1840. Bailey argued that a vote for Birney would help elect Van Buren, and that although the Whigs, if elected, would be no more friendly to abolitionists than would the Democrats, abolitionists could exert more influence on the Whigs. Within a year, however, Bailey went over to the Liberty party. His conversion is noted in Bretz, "The Economic Background of the Liberty Party," *American Historical Review,* XXXIV (January 1929), 256.

19. "The Liberty Party . . . ," *The Liberator,* March 12, 1847. Expressing the same thought in negative terms, he wrote, "Political action is not moral action, any more than a box on the ear is an argument." "James G. Birney—the Liberty Party," *ibid.,* March 13, 1846.

MICHAEL B. KATZ

EDUCATIONAL PROMOTERS
AND THE HIGH SCHOOL

*Improving educational opportunity for children of the
poor and lower-middle classes was a reform strenuously
advocated throughout the Jacksonian era. Although the
beneficiaries of this movement were to be the sons and
daughters of the humble, its leaders were usually of the
socioeconomic elite. In the following passage Michael
Katz carefully examines the motives of high school
reformers in Massachusetts. Arguing that the idea of
intermediate schooling for the children of havenots was
related to, if not directly triggered by, the accelerating
rate of industrialism and urbanism, Katz stresses the
diverse social goods that the educational reformers
anticipated would flow from the establishment of public
high schools. Industrial productivity would increase, as
would community wealth, while the upward mobility
experienced by students, most of them of plebeian
background, would promote social order and harmony.
Unfortunately from the point of view of their promoters,
the new schools failed to attract substantial numbers of
the children of the poor, largely because both their
purposes and their actual operations were largely
irrelevant to the lives and experiences of those they hoped
to uplift. Since Katz is a scholar attendant to the nuances
and complexities of life and thought, he notes too the
paradoxes and contradictions in a way of thought which
appeared to glorify technological advance while
simultaneously bemoaning its social consequences.*

Reprinted by permission of the publishers and the author from *The Irony of Early School
Reform: Educational Innovation in Mid-Nineteenth Century Massachusetts* by Michael B.
Katz, Cambridge, Mass.: Harvard University Press, Copyright © 1968 by the President and
Fellows of Harvard College. Pages 27-50. Notes have been omitted.

Massachusetts educational promoters proudly argued that education had fostered the impressive economic progress of the commonwealth. The relation between education and the creation of wealth was, in fact, the thesis of Horace Mann's fifth report, in which he elaborated at length his contention that the progress and prosperity of a manufacturing economy were dependent upon the education of the entire population. Elsewhere, he claimed that "education is not only a moral renovator, and a multiplier of intellectual power, but . . . also the most prolific parent of material riches." Education, therefore, should "not only be included in the grand inventory of a nation's resources," but should "be placed at the very head of that inventory." The connection between education and industrial prosperity and the enthusiasm with which schoolmen welcomed economic transformation were well illustrated in the first report of George Boutwell, third secretary of the Massachusetts Board of Education.

Boutwell stressed that education had been of the utmost importance in the development of Massachusetts into an industrial state. The role of the schools was increasingly potent since "labor," in its "leading characteristics," had been previously a "manual process," but now had become, "in its force and value, essentially intellectual." The fruits of intelligence were harvested in improved agricultural production and especially in industry. "The prosperity of the mills and shops is based quite as much upon the intellectual vigor as upon the physical power of the laborers." In his rapturous description of the qualities of intellectualized industry Boutwell demonstrated one side of the ambivalence of Massachusetts educators to industrial society:

Labor is not imitative merely,—it is inventive, creative. The laborer is no longer servile, yielding to laws and necessities that he cannot comprehend, and therefore cannot respect, but he has been elevated to the regions of art and works by laws that he appreciates, and aspires to a perfection as real, at least, as that of the sculptor, painter, or poet . . . The laws of labor are the laws that exist and are recognized in art, eloquence and science. The great law of these latter unquestionably is, that every student shall be at the same time an original thinker, investigator, designer and producer.

The artist-laborer had a central role to play in the state since, claimed Boutwell, "Massachusetts, from its history and position, is necessarily a manufacturing and commercial state." Manufacture and commerce, he continued, require intellectual cultivation and "a high order of learning." Consequently, the industrial and commercial success of Massachusetts depended "for the materials of its growth and prosperity on the intelligence of the laboring classes upon the land and in the shops and mills. Thus we connect the productive power of our state with its institutions of learning."

"Now the increased means for education for the last sixty years," wrote Horace Mann to J. A. Shaw in 1840, "have not kept pace with the increasing obligations, duties, and temptations of the community." Here Mann sounded a widely echoed theme. In the past, educators argued, the common schools had made Massachusetts prosperous, but the educational institutions sufficient for the needs of a simple agrarian commonwealth would not meet the demands of an urban-industrial society. As the Winchendon school committee proclaimed: it was a "fixed point" that all should receive a good education but the term "good" itself was "movable." In educational requirements the "tendency was upwards." The occupations previously open to a boy with only an elementary common school background now required a secondary education. In every variety of work "rapid progress," commented the Brookline school committee in 1855, called for a "corresponding expansion . . . in education." "Modern commerce" required the "young merchant" to have "a more adequate knowledge of the great globe he dwells on than can be acquired from the pages of a Grammar School textbook"; the farmer could not "much longer dispense with some scientific knowledge of the soil he cultivates." Similarly, "the ships, the mills, and warehouses we need can no longer be built by the 'rule of thumb' of an ignorant mechanic." In short, "whole classes in our community who, not a generation ago, would have been content to earn their living by unskilled labor, are now thrust from that lower market, and forced to add knowledge and intelligence to the labor of their hands." The answer, to the committee, was "not to regret this state of things, but . . . to provide for it." And provision to them meant a high school. Similarly, Rantoul may have had a high school in mind when he complained that some parents scoffed at the newer, more advanced subject matter of education with the attitude "that as they did not attend, when young, to those studies, therefore it is not important for their children to attend to them." But this was a fallacy "inasmuch as their children come into life in a community much better taught than was the society in which their parents began life."

Intertwined with the arguments relating the necessity of improved education, especially a high school, to the economic requirements of an industrializing society are contentions stressing the relationship between the high school and social mobility. The Winchendon committee argued that the availability of foreigners to perform the "least desirable" sorts of work enabled "our sons to rise to other employments." To seize the new opportunities for its children a town required an advanced educational system, especially a high school; there was no other alternative if parents desired their children to rise on the economic and social scale. "Shall we," asked the committee, "stand still, and see our children outstripped in the race of life, by the children of those who are willing to pursue a liberal and far-sighted policy?"

The relation between the high school and both communal prosperity and mobility was driven home to the people of Beverly by Rufus Putnam, part-time superintendent and principal of a high school in neighboring Salem. He informed the town that there was a direct correlation between educational facilities and the wealth of a community. He told the citizens of Beverly that to develop their economy they would have to develop their schools, and, he maintained, no improvement was more crucial than a high school. "The best educated community" will "*always* be the most prosperous community . . . nothing so directly tends to promote the increase of *wealth* of a community as the thorough mental training of its youth." When he had taken charge of the Bowditch (English) High School in Salem, Putnam told the people of Beverly in 1853, parents had difficulty finding employment for children who had attended. But technological change had completely altered the situation: "the introduction of Machinery in the arts had increased the demand for education inasmuch as there was more mind required in the use of machinery than without it . . . and an increase in a greater proportion of mental process to produce the increased results called for more education." In fact, "there was such a demand for well educated boys that some were induced to leave school before they had completed their regular course of study."

The argument that a high school would foster mobility probably appealed to parents of limited or moderate means, for they are the ones who would not be able to provide their sons with the capital or influence that might make a good education less necessary. It is likely that these arguments influenced many of the artisans and less wealthy businessmen who voted for the retention of Beverly High School. Similarly, it is likely that the affluent supporters were influenced by the appeal to communal wealth, since as owners of real estate and as investors they stood to gain the most from urban and industrial development. But would the arguments concerning mobility appeal to them? Had they an interest in paying taxes to develop competition for themselves and their children? Another prominent high school promoter from Beverly helps answer these questions.

Dr. Wyatt C. Boyden, next-door neighbor of Robert Rantoul, was the leading town physician. The two promoters did not always agree. Boyden was a Whig, a friend of Rufus Choate, an admirer of Webster. Rantoul was a Democrat. In 1836 Boyden was one of four physicians whose united raising of fees evoked a petition from a town meeting, a petition urged by Rantoul. Both Rantoul and Boyden were charter members of the Beverly Academy, which flourished from the 1830's to the mid-50's, but a fight between the trustees and proprietors led to Rantoul's resignation. The fight had been over the appointment of a teacher, one James Woodbury Boyden, the doctor's eldest son. However, the two men must frequently have submerged their differences. For nearly two decades they served together on the town school committee; and both were among the ten original members of the Republican party in Beverly. The cooperation of Boyden, the Whig, and Rantoul, the Democrat, underlines the fact that on the local level partisan politics was simply irrelevant, in this period, to educational reform.

The son of a financially struggling country doctor, Boyden was born in Tamworth, New Hampshire, in 1794. A combination of common schools, a brief spell at an academy, and private tutoring by a local minister prepared

Boyden for Dartmouth, which he entered in 1815. In 1819 he became the first Tamworth resident to receive a Dartmouth A.B. From 1815 to 1826 Boyden alternated going to college with school teaching and, finally, studying medicine at Dartmouth. As was common in that period, he actually started to practice before he had received his degree. During one term Boyden taught school in Beverly Farms, where he met Elizabeth Woodbury. They married in 1821 and settled in New Hampshire until pressure from Elizabeth's parents and the offer of an attractive junior partnership in a flourishing practice attracted them back to Beverly.

Unlike his father, Boyden was a prosperous doctor. "During the healthy and active part of my life," he wrote, "I have had a leading and somewhat lucrative business . . . My yearly income has from the beginning more than supported me." Boyden's financial status was not, however, solely the result of his income from fees. With considerable shrewdness he early perceived the future of the shoe business in Lynn, and his considerable investments there, claimed his grandson, "have proved of substantial benefit to the family." Boyden also provided his sons with capital. "When he found that his son Albert was a shrewd and safe man," wrote Byden's grandson, "he entrusted money to him for investment in Illinois farm-mortgages at rates of interest which, though normal for their times, seem fancifully high in our days of cheap money." Dr. Boyden died in 1879 and left an estate valued at $75,000, "this sum being almost entirely the result of his own earnings, savings and investments."

This physician-promoter also engaged actively in the affairs of Beverly. Boyden's learning and his love of the classics made him a leader in educational matters; and he served for twenty-four years as a member of the school committee. He was also, as has been noted, a charter member of the Beverly Academy. According to his grandson, he was the town's most active and influential exponent of graded schools. Despite his long interest in education, the decision to vote for the high school was not an easy one for Boyden to make. In a fragment of a letter, perhaps never sent, Boyden admitted his unwillingness to increase "the high rate and pressure of our Town Expenses— for schools, and all other purposes. I confess I have had some reluctance to add to them the expense of a high school."[33] But Boyden's fundamental assumption regarding education was that "the prosperity of the country— and the permanence of our civil, political and religious Institutions . . . depend on the intelligence and virtue of the people." To insure these conditions the founders of New England, Boyden explained, had established free common schools open to all and a college generously aided by public funds. But, he continued, "There was still a course of education wanted, intermediate between the common school and the college." The "academies . . . private schools and private tuition" hardly met this need and, moreover, served the rich rather than the "middling and poorer classes." The lack of higher educational opportunities for the poorer class was a serious situation: "The State had an interest in the education of the best talent of the community. And this talent was as often found among the middling and lower classes as among the rich—perhaps oftener. For the rich are apt to become luxurious, indolent and lazy. They have not the stimulus of necessity—which is not only the mother of invention—but of diligence—of great effort and progress." Because academies and private schools proved "unacceptable to the people at large, by reasons of distance and expense . . . our Legislature established the high school system." The purpose of the high school system, he emphasized, was to make available "preparation for college and the higher branches of learning . . . to distinguished industry and talent, in whatever condition and circumstances it might be found."

Boyden made it clear that his vote for the high school, should he so cast it, would not be on his "own account" because he could afford to educate his own children. Nor would he vote for one "to supply the rich. They can supply themselves with the means of education." His vote, rather, would be, first, for those individuals "who have not the means of a higher education within themselves." His motivation for providing that means was his conception of "the public good"; "for the interest of the State . . . the best talent of the community should be educated, wherever it may be found." Ironically, the very people for whose good Boyden eventually supported a high school had not the enlightened self-interest to accept his graciousness.

But who would a high school educate? Would all attend? Boyden neither advocated nor believed in a democracy of intellect, and his social convictions become even clearer from his remarks on the distribution of ability. Some had not the "capacity" to learn the "higher branches"; others would have no opportunity; many would not want to; and a number would not find the higher learning in "their interest." To imagine that all could learn the higher branches was, in fact, a dangerous illusion: besides being untrue, it threatened to alter a delicate social balance, which required hewers of wood and drawers of water. Society needed learned men, "preachers, teachers and authors," but it also required "food, shelter and clothing." And food, shelter, and clothing were "not the higher branches of learning." Neither was higher learning "merchandise" which could be bought and sold. In fact, those who had not the need for higher learning had better avoid it: "As a little learning is a dangerous thing—'drink deep or taste not the Pierian Spring.' " Only common school education was "fundamental . . . for practical life and it should be made as universal and practical as possible." Indeed, "knowledge of the common branches is about as much as the mass of scholars can acquire during the period of their childhood and youth."

In proper doses education was a fine tonic. Too little and prosperity faltered while deserving talent went unrewarded. Too much and the intricate social organism no longer functioned properly. Dr. Boyden, essentially, prescribed a meritocracy which would absorb and assimilate the bright, ambitious, hard-working boy, as he himself had been. But he had no desire to alter the hierarchy which made a social ladder necessary, and with more than a little of the smugness of the man who had made it the hard way, he wanted the ladder itself neither easy to climb nor wide.

As in Beverly, school promoters throughout Massachusetts were people intimately connected with the economic transformation of the state. On the state level James Carter, the first great advocate of school reform, based an argument for extended education on the fact that Massachusetts had to industrialize in order to survive. Horace Mann helped push through the Massachusetts legislature bills supporting and assisting railroad construction. George Boutwell was a merchant. In Lawrence, Henry K. Oliver, the most vocal school promoter and a leading candidate for appointment as the third secretary of the Board of Education, was agent for one of the largest cotton mills in the state. This was the former occupation of Joseph White, fourth secretary of the Board of Education. School committeemen had to represent the most educated citizens; for they had to be able to examine intelligently teachers, inspect schools, and write reports. Often the ministry played an active role, but in most towns lay participation was important and critical. For many years one of the most active educational reformers in Beverly was William Thorndike, a rich merchant. And so it was throughout the commonwealth. The supporters of education wrote the legislation, invested the money, and ran the enterprises that brought about the economic and social transformation of Massachusetts.

To note the business connections of education promoters is to highlight a key feature of the reform process. Educational reform at this time was essentially a *lay* (or amateur) achievement. On the state level the men who did the most to arouse the reform spirit, like Horace Mann, came to education from other fields; on the local level it was influential laymen who, for the most part, supervised and administered educational innovation. As we shall see, these lay reformers were often short-sighted and insensitive; however, despite its shortcomings, their style of educational reform had one great virtue: it represented a degree of participation in public education by lay communal leadership perhaps never again equalled in the history of American society. Whatever our opinion of their motives or their results may be, we must recognize that for about two decades at mid-century the men in communities busiest with their own complicated affairs expended immense amounts of time and effort in their commitment to improve and extend public education.

Wealthy groups had interests other than developing communal resources and promoting limited mobility when they advocated high schools. As changes in the nature of commercial life made a prolonged apprenticeship unnecessary, some merchants wondered what to do with their adolescent boys. On the night of June 9, 1834, a group of men, "chiefly engaged in commerce," gathered to discuss the education of their sons. Among those present was

Nathan Appleton, and the secretary of the meeting was the eminent William Ellery Channing. The merchants agreed that the present system of apprenticeship had become inefficient and wasteful of their sons' time. The men also agreed that "gentlemen, who decline to send their sons to college as being an institution not suited to their preparation for active life, are bound to give them a better education than they now receive." The men had definite educational objectives for their sons, and these objectives suggest a portrait of the ideal New England merchant: astutely making a fortune, conscious of a deep sense of responsibility to society, and desirous of continually improving his mind. To the merchants the ideal school would be anything but a place of leisure since it was to provide an arduous preparation for a life in the counting room. A new type of institution was clearly needed, and the merchants thought they saw one at hand; "the present English high school (a very valuable institution) might be so extended as to give all the advantages which are needed."

Certainly, many school committees, desiring to establish a high school, must have concentrated on convincing those with a stake in the economic progress of their towns. The Dalton school committee, for one, wrote in 1860 that a high school would offer "greater inducements . . . to capitalists from abroad to come and occupy your unoccupied building sites and unimproved water power." Likewise, the Athol committee in 1855 contended that a high school would attract people "who have large scholars to educate . . . thereby increasing the population and business of the place." Aside from attracting capital and population, the committee continued, a high school "would greatly enhance the value of property in town, to a percentage, it is believed, which would of itself more than pay the expenses of the school." The committee concluded that "the town could not make a better pecuniary investment."

If the promoters were correct, then towns which established high schools should have had a far higher per capita valuation than ones which did not. There should have been a significant and positive correlation between valuation and high school establishment. In a large sample of towns studied in both 1840 (before almost any of them had established a high school) and in 1865, those with high schools had a slightly higher per capita valuation than those which did not.* But there was no significant correlation between high school establishment and valuation for either year. Towns which established high schools were, and continued to be, more prosperous than ones which did not. Apparently, in spite of promoters' predictions, the high school had no effect on communal wealth.

*Throughout Part I, I shall refer to the statistical study of the state. This study employed a variety of statistical techniques and was performed by computer. In the body of this study I present only the relevant conclusions of the statistical analysis. Interested readers will find a full discussion of method as well as tables in Appendix B. [of *The Irony of Early School Reform*].

From the analysis of the vote in Beverly we would predict that the more wealthy members of the community, as well as middle-class parents particularly concerned about their children's mobility, would not only support the high school but would also send the most students to it. This prediction is strengthened by the general tenor of the pro-high school arguments so far. The high school was billed as the harbinger of communal wealth, individual prosperity, continued industrialization, and social mobility. From the reaction of the Beverly working class we would expect but few of their children in the high schools. We should expect that high school students would comprise a minority of the eligible children in the town. We should expect, further, that the proportion of eligible children attending was inversely related to the size and rate of growth of the town: it was mainly immigrants and other laborers arriving to man new mills and factories who swelled the population of towns; thus, as towns grew, the working-class elements, who we are supposing did not use the high schools very much, would become disproportionately larger.

This expectation may seem contrary to current sociological theory, which stresses that an increase in the size of the middle class, or in the number of non-manual workers, often accompanies population growth. Current theory, however, is based on contemporary conditions. In the nineteenth century the structure of communities may well have been quite different. Although urbanization probably brought an increase in the number of white-collar jobs, the technological state of industry undoubtedly required a much lower proportion of white-collar to manual workers than in the twentieth century. (The whole topic of the historical relationship between urban population growth and social structure is one that requires much investigation.) As figures cited by Lipset and Bendix clearly imply, the transition from a rural, farming community to a non-farming community, the particular type of shift with which we are here concerned, is usually accompanied by a large increase in the proportion of manual workers. Moreover, in the nineteenth century it was immigrants who swelled the population, and such people usually congregated in the lowest status occupations.

From a random sample of 10 percent of towns and cities that had high schools in 1860 both predictions are definitely confirmed: In the sample as a whole under 20 percent of the estimated eligible children went to high school. In the smallest and most static towns (1,000-3,000), about 28 percent of the eligible attended. In the medium-size ones (6,000-8,000), about 15 percent, and in the large, expanding cities (over 14,000), approximately 8 percent.

The analysis of high school enrollment in individual communities supports the general finding that high schools were minority institutions probably attended mainly by middle-class children. One hundred and eighty-one students entered Somerville High School between 1856 and 1861; information about the parents of 135 of these has been gathered. These 135 children represent 111 families. In these 111 families, 44 fathers were owners of businesses (stores or manufacturing concerns), self-employed as merchants or brokers, or masters employing artisans. An additional 8 fathers were employed in businesses, mostly as clerks. Five were professionals and 6 public employees; 1 was a master mariner and 1 a shipwright. If we lump these people together as "upper middle class" they comprise 57 percent of the fathers of high school children. If we consider as slightly lower on the occupational scale, but still middle class, artisans and farmers, there were 26 fathers in the former and 9 in the latter category. There was 1 father who was a farm laborer and for 10 parents no occupation was listed. (Some of the latter were obviously widows.) No child of a factory operative or of an ordinary laborer entered Somerville High School in these years. Although there were over 1,500 Irish immigrants in Somerville, none of their children entered, and only 3 of the fathers were foreign born: 1 each in England, Nova Scotia, and Bavaria. Only 25 of the 111 families had children who graduated, but there was little difference in their social background. How typical was Somerville? An analysis of the graduates of Chelsea High School between 1858 and 1864 produces similar conclusions. In our "upper middle class" category were 29 out of the 43 parents. Eleven were artisans, 3 had no occupation listed. Again, no operatives, no laborers, no Irish sent children to the high school. In both Chelsea and Somerville it is reasonable to estimate that the lowest occupational categories included at least 40 to 50 percent of the population. The high school was indeed a strictly middle-class institution.

So far there is a certain consistency between ideology and action on the part of high school supporters. These well-to-do individuals and these more middle-class supporters argued that high schools were desirable because they would foster communal and individual prosperity and promote social mobility. They assumed that industrialization was good and that it should be fostered; they felt high schools would serve this purpose, and they sent their children to the institutions that they established. However, high school supporters were often complex individuals, and another aspect of their reaction to social development is less consistent than the one already discussed. Educational promoters were ambivalent about the very industrial society that the high schools they supported were supposed to help develop. They felt that industrial and urban life produced the most frightening kinds of social and moral decay. Horace Mann, for one, maintained that a "cardinal object" of the state was the "physical well-being of all the people,—the sufficiency, comfort, competence, of every individual in regard to food, raiment, and shelter." But the "industrial condition . . . and business operations" of Massachusetts were producing "fatal extremes of overgrown wealth and desperate poverty." Class divisions, moreover, were being intensified by the growth of cities, for "density of population has always been one of the proximate causes of social inequality." There was a danger, he warned, that America would follow the course of England, where agricultural feudalism had receded before a new industrial serfdom accompanied by novel forms of degradation and vice. Mann complained to J. A. Shaw of "the new exposure to error, with new temptations to dishonesty, which grow out of a more dense population." The problem became acute because of the shift from a farm to an industrial society: "If the spontaneous productions of the earth were sufficient for all," Mann claimed, "men might be honest in practice, without any principle of rectitude because of the absence of temptation." But the growth of cities and the introduction of machinery were the serpent in Mann's Eden: "as population increases, and especially as artificial wants multiply, the temptations increase, and the guards and securities must increase also, or society will deteriorate." Of all the "guards and securities," none, it will become clearer presently, was of more worth to Mann and his contemporaries than education.

Another problem posed by the growth of cities and factories was the hostility of manual laborers to the cultivation of refined manners and taste as well as to benevolence and kindness. To Mann poverty bred barbarity. In cities, "poverty casts its victims into heaps, and stows them away in cellars and garrets"; and in cellars and garrets family life and morality degenerated into a mere mockery of their proper form. For Mann the results of urbanization were poverty, crime, and vice. Civilization itself was threatened by the rapid and uncontrollable growth of cities, and there was a consequently urgent duty to save "a considerable portion of the rising generation from falling back into the conditions of half-barbarous or of savage life."

The second and third secretaries of the Board of Education, Barnas Sears and George Boutwell, also feared for the destruction of individual morality, the family, and society. To Sears immigrants and cosmopolitanism were particularly pernicious. Cities, he claimed, "furnish peculiar facilities for the diffusion of corrupt principles and morals." Migrants to the cities found "in their new places of abode, pleasures set before them appealing to every sense, and in gradations adapted to every intellect." So strong was the "current of sensuality," warned a shocked and fearful Sears, "that it too often sweeps almost everything before it . . . This life of congregated human beings, where money, leisure, shows, and a succession of excitements are the objects of pursuit, is now, with inconceivable power, educating myriads of children."

Boutwell emphasized the collapse of the family. In one report he listed the "facts to be considered when we estimate the power of the public school to resist evil and to promote good"; these were "the activity of business, by which fathers have been diverted from the custody and training of their children; the claims of fashion and society which have led to some neglect of family government on the part of mothers; the aggregation of large populations in cities and towns, always unfavorable to the physical and moral welfare of children; the comparative neglect of agriculture and the consequent loss of moral strength in the people." Elsewhere he was equally direct. "As in some languages there is no word which expresses the true idea of home," he proclaimed, "so in our manufacturing towns there are many persons who know nothing of the reality." Among this group were "multitudes of children and youth." In agricultural areas "such cases are rare: and I cannot doubt that much of the moral and intellectual health enjoyed by the agricultural population is due to this circumstance." And this was the man who, practically simultaneously, delivered rapturous descriptions of the artist-laborer made possible by the machine.

To Massachusetts schoolmen the young, unknowingly, were caught in a Faustian dilemma, and Mephistopheles lurked in the cities. The reports of Sears were particularly gloomy. With all of society conspiring against them, what could the schools do? The question Sears and indeed everyone else refused to ask was: If the public schools aided and sustained the growth of urban-industrial civilization, and if, in turn, they were powerless to check its pernicious effects, then was not the extension of public education really the pursuit of social self-destruction?

Faced with the decline of the family and the disintegration of society, Massachusetts schoolmen proclaimed that the state must assert itself and emphasize its character as a parent who should guard its family of children. Mann stressed the natural right of the child to education and the duty of society, acting as a trustee and the final arbiter of property, to assure the fulfillment of the child's rights. The infant, he said, needed "sustenance, and shelter, and care." If its "natural parents" were removed, or "parental ability" failed, it was the clear duty of "society at large . . . the government . . . to step in and fill the parent's place." Massachusetts, to Mann, was a particularly good state since it was "parental . . . in government." To Sears, too, the state was kindly, a "nourishing mother, as wise as she is beneficient." But the softness of the mother turned into the sternness of the patriarch as problems increased. In the writings of Boutwell and the fourth secretary, Joseph White, the state through its school system became an engine for instilling social discipline. To Boutwell the school "inculcates habits of regularity, punctuality, constancy and industry in the pursuits of business; through literature and the sciences in their elements, and, under some circumstances, by an advanced course of study, it leads the pupil towards the fountain of life and wisdom; and by moral and religious instruction daily given, some preparation is made for the duties and temptations of the world." The school became the means of instilling in the population the qualities necessary for success in industrial society. Boutwell's successor, White, also stressed the formative qualities of education. "How great and good a thing," White wrote, "is the legislation which wisely seeks to train the intellect and form the character of a people." The state, through the schools, should transform the tyranny of the majority into an organized and effective mechanism for social discipline.*

*With Joseph White the tradition of eminent secretaries of the Board ended. White, unlike his predecessors, came from a well-to-do family of merchants in Worcester County. He attended Williams College and started to prepare for a legal career. Deciding against the law as a career, he instead took a position in Lowell as an agent for one of the largest cotton mills in the state. An ardent Presbyterian and a devoted Whig, White entered politics as a state sentator. His term as secretary to the Board lasted seventeen years, and after his retirement he evidently devoted himself to the local affairs of the Berkshires, to the business of his church and of Williams College, and to the promotion of local historiography. One memorialist claimed that his term at the Board represented "much the most successful work of his life."

Local high school promoters shared the secretaries' analysis of the disastrous course of society and argued that the high school would solve at least three outstanding community problems. In the first place, the high school in theory catered to the poor as well as the rich and was a vital antidote to the stratification, strife, and social disintegration that educators thought they saw around them. The Winchendon school committee claimed that the influence of the high school "in binding the population together, and promoting good feeling and harmony, must be obvious to everyone." To many Massachusetts educators an ideal society, one which represented the aims of the founding fathers, was free of rigid stratification, harmonious and without acrimony. To achieve this harmony, to recreate the alleged social unity of pre-industrial civilization, high schools were a necessity. Joseph White wrote of high schools:

The children of the rich and the poor, of the honored and the unknown, meet together on common ground. Their pursuits, their aims and aspirations are one. No distinctions find place, but such as talent and industry and good conduct create. In the competitions, the defeats, and the successes of the schoolroom, they meet each other as they are to meet in the broader fields of life before them; they are taught to distinguish between the essential and true, and the fractious and false, in character and condition . . . Thus a vast and mutual benefit is the result. Thus, and only thus, can the rising generation be best prepared for the duties and responsibilities of citizenship in a free commonwealth. No foundation will be laid in our social life for the brazen walls of caste; and our political life, which is but the outgrowth of the social, will pulsate in harmony with it, and so be kept true to the grand ideals of the fathers and founders of the republic.

When we understand the longing for unity of high school promoters and their essential ambivalence to the society they were helping to create, then we can appreciate better the attitude of Robert Rantoul and high school promoters in Beverly. Both Rantoul and Boyden stressed the desirability of a more organic, closely knit social order. Surely, they must have been aware that throughout the state people were arguing that a high school would promote this goal. The high school would provide a counter-balance to the same divisive economic forces that it was to help unleash. Thus, support for a high school was a complex reaction related in part to an essentially ambivalent perception of society. The high school was an ideal innovation because it would allegedly serve the frequently conflicting values and interests of educational reformers.

The high school was supposed to solve still other community problems. Promoters claimed that the school would serve as an agent of community civilization. The tone of the community would be raised; cultural as well as social unity would prevail and upwardly mobile youths could be socially as well as intellectually prepared for their new status. For example, the Lincoln school committee stressed that the effect of a well conducted high school was "to elevate the sentiments, the taste, the manners of the pupils." In the high school there would be "no room for the awkwardness, vulgarity and rudeness in behavior and speech, that are too generally tolerated and some times encouraged even, in common district schools." The high school inducted pupils into "a higher civilization and refinement, and does what otherwise might not be done, to prepare them for occupying exalted positions in social life, and for doing much for the welfare of their fellow men." Perhaps best of all, the benefits of the high school extended to the whole community: "the spirit of improvement here imbibed, goes home" with the students, "and the whole family feels its inspiration. The intellectual light that is kept burning here, sends its rays abroad through the community. The refining process here commenced, is carried into the social circle."

Another problem was the attitude of parents, continually lamented by school committees. "The great defect in our day," observed the Barnstable school committee, "is the absence of governing or controlling power on the part of parents, and the consequent insubordination of children." As for the children, "self-will is their law; hence flows conceit, and a monstrous precocity . . . What the parent makes them, the teacher finds them." Concluded the committee, "Our schools are rendered inefficient by the apathy of parents." Parents failed to appreciate the values of education, spoiled their children, and frustrated the efforts of the school. The failure of parents to provide moral discipline and their general lack of interest in the schools was a persistent theme in every school report consulted. To school committees the problem was extremely serious because parental apathy and hostility were not only thwarting educational advance but promoting those very social tendencies that educators were trying to check.

The high schools, Barnas Sears argued in 1854, were a means of overcoming the problem of parental apathy. The establishment of high schools, he wrote, "gives the schools themselves a place in the estimation of the people, which they never held before." Sears continued, "We need not go back many years to find a prejudice against the public schools," but the high schools had dispelled antipathy and apathy to public education. "There are no better schools in the Commonwealth than some of our public high schools, and to these families of the highest character now prefer to send their children." But that parents of the "highest character," meaning probably the socially and financially prominent, used the high schools is no proof that the antipathy of the working class was overcome. In fact, the undisguised harangues of school committees made one aspect of educational reform particularly clear. The committees saw themselves arrayed against the mass of parents, whom they considered uncomprehending and indifferent. School committees were unashamedly trying to impose educational reform and innovation on this reluctant citizenry. The communal leaders were not answering the demands of a clamorous working class: they were imposing the demands; they were telling the majority, your children shall be educated, and as we see fit.

Promoters represented educational reform, especially the high school, as an innovation directly aimed at urbanizing, industrializing communities. The high school was simultaneously to foster mobility, promote economic growth, contribute to communal wealth, and save towns from disintegrating into an immoral and degenerate chaos. If these contentions were heeded, then it should have been in the communities undergoing the most rapid and severe transformation, the most urban and industrial areas, that high schools were established. It should have been in these places that schoolmen were contending most vigorously for innovation, most actively trying to overcome the apathy of the mass. In these areas the concern for education should have been most marked by both innovation and high expenditures on schooling.

An extensive statistical study of the state has demonstrated that these suppositions are, for the most part, valid. The establishment of high schools was related to all the dominant patterns of urbanism and industrialism; and it was in the more urban and industrial areas that greater numbers of children over fifteen attended school. High school establishment was, however, relatively more associated with urban than with manufacturing characteristics. This is not surprising, for it was more specifically the urban phenomena that were singled out by promoters as susceptible to correction by a high school. The harangues against the new society that have been presented stressed the problems of urban poverty, squalor, and social disorganization. Moreover, high schools were especially associated with large numbers of people employed in commerce. This is an expected conclusion, since it was to solve the problem of an anachronistic apprenticeship for adolescents headed toward a commercial career that the Boston merchants advocated a high school. The association of high school establishment with urban and industrial characteristics does not contradict the finding, already noted, that the lowest percentage of children attended high school in the most urban areas. High school establishment and high school attendance were very different phenomena. It was in the rapidly urbanizing places that communal leaders and middle-class parents most readily saw a need for a high school; it was also these places that had the most children from social groups least attracted by the high school and least able economically to make use of it.

As for measures of school spending, both high per-pupil expenditure and a high school tax rate were usually associated with the establishment of a high school. But this general relation obscures subtle differences. Spending on education was by no means as clearly related to social measures as was high school establishment. Usually, the higher the per-capita valuation of a town, the lower was its tax rate. The converse was true for per-pupil expenditure. These relations are predictable. The more money a town had the smaller the proportion needed to sustain a high per-pupil expenditure. In one situation, however, both measures of school spending were high. This was in wealthy suburban towns. This finding supports the contention that educational concern was primarily a characteristic of the middle and upper social groups, for in these towns, where manufacturing was not extensive, there would be fewer of the kinds of people who stood in the way of the improvement of schools. Similarly, in towns where agriculture became of increasing importance the school tax rate was particularly low. In these areas the townspeople would see but little relation between their own welfare and the furtherance of industrial growth, and they would be affected little by social disorder at their doorstep. Yet somewhat surprisingly, per-pupil expenditure was depressed by the rapid and sharp development of manufacturing. In this situation the lower expense was undoubtedly as much the result of an influx of immigrants with large families and few taxable resources as of parsimony.

To sum up the argument thus far: the vote on the abolition of Beverly High School and other data imply that the people of most wealth and prestige in communities, often joined by those of more middle-level social position, supported educational innovations, especially the establishment of high schools. These people shared an ambivalent perception of the growing urbanism and industrialism that marked the commonwealth. Cities and factories were necessary, good, and should be promoted; cities and factories brought social and familial disintegration and chaos. Related to their ambivalent perception of society were their contentions concerning the virtues of educational reform in general and the high school in particular. The high school would foster urbanism and industrialism by creating communal wealth, by training skilled workmen, by assuming the functions of outmoded apprenticeships, by providing necessary channels for mobility. The high school would curb the evils of urbanism and industrialism by unifying and civilizing the community and the family, by overcoming the hostility and apathy of parents to education. Essentially, the reformers looked to a parental state to sponsor education that would help build modern industrial cities permeated by the values and features of an idealized rural life. The relation between expenditures on education, high school establishment, and the nature of communities reveals the depth of commitment to this ideology, for it was in the more urban and industrial communities, those most in need of educational innovation according to the ideology, that educational change was most apparent. Educational change, however, was not a gentle process: educational promoters, convinced of the value of their wares, harangued and badgered the mass of reluctant citizens; the style of reform was imposition. Already, then, disturbing problems arise: the high school was not usually attended by the working class whom it was allegedly intended to benefit; it was not welcomed by the people for whom it was supposedly established.

DAVID J. ROTHMAN

ANTEBELLUM CONCEPTS OF PRISON REFORM

Prison reform was one of the Jacksonian era's great enthusiasms. Alexis de Tocqueville, author of the penetrating and influential Democracy in America, *had been sent here in 1831 by the French government to prepare a report on the admired American penitentiary system. Influenced by the ideals of the Enlightenment, Americans 150 years ago were convinced that criminals could be regenerated within the walls of prisons organized on correct principles. David Rothman argues that the optimism of the era's prison reformers flowed from their explanation of criminality. Good environmentalists all, they attributed deviancy not to inherited or biologically-grounded deficiencies in the individual criminal, but rather to the circumstances surrounding his or her life, above all during childhood. The elite who predominated in this as in other reform movements blamed crime on society. However, by "society" they meant neither private property nor social inequality, as did contemporary radicals, but the temptations attendant on the fluidity and disorder supposedly upsetting American life at the time. In Rothman's arguable but interesting interpretation, the reformers were less interested in discovering the actual causes of criminal behavior than they were in "proving" their own preconceptions, thus justifying the particular ameliorative measures they were intent on pursuing.*

Americans in the pre-Civil War era intently pondered the origins of deviant behavior. Philanthropists organized themselves into societies to investigate the question, hoping to devise an effective method of punishment. Legislators, no less interested in a theory for crime, prepared to amend the statutes and appropriate the funds for a new system. To judge by the numerous periodical articles, laymen were also concerned with a subject that had a direct and obvious bearing on their daily lives. Traditional answers were no longer satisfactory.

One of the best examples of their effort appeared in the early reports of the inspectors of New York's Auburn penitentiary. These officials, charged with the management of the prison, attempted to understand the causes of deviancy by collecting and appending to their 1829 and 1830 reports to the state legislature biographical sketches of inmates about to be discharged. The purpose of these brief ten- to twenty-line vignettes, the inspectors explained, was to exhibit "facts which must be interesting, as well to the legislator as to the philanthropist and the Christian." Here, in the life stories of several hundred convicts, they could discover the origins of crime. Impatient with theology and disappointed in the law, they turned to the careers of offenders for the information they wanted.

At first glance, these acounts are curiously naïve. Officials obtained the facts, we are told, in interviews with the convicts just before their release, and obviously made no effort to check the accuracy of the statements. When the sketches recount the events that led up to the prisoner's conviction, each convict emerges as the innocent victim of some misunderstanding. He sold goods he did not know were stolen, or passed bills he did not recognize were counterfeit, or took a horse he did not realize belonged to a neighbor. The investigators, however, did not contradict these assertions or declare their own skepticism. They were not trying to prove that the courts of justice always convicted the right man, that the legal system was infallible. Clearly their concern was different. No record survives of how interrogators conducted the interviews or how they phrased their questions, what kinds of suggestions they openly or covertly made to the convicts. But the finished products follow so set a pattern, and officials were so eager to publicize them, that undoubtedly they heard what they wished to hear, learned what they wished to learn. Their interest was not in the process of conviction, they were quite certain that a collection of criminals stood before them. No, they were preoccupied with the convicts' early years, their growing up in the family, their actions in the community. And of the reliability and pertinence of this information they were certain.

In their search for the roots of deviant behavior, investigators concentrated on the convicts' upbringing, devoting the most space to it in almost every one of these biographies. They focused their questions on the criminals' childhood, recording what they wanted legislators and philanthropists to learn. No matter at what age the deviant committed an offense, the cause could be traced back to his childhood. Prisoner number 315, discharged in 1829, had been convicted for forgery at the age of fifty-five. Until then, he had apparently "maintained a respectable standing in the society." Why had a man of property with no previous record been guilty of such an act? His history provided the answer:

No. 315.—A.N., born in Massachusetts; father was killed at Quebec when he was very young; family soon after scattered, and he was bound out to a farmer, with whom he lived till of age; was a wild, rude boy, and early addicted to some bad habits, drinking, swearing, etc.

In the early years, if you looked carefully, were the origins of deviancy.

And look carefully they did. The 1829 and 1830 reports of the Auburn penitentiary contained 173 biographies, and in fully two-thirds of them, the supervisors selected and presented the data to prove that childhood made the man. Almost always a failure of upbringing—specifically, the collapse of family control—caused deviant behavior. In these sketches, one of three circumstances characterized the failure. First, the children duplicated the parents' corrupt behavior. Prisoner 339 was typical: "Brought up . . . under the influence of a bad example; says his father has been in the New York prison." Or case 317: "Father a very intemperate man, and brought him up to it." Second, the family disintegrated because of death or divorce or desertion, turning an undisciplined child loose on the community. Inevitably, the results were disastrous. H. L., "born in Vermont; after his father's death, when he was a mere boy, worked out for a living and had his own way." And M. R. R.: "His father went off before his remembrance, and never returned . . . his mother married again . . . to a very intemperate bad man, who drove his stepchildren off, and told them he would kill them if they ever came home again." And J. L.: "Parents separated when he was seven on account of his father's going after other women; was then bound out to a farmer . . . ran away from him." Third, the child, through no obvious fault of the parents, left home. M. H., a girl born in Massachusetts, "ran away from her parents at thirteen years of age, and went into Rensselaer county . . . where she . . . soon became a common prostitute."

Investigators had no need to question the truth of these facts. The very presence of the convict at the interview made them self-confirming. They did not doubt that the common whore had run off from her fmaily, that the father of a thief was a drunkard, that a counterfeiter had been on his own from an early age. The moral was clear to them and could not be lost on their readers: deviancy began with the family.

Officials had no difficulty in tracing criminal behavior directly to circumstances of family life. They were certain that children lacking discipline quickly fell victim to the influence of vice at loose in the community. Inadequately prepared to withstand the temptations, they descended into crime. To document this idea, investigators inquired into and reported upon convicts' drinking habits, and those of their companions, and tried to discover other corruptions to which they had succumbed. Once again, they assembled the right facts for the story. In these sketches, the vices permeating the society made the family's failure decisive.

The undisciplined youth typically began to frequent taverns, soon became intemperate, and then turned to crime to support his vice. J. A., a French Canadian, "lost his parents when young, and was thrown friendless upon the world; had troubles which led him to excessive drinking. . . . Convicted of grand larceny." J. T., who had the misfortune to serve an apprenticeship under a drunken master, also "fell into the habit of drinking too much himself; it was in a grocery where he had been drinking too freely, that he committed the crime [theft] that brought him to prison." The temptation of liquor was so great that occasionally those properly raised succumbed to it in time of crisis. J. M. "was a steady young man and continued so till after his wife died . . . when he broke up housekeeping and went about from place to place; soon got to drinking too freely, became very intemperate, and at length took to stealing." R. R., "a steady industrious and moral young man . . . has been worth $3000; on account of domestic trouble took to drinking, and followed it up till he came to prison." If the best of sorts might yield to vice, those without rigorous moral training were certain victims.

Persons outside family government often began to wander, falling in with bad company and acquiring the worst habits. Some first became intemperate and then committed crimes, others went directly to theft and burglary. Predictably, M. S., having run away from his apprenticeship at age fourteen, then roamed "about the country, with no other business than stealing." In another common variation, those lacking family counsel took up an occupation that was almost certain to lead to vice and crime. Enlistment in the army was one such step. The authors of these sketches were convinced that military service was a "school for vice." T. L. ,in their estimation, had proved himself an "apt scholar": while serving with the British forces in Canada, he "gave himself up to drinking, stealing, etc. and was ripe for crime when he came into this state." The American situation was no different: J. L., born in Albany, New York, enlisted after running away from a local farmer. "Had previously been a sober, industrious boy but in the army became very intemperate and vicious; after his discharge, strolled about the country, drinking more and more till he came to prison." Soldiers suffered from too little supervision once they left the barracks. The trouble with the military was that it was not military enough.

The sailor's life also offered an education in immorality. At sea, J. H. "became excessively intemperate, and addicted to all sorts of vice; had no sense of moral obligation; lived without God in the world. When he quit the seas, came into this state . . . through intemperance was led to the commission of a crime." Officials believed it axiomatic that anyone who "has been in almost every seaport in the world," would be "addicted to every bad habit in the world." Some civilian occupations were equally dangerous—

for example, digging New York's new canal. J. P., typical of those leaving home without parental consent, "came to work on the [Erie] canal; fell into vicious company, and consequently vicious habits; became intemperate." Soon the courts convicted him for passing counterfeit money. G. J. "had previously been sober and industrious." But on the canal, "he soon got into many bad habits, drinking, gambling, stealing, etc.," till he arrived at the Auburn penitentiary.

These carefully designed, really contrived biographies, undoubtedly strike the modern reader as crude and simplistic versions of later, more sophisticated analyses. Yet when looked at from the vantage point of the eighteenth century, they are in many ways important and different. For one thing, they are highly secular documents. Officials were interested in crime, not sin, and had no inclination to view legal offenses as Lucifer's handiwork or the retributive judgment of an angry God. The accounting system of the colonial period—where crime rates reflected both the community's religiosity and divine judgment on it—was outdated. Officials, in fact, gave surprisingly little attention to the convicts' religious history. Occasionally they noted if someone was raised without family prayer or had never regularly attended church. But even then religious training was an indicator of the quality of his upbringing, and without intrinsic importance. It revealed in one more way how the family had failed to educate and discipline the child.

Nor did these vignettes show the Revolutionary War generation's concern for legal reform. Officials now looked to the life of the criminal, not to the statutes, in attempting to grasp the origins of deviancy. They presented biographical sketches, not analyses of existing codes. They did not bother to gather information about or report upon convicts' previous encounters with the law, what kinds of punishments they had received, or their feelings about them. Such questions were for the 1790's, not the 1820's and '30's.

In a still more crucial way the concept of deviant behavior implicit in these sketches signaled a new departure. Although the colonists had blamed inadequate parental and religious training for crime, they were preoccupied with the sinner himself. Convinced that the corrupt nature of man was ultimately at fault, they did not extensively analyze the role of the criminal's family or the church or the general society. Furthermore, they shared a clear understanding of what the well-ordered community *ought to* look like, and this too stifled any inclination to question or scrutinize existing arrangements. Their religious and social certainty covered the discrepancies between ideas and realities, obviating new approaches and theories. Americans in the Jacksonian period stood in a very different position. They learned that men were born innocent, not depraved, that the sources of corruption were external, not internal, to the human condition. Encouraged by such doctrines to examine their society with acute suspicion, they quickly discovered great cause for apprehension and criticism.

But why did they become so anxious in their concern? Why did they so easily discover corruption? They were, it is true, predisposed to this finding, yet it is puzzling that they located all that they looked for. Communities were not overrun with thieves and drunkards, prostitutes and gamblers; the rate of crime, for example, probably did not increase over these years. Rather, Americans conducted this examination with grandiose expectations. Assuming that deviant behavior was symptomatic of a failing in society, they expected to ferret out corruption and eliminate crime. With the stakes so high, they could ignore no possible malfeasance.

Another consideration expanded their list of social evils. Many Americans in the Jacksonian period judged their society with eighteenth-century criteria in mind. As a result, they defined as corrupting the fluidity and mobility that they saw. Thinking that an orderly society had to be a fixed one, they judged the discrepancies between traditional postulates and present reality as promoting deviant behavior. Not having evolved an alternative to the colonial vision of society, they looked back both with envy and discomfort. They were embarrassed about the cruelty and shortsightedness of earlier punishments, and hoped to be humanitarian innovators. Yet they also believed that their predecessors, fixed in their communities and ranks, had enjoyed social order. But how were they now to maintain cohesion in so fluid and open a society? This ambivalence gave a very odd quality to their thinking. On the one hand, they aimed at the heights, about to eliminate crime and corruption. On the other, they doubted the society's survival, fearing it might succumb to chaos. They confronted, it seemed, unprecedented opportunity, and unprecedented peril.

Holding such a position, American students of deviant behavior moved family and community to the center of their analysis. New York officials accumulated and published biographies because this technique allowed them to demonstrate to legislators and philanthropists the crucial role of social organizations. Accordingly, almost every sketch opened with a vivid description of an inadequate family life and then traced the effects of the corruptions in the community. While many a convict may possibly have come from a broken home or been prone to drink, no one ought to take the inspectors' findings as straight facts. They had a prior commitment to gathering and publicizing this type of information to explain the origins of crime. Interviewers probably induced the convicts to describe, whether accurately or not, their early life in grim terms. Sympathetic questioners, letting the criminal know that they thought that much of the blame for his fate rested with his parents, would soon hear him recount his father's drinking habits and the attraction of the tavern around the corner. These sketches reflected the ideas of the questioner, not some objective truth about the criminal. The doctrine was clear: parents who sent their children into the society without a rigorous training in discipline and obedience would find them someday in the prison. The case of W. S. can summarize both the approach and the message: "Lived with his parents who indulged him too much for his good;

was a very wild unsteady boy; fond of company and amusements; when he could not get his parents' consent, would go without it." The result? "Convicted of an attempt to rape . . . and sentenced to three years."

The pessimism and fear underlying this outlook pointed to the difficulty Americans had in fitting their perception of nineteenth-century society as mobile and fluid into an eighteenth-century definition of a well-ordered community. Their first reaction was not to disregard the inherited concept but to condemn present conditions. Hence, in these biographies a dismal picture emerged of a society filled with a myriad of temptations. It was almost as if the town, in a nightmarish image, was made up of a number of households, frail and huddled together, facing the sturdy and wide doors of the tavern, the gaudy opening into a house of prostitution or theater filled with dissipated customers; all the while, thieves and drunkards milled the streets, introducing the unwary youngster to vice and corruption. Every family was under siege, surrounded by enemies ready to take advantage of any misstep. The honest citizen was like a vigilant soldier, well trained to guard against temptation. Should he relax for a moment, the results would be disastrous. Once, observers believed, neighbors had disciplined neighbors. Now it seemed that rowdies corrupted rowdies.

Yet for all the desperation in this image, Americans shared an incredible optimism. Since deviant behavior was a product of the environment, the predictable result of readily observable situations, it was not inevitable. Crime was not inherent in the nature of man, as Calvinists had asserted; no theological devils insisted on its perpetuation. Implicit in this outlook was an impulse to reform. If one could alter the conditions breeding crime, then one could reduce it to manageable proportions and bring a new security to society.

One tactic was to advise and warn the family to fulfill its tasks well. By giving advice and demonstrating the awful consequences of an absence of discipline, critics would inspire the family to a better performance. (The biographical sketches, then, were not only investigations but correctives to the problem.) One might also organize societies to shut taverns and houses of prostitution, an effort that was frequently made in the Jacksonian period. But such measures, while important, were slow-working, and by themselves seemed insufficient to meet the pressing needs of this generation. Another alternative then became not only feasible but essential: to construct a special setting for the deviant. Remove him from the family and community and place him in an artificially created and therefore corruption-free environment. Here he could learn all the vital lessons that others had ignored, while protected from the temptations of vice. A model and small-scale society could solve the immediate problem and point the way to broader reforms.

Almost everyone who wrote about deviancy during the Jacksonian era echoed the findings of Auburn's inspectors and many emulated their methodology. Officials at other prisons conducted similar surveys among convicts, validating the general conclusions reached in New York. Interested laymen, organized into such benevolent societies as the New York Prison Association and the Boston Prison Discipline Society, made their own investigations and then helped to publicize the same ideas among a still broader portion of the population. Well-known reformers, like Dorothea Dix, Francis Lieber, and Samuel Gridley Howe, concerned with a spectrum of causes, paid great attention to the problem of crime and its correction and further popularized the concepts. Family disorganization and community corruption, an extreme definition of the powers of vice and an acute sense of the threat of disorder were the standard elements in the discussions. A wide consensus formed on the origins of crime.

Prison officials everywhere informed state legislators of the crucial role of the family and community in causing deviant behavior. "The mass of criminals," explained the inspectors of Pennsylvania's Eastern State Penitentiary, "is composed of persons whose childhood and youth were spent in the uncontrolled exercise of vicious instincts." The warden of the Ohio penitentiary listed the breakdown of the household among the leading causes of crime. "Unhappy orphanage," he lamented, "leaves the susceptible youth without those restraints and safeguards which conduct to a life of probity." To buttress this argument one official calculated that of the 235 men committed to the prison in one year, 86 were under twenty-five years of age, a sure sign that the failure of the family was at the root of the problem. Another appropriately conducted interviews and compiled case histories. His most important finding, he believed, was that 221 convicts from a sample of 350 had been "thrown out from under parental influence and restraint," before reaching the age of twenty-one; in fact, 89 of them were without guardians by the time they were twelve. They had "never learned to submit to proper authority," or to understand that "their own safety and happiness are secured by such obedience."

All observers agreed that the forces at work in the community aggravated the family's errors. The future convict, concluded the Pennsylvania group, "social to a fault," took his cues from his surroundings; predictably, "the vices of social life have heralded the ruin of his fortunes and his hopes." Ohio's officials shared this view: "Without the refining and elevating influences of the home, without parental restraint and example, they were thrown upon a cold and selfish world, and often wronged. . . . They have done as might have been expected."

An identical interpretation appeared in the opening pages of the first annual report (1844) of the New York Prison Association. According to one of its founders, the Unitarian minister William H. Channing, the association was formed to aid persons awaiting trial, to help reform convicts, and to assist released prisoners. This commitment, he explained, was not only testimony to a Christian desire to have good triumph over evil and to avoid "the vindictive spirit," but also reflected the community's ultimate responsibility, because of its "neglect and bad usages," for "the sins of its children." The first part of this formulation needed little clarification, but the second did, and so he elaborated on the role of the family and community in the origins of crime.

"The first and most obvious cause," began Channing, "is an evil organization derived from evil parents. Bad germs bear bad fruit." Although his language suggested that a biological process was at work, he did not consider heredity anything more than a predisposing force that could be "cleansed away by a healthful moral influence." A properly organized social system would "purify away what is bad," and shield its members "from the temptations beneath which they are peculiarly liable to fall." The existence of crime pointed to the community's inability to fulfill its task, not the influence of heredity. Channing went on to link the failure of family training directly to deviant behavior. Of the 156 inmates recently admitted to Pennsylvania's Eastern State Penitentiary, he reported, fourteen had been orphaned by age twelve, thirty-six were missing one parent or another soon thereafter, 143 had received no religious instruction, and 144 never attended Sabbath school. "Such statistics," affirmed the minister, "tell at a glance that early neglect was certainly, in part, probably in great part, the cause of after crime."

Channing too believed that the corruptions pervading the community made early parental neglect so injurious; in fact, he was surprised that the power of vice did not debilitate still more people. "We seldom appreciate," he declared, "how easily, if left alone, unsustained by worthy example . . . we might become lawless and perverse. . . . Slight deviations, uncorrected, hurry the transgressor into a rapid downward course. . . . Tempters ensnare the inexperienced. . . . The spirit of mere adventure entangles the careless into a web of vile associations, from which there is no after escape. . . . How many a young man . . . took, almost without a thought, the first step in that path which ended in the gambler's hell, the plausible deceits of the forger and counterfeiter." Well-baited traps were so pervasive that the slightest miscalculation brought terrible consequences. "The sight of evil, as by contagion, awakens the desire to commit evil." Yet, for all his anxiety about society, Channing, like other Americans in the Jacksonian period, did not succumb to despair. "The study of the *causes* of the crime," he concluded, "may lead us to its *cure.*" His environmental theory encouraged rather than stifled action.

Succeeding reports of the New York Prison Association repeated these themes. Continuously stressing the critical role of the family, they reminded parents of the "importance of exercising careful superivsion and wholesome discipline." Otherwise, the contagion of vice would be irresistible. Intemperance was "the giant whose mighty arm prostrates the greatest numbers, involving them in sin and shame and crime and ruin." And behind it, "never let it be forgotten, lies the want of early parental restraint and instruction." Readers even learned that "the loss of the father more frequently than that of the mother leads to criminal conduct on the part of the children"; for "mothers, as a general thing, are less able than fathers to restrain their sons."

The catalogue of seductions that led hapless youngsters to the penitentiary did not become thinner with time. The 1855 association report devoted a lengthy appendix to the sources of crime, first paying due regard to the position of the family as the "bulwark against temptation," and then spelling out the social evils rampant in the community. There was the tavern and the brothel house—appropriately joined with a quote from Hosea, "whoredom and wine . . . taketh away the heart"; the theaters and the gambling houses were menaces, and so were the men who sold licentious books and pictures at the railroad station and boat landings. Still, no matter how lengthy the list, the organization assured its followers that "energetic and enlightened action of the people in . . . social and individual capacities" would effectively combat crime.

A rival and perhaps more famous association, the Boston Prison Discipline Society, differed on many substantive issues with its New York counterpart, but both agreed on the sources of deviant behavior. Founded in 1825 by Louis Dwight, a onetime agent of the American Bible Society, the Boston group set down a very familiar creed. "This society," announced one of its early reports, "shows the importance of family government. . . . It is the confession of many convicts at Auburn [New York] and Wethersfield [Connecticut] that the course of vice, which brought them to the prison, commenced in disobedience to their parents, or in their parents' neglect." No one was probably surprised to learn that "youth, when unrestrained and neglected by their parents, find their way to the tavern and the grog shop." This was the meaning of member Samuel Gridley Howe's pronouncement: "Thousands of convicts are made so in consequence of a faulty organization of society. . . . They are thrown upon society as a sacred charge; and that society is false to its trust, if it neglects any means for their reformation." Those to blame for this state of affairs had the duty, and seemingly the power to effect reform.

Two of the most important figures in the New York and Boston organizations, Channing and Dwight, had first followed religious careers—the former was actually a minister, the latter had studied for it and then worked for the Bible Society. But one must define very carefully the religious influence in reform societies. The changes in Protestant thinking from the eighteenth to the nineteenth century had certainly increased the clergy's concern and attention to social reform, and because of their insistence that men were to do good by improving the common weal, many Americans participated in benevolent activities. Nevertheless, the prescriptions of what was right action, the definition of the policy that men of goodwill were to enact, revealed more of a secular than a religious foundation. Channing and Dwight echoed prevailing social anxieties; they did not make a uniquely religious perspective relevant. Their vision of the well-ordered society did not indicate the influence of their special training. In this sense, they, unlike their predecessors, followed the pack rather than heading it.

Noted reformers and pamphleteers in pre-Civil War America were keenly interested in the predicament of the criminal. Francis Lieber was distressed by the treatment of offenders as well as of slaves. "The history of by far the greatest majority of criminals," insisted Lieber, "shows the afflicting fact, that they were led to crime by the bad example of their parents." From this first cause flowed a sequence of events, "a gradual progress in vice, for which society often offers but too many temptations." No effort to assist the deviant should be spared, he argued, for "society takes upon itself an awful responsibility, by exposing a criminal to such moral contagion, that, according to the necessary course of things, he cannot escape its effects."[30] A more celebrated contemporary, Dorothea Dix, wrote about the convict as well as the insane, publishing an important pamphlet, *Remarks on Prisons and Prison Discipline in the United States.* "It is to the defects of our social organization," declared Dix, "to the multiplied and multiplying temptations to crime that we chiefly owe the increase of evil doers." And like Lieber, she too announced that the community had the responsibility and the resources to confront and eliminate the problem.

The Jacksonians' conception of the causes of crime had an obvious and precise relevance for understanding juvenile delinquency. The child offender, no less than the adult one, was a casualty of his upbringing. The importance of family discipline in a community pervaded with vice characterized practically every statement of philanthropists and reformers on delinquency. Both mature and immature offenders were victims of similar conditions. Not that Americans, insensitive to an idea of childhood, unthinkingly made children into adults. Quite the reverse. They stripped the years away from adults, and turned everyone into a child.

The custodians of juvenile delinquents asked the same questions and drew the same conclusions as wardens in state prisons. No sooner did New York, for reasons we shall soon explore, establish a house of refuge in 1824 to incarcerate minors guilty of criminal offenses, than its managers collected and published case histories. Their inquiries, following a set form, indicated a common perspective on deviant behavior. How long had the youngster been under family government? How often, and how long, had he served as an apprentice? What was the moral character of his parents and his masters? Did the delinquent drink? Or have other vices? What about his companions? What was his first illegal act? His second and his third? The very thoroughness of the examination reflected how much the interrogators valued the information.

Refuge managers located in parental neglect the primary cause of deviant behavior. In typical instances: J. C., at fourteen, ran away from an inattentive and corrupt father. He soon returned, to steal six watches; his father helped to sell the loot. R. W., whose parents were intemperate, roamed the streets, and stayed away from home for weeks on end; he pilfered or begged his daily subsistence until arrested. J. L., another inmate caught stealing, recounted that after his father's death, his mother began drinking, "and then we all went to destruction, mother, brothers, sisters, all." Each case was proof that the child who became "his own boss and went in the way that was right in his own eyes," was a prison convict in the making.

The sketches demonstrated the dire consequences of even minor acts of disobedience. The delinquent moved inexorably from petty to major crimes. W. O. first stole one shilling from his father, then some items of clothing from a stranger, later robbed a watch and some broadcloth from a shop, and finally wrecked, burned, and looted a house. E. M. began his career by pilfering small change from drunkards and graduated to highway robbery. J. R. went from pennies to dollars, and C. B. from fruits and cakes in the kitchen cupboard to cash in store registers. What a careless parent dismissed as a comparatively harmless prank was a crucial event. A few pennies and some sweets, as these biographies revealed, were the first symptoms of a criminal life.

The vices at loose in the community invariably brought the unwary and untrained child to the prison gates. Delinquents' careers demonstrated the debilitating influences of the tavern, where they first began to drink, and the noxious quality of theaters and the houses of prostitution, where they learned other corruptions. Temptations seemed so omnipresent that when dedicating a new building at the New York refuge, the presiding minister reminded his audience that, had their parents been less vigorous or their training less thorough, they too might have become delinquent. "Who of us dare to say," he asked, "that if he had been exposed to the same influences, he would have preserved his integrity and come out of the fiery ordeal unscathed? The sight of such a group of children . . . in yonder gallery should fill us with humility and teach us lessons of mercy!"

Thus, Jacksonians located both the origins of crime and delinquency within the society, with the inadequacies of the family and the unchecked spread of vice through the community. The situation appeared bleak, almost desperate. What elements would now stabilize the community? What kind of social order would keep deviancy within bounds? But if the dangers were immense, so were the possibilities. Convinced that crime was the fault of the environment, not a permanent or inevitable phenomenon, and eager to demonstrate the social blessings of republican political arrangements to the world, Americans set out to protect the safety of the society and to achieve unprecedented success in eradicating deviancy. Their analysis of the origin of crime became a rallying cry to action.

LOIS W. BANNER

RELIGIOUS BENEVOLENCE AS SOCIAL CONTROL: A CRITIQUE OF AN INTERPRETATION

Few topics fascinate historians as much as the motives of historical actors. Few questions are less likely to yield definitive answers. For who can ever know why dead men and women behaved as they did? The impossibility of attaining exact answers has not deflected American social historians from seeking to throw further light on the motives of antebellum reformers. As Lois Banner indicates, many modern historians have explained the leaders of antebellum Protestant benevolence as social conservatives who hoped above all to instill acquiescence in the prevailing social order. Religion in general, the Bible, tract, and Sunday School societies of the "Benevolent Empire" in particular, were thus viewed as means whereby the well-to-do financial supporters of these Protestant enterprises would exercise social control over society. Professor Banner's essay seeks to refute this thesis. Using diverse data drawn from a variety of sources, she argues that religious reformers were concerned primarily with the interests of their denominations, were motivated by religious zeal, and had on their minds things other than the maintenance of a hierarchical social order. No last word is likely to be said on this subject, nor is one stated in this paper. Not its least useful feature is its reminder that motives are likely to be complex. That certain organizations did in fact exercise social control does not mean that those who founded them had nothing else in mind. People rarely anticipate the actual consequence of the things they strive to achieve.

Originally published in the *Journal of American History*, LX (June 1973), 23-41. Reprinted with the permission of the copyright holder, the Organization of American Historians.

Among social historians of the last two decades it has become standard to classify the post-Revolutionary generation of religious humanitarians as conservative and self-serving. Fearful of rising currents of secularism and egalitarianism in the new nation, these churchmen, so many students would have it, mounted a campaign of religious evangelism and created a system of local and national religious and benevolent societies in order to preserve their own declining status and to regain their earlier colonial position as the moral arbiters of American society. Such a conclusion about the nature of religious humanitarianism was first advanced in 1954 by John R. Bodo and Charles C. Cole. Charles I. Foster and Clifford S. Griffin offered in 1960 important variations on the main theme. Each approached the subject from a different perspective. While Bodo and Cole organized their studies around individual representatives from the clergy and focused on sermons as their sources, Foster and Griffin centered on both ministerial and lay members of the interdenominational societies and focused on the societies' reports. Yet all agreed that when these religious humanitarians founded Bible and tract societies, or promoted temperance and Sabbath observance, or tried to aid the urban poor, what they wanted in reality was to gain power over society for their own conservative, if not reactionary, ends. It was the desire for "social control," not social improvement, which lay behind their seemingly benevolent schemes.[1]

Moreover, it has recently been customary to stress the differences rather than the similarities in ideology and motivation between these religious humanitarians and the later antislavery reformers, thereby isolating the former from the historical plaudits now accorded the latter. In the past two decades few figures who would be classified as reformers have escaped the sweeping and often profound criticism of the American reform tradition launched by a generation of historians of the right and left. The abolitionists, however, have been more fortunate. Attacks against them for racism, for fanaticism, for ideological rigidity and methodological naïveté have been powerfully resisted and in large measure turned back.[2] And, as if further to maintain the abolitionists' claim to moral integrity, some historians have found it important to deny their connection with the earlier Protestant humanitarians of the century. For example, building on arguments first advanced by Bodo, Cole, Foster, and Griffin, John L. Thomas has argued that Protestant benevolence before the 1820s was in no sense humanitarian. This earlier generation, according to Thomas, was interested solely in furthering Christianity and morality, not humane improvements. Not until the flowering of liberal theology in Unitarianism and Transcendentalism and of Christian perfectionism under Charles Grandison Finney, Thomas argues, did Protestants become truly humanitarian and reform-minded. From Thomas' perspective, the connection between the abolitionists and their religious predecessors in reform was only indirect. The earlier generation was the last dying gasp of an old order rather than the herald of a new. Their influence was negligible, and their motives were suspect.[3]

Yet however satisfying to the liberal conscience such criticism may be, it
ignores some significant factors about the genesis and goals of religious
humanitarianism. The not-surprising devotion of these men to Protestant
morality, their attachment to the capitalist economy, and their fear of
democracy comprised only one strand in a complex of attitudes toward
politics and society. To abstract this one strand as their "real" motivation
is to fall into the error which plagued the Progressive historians: the belief
that reality is always mean, hidden, and sordid and that men normally act
not out of generosity but from fear and from considerations of status and
gain. Equally important, the historians who advance such a thesis have for
the most part failed to take into account a large literature on the subject
written by sympathic students, beginning with Robert Baird in 1844 and
continuing more recently to Perry Miller and Sidney Mead. These authors
argue that, rather than trying to control the steady growth of egalitarianism
in America, the men of the older order were trying to adjust to it.[4] Above all,
their studies suggest that there are some major weaknesses within the "social
control" argument.

These weaknesses warrant analysis. Foster, Griffin, Bodo, and Cole suggest that the religious humanitarians comprised a group of Calvinist clergymen whose roots lay in New England; who drew their inspiration directly
from Congregationalist Samuel Hopkins' notion of "disinterested benevolence"; whose status in the community was in decline; who were bent on
establishing some sort of theocratic control over society and politics; and
whose most characteristic representative was Lyman Beecher. All these assertions are highly debatable.

First, the idea of benevolence was a general inheritance from a number of
eighteenth-century sources and was not of narrow New England origin.
The Scottish philosopher Francis Hutcheson, the Quakers, and Anglican
reformers like George Whitefield and John Wesley all presented versions of
it.[5] Moreover, the self-assertive New Englanders aroused as much hostility
as imitation among their Protestant coreligionists. In part out of personal
and denominational rivalry and in part because Hopkins substituted universal salvation for Calvinist determinism, even the Presbyterians in the middle
region came to reject Hopkinsianism.[6] That historians have singled out
Hopkins as the originator of religious benevolence has much to do with
Congregational allegiance to their own men and ideas, to the strength and
vitality of the organizations they established, to the popularity of their
American Board of Commissioners for Foreign Missions (ABCFM)—the
first organization of its kind in America—and to the romantic story of its
founding in 1810, through the efforts of six college students who, inspired
by Hopkins' theories, subsequently became the first American foreign missionaries under the auspices of ABCFM.[7] Moreover, there were important
institutional precedents for post-Revolutionary humanitarianism in the
Anglican's Society for the Propagation of the Gospel and in Quaker and
Moravian charitable societies, not to mention the organizations for fraternity

and for social improvement which Benjamin Franklin and others had established throughout the colonies. Institutional needs and goals, as well as ideologies, can powerfully affect motivation and action.[8]

Second, it is also questionable whether the clergy of the early republic considered their authority to be on the decline. Here, too, scholars have appropriated certain well-known Congregational complaints to explain the attitudes and situation of the entire ministerial profession.[9] Those Congregational ministers who nurtured the romantic version of an idyllic, theocratic past may have felt such status anxieties, but none of the other denominations looked back to such a golden era from which to draw inspiration and example. Their way had always been beset by that inattention to spiritual matters which the new and unorganized continent engendered: the revivalism of the so-called "Second Great Awakening" was on one level a well-tested response to a familiar situation of religious indifference. Moreover, most ministers, even among Presbyterians and Congregationalists, came from farming families of moderate means.[10] To these families the ministry represented a significant social advance. Moreover, no other profession offered such extensive scholarship funds and part-time work opportunities to its practitioners in training. In some places and among some groups ministers may have been scorned, but in a shifting social order so were doctors and lawyers. To no less a degree than the latter, clergymen had access to local prominence and community deference.[11]

Third, it was the Presbyterians and not the Congregationalists who dominated the boards of the two major post-Revolutionary interdenominational societies—the American Bible Society and the American Sunday School Union. Presbyterianism, despite what seems an almost common assumption, was not a replica of Congregationalism. Most important, Presbyterianism, except for some areas in New Jersey, was a dissenting church. Unlike Congregationalism, it did not have a tradition of establishment in America. Religious diversity had always characterized the situation in the middle states. Presbyterians had always lived in cooperation and competition with a variety of other churches, and in Virginia, where there was an Anglican establishment, the Presbyterians had vigorously fought for disestablishment.[12] As if to underscore this diversity, the American Bible Society and the American Sunday School Union always tried to preserve an interdenominational character: Methodists, Baptists, Quakers, and Episcopalians were always included on their boards of directors, and representatives of all these churches—at least until the 1830s, when denominationalism began to predominate—participated in the decision-making and activities of these two societies.[13] In contrast, the two major Congregational societies, the American Education Society and the American Board of Commissioners for Foreign Missions, could lay little claim to interdenominationalism.[14] Centered at mid-continent and with a more diverse membership, the "Presbyterian" societies were more truly interdenominational in character.

To institute denominational control over the state was not the goal of mid-state and southern Presbyterians, Baptists, and Methodists. Nor were they intent on gaining some sort of direct control over political affairs. Scholars base too many interpretations upon Beecher's famous 1818 statement that before disestablishment in Connecticut the clergy controlled politics and after disestablishment they seized on the voluntary societies as an indirect means of political control. What is in fact significant about Beecher's claim is its uniqueness.[15] No other clergyman left such witness. Rather, one of the more important themes of clerical thought under the early republic was a distaste for politics, a belief that political life in America was corrupt, that acrimonious political divisions were undermining national unity, and that the clergy had no business in the political arena.[16] Historians like Griffin, who argue that the clergy were politicians with a Machiavellian cunning that would do credit to the most sophisticated party leader, overlook these themes.

Among the dissenting sects and on the frontier, it is true, ministers did run for elective office, and no clergyman would freely relinquish his traditional right of commenting on politics from his pulpit or fail to utilize the petition, that time-honored tool of registering popular attitudes, in favor of religious campaigns like temperance and Sabbath observance. Few, however, were willing to go further. Scholars have vastly overrated the importance of Ezra Stiles Ely's published appeal in 1828 that denominations and groups of Christians issue statements backing political candidates, for it found little open support among the ecclesiastical community.[17] It was not until the 1840s that a reform group was able to overcome the anti-political bias of American Protestantism and to launch a genuine political movement in the Liberty party.

Finally, the "social control" school has erred in identifying the membership of religious benevolence in the antebellum years so closely with the Congregationalists and Presbyterians. To do good works was a universal Christian sentiment, to fear secularism was a common reflex among Protestants after the Revolution.[18] Historians of benevolence who slight this fact do so because they have not paid sufficient attention to the large body of writing on the development of the denominations in America—works which suggest that the structure and dimension of benevolence during the years of the early republic were greatly influenced not only by the political, social, and ideological factors which most social historians have stressed, but also by the institutional needs and growth patterns of the American Protestant denominations themselves. It is axiomatic to social scientists that an important determinant of individual action lies within the norms and standards of the groups with which the individual identifies himself.[19]

In explaining motivation, the institutional dimension cannot be overlooked. Congregationalists, for example, took up benevolence several decades before the Methodists largely because they had earlier reached a more complex stage of institutional development. By the 1800s their churches were formed; their ministers were settled; but their associations and consociations too often lacked vigor or were prevented from taking decisive action because of the Congregational devotion to the autonomy of local churches. New leaders were tired of old habits, were desirous of advancing themselves, and, given the massive defections to the Baptist faith and to liberalism which the Great Awakening of the eighteenth century had produced, were eager to find some new way of assuring the loyalty and sustaining the enthusiasm of a newly "awakened" constituency. Voluntary societies for missions, for distributing Bibles and tracts, and even for broader humanitarian ends suited all these purposes.[20] As for the Quakers and Anglicans in the eighteenth century, organizational innovation plus new and broadened religious objectives became the way to translate piety into action, to bypass indecision and conflict in regular organizations, and to gain new respect and influence in the community at large.[21]

Methodism, however, which had not appeared on the American continent until 1767, in the early 1800s still preserved its unified sectarian zeal. Within its tightly centralized and hierarchical structure, conflicts of opinion had not yet appeared; there was still no discontent with Methodist programs for enlisting and retaining church members through the preaching of itinerant pastors who served a number of churches and who were transferred to a different section of the country each year. In short, the denomination had not yet experienced a sense of failure.[22] Because Methodist ministers kept aloof from secular affairs, did not preach political sermons, and did not hold settled pastorates, they did not make the kind of local connections which might have increased their interest in extra-ecclesiastical matters. Nor was Methodism strong in those urban areas where human suffering was concentrated. Methodist preachers missed the cosmopolitan influences, the wide-ranging contacts, the air of change and experimentation that the city brought to the clergy of other denominations. Like Baptists, Congregationalists, and Presbyterians, they held revivals, but instead of forming missionary and benevolent societies as a result of revivals, they formed churches.[23] When it suited their purposes they utilized the interdenominational societies, but they did not become deeply involved with them.

Moreover, the organization of individual Methodist churches was directed toward individual piety, not social improvement. Individuals met in groups called "classes" and "bands," not to discuss missions or to give Sunday instruction to the young, but to seek for the state of holiness, unique at this point to the Methodist church, called "Christian perfection." The duty of the early Methodist was to perfect himself and to help others attain sanctification, not to engage in benevolence as a means of social improvement. Society would be perfected only when all its individual members were.

By the 1820s, however, as its early sectarian zeal waned, Methodist development began to parallel that of Congregationalism. Its ministers demanded settled pastorates; conflict appeared in the hierarchy; and a group of younger

New York City ministers successfully agitated for the formation of denominational missionary and religious benevolent societies. Subsequently, Methodists began to exhibit a strong interest in temperance and African colonization. Indeed, that temperance and antislavery causes spread so rapidly in
the late 1820s and 1830s when they had previously met with indifference had
much to do with Methodist espousal of them, since by then Methodism was
the largest denomination in the country.[24] In the final analysis, one can
make a strong case that Congregationalists and Methodists took up benevolence because it suited the particular institutional needs of denominations
trying to make the best possible adjustment to the conditions of religious
life in America.[25]

Historians of religious benevolence have not only slighted the denominational dimension of their subject but also have not made clear exactly what
projects were included as part of the broad movement of religious humanitarianism nor to what extent and where secular and religious humanitarianism
intersected in personnel and programs. For the most part, those who advance
the "social control" thesis give the impression that men of religion were
interested in little beyond their missionary, Bible, and tract societies, except
for those few reforms—like temperance, poor relief, and African colonization—through which they could extend their plans to manipulate society for
conservative ends. Except for the Quakers and Unitarians, who have always
had their staunch champions, the prevailing literature often suggests that,
indeed, secular and religious reform associations had little in common except
the accident of proximity in time. Yet it is clear that the various churches'
enthusiasm for voluntarily joining behind social programs, their desire to
institutionalize the revival and gain increased social relevancy, and certain
ideological concerns like millennialism and nationalism may have been
more crucial to the genesis of many more humanitarian movements than
historians have heretofore realized.

Clerical involvement in education is a useful example. Assuredly, one
cannot deny that the inculcation of morality often seemed to take precedence
over goals more strictly educational in the schools that the religious humanitarians established and that eventually, in a number of locales, they chose to
oppose the public schools over the issue of Bible instruction. Yet to stress
these features is too often to overlook the real variety and number of educational innovations they supported. In most cities of the nation, benevolent
leaders established free school systems for the children of the poor, who
previously had received little or no education.[26] They chided legislatures for
not providing sufficient funds for public systems of education.[27] They pres-
sured local governments into establishing special juvenile reformatories
where youthful convicts could learn the rudiments of education, a trade,
and the tenets of Christian morality. They established libraries for young
mechanics and apprentices and in a number of areas were the major force
behind the founding of lyceums, for which they were in constant demand as
speakers.[28] They founded Sunday schools as centers for religion and educa-

tion.[29] And throughout the nation, pastors of all churches conducted elementary schools, often as a way of supplementing inadequate salaries, but also because of clerical concern that Americans be educated at a time when the public authorities had not yet assumed full responsibility for public education.[30] Not the least of their activities on behalf of education was the founding of the majority of American colleges and universities in existence at that time.

Moreover, religious benevolence for many was a transitional activity on the way to humanitarian reform. Local Bible, tract, and particularly missionary projects did not always remain stagnant endeavors. Missionaries to the Cherokee and Choctaw Indians found, for example, that the tribes were often more interested in learning the white man's methods of cultivating crops and organizing his civilization than in listening to Christian preaching or acquiring Bibles.[31] There was also a dynamic interaction between those men and women who distributed Bibles and tracts in the cities and the subjects of their charity. Often these benevolent partisans met with hostility, but until the 1820s, in New York City at least, it was they, and not public officials, who toured the poverty wards and came into contact with the disadvantaged. It was from their reports that the directors of the many private welfare organizations in existence in a city like New York—men who in addition often headed the religious benevolent societies—planned their schemes to establish schools, churches, savings banks, juvenile reformatories, and asylums.[32] Throughout the nation the columns of religious periodicals were consistently filled with news of humanitarian organizations of every variety because their readers were interested in and involved with these organizations.

Furthermore, one suspects that restless Americans, enthused by their ministers' nationalist and millennial rhetoric to expect rapid social improvement in their country free from the vices of Europe, would not long remain satisfied with the obvious inability of Bible and tract distribution to accomplish the revolutionary social effects their promoters claimed for these charities. When it became clear, especially after the excitement over the extensive and highly publicized campaigns to provide every family in the United States with a Bible in the early 1830s died down, that simply putting the Bible into the hands of all Americans was not sufficient to convert them to Christianity and to eliminate poverty and other social ills, many supporters of religious benevolence obviously were attracted toward reforms, like temperance and antislavery, whose potential to effect social change was without question greater. And in the case of the many women who, because of their piety and leisure time, were often the benevolent societies' most faithful workers, employment outside the home in contact with the disadvantaged often made them more cognizant of their own disabilities. They formed the ranks from which the emerging women's rights movement would later draw its members.[33]

Similarly, it is becoming increasingly apparent that a prime consideration in the motivation of many early American reformers was their religious background and training.[34] Thomas Hopkins Gallaudet, for example, founder of the first asylum and school for the training of the deaf in the United States, was an ordained Congregational minister and a graduate of the Andover Seminary, which was renowned as a center for missionary training. Recruited by a number of prominent laymen from his home town of Hartford, Connecticut, Gallaudet spent a year in Europe learning the most advanced techniques in the field and returned to the United States in 1817 to apply what he had learned abroad. Gallaudet would have disavowed the scholarly custom of classifying his efforts as "secular" humanitarianism. He had chosen a career in humanitarianism rather than the ministry because he wanted to be a part of "the great system of good" which looked forward to "the millennium." And that his endeavors were conducted along "Christian principles" was, he judged, crucial to their very nature.[35] Just as so many of his classmates from Andover chose to become missionaries, so Gallaudet defined his work as a mission to a particular group of the disadvantaged at home.

And who more than the missionary personified to American society the self-abnegation and concern for others which reform itself demanded? To a generation raised on romantic tales of the lives of eighteenth-century Indian missionaries like David Brainerd—who died an early death from smallpox and left behind a pietistic and popular diary—and eagerly followed the exploits of youthful missionaries to foreign lands, most of whom died tragically after a few years of service, the missionary life was the acme of heroic self-sacrifice for society's greater good. It was characteristic, for example, that when future antislavery lecturer Marius Robinson was converted to Christian service in Finney's revivals in 1827, he could at first think of no more idealistic pursuit to follow than foreign missionary service.[36] And it was only through the extraordinarily persuasive powers of Theodore Dwight Weld that he and other students at Lane Seminary, to which many of Finney's converts had transferred, were persuaded to substitute antislavery for missionary activity as their life work.[37] The shift in careers, however, was in reality much less sharp than it has often appeared. Many antislavery reformers had previously worked as missionary agents for tract, temperance, and Bible societies, and their antislavery careers of constant traveling, preaching, and converting resembled nothing so much as that of the missionary.[38] They were the itinerants of a new sectarian faith, the radical sons of liberal fathers who had learned about humanitarianism and its methods from the older generation but who, without the institutional attachments of their fathers, could more easily take up new reform and career pursuits.[39]

Finally, in addition to overemphasizing the Puritan origins of religious humanitarianism and underemphasizing its full extent and its denominational setting, some historians have been less than fair in discussing the ideological content of the humanitarians' appeal. Behind all clerical revivals and benevolent endeavor lay several major concerns which historians anxious to expose the failings of their subjects have overlooked. The foremost of these—a theme which religious historians stress and which historians like Bodo, Foster, and Griffin ignore—was millennialism.[40] The second, which parallels an underlying and recently discovered theme of political discourse during the young republic, can be called "Christian republicanism."[41] Both millennialism and republicanism were central to the humanitarians' conception of their role in America, and one cannot completely understand their motivation and their actions without taking these concepts into account.

The belief that Christ was to come to earth, eradicate all social ills, and reign for a thousand years before the final judgment had been a standard Christian belief since the time of Saint Paul and had played a role in Edwardian and Wesleyan doctrines. But the eighteenth-century revolutions, the birth of the American Republic, and the beginnings of a worldwide Protestant missionary movement seemed to give it special urgency in the early nineteenth century. By about 1800 the Protestant community had largely abandoned Edwards' postmillennialism (the belief that human society had already entered the millennial age); but whether Protestants saw its initiation as imminent or in the future, the millennial belief colored all their missionary and benevolent activities.

The doctrine itself had a double-edged effect on them. First, as Alan Heimert has argued with regard to the eighteenth century, the society they imagined was clearly utopian and often radical in its implications. Timothy Dwight, in a typical description of the future age, predicted that there would be neither poverty nor illness, neither wars nor civil strife. There would be no need for politicians, for "all distinctions of party and sect, of name and nation, of civilization and savageness, of climate and colour, will finally vanish."[42] But as different from the present as the future was to be, by the early nineteenth century clerics generally did not expect that radical human actions would precede the millennium's appearance. Rather, they interpreted their Bible and missionary societies to be God's special way of converting the world to Christianity and inaugurating the millennial age. "We have all been praying for the coming of the Millennium," explained James Blythe, speaking in 1814 before the Presbyterian Synod of Kentucky in Lexington, "and by most Christians it has been thought to be very nigh at hand; but who until a few years ago, apprehended that an high way for our God was to be prepared among the heathen, simply by *multiplying the Bible,* or that this great event was to be ushered in by awakening a *missionary spirit*, and the erection of *theological schools*?"[43]

Those critics who might scoff at such a naïve program for effecting social change were irrelevant to them, for they were certain that behind their endeavors lay what might be called a "powerful magic." When Lewis and

Arthur Tappan, the New York philanthropists, were criticized by their brother Benjamin, an Ohio politician and religious skeptic, for supporting senseless causes like Bible and tract distribution in addition to their more worthwhile ventures into education and antislavery, they retorted that in God's sight all humanitarian endeavors were of equal importance. What was needed for the divine favor, they explained, was simply that the "benevolent principle" be in operation.[44] Millennialism was a powerful spur to benevolence; but it was just as much a stimulus to unrealistic thought on the matter. For since the coming of the millennial age was inevitable as long as men worked and prayed for its appearance, religious humanitarians could justify any legitimate action, however foolhardy, that seemed to further the Christian hope for a perfect society.

In addition to millennialism, clerical ideas about the nature of the American polity underlay most benevolent actions. It was not simply that most Protestant clerics were, as many historians point out, devoted nationalists, but they were also ardent republicans as well. Like the Federalists and Jeffersonians who governed the new nation, their reading of history and their own experience during the troubled post-Revolutionary years had demonstrated to them that a republic could survive the constant threat of demagoguery and dictatorship only if its citizens were alert and self-reliant. Virtue was the key, in the republican point of view, to the maintenance of a successful state. Yet on all sides they saw impending disaster. Politics had quickly degenerated into division, and politicians had become sycophants, not statesmen. Political differences had degenerated into that political factionalism which had heralded the downfall of all previous republics, and the parties themselves had become little more than vehicles for personal ambition. Politicians had no concern for the "intelligence and virtue of coming generations," and electoral contests had "cast a shade over our national character, wasted our strength, endangered our union, assaulted the basis of our constitution, and placed in jeopardy our existence as a nation."[45]

Such lack of concern for the true national interest, however, only reflected, according to Protestant analysts, the prevailing attitudes of the citizenry. Too many Americans, clerics judged, had little concern for their own souls, for their fellow men, or for their country. Too many men lusted after power, fame, or wealth. "We must be rich," wrote one spokesman with scorn, "and that in a few years."[46] No longer could humanitarians view the individual accumulation of wealth as an unmixed blessing, for behind the actions of the rising entrepreneurs, professionals, and politicians too often lay a ruthless self-aggrandizement to which virtues like humility and philanthropy seemed irrelevant. The national ideal seemed no longer the self-reliant and honorable merchant and mechanic which these Protestant clerics envisioned— a man whose life was simple and whose charity was manifold; a man who had the strength of character to scorn prevailing social customs and styles; and a man behind whose entrepreneurial ambition lay the desire to help others. Instead, men of position and wealth were attacking the religious humanitarians as theocrats, refusing to support their charities, paying little attention to their strictures against materialism and high-living, and devoting their energies to the more self-satisfying and less morally demanding requirements of the worlds of business and politics, while men of lesser rank who aspired after success followed their example. The Tappans as philanthropists, who confessed that their sole reason for making money was to enable them to do good, were the exception, not the rule.[47]

From their perspective, three remedies to the evils they diagnosed suggested themselves. First was the establishment of effective systems of education, where young and old could learn republican virtues such as civic responsibility, personal simplicity, and charity. Like Thomas Jefferson and many nineteenth-century liberal reformers, Protestant humanitarians looked on education as a panacea for many social ills: it was, for example, the "universal antidote" to end poverty. For if Americans—and particularly the young, still impressionable and idealistic—were effectively taught right conduct in schools, in prisons, in reformatories, and through public lectures and lyceums, there was a chance they could transcend their natural selfishness and licentiousness and work together to achieve that millennial utopia which Protestant thought envisioned. If ignorance, according to Protestant humanitarian De Witt Clinton, was "the cause as well as the effect of bad governments," then education was the way to achieve a successful republican state. Educator Philip Lindsley agreed: "The want of it [education] has occasioned most of the misery and crime which have been inflicted on our world under the specious names and imposing authority of religion and liberty."[48]

Religion, too, was the key to a successful republican state. No matter the inaccuracy of their analysis, Protestant humanitarians believed that Christianity and especially the liberating spirit of the Reformation had been responsible for all the liberal achievements of their era, including the founding of the American colonies and the formation of the United States itself. In freeing men from Catholicism, the Protestant Reformation had liberated them from their attachment to the feudal state and had stimulated them to develop representative governments and liberal societies. Contained everywhere in the religious journals of the early republic are highly selective and self-interested studies comparing the progressive institutions of Protestant countries with the decadent and despotic institutions of pagan states. As one speaker before the Baltimore Women's Sunday School Society, drawing on an undeniably partisan interpretation of human history and human character, exulted, "The obvious tendency of our holy religion is to make men republicans."[49]

For not only did the Protestant faith teach men humility and humanitarianism but also it taught them, according to its apologists, to be self-motivated and self-reliant. Unlike the professional man or the politician, anxious to please demanding clients and constituencies and intent on gratifying desires dictated by social customs and fads, the Christian was truly independent; he was subject only to God's law. Among Christians, the primary effect of the Reformation had been "the emancipation of the mind from subjection to every restraint but that which common sense and truth imposes. . . ." "Few men in any profession or party ever think for themselves," wrote Lindsley; it was the Christian alone who followed his reason and his conscience. Benevolent partisans could not often comprehend the quite legitimate attacks on their humanitarian activities, like temperance or Sabbath observance, for being authoritarian: it was not, according to one Unitarian source, the temperance reformers who were establishing a new orthodoxy, but rather the "self-styled gentlemen" who set the fashion for drink. Religious humanitarians saw themselves as the last survivors of that slowly dying American who acted according to universal and time-honored standards and who did not adopt current fad and fashion as his guide. Religion made men republicans; it also made them individualists.[50]

In addition to religion and education, the third major ingredient of "Christian republicanism" was the voluntary association. It was a form of organization long employed to give permanency to citizen initiative and group endeavor. Many reformers came to view the voluntary society as the perfect means whereby benevolence could be institutionalized without granting additional and potentially dangerous powers to the central government.[51] It was, moreover, a way of involving citizens with their government and thus insuring that democracy would actually function within the republican framework, of bringing together in harmony people of the various competing classes and sections, and of providing stable organizations and a sense of community within a society in continual flux. In sum, the benevolent leaders planned their societies as workshops in republicanism, which could "bind together as with a cord of love the citizens of this great country" and which could "divert the attention of enlightened minds from the visions of political speculation, and the angry disputes of party, to the substantial good of lessening the miseries and multiplying the comforts of human life."[52]

Benevolent spokesmen envisioned that employer and worker, wealthy and poor, would participate in these voluntary associations and that through this "true American Union" the wealthy would learn frugality and charity and the poor would learn self-reliance and industriousness. William Ellery Channing, often incorrectly cited as a critic of voluntarism because he, unlike others involved in benevolence, saw the potential danger to the republic from large-scale organizations which could be perverted to political ends, in reality supported their aims. He looked "with interest and hope on the spirit of association" for he regarded the central government with suspicion. "Our social principles and relations are the great springs of improvement, and of vigorous and efficient exertion," he wrote. When united with others, he observed, the individual's resolve became firm, and men became conscious of unknown powers.[53] Voluntary associations, then, could be an important contribution to the success of republicanism.

In their analyses of voluntary organization, men like Channing offered an important contribution to the republican ideology of their age. Many literate Americans after the Revolution regarded the republican form of government with apprehension. Only too often such fears limited the ability of republican theorists to view American institutions from other than a negative perspective: they were concerned with how to check power, not how to create it. The most representative minds of the American enlightenment, Jefferson and James Madison, judged that society could best protect itself against the destructive energy of factions, the corrupting influence of power, and the evil inherent in all men by federalizing territorial states and by dividing the powers and functions of government among many branches. The benevolent leaders, however, ventured in a more positive direction. Excluded from politics, they looked toward society to find their solution to the supposed defects inherent in the republican order. The mechanistic division of power they left up to political theorists; what concerned them was how best to channel social power for useful, democratic ends.

Such was the theory of voluntarism which underlay their benevolent organizations. In practice, of course, it did not often work out as they had planned. Individuals could easily enough be persuaded to join their societies; the problem was to maintain interest for any period of time. Rather than acting as coordinators for active local chapters, however, directors of the national religious societies spent their time as publicity agents, as fund raisers, and as employers of paid agents sent out to invigorate local auxiliaries and to try to form new ones. Nor was the hope that the wealthy and the poor might learn from one another any more than a romantic and naïve vision. Men of position quickly assumed prominence in the societies, and, although they did not hesitate to proclaim their own values to the poor, one wonders to what extent they put into practice in their own lives their rhetorical commitment to virtues like humility, asceticism, and self-abnegation.

Like many groups dedicated to a common purpose, the religious humanitarians were often blind to those evils in their own organizations which they saw clearly in the associations of others. They had little conscious desire to control society or to resurrect an older social order in which clerical wisdom was supreme. They wanted rather, like their Federalist and Jeffersonian contemporaries, to insure the success of the American republic and ultimately to attain a stable democratic order. But because their organizations were subject to all the frailties of human institutions, it was inevitable that their results would fall far short of the goals they had set for themselves and that, from the perspective of history, their moralism would seem to outweigh their benevolence. Yet when they excoriated materialism and called for humanitarian endeavor, they provided a signal service for their generation. Few men in that age were willing to challenge the universal devotion to wealth; few men were able to see that contemporary materialism had in it a ruthlessness which disregarded spiritual and humane qualities. The religious humanitarians of the early nineteenth century called into question the goals of America and forced their generation to examine their values. Not the least of the results of this examination was to direct the thoughts of many Americans toward reform.

Notes

1. John R. Bodo, *The Protestant Clergy and Public Issues, 1812-1848* (Princeton, 1954); Charles C. Cole, Jr., *The Social Ideas of the Northern Evangelists, 1820-1860* (Princeton, 1954); Charles I. Foster, *An Errand of Mercy: The Evangelical United Front, 1790-1837* (Chapel Hill, 1960); Clifford S. Griffin, *Their Brothers' Keepers: Moral Stewardship in the United States, 1800-1865* (New Brunswick, 1960). For the most recent analyses of Protestant humanitarianism from the "social control" perspective, see M. J. Heale, "Humanitarianism in the Early Republic: The Moral Reformers of New York, 1776-1825," *Journal of American Studies,* 2 (Oct. 1968), 161-75; W. David Lewis, "The Reformer as Conservative: Protestant Counter-Subversion in the Early Republic," Stanley Coben and Lorman Ratner, eds., *The Development of an American Culture* (Englewood Cliffs, 1970); Raymond A. Mohl, *Poverty in New York, 1783-1825* (New York, 1971). The term "social control" was first used by Clifford S. Griffin. See Clifford S. Griffin, "Religious Benevolence as Social Control, 1815-1860," *Mississippi Valley Historical Review,* XLIV (Dec. 1957), 423-44.
2. For criticism of the abolitionists, see David Donald, "Toward a Reconsideration of Abolitionists," *Lincoln Reconsidered: Essays on the Civil War Era* (New York, 1956), 19-36; Stanley M. Elkins, *Slavery: A Problem in American Institutional and Intellectual Life* (Chicago, 1959), 140-206; and Avery Craven, *The Coming of the Civil War* (rev. ed., Chicago, 1957), 134-50. For defenders of the abolitionists, see Martin Duberman, "The Northern Response to Slavery," Martin Duberman, ed., *The Antislavery Vanguard: New Essays on the Abolitionists* (Princeton, 1965), 395-413; Merton Dillon, "The Abolitionists as a Dissenting Minority," Alfred F. Young, ed., *Dissent: Explorations in the History of American Radicalism* (DeKalb, 1968), 83-108; Aileen Kraditor, *Means and Ends in American Abolitionism* (New York, 1967).
3. John L. Thomas, "Romantic Reform in America, 1815-1865" *American Quarterly,* XVII (Winter 1965), 656-81.
4. Robert Baird, *Religion in America; Or, an Account of the Origin, Process, Relation to the State, and Present Condition of the Evangelical Churches in the United States. With Notices of the Unevangelical Denominations* (New York, 1844); Sidney E. Mead, *The Lively Experiment: The Shaping of Christianity in America* (New York, 1963); Perry Miller, *The Life of the Mind in America: From the Revolution to the Civil War* (New York, 1965). See also Oliver Wendell Elsbree, "The Rise of the Missionary Spirit in New England, 1790-1815," *New England Quarterly,* I (July 1928), 295-322; Oliver Wendell Elsbree, *The Rise of the Missionary Spirit in America, 1790-1815* (Williamsport, Pa., 1928); Timothy L. Smith, *Revivalism and Social Reform: American Protestantism on the Eve of the Civil War* (New York, 1957).
5. Miller, *Life of the Mind in America,* 78; Edward A. Park, *Memoir of the Life and Character of Samuel Hopkins* (Boston, 1854), 120. For the interdependence of eighteenth-century benevolent thought, see Michael Kraus, *The Atlantic Civilization: Eighteenth-Century Origins* (Ithaca, 1959).
6. For the negative reaction to Hopkinsianism, see Edmund S. Morgan, "The American Revolution Considered as an Intellectual Movement," Arthur M. Schlesinger, Jr., and Morton White, eds., *Paths of American Thought* (Boston, 1963), 11-33. For the Presbyterian-Congregational rivalry, see Samuel Miller to Jedidiah Morse, Dec. 22, 1807, Feb. 14, 1809, Samuel

Miller Papers (Princeton University). For the Presbyterian dislike of Hopkinsianism, see Gardiner Spring, *Personal Reminiscences of the Life and Times of Gardiner Spring . . .* (New York, 1866).

7. Clifton Jackson Phillips, *Protestant America and the Pagan World: The First Half Century of the American Board of Commissioners for Foreign Missions, 1810-1860* (Cambridge, Mass., 1968). 1-31.

8. For voluntary organizations, see Arthur M. Schlesinger, "Biography of a Nation of Joiners," *American Historical Review,* L (Oct. 1944), 1-25; Carl Bridenbaugh, *Cities in the Wilderness: The First Century of Urban Life in America, 1625-1742* (New York, 1938); Carl and Jessica Bridenbaugh, *Rebels and Gentlemen: Philadelphia in the Age of Franklin* (New York, 1942). For voluntary humanitarian associations in the early nineteenth century, see Frank Crow, "The Age of Promise: Societies for Social and Economic Improvement in the United States, 1783-1815" (doctoral dissertation, University of Minnesota, 1952).

9. Historians of the "social control" persuasion have relied too heavily on Lyman Beecher's famous lament of the passing of "cocked hats, and gold-headed canes." Barbara M. Cross, ed., *The Autobiography of Lyman Beecher* (2 vols., Cambridge, Mass., 1961), I, 253.

10. *Christian Spectator,* V (Jan. 1823), 16-17. For biographies of early nineteenth-century ministers of all denominations, see William B. Sprague, *Annals of the American Pulpit; Or Commemorative Notices of Distinguished American Clergymen of Various Denominations, from the Early Settlement of the Country to the Close of the Year Eighteen Hundred and Fifty-Five* (9 vols., New York, 1857-1869).

11. Baird, *Religion in America,* 306; Sidney E. Mead, "The Rise of the Evangelical Conception of the Ministry in America (1607-1850)," H. Richard Niebuhr and Daniel D. Williams, eds., *The Ministry in Historical Perspectives* (New York, 1956), 234.

12. For the history of Presbyterianism, see E. H. Gillett, *History of the Presbyterian Church in the United States of America* (2 vols., Philadelphia, 1864); Leonard J. Trinterud, *The Forming of an American Tradition: A Reexaminaton of Colonial Presbyterianism* (Philadelphia, 1949); William Warren Sweet, *Religion on the American Frontier: The Presbyterians; A Collection of Source Materials* (New York, 1936); Walter Brownlow Posey, *The Presbyterian Church in the Old Southwest, 1778-1838* (Richmond, 1952); Ernest Trice Thompson, *Presbyterians in the South* (2 vols., Richmond, 1963); Elwyn A. Smith, "The Forming of a Modern American Denomination," *Church History,* XXXI (March 1962), 74-99; Fred J. Hood, "Presbyterianism and the New American Nation, 1783-1826: A Case Study of Religion and National Life" (doctoral dissertation, Princeton University, 1968).

13. See American Bible Society, *Annual Reports* (New York, 1817-1840); American Sunday School Union, *Annual Reports* (Philadelphia, 1825-1840). For example, the first Board of Managers of the Amrican Bible Society included seven Episcopalians, five Presbyterians, two Baptists, one Methodist, and one Congregationalist. See manuscript by Margaret Hills and Elizabeth Eisenhard, "The Founders of the American Bible Society," Eric North, ed., "History of the American Bible Society" (American Bible Society, New York City). In 1832 of the seventy-six officers and managers of the American Sunday School Union, twenty-six were Presbyterians, fourteen Episcopalians, ten Baptists, ten Methodists, eight Congregationalists, four Dutch Reformed, one Moravian, and one Quaker. See American Sunday School Union, *Eighth Annual Report* (1832), 32.

14. Although one apologist for the Congregationalists contended that the directors of American Board of Commissioners for Foreign Missions (ABCFM) had tried without success to enlist representatives of other denominations. *Address to the Public on the Proposed Union between the American Board of Commissioners for Foreign Missions and the United Foreign Missionary Society* (Boston [1826]), 6.

15. Cross, ed., *Autobiography of Lyman Beecher,* I, 253. Elwyn A. Smith significantly modifies the common notion that even Beecher was intent on some sort of "social control." Elwyn A. Smith, "The Voluntary Establishment of Religion," Elwyn A. Smith, ed., *The Religion of the Republic* (Philadelphia, 1971), 154-82.

16. *Panoplist,* II (Aug. 1806), 117; *Christian Magazine,* I (Dec. 1806), vi; *Weekly Reorder,* III (July 30, 1817), 413; *Christian Spectator,* V (April 1823), 189-90; *American Baptist Magazine,* VII (March 1827), 94, VIII (Aug. 1828), 243; *Christian Secretary,* XVI (May 27, 1837), 77; *Christian Examiner,* XXII (May 1837), 154; *Methodist Magazine,* X (Feb. 1827), 43; Nathan Bangs, *A History of the Methodist Episcopal Church* (4 vols., New York, 1845), II, 147-49; David Benedict, *A General History of the Baptist Denomination in America, and Other Parts of the World* (2 vols., Boston, 1813), I, 352. See also Lois W. Banner, "The Protestant Crusade: Religious Missions, Benevolence, and Reform in the United States, 1780-1840" (doctoral dissertation, Columbia University, 1970).

17. Moreover, the sermon does not prove that the benevolent community was anti-Jackson and, thus, "anti-democratic." Ely endorsed neither candidate in the sermon, and he added an appendix to the 1828 printed version of the 1827 sermon, in which he admitted a preference for John Quincy Adams, but he thought that Andrew Jackson was a "friend and supporter of Christianity" and deserved the presidency in the future. Ezra Stiles Ely, *The Duty of Christian Freemen to Elect Christian Rulers: A Discourse Delivered on the Fourth of July 1827* Philadelphia, 1828).

18. Bangs, *History of the Methodist Episcopal Church,* I, 26-27; Charles Roy Keller, *The Second Great Awakening in Connecticut* (New Haven, 1942), 191; Isaac Backus, *A History of New England with Particular Reference to the Denomination of Christians Called Baptists* (2 vols., Newton, Mass., 1871), II, 385.

19. Robert Bierstadt, *The Social Order: An Introduction to Sociology* (New York, 1957). For a historian who takes cognizance of the denominational dimension, see Foster, *Errand of Mercy.*

20. Data on the Congregationalists is vast and scattered. For developments in Massachusettss, see Evarts B. Greene, "A Puritan Counter-Reformation," *Proceedings of the American Antiquarian Society,* 42 (April 1932), 17-46; Samuel Worcester, *The Life and Labors of Rev. Samuel Worcester D.D., Former Pastor of the Tabernacle Church, Salem, Mass.* (Boston, 1852); William Sprague, *The Life of Jedidiah Morse D.D.* (New York, 1874); and James King Morse, *Jedidiah Morse: A Champion of New England Orthodoxy* (New York, 1939). On Connecticut, see Keller, *Second Great Awakening in Connecticut;* M. Louise Green, *The Development of Religious Liberty in Connecticut* (Boston, 1905); Richard J. Purcell, *Connecticut in Transition, 1775-1818* (Washington, 1918). The two histories of Congregationalism as a denomination, Williston Walker, *A History of the Congregational Churches in the United States* (New York, 1894), and Gaius Glenn Atkins and Frederick L. Fagley, *History of American Congregationalism* (Boston, 1942), are unsatisfactory.

21. For a study of the institutional development from sectarianism to denominationalism and benevolence, see Sydney V. James, *A People Among Peoples: Quaker Benevolence in Eighteenth-Century America* (Cambridge, Mass., 1963).

22. For this discussion of Methodism, see Bangs, *History of the Methodist Episcopal Church;* Wade Crawford Barclay, *Early American Methodism, 1769-1844* (2 vols., New York, 1949); Elizabeth K. Nottingham, *Methodism and the Frontier: Indiana Proving Ground* (New York, 1941); William Warren Sweet, *Religion on the American Frontier, 1783-1840; The Methodists* (Chicago, 1946); Walter Brownlow Posey, *The Development of Methodism in the Old Southwest, 1783-1824* (Nashville, 1933); W. M. Gewehr, "Some Factors in the Expansion of Frontier Methodism, 1800-1811," *Journal of Religion,* VIII (Jan. 1928), 98-120; Elmer T. Clark. J. Manning Potts, Jacob S. Payton, eds., *The Journal and Letters of Francis Asbury* (3 vols., London, 1958); Nathan Bangs, *An Authentic History of the Missions under the Care of the Missionary Society of the Methodist Episcopal Church* (New York, 1832).

23. Donald G. Mathews, "The Second Great Awakening as an Organizing Process, 1780-1830: An Hypothesis," *Americn Quarterly,* XXI (Spring 1969), 23-43.

24. Barclay, *Early American Methodism,* II, 37. According to Donald G. Mathews, it was not until 1832 that the General Conference of the Methodist Church ended its official reluctance to support non-Methodist organizations and resolved to allow the bishops to appoint

agents for the American Colonization Society from among members of the denomination. Donald G. Mathews, *Slavery and Methodism: A Chapter in American Morality, 1780-1845* (Princeton, 1965), 94.

25. The institutional imperatives behind Presbyterian benevolence were much the same as for the Congregationalists. See Gillett, *History of the Presbyterian Church*; Ashbel Green, *The Life of Ashbel Green V.D.M.* (New York, 1849); Ashbel Green, *Presbyterian Missions* (New York, 1893); William O. Brackett, Jr., "The Rise and Development of the New School in the Presbyterian Church in the U.S.A. to the Reunion of 1869," *Journal of the Presbyterian Historical Society,* XIII (Sept. 1928), 128-29; Hood, "Presbyterians and the New American Nation." Congregationalism and anti-intellectualism impeded the efforts of eastern educated Baptist leaders to create denominational missionary and benevolent organizations. See Robert G. Torbet, *A History of the Baptists* (Philadelphia, 1950); Robert G. Torbet, *A Social History of the Philadelphia Baptist Association: 1707-1940* (Philadelphia, 1944); Robert G. Torbet, *Venture of Faith: The Story of the American Baptist Foreign Mission Society and the Woman's American Baptist Foreign Mission Society 1814-1954* (Philadelphia, 1955); and Albert Henry Newman, *A History of the Baptist Churches in the United States* (New York, 1894). For a discussion of the general relationship between denominationalism and benevolence, see Banner, "The Protestant Crusade."

26. Rush Welter, *Popular Education and Democratic Thought in America* (New York, 1962), 34. See also Timothy L. Smith, "Protestant Schooling and American Nationality, 1800-1850," *Journal of American History,* LIII (March 1967), 679-95.

27. John Romeyn to John Van Shaack, Feb. 2, 1800, Gratz Collection (Pennsylvania Historical Society); *Christian Spectator,* I (Aug. 1819), 405; James B. Taylor, *The Exigencies and Responsibilities of the Present Age. A Sermon, Preached in the First Baptist Church, Philadelphia, May 23, 1836* (Philadelphia, 1836); F. W. P. Greenwood, *A Sermon, Delivered on the 25th Anniversary of the Boston Female Asylum, Sept. 23, 1825* (Boston, 1825), 4; *American Sunday-School Magazine,* I (July 1824), 2; *American Annals of Educattion and Instruction,* I (Aug. 1830), 2-3, I (March 1831), 116; Thompson, *Presbyterians in the South,* I, 237.

28. William B. Sprague, *A Discourse, Delivered on Sabbath Evening, March 17, 1833, in St. Peter's Church, in Aid of the Albany Apprentices' Library* (Albany, 1833); Dorothy C. Barck, ed., *Letters from John Pintard to His Daughter: Eliza Noel Pintard Davidson, 1816-1833* (4 vols., New York, 1940), I, 349-50; Lewis Tappan, Journal, May 27, 1829, Lewis Tappan Papers (Manuscript Division, Library of Congress). Although Carl Bode points out that most of the lyceum speakers were ministers, he does not discuss the dynamics of the formation of local societies. On the lyceum, see Carl Bode, *The American Lyceum: Town Meeting of the Mind* (New York, 1956), 31. For an indication of the extent of the influence of ministers and pious laymen, see *American Annals of Education and Instruction,* I (June 1831), 273.

29. The *Twelfth Annual Report* of the American Sunday School Union stated that the rising concern for public systems of education was one of the major results of their efforts. American Sunday School Union, *Twelfth Annual Report* (Philadelphia, 1836), 29. See also *Religious Intelligencer,* I (May 17, 1817), 805.

30. Walter Brownlow Posey, *Frontier Mission: A History of Religion West of the Southern Appalachians to 1861* (Lexington, Ky., 1966), 409. Certain of the Protestant missionary societies and missionaries also became involved in trying to establish or improve public systems of education. Rufus Babcock, ed., *Forty Years of Pioneer Life: Memoir of John Mason Peck, D.D.* (Carbondale, Ill., 1965), 122-23; Records of the Society for Propagating the Gospel Among the Indians and Others of North America (Massachusetts Historical Society); Smith, "Protestant Schooling," 689-94.

31. Thompson, *Presbyterians in the South,* I, 189-203; Jedidiah Morse, "Journal of a Mission to the Isle of Shoals, performed at the request and expense of the Society for Propagating the Gospel among the Indians and Others," Aug. 5-15, 1800, Jedidiah Morse Papers (New York Public Library).

32. According to Baird, in distributing Bibles and tracts, members of voluntary associations

often discovered cases of poverty and disease and reported them to associations or individuals qualified to attend to them. Baird, *Religion in America*, 177. See Mohl, *Poverty in New York*, 121-58.

33. Keith Melder, "Ladies Bountiful: Organized Women's Benevolence in Early 19th-Century America," *New York History*, XLVIII (July 1967), 231-54; R. Pierce Beaver, *All Loves Excelling: American Protestant Women in World Missions* (Grand Rapids, 1968).

34. Thomas, "Romantic Reform in America," 159.

35. Henry Barnard, *Tribute to Gallaudet. A Discourse in Commemoration of the Life, Character and Services of the Rev. Thomas H. Gallaudet L.L.D., Delivered before the Citizens of Hartford, January 7, 1852* (Hartford, 1852); Thomas H. Gallaudet, *A Sermon Delivered at the Opening of the Connecticut Asylum for the Education and Instruction of Deaf and Dumb Persons, April 20, 1817* (Hartford, 1852), 169.

36. Russel B. Nye, "Marius Robinson, A Forgotten Abolitionist Leader," *Ohio State Archaeological and Historical Quarterly*, LV (April-June 1946), 139. So powerful was the impulse toward religious missions that by 1836 even Charles G. Finney was recommending that Christians ought to give up social reform causes for missions and evangelism—a fact which John Thomas and others overlook. See Finney to Theodore Dwight Weld, July 21, 1836, Gilbert H. Barnes and Dwight L. Dumond, eds., *Letters of Theodore Dwight Weld, Angelina Grimke Weld and Sarah Grimke, 1822-1844* (2 vols., New York, 1934), I, 319.

37. See Gilbert Hobbs Barnes, *The Antisalvery Impulse, 1830-1844* (New York, 1933), 64-73.

38. John Lytle Meyers, "The Agency System of the Anti-Slavery Movement, 1823-37, and its Antecedents in Other Benevolent and Reform Societies" (doctoral dissertation, University of Michigan, 1961).

39. Lois W. Banner, "Religion and Reform in the Early Republic: The Role of Youth," *American Quarterly*, XXIII (Dec. 1971), 677-95.

40. For millennialism, see Elsbree, *Rise of the Missionary Spirit*; Ira V. Brown, "Watchers for the Second Coming: The Millenarian Tradition in America," *Mississippi Valley Historical Review*, XXXIX (Dec. 1952), 441-58; David E. Smith, "Millenarian Scholarship in America," *American Quarterly*, XVII (Fall 1965), 535-49; Ernest Lee Tuveson, *Redeemer Nation: The Idea of America's Millennial Role* (Chicago, 1968); and J. F. Maclear, "The Republic and the Millennium," Elwyn A. Smith, ed., *The Religion of the Republic* (Philadelphia, 1971), 183-216.

41. For republican thought after the Revolution, see John R. Howe, Jr., "Republican Thought and the Political Violence of the 1790's," *American Quarterly*, XIX (Summer 1967), 147-65; Gordon S. Wood, *The Creation of the American Republic, 1776-1787* (Chapel Hill, 1969); James M. Banner, Jr., *To the Hartford Convention:The Federalists and the Origins of Party Politics in Massachusetts, 1789-1815* (New York, 1970).

42. Alan Heimert, *Religion and the American Mind: From the Great Awakening to the Revolution* (Cambridge, Mass., 1966); Timothy Dwight, *A Sermon Delivered in Boston, Sept. 16, 1813, before the American Board of Commissioners for Foreign Missions at Their Fourth Annual Meeting* (Boston, 1813), 7.

43. James Blythe, *A Portrait of the Times; Being a Sermon, Delivered at the Opening of the Synod of Kentucky . . . Sept. 7, 1814* (Lexington, Ky., 1814).

44. Lewis Tappan to Benjamin Tappan, Sept. 26, 1829, Jan. 8, 1833, Benjamin Tappan Papers (Manuscript Division, Library of Congress).

45. *Panoplist*, II (May 1807), 570; *Weekly Recorder*, III (July 30, 1817), 413. For further documentation, see footnote 16.

46. *An Address, from the Convention of Massachusetts Congregational Ministers, 1709; Panoplist*, II (Aug. 1806), 117. See also *Evangelical and Literary Magazine*, I (July 1818), 323; *Connecticut Evangelical Magazine*, VI (Nov. 5, 1805), 171; *Methodist Magazine*, XII (Oct. 1830), 402; *New York Evangelist*, VII (July 30, 1836), 121.

47. For evidence of the societies' difficulties in retaining members and in raising money, see Mathew Carey, *Essays on the Public Charities of Philadelphia: Intended to Vindicate Benevolent Societies from the Charge of Encouraging Idleness, and to Place in Strong Relief, before

an Enlightened Public the Sufferings and Oppression under which the Greater Part of the Females Labour, Who Depend on Their Industry for a Support for Themselves and Children (Philadelphia, 1830), 13-14; Barck, ed., *Letters from John Pintard,* II, 155-56; J. Orin Oliphant, *Through the South and the West With Jeremiah Evarts in 1826* (Lewisburg, Pa., 1956), 84-87; Bela Bates Edwards, *Memoir of the Rev. Elias Cornelius* (Boston, 1833), 297. On the motivation of the Tappans, see Lewis Tappan to Benjamin Tappan, Sept. 26, 1829, Jan. 8, 1833, Benjamin Tappan Papers.

48. *Quarterly Christian Spectator,* II (June 1830), 221; Charles Fenton Mercer, *A Discourse on Popular Education; Delivered in the Church at Princeton, . . . the evening before the annual commencement of the College of New Jersey, Sept. 28, 1826* (Princeton, 1826), 36; De Witt Clinton's address to Free School Society, Dec. 11, 1809, William W. Campbell, ed., *The Life and Writings of De Witt Clinton* (New York, 1849), 312; Philip Lindsley, "The Cause of Education in Tennessee: An Address Delivered to the Young Gentlemen Admitted to the Degree of Bachelor of Arts, at the First Commencement of the University of Nashville, Oct. 4, 1826," LeRoy J. Halsey, ed., *The Works of Philip Lindsley, D.D.* (3 vols., Philadelphia, 1866), I, 126.

49. "Extracts from an Address, Delivered before the Managers and Teachers of Female Union Society of Baltimore, for the Promotion of Sabbath Schools, Nov. 3, 1828," *American Sunday-School Magazine,* VI (Jan. 1829), 3. See also John B. Romeyn, *Christ the Light of the World* [n.d.], Romeyn, ed., *Sermons,* I, 1-61; Clinton's address to American Bible society, May 8, 1823, William W. Campbell, ed., *The Life and Writings of De Witt Clinton* (New York, 1849), 305; I. L. Skinner, *An Address, Delivered before the Missionary Society of the City of Washington, Auxiliary to the Board of Commissioners of Foreign Missions* (Washington, 1826), 9-10; John M. Peck, "Fifty Years's Retrospect. A New Year's discourse delivered in St. Louis, Lord's-day, January 2d, and in the Legislative Hall in St. Charles, January 3, 1825," *Christian Watchman,* VI (March 12, 1825), 53-54.

50. Philip Lindsley, "Baccalaureate Address Pronounced on the Evening of the Anniversary Commencement of the University of Nashville, October 3, 1827," Halsey, ed., *Works,* I, 186-201; Albert Barnes, *The Power of Holiness in the Christian Ministry. A Discourse Delivered before the Directors, Professors, and Students of the Theological Seminary of the Presbyterian Church at Princeton, September 29, 1834* (Philadelphia, 1834), 8; *Christian Examiner,* XIV (July 1833), 273-78.

51. Mead alone notes that there was an ideological thrust behind the formation of voluntary societies. See Sidney Mead, *Lively Experiment,* 92.

52. *Virginia Evangelical and Literary Magazine,* II (Feb. 1819), 91-92; *Christian Monitor,* II (Oct. 26, 1816), 49-51. See also *Panoplist,* XIV (Dec. 1818), 542-45; *Quarterly Christian Spectator,* VI (March 1834), 48; *Methodist Magazine and Quarterly Review,* XVIII (July 1836); *Quarterly Observer,* I (July 1833), 59; Wheeler, *A Sermon . . . before the . . . Missionary Society . . . 1826,* p. 7; John Sergeant, *A Sermon before the Philadelphia House of Refuge, 1826* (Philadelphia, 1826), 11.

53. For a representative statement of the "true American Union" idea, see Heman Humphrey, *The Way to Bless and Save our Country: A Sermon, Preached in Philadephia at the Request of the American Sunday-School Union, May 23, 1831* (Philadelphia, 1831), 15. William Ellery Channing subscribed to the idea of a "fraternal union" of classes. See William Ellery Channing, *Memoir of William Ellery Channing: With Extracts from His Correspondence and Manuscripts* (3 vols., Boston, 1848), III, 38. For Channing's discussion and criticism of voluntary organization, see *Christian Examiner,* VII (Sept. 1829), 105-40. Lyman Beecher attacked Channing's fears of the dangers of associations as a "vague, indefinite prejudice," and contended that the real reason for Channing's complaints was to excuse the failure of the Unitarian mission to India. Lyman Beecher, *Spirit of the Pilgrims,* III (Feb. 2, 1830), 129-41.

BIBLIOGRAPHICAL NOTE

There is of course a vast literature on each of the general areas under discussion. The point of this brief note is not to attempt a comprehensive bibliography of these fields but rather to suggest a small number of recent publications, in addition to the essays selected for inclusion, that offer new interpretations of and approaches to the topics discussed in this book.

Edward Pessen, *Riches, Class, and Power Before the Civil War* (Lexington, Mass., 1973), discusses the distribution of wealth, social mobility, class, and power in the major cities of the Northeast. The distribution of wealth is also dealt with in George Blackburn and Sherman L. Richards, Jr., "A Demographic History of the West: Manistee County, Michigan, 1860," *Journal of American History,* 57 (Dec. 1970), 600-618; Gavin Wright, " 'Economic Democracy' and the Concentration of Agricultural Wealth in the Cotton South," *Agricultural History,* 44 (Jan. 1970), 63-94; Richard Lowe and Randolph Campbell, "Slave Property and the Distribution of Wealth in Texas, 1860," *JAH,* 63 (Sept. 1976), 316-324; and Lee Soltow, *Men and Wealth in the United States, 1850-1870* (New Haven, Conn., 1975), an at times inaccessible but important examination of mid-century census data. For social mobility see Stuart Blumin, "Mobility and Change in Ante-Bellum Philadephia," in Stephan Thernstrom and Richard Sennett, eds., *Nineteenth-Century Cities: Essays in the New Urban History* (New Haven, Conn., 1969), 165-208; Gary B. Nash, "The Philadelphia Bench and Bar, 1800-1861," *Comparative Studies in Society and History,* 7 (Jan. 1965), 203-220; and Clyde Griffin, "Making It in America: Social Mobility in Mid-Nineteenth Century Poughkeepsie," *New York History,* 51 (Oct. 1970), 479-499. Women are discussed interestingly in Ann D. Wood, " 'The Fashionable Diseases': Women's Complaints and Their Treatment in Nineteenth-Century America," *Journal of Interdisciplinary History,* 4 (Summer 1973), 25-52; Anne Firor Scott, *The Southern Lady From Pedestal to Politics* (Chicago 1970); Ronald W. Hogeland, " 'The Female Appendage': Feminine Life Styles in America, 1820-1860," *Civil War History,* 17 (June 1971), 101-114; and Carroll Smith-Rosenberg, "Beauty, the Beast, and the Militant Woman: A Case Study in Sex Roles and Stress in Jacksonian America," *American Quarterly,* 23 (Oct. 1971), 562-584. For examples of the new urban history see Thernstrom and Sennett, *Nineteenth-Century Cities*; Leo F. Schnore, ed., *The New Urban History: Quantitative Explorations by American Historians* (Princeton, 1975); Lyle W. Dorsett and Arthur H. Shaffer, "Was the Antebellum

South Antiurban? A Suggestion," *Journal of Southern History,* 38 (Feb. 1972), 93-100; Michael H. Frisch, *Town Into City: Springfield, Massachusetts, and the Meaning of Community, 1840-1880* (Cambridge, 1972); Sam Bass Warner, Jr., *The Private City: Philadelphia in Three Periods of Its Growth* (Philadelphia, 1968); and Edward Pessen, "The Social Configuration of the Antebellum City: An Historical and Theoretical Inquiry," *Journal of Urban History,* 4 (May 1976), 267-306.

The economy is analyzed from the standpoint of the new economic history in Robert W. Fogel and Stanley L. Engerman, eds., *The Reinterpretation of American Economic History* (New York, 1971); Douglas S. North, *The Economic Growth of the United States, 1790-1860* (New York, 1965); Albert Fishlow, *American Railroads and the Transformation of the Ante-Bellum Economy* (Cambridge, 1965); Paul A. David, "The Growth of Real Product in the United States Before 1840: New Evidence, Controlled Conjectures," *Journal of Economic History,* 27 (June 1967), 151-195; and Harry N. Scheiber, "Government and the Economy: Studies of the 'Commonwealth' Policy in Nineteenth-Century America," *Jour. Interd. Hist.,* 3 (Summer 1972), 135-154. For a criticism of Robert W. Fogel's interpretation of antebellum railroads and their role, see Peter D. McClelland, "Railroads, American Growth, and the New Economic History: A Critique," *Jour. Eco. Hist.,* 28 (March 1968), 102-123. Black labor, slave and free, is discussed in Robert W. Fogel and Stanley L. Engerman, *Time on the Cross* (Boston, 1974); Eugene D. Genovese, *Roll, Jordan, Roll: The World the Slaves Made* (New York, 1974); John W. Blassingame, *The Slave Community: Plantation Life in the Antebellum South* (New York, 1972); Richard Sutch, *The Treatment Received by American Slaves: A Critical Review of the Evidence Presented in Time on the Cross* (Berkeley, 1974); Charles B. Dew, "Disciplining Slave Ironworkers in the Antebellum South: Coercion, Conciliation, and Accommodation," *AHR,* 79 (April 1974), 393-418; Robert S. Starobin, *Industrial Slavery in the Old South* (New York, 1970); Ira Berlin, *Slaves Without Masters: The Free Negro in the Antebellum South* (New York, 1974); and Theodore Hershberg, "Free Blacks in Antebellum Philadelphia," *Journal of Social History,* 5 (Winter 1971-1972), 183-209. Interesting examples of the new labor history are Paul Faler, "Cultural Aspects of the Industrial Revolution: Lynn, Massachusetts, Shoemakers and Industrial Morality, 1826-1860," *Labor History,* 15 (Summer 1974), 367-394; Bruce Laurie, " 'Nothing on Impulse': Life Styles of Philadelphia Artisans, 1820-1850," *Labor History,* 15 (Summer 1974), 337-366; Herbert G. Gutman, "Work, Culture, and Society in Industrializing America, 1815-1919," *AHR,* 78 (June 1973), 531-588; and Theodore Hershberg, Michael B. Katz, Stuart Blumin, Laurence Glasco, and Clyde Griffin, "Occupation and Ethnicity in Five Nineteenth-Century Cities: A Collaborative Inquiry," *Historical Methods Newsletter,* 7 (June 1974), 174-216.

New treatments of Jacksonian politics and political issues include Joel Silbey, ed., *Political Ideology and Voting Behavior in the Age of Jackson* (Engelwood Cliffs, N.J., 1973); Ronald P. Formisano, *The Birth of Mass Political Parties: Michigan, 1827-1861* (Princeton, 1971); Formisano, "Deferential-Participant Politics: The Early Republic's Political Culture, 1789-1840," *American Political Science Review,* 68 (June 1974), 473-487; and Wiliam G. Shade, "Pennsylvania Politics in the Jacksonian Period: A Case Study, Northampton County, 1824-1844," *Pennsylvania History,* 39 (July 1972), 313-333 (which, together with Formisano's work and Lee Benson's *The Concept of Jacksonian Democracy: New York As a Test Case* [Princeton, 1961], offers an "ethnocultural" interpretation of Jacksonian politics and voter behavior.) Effective critiques of this approach include Richard L. McCormick, "Ethno-Cultural Interpretations of Nineteenth-Century American Voting Behavior," *Political Science Quarterly,* 89 (June 1974), 351-377; and J. Morgan Kousser, "The 'New Political History': A Methodological Critique," *Reviews in American History,* 4 (March 1976), 1-14. Also useful is Richard B. Latner and Peter Levine, "Perspectives on Antebellum Pietistic Politics," *Reviews in Amer. Hist.,* 4 (March 1976), 15-24.

Political issues are explored in James R. Sharp, *The Jacksonians Versus the Banks: Politics in the States After the Panic of 1837* (New York, 1970); John M. McFaul, *The Politics of Jacksonian Finance* (Ithaca, N.Y., 1972); Michael Paul Rogin, *Fathers and Children: Andrew Jackson and the Subjugation of the American Indian* (New York, 1975), a provocative but unpersuasive psychoanalysis; James C. Curtis, *The Fox at Bay: Martin Van Buren and the Presidency, 1837-1841* (Lexington, Ky., 1970); (Curtis's *Andrew Jackson and the Search for Vindication* [Boston, 1976], is a critical but balanced biography); Matthew A. Crenson, *The Federal Machine: Beginnings of Bureaucracy in Jacksonian America* (Baltimore, 1975); Edwin A. Miles, "After John Marshall's Decision: Worcester v. Georgia and the Nullification Crisis," *Jour. South. Hist.,* 39 (Nov. 1973), 519-544; Donald B. Cole, *Jacksonian Democracy in New Hampshire, 1800-1851* (Cambridge, 1970); Ronald N. Satz, *American Indian Policy in the Jacksonian Era* (Lincoln, 1975); Robert Charles Thomas, "Andrew Jackson Versus France: American Policy Toward France, 1834-1836," *Tennessee Historical Quarterly,* 35 (Spring 1976), 51-64, succinct and informative; and Peter Levine, "State Legislative Parties in the Jacksonian Era: New Jersey, 1829-1844," *JAH,* 62 (Dec. 1975), 591-608, which throws much light on state politics not in New Jersey alone. Useful discussions of party memberships include Burton W. Folsom II, "The Politics of Elites: Prominence and Party in Davidson County, Tennessee, 1835-1861," *Jour. South. Hist.,* 39 (Aug. 1975), 180-206; Donald V. Ratcliffe, "The Role of Voters and Issues in Party Formation: Ohio, 1824," *JAH,* 59 (March 1973), 847-870; and Whitman H. Ridgway, "McCulloch vs. the Jacksonians: Patronage and Politics in Maryland," *Maryland Historical Magazine,* 70 (Winter 1975), 350-362.

In recent years students of nineteenth-century reform have focused increasingly on the diverse local reforms pursued by voluntary associations, in addition to the great national movements such as abolition, that used to preoccupy them. Useful collections that treat the older themes are Martin Duberman, ed., *The Antislavery Vanguard: New Essays on the Abolitionists* (Princeton, 1965); David Brion Davis, ed., *Ante-Bellum Reform* (New York, 1967); and Walter Hugins, ed., *The Reform Impulse, 1825-1850* (New York, 1972). C. S. Griffin, *The Ferment of Reform* (New York, 1967), is an informative bibliograhical study. Examples of the newer studies are Carroll Smith-Rosenberg, *Religion and the Rise of the American City: The New York City Mission Movement 1812-1870* (Ithaca, 1971); Bertram Wyatt-Brown, "The Antimission Movement in the Jacksonian South: A Study in Regional Folk Culture," *Jour. South. Hist.,* 36 (Nov. 1970), 501-529; Raymond A. Mohl, "The Humane Society and Urban Reform in Early New York, 1787-1831," *New-York Historical Society Quarterly,* 54 (Jan. 1970), 30-52; William W. Cutler, III, "Status, Values, and the Education of the Poor: The Trustees of the New York Public School Society, 1805-1853," *Amer. Quar.,* 24 (March 1972), 69-85; Robert S. Pickett, *House of Refuge: Origins of Juvenile Reform in New York State, 1815-1857* (Syracuse, 1969);

Ronald Story, "Class and Culture in Boston: The Athenaeum, 1807-1860," *Amer. Quar.,* 28 (May 1975), 178-199; Michael B. Katz, ed., *Education in American History: Readings in the Social Issues* (New York, 1973); Gerald N. Grob, *Mental Institutions in America: Social Policy to 1875* (New York, 1973); and the following essays by M. J. Heale: "The New York Society for the Prevention of Pauperism, 1817-1823," *New-York Hist. Soc. Quart.,* 55 (April 1971). 153-176; "The Formative Years of the New York Prison Association, 1844-1862: A Case Study in Antebellum Reform," *New-York Hist. Soc. Quart.,* 59 (Oct. 1975), 320-347; and "From City Fathers to Social Critics: Humanitarianism and Government in New York, 1790-1860," *Journ. Amer. Hist.,* 63 (June 1976), 21-41.

INDEX

ABOUT THE EDITOR

Edward Pessen, Distinguished Professor of History at Baruch College and Graduate Center, C.U.N.Y., specializes in American social, political, and intellectual history. He has written articles for *The Political Science Quarterly*, the *Journal of Urban History*, *The American Historical Review*, *The Journal of American History*, and other journals. His previous books include *Most Uncommon Jacksonians*, *Jacksonian America*, *Three Centuries of Social Mobility in America*, and *Riches, Class, and Power Before the Civil War*. He has recently been awarded a Guggenheim Fellowship to study the extent and significance of social mobility in American history.